PATERNOSTER THEOLOGICAL

Beyond Suspicion

**Post-Christendom Protestant Political Theology
in John Howard Yoder and Oliver O'Donovan**

PATERNOSTER THEOLOGICAL MONOGRAPHS

A full listing of all titles in this series
appears at the close of this book.

PATERNOSTER THEOLOGICAL MONOGRAPHS

Beyond Suspicion

Post-Christendom Protestant Political Theology in John Howard Yoder and Oliver O'Donovan

Paul Doerksen

Foreword by P. Travis Kroeker

MILTON KEYNES · COLORADO SPRINGS · HYDERABAD

Copyright © Paul Doerksen 2009

First published 2009 by Paternoster

Paternoster is an imprint of Authentic Media
9 Holdom Avenue, Bletchley, Milton Keynes, MK1 1QR, UK
1820 Jet Stream Drive, Colorado Springs, CO 80921, USA
OM Authentic Media, Medchal Road, Jeedimetla Village,
Secunderabad 500 055, A.P., India

www.authenticmedia.co.uk
Authentic Media is a Division of IBS-STL UK, a company limited by guarantee
(registered charity no. 270162)

15 14 13 12 11 10 09 7 6 5 4 3 2 1

The right of Paul Doerksen to be identified as the Author of this Work
has been asserted by him in accordance with the Copyright, Designs
and Patents Act 1988

All rights reserved. No part of this publication may be reproduced, stored in a retrieval system, or transmitted in any form by any means, electronic, mechanical, photocopying, recording or otherwise, without the prior permission of the publisher or a license permitting restricted copying. In the UK such licenses are issued by the Copyright Licensing Agency, 90 Tottenham Court Road, London W1P 9HE.

British Library Cataloguing in Publication Data
A catalogue record for this book is available from the British Library

ISBN 978-1-84227-634-1

Typeset by the Author
Printed and bound in Great Britain
for Paternoster
by AlphaGraphics Nottingham

Series Preface

In the West the churches may be declining, but theology—serious, academic (mostly doctoral level) and mainstream orthodox in evaluative commitment—shows no sign of withering on the vine. This series of *Paternoster Theological Monographs* extends the expertise of the Press especially to first-time authors whose work stands broadly within the parameters created by fidelity to Scripture and has satisfied the critical scrutiny of respected assessors in the academy. Such theology may come in several distinct intellectual disciplines—historical, dogmatic, pastoral, apologetic, missional, aesthetic and no doubt others also. The series will be particularly hospitable to promising constructive theology within an evangelical frame, for it is of this that the church's need seems to be greatest. Quality writing will be published across the confessions—Anabaptist, Episcopalian, Reformed, Arminian and Orthodox—across the ages—patristic, medieval, reformation, modern and counter-modern—and across the continents. The aim of the series is theology written in the twofold conviction that the church needs theology and theology needs the church—which in reality means theology done for the glory of God.

Series Editors

Oliver Crisp, Reader in Theology, University of Bristol, UK

Trevor A. Hart, Head of School and Principal of St Mary's College School of Divinity, University of St Andrews, Scotland, UK

Anthony N.S. Lane, Professor of Historical Theology and Director of Research, London School of Theology, UK

Anthony C. Thiselton, Emeritus Professor of Christian Theology, University of Nottingham, Research Professor in Christian Theology, University College Chester, and Canon Theologian of Leicester Cathedral and Southwell Minster, UK

Kevin J. Vanhoozer, Research Professor of Systematic Theology, Trinity Evangelical Divinity School, Deerfield, Illinois, USA

For Julie

Contents

Foreword by P. Travis Kroeker	xiii
Acknowledgements	xv
Introduction	1
Political Theology	7
Chapter 1: "God is King": The Hebrew Scriptures in the Theopolitical Thought of John Howard Yoder and Oliver O'Donovan	**15**
Introduction	15
Reading The Bible: Yoder's Ecclesial Epistemology	17
'Stance'	18
Bible As Story	20
'Biblical Realism'	21
Reading The Bible: O'Donovan's Theological Epistemology	28
Thinking From Scripture	29
The Search For Political Concepts In Scripture	30
The Hebrew Scriptures in Yoder's Theopolitical Thought	36
God As King	36
Ambivalence To The Human Monarchy In Israel	40
The Sad, Tragic Prophet: The Jeremian Shift	42
The Hebrew Scriptures in O'Donovan's Theopolitical Thought	50
God's Kingship As The Basis Of Authority	51
Political Themes Drawn From The Claim That God Is King	53
Juridical Authority And Prophetic Tradition	57
Six Political Theorems For Political Theology	59
Comparative Observations	63
Chapter 2: A Political Rendering of the Claim that Jesus is Lord: Yoder and O'Donovan's Theopolitical Reading of the New Testament	**69**
Introduction	69
The Logic of Cross and Resurrection	71
The Vindication of the Way of the Cross: Yoder's Logic of Cross and Resurrection	72
The Vindication of Creation: O'Donovan's Logic of Cross and Resurrection	78
The Life, Teaching, and Ministry of Jesus	85

The Politics of Jesus: Yoder on Jesus' Earthly Life, Teaching, and Ministry	86
God's Rule Displayed in Christ: O'Donovan on Jesus' Earthly Life, Teaching, and Ministry	94
Eschatology	98
Yoder: Eschatology and the Powers	99
O'Donovan: Eschatology and the Powers	104
Ecclesiology	108
Yoder: Body Politics	109
O'Donovan: The Church as Political Society	117
Political Authority and the State	119
Yoder: 'No State as Such"	120
O'Donovan: Separate Authorization of Secular Power	123
Jesuology and Christology in Political Theology	126

Chapter 3: The Secular and the Eternal: A Contested Reading of Christendom — 128

Introduction	128
Christendom: Great Reversal or Great Tradition?	130
Yoder and the 'Constantinian Shifts' of Christendom	135
O'Donovan and the Temptations of Christendom	139
Yoder's Conflation of Constantinianism and Christendom	141
O'Donovan's View of Christendom as Church on Mission	149
The Visibility of the Church	150
Theology of History	156
Yoder's Apocalyptic Historiography	156
O'Donovan's Contested History	160
Christian Political Responsibility	163

Chapter 4: The Just War Revisited: The Just War Rejected — 171

Introduction	171
The Nature of the Disagreement between Yoder's Pacifism and O'Donovan's Just War	172
Judgment and Justice	176
Eschatology	185
Ecclesiology	192
Peace, War, and Responsibility	200

Concluding Reflections on Post-Christendom Christian Political Theology — 208

Appendix — 217

Bibliography 219

General Index 229

Foreword

Political theology in the past century has often been more about politics than about theology, more about philosophical and conceptual analysis than about biblical interpretation, more about statist sovereignty than about the church's affirmations concerning messianic sovereignty. This is in keeping with the rise of post-Enlightenment liberalism both in influencing the dominant political theories of our time and in setting the agendas for theology and theological ethics in late modernity. No two contemporary thinkers have more radically redefined the tasks and basic questions of political theology in a theological, exegetical direction than John Howard Yoder and Oliver O'Donovan, even while remaining fully attuned to the historical and political conceptual traditions and issues of the Christian West. Although each is clearly influenced by the anti-liberal and exegetical, apocalyptic messianism of Karl Barth—thus warranting Paul Doerksen's comparative analysis under the rubric of "post-Christendom Protestant political theology"—Yoder and O'Donovan are by no means slavish Barthians, nor are they in agreement about the political or theological implications of this basic approach. Doerksen's book provides us with the first systematic, comparative treatment of these two important thinkers and it is a deceptively fine account. I say it is deceptive because what Doerksen's work offers is a non-polemical and fair-minded, nuanced and non-defensive account of the similarities and differences between these two Barth-influenced political theologians who are themselves highly polemical and agonistic thinkers. That is to say, Doerksen brings Yoder and O'Donovan into dialogue with one another beyond the caricatures that characterize the polemical exchanges, thus showing with descriptive clarity what is at stake for contemporary political theology in this dialogue—regarding the interpretation of Scripture, Christology, war and peace, and political authority.

The sovereignty question is rightly central in Doerksen's book: "Yahweh is King" and "Jesus is Lord" are the central biblical tropes informing the political theologies of both Yoder and O'Donovan, though they lead each to very different readings of Christendom and of just war. As one might expect, Yoder the Anabaptist radical is a strong critic of the history of Christendom as a "Constantinian" betrayal of the messianic pacifism of the early church, while O'Donovan the Anglican divine provides the most compelling architectonic account of the basic features and conceptual resources of Christendom traditions for post-Christendom political theology that we have. Yet both thinkers write out of a reforming freedom from traditional constraints (denominational, exegetical, ideological) that is rooted for each in the primacy of Scripture and a theological openness to the continuing authority of divine agency in revealing new political pathways for obedience to messianic sovereignty. For these reasons Yoder and O'Donovan make for stimulating, rigorous and lively conversation partners. Paul Doerksen's book offers us a reliable and thoughtful guide to the basic contours and importance of this conversation for an emergent Christian political theology that is biblical but not biblicist, historically informed but not historicist, ecclesial but neither sectarian nor anti-secular, apocalyptic but not triumphalistic. Nothing is more important for the messianic body than to catch sight of the faithful enactment of messianic sovereignty (the "mind of Christ," to use Pauline language) in its own time and place. The prophetic explorations of Yoder and O'Donovan are richly relevant to the church's ongoing conversation about the political implications of such a vision, and Doerksen's study helps us understand why this is so.

P. Travis Kroeker

Acknowledgements

The taking on of scholarly work is a complex mixture of individual (sometimes isolated) work and dependence on the contribution of and participation in a variety of communities. So it is my happy task to acknowledge the essential involvement of several communities in this project.

The academic community in which this book has its genesis has of course been central in shaping my work. The care and rigour with which I have been supervised by Professor P. Travis Kroeker has been exemplary. It has been my privilege to be mentored by this scholar of international reputation, who, when my work was on the table, pushed hard for quality of argument and clarity of thought, and also found room to develop with me a friendship that I treasure. My gratitude is also extended to the other members of my supervisory committee, Professor Peter Widdicombe and Professor Zdravko Planinc. Among others who have also provided important input along the way, I should mention James Reimer, Craig Carter, Reinhold Kramer, Justin Neufeld, Justin Klassen, Greg Hillis, Russell Snyder-Penner, and Daryl Culp.

I am grateful to the faculty and administration at MBCI, who have been flexible in providing leaves, part-time arrangements, and interest in my work. My thanks especially to the group that meets on Fridays from time to time – my hope is that you know how much our fecund exchanges have meant to me over the years. And I am also indebted to other friends too numerous to list, both in Kitchener/Waterloo and Winnipeg, including the 'Tall Foreheads' reading group. Nonetheless, I must mention Denny and Mary, whose friendship has meant so much to us throughout this process. Thanks also to my colleague Shane Cooney whose cheerful help with final preparation of the manuscript is much appreciated.

I feel as though I owe a word of thanks to a variety of coffee shops in Kitchener/Waterloo and Winnipeg, since much of my work has been completed while sitting for hours in settings where I have never been asked to 'move along,' but have been granted the space to work in freedom. So, thanks to Williams' Coffee Pub, the Huether, Chapters, Stella's, Bread and Circuses, Second Cup, and Starbucks.

I must also acknowledge the financial support of an Ontario Graduate Scholarship, as well as the funding provided by the Social Science and Humanities Research Council of Canada during much of the time when my research was conducted.

My deeply felt thanks go to family. Mom and Dad Suderman have been very supportive, traveled many times to see us, and looked after our girls for several extended weekends. Thanks also to my Mom, who even as she struggled with her health, has remained supportive, and I hope to live up to her suggestion that I use my education "wisely." Mom's apparent mystification as to why her children 'like books' so much is no mystery to us – we come by this interest honestly from her and our late father, whom I think of often, and wish that he was with us – I like to think that he would be interested in my work.

To our girls – Cecely, Hannah, and Greta – who have become familiar with a vocabulary of 'dissertation, defense, Yoder, O'Donovan' and so on, I extend my affection and appreciation for patience through the many evenings and weekends when I was absent, or might as well have been. Finally, I reserve my deepest, heartfelt gratitude to the grace and love freely given to me by my beloved wife Julie. Not once have I been the recipient of a chastening word that might suggest a lack of support and confidence in me, this despite the disruption of major proportions that 2 cross-country moves (and so on) have imposed on our family. To you, Julie, I dedicate this project, as a gesture toward the patient love freely given across the years.

Introduction

This project, through a comparative analysis of John Howard Yoder and Oliver O'Donovan, will show how, in a post-Christendom, secular, liberal Western society, Protestant political theology has tried in two different ways to relate discourse about God to political thought and social structure. Within the modern Western political tradition, it is most often taken as a given that church and state must remain separate, a notion that has its roots in the work of such influential thinkers as Jean-Jacques Rousseau and Thomas Hobbes. Such an understanding might be seen as a reaction to more than a millennium of Christendom, when church and secular authority worked in close relation to govern society.[1] This arrangement, heavily critiqued and subsequently dismantled in Western society, has given way to the current post-Christendom era.

It is important to pay attention to the voices of Yoder and O'Donovan in these early years of the twenty-first century, which began with the attacks of September 11, 2001 on the World Trade Center in New York, a dramatic but surely not unique example of violence that includes a significant religious dimension, albeit one that is impossible to extricate from other contributing factors such as economics, politics and so on. It is clear that the renewed optimism of Western liberalism, so evident in the wake of the collapse of the Soviet Union and the tearing down of the Berlin Wall in 1989, was not sustainable for very long, if at all. The 'end of history' had *not* arrived, and religion refused to stay where liberalism would prefer to put it, that is, on the margins, on the level of personal piety. Therefore, the current situation includes the presence of theological voices of many kinds which continue to clamour to analyze and critique political arrangements from the perspective of differing interpretations of God's ways with the world.[2]

---

[1] The term 'Christendom' can describe a specific historical era in which the Christian church was identified with the whole of organized society, or the merging of the religious and political community. See R.W. Southern, *Western Society and Church in the Middle Ages* (Middlesex: Penguin Books, 1970), 16. As a concept, 'Christendom' might be described an attempt to take seriously the political nature of the church and its instrumental role in the salvation of the world. See William Cavanaugh, "Church," in William Cavanaugh and Peter Scott, eds. *Blackwell Companion to Political Theology* (Oxford: Blackwell Publishers, 2004), 397. In Craig Carter's use of the term, Christendom is "a concept of Western civilization as having a religious arm (the church) and a secular arm (civil government), both of which are united in their adherence to Christian faith, which is seen as the so-called soul of Europe or the West." Craig Carter, *Rethinking 'Christ and Culture': A Post-Christendom Perspective* (Grand Rapids: Brazos Press, 2006), 14.

[2] William Cavanaugh and Peter Scott, eds. *Blackwell Companion to Political Theology* (Oxford: Blackwell Publishers, 2004), 1.

This is not to say that theological voices of the previous century has been completely marginalized in the arenas of politics and social ethics.[3] However, it can be argued that most theological voices in Western Christianity were framed within a widespread acceptance of a basically unified reality of Christendom in its many forms, a reality which has been largely eroded, and in any case, not accepted by many theologians, leaving the West in a post-Christendom era.[4] Therefore, theological discourse must work within this post-Christendom reality, without relying implicitly or explicitly on the presumptions of Christendom.

Put another way, Christian political thought in the twentieth century has largely proceeded along the lines of what might be termed a "dominant tradition," wherein the institutions of the state and civil society take on the primary role as agents of freedom and organizers of the human community, while the church takes on a truncated political role as custodian of values and propagator of ideals deemed necessary to sustain the state and civil society.[5] However, in the post-Christendom era, this dominant tradition of political theology has begun to be challenged by what may be termed as an "emergent tradition," which recognizes the distortion of the mission of the church within the dominant tradition, and therefore "rejects politics as statecraft and envisions the church as a concrete public, political space in its own right."[6]

It is within this so-called emergent tradition of post-Christendom political theology that the theological voices of Yoder and O'Donovan find their place, although they do so from differing social locations – Yoder as an American Anabaptist, representing a tradition descended from a dissenting branch of the

---

[3] Any number of sources could be cited to narrate the basic story of twentieth century Christian social ethics and political thought. For example, see J. Philip Wogaman, *Christian Perspectives on Politics* (Louisville: Westminster John Knox Press, 2000); Wogaman, *Christian Ethics: A Historical Introduction* (Louisville: Westminster John Knox Press, 1993); William Cavanaugh and Peter Scott, eds. *Blackwell Companion to Political Theology* (Oxford: Blackwell Publishers, 2004); Stanley Hauerwas and Samuel Wells, eds. *Blackwell Companion to Christian Ethics* (Oxford: Blackwell Publishers, 2006).

[4] A fuller discussion of Christendom will follow below, especially as this is understood by Yoder and O'Donovan in their respective thought. The fuller discussion requires taking up the concept of Constantinianism as well as Christendom, which will be addressed in detail in chapter three.

[5] Daniel Bell, Jr., "State and Civil Society," in *Blackwell Companion to Political Theology* (Oxford: Blackwell Publishers, 2004) 428, 429. Bell sees this dominant tradition manifested within three strands of twentieth century Christian political thought: a) the political theology of thinkers such as Johann Baptist Metz, Jürgen Moltmann, and Dorothee Sölle; b) Latin American liberation theology; and c) the 'public theology' of theologians such as John Courtney Murray, Richard John Neuhaus, Ronald Thiemann, and Max Stackhouse. Bell, 430-432.

[6] Bell, 433.

Reformation; O'Donovan as a British Anglican, representing a state church tradition descended from the magisterial Reformation – two traditions that only recently have begun to dialogue seriously with each other.[7] This book will therefore take a close look at the particular theopolitical visions of these Western theologians as a way of seeing how they go about their work, what kinds of claims they make, how they use the Scriptures and so on. Briefly put, I want to make sense of their claim that they are providing a political rendering of the claim that Jesus is Lord within a post-Christendom context.

O'Donovan claims that he is trying to recover the ground that has been traditionally held by the notion of authority – he does so by way of a matrix of political authority/political act/judgment, which serve as the nuclear core of what he is trying to investigate theologically. Yoder is fully engaged in trying to uncover an ever-refined understanding of peoplehood – people in covenant with God, a community in covenant with God, which by its very existence and embracing of the politics of Jesus is fully political, or so he claims. The order of the faith community constitutes a public offer to all of society.

In short, if "the work of political theology is to shed light from the Christian faith upon the intricate challenge of thinking about living in late modern Western society,"[8] then it is very important to listen to Yoder and O'Donovan in this post-Christendom era. In the course of examining their respective works, we will see that they deal with a wide range of relevant issues such as judgment, the nature of freedom, the possibility and shape of public deliberation and communication, the role of power and coercive force, the powers that any given institution should or should not have, the nature of representation, the nature and locus of authority, role and form of punishment, sharing and husbanding of resources, discussions of what constitutes meaningful action in history, the intelligibility of suffering, and all of this without making a case for hegemony of the church or some version of theocracy, for the revival of Christendom or even the establishment of the church. In common with other Christian thinkers, but also with other political theorists, Yoder and O'Donovan seek to move beyond assumptions that reduce politics to actions that are simply assertions of the will.[9]

Interpretations advocating the separation of church and state in the modern era have been shaped by a liberal tradition of radical two-fold suspicion - the suspicion that politicians corrupt morality, and that politics is corrupted by theology.[10] To address this pervasive suspicion, it is thought that church and

---

[7] I am indebted here to comments made by Craig Carter.

[8] O'Donovan, *The Ways of Judgment*, x.

[9] Rowan Williams, "Introducing the Debate: Theology and the Political." in *Theology and the Political: The New Debate,* ed. Creston Davis, John Milbank, and Slavoj Zizek, (Durham and London: Duke University Press, 2005), 1.

[10] Oliver O'Donovan, *The Desire of the Nations: Rediscovering the Roots of Political Theology* (Cambridge: Cambridge University Press, 1996), 6-8.

state must be kept separate, and further, that it is the important prerogative of the state to determine the place of the church within society. O'Donovan and Yoder refuse to allow political theology to be defined in conventional liberal categories. That is, their work can be understood as constructing Protestant political theologies that challenge liberal suspicions, but they do so in significantly different ways that need to be clarified and compared. Both O'Donovan and Yoder claim to find authorization for their respective projects in the Christian scriptures,[11] although their readings and use of particular biblical texts relating to political theology differ significantly. Broadly put, it might be said that O'Donovan's use of the Bible is indebted to the magisterial Reformers, while Yoder tries to read the Bible in the spirit of the early Anabaptists.[12] Thus Yoder's reading of the Bible tends to have a more distinctively counter-culture dimension than does that of O'Donovan. Throughout the course of this project, I will explore the contours of these two theopolitical visions that claim to be based on the Bible via a critical comparison that brings into relief significant differences and similarities, and culminates in an analysis of what is perhaps their most telling disagreement regarding the use of coercive power by the state.

The term 'political theology' will be used in a descriptive way, although the phrase is surrounded by an important debate that centers on the question of whether politics or theology forms the primary horizon for the enterprise of discussing the relation of church and state. Therefore, the project begins by placing the term 'political theology' itself in context as a way of setting the stage for a further understanding of how O'Donovan and Yoder fit into this ongoing conversation.

The first chapter of the project consists in a critical comparison of the use of the Hebrew Scriptures by these two Christian theologians. O'Donovan's reading of the Hebrew Scriptures focuses on God's kingly rule of Israel (a 'royal' reading) as the nexus of power, law and tradition. Yoder's reading of the Hebrew Scriptures centers on what he calls the diaspora vision that he finds originating in the Abrahamic call and culminating especially in the ministry of the prophet Jeremiah (an 'antiroyal' reading). This signals that Yoder is interested in how Israel, and subsequently, Christian believers, find their place in society as pilgrims, exiles or resident aliens.

---

[11] See O'Donovan, *The Desire of the Nations*, 15; John Howard Yoder, *The Politics of Jesus: Vicit Agnus Noster*, 2d ed. (Grand Rapids: Eerdmans Publishing, 1994), 2. The first edition was published in 1972 – all references in this book are from the second edition. See also Yoder, *The Jewish-Christian Schism Revisited*, Michael Cartwright and Peter Ochs, eds. (Grand Rapids: Eerdmans, 2003).

[12] Christopher Rowland applies this characterization within his discussion of the role of the Apocalypse in O'Donovan's work. See Christopher Rowland, "The Apocalypse and Political Theology," in Craig Bartholomew, Jonathan Chaplin, Robert Song, and Al Wolters, eds. *A Royal Priesthood? The Use of the Bible Ethically and Politically – A Dialogue with Oliver O'Donovan* (Grand Rapids: Zondervan Press, 2002), 241-254.

Introduction 5

The second question to be addressed is the understanding of Jesus and the church in the political theologies of O'Donovan and Yoder. In O'Donovan's case, his focus on God's kingly rule in Israel does not lead him to assert that Christ calls the church to rule society. Rather, the authorization of secular space comes from the new reality created by the resurrection and exaltation of Jesus Christ, which redeems and vindicates creation, and has a crucial ecclesiological mode, "which takes the church seriously as a society and shows how the rule of God is realized there."[13] It is precisely within this framework that a space for limited secular authority arises. "If the mission of the church needs a certain social space, for men and women of every nation to be drawn into the governed community of God's Kingdom, then secular authority is authorized to provide and ensure that space."[14] The authorization of secular space is provisional and penultimate, but fully real, as a place where judgment can take place, where real authority, including the use of force, is wielded. For O'Donovan, then, the church's internal focus has to do with ultimate things, and therefore it does not pass judgment, but offers forgiveness and reconciliation.[15] But the church is differently authorized than the state,[16] and so the church works to help society and rulers to extend mercy in judgment, but nonetheless to judge, as a way of shaping larger secular society, and of extending God's rule beyond the experience of the church.

Yoder reads the New Testament with a focus on the cross of Jesus Christ – he maintains that Jesus led a life that challenged the powers that be, which led in turn to his being crucified as a political criminal. The resurrected Christ calls into existence a church community that is called to live according to this same cruciform pattern – Yoder calls this 'the politics of Jesus.' Jesus is to be understood as the model of radical political action. The church community is thus seen as paradigmatic – the order of the faith community constitutes a public offer to all of society. The church is, as it were, a vision of the kingdom come, but there is no separate authorization for secular society. It has a mandate from God to provide space for the church to fulfill its mission.[17] The difference between O'Donovan and Yoder at this point is important. In both cases, there is 'space' for secular society and 'space' for the church to fulfill its mission. However, O'Donovan sees the secular space as having an authorized status, while for Yoder, God does not grant secular society a separate authorization, but nonetheless orders it. So, for Yoder, political theology entails a particular kind of focus on the church as a community of suffering love, where "the very shape of the people of God in the world is a public witness, or is 'good news,'

---

[13] O'Donovan, *The Desire of the Nations*, 123.
[14] O'Donovan, *The Desire of the Nations*, 146.
[15] O'Donovan, *The Desire of the Nations*, 256-258.
[16] O'Donovan, *The Desire of the Nations*, 158.
[17] Yoder, *Discipleship as Political Responsibility*, trans. Timothy Geddert (Scottdale: Herald Press, 2003). See especially the essay "The State in the New Testament."

for the world, rather than first of all rejection or withdrawal."[18] In sum, his contention is that a church formed by the politics of Jesus can be a Christian witness to the state, and thus exist for the nations without committing itself to underwrite the violence used by the state.

These divergent conceptions of the role of the church lead to a sharp disagreement regarding Christendom, which will be the focus of the third chapter. O'Donovan believes that Christendom, which he understands as the era stretching from the fourth century to the First Amendment of the Declaration of Independence (1791), is a positive resource that offers a way to understand the shape of secular space as part of a theologically conceptualized politics. Historical Christendom has given us the unique opportunity to see how this relationship might shape society. Yoder is critical of theological projects that underwrite either civil religion or the state establishment of any particular religion. Any such initiatives are interpreted as "Constantinian," to use Yoder's technical term. While Yoder defines Constantinianism as "the identification of church and world in the mutual approval and support exchanged by Constantine and the bishops," the concept is not primarily historical, but representative of an attitude toward the relation of state and church which Yoder sees as unfaithful to the Christian vision.[19] That is to say, he calls into question all tendencies of the church to establish relations of political compromise with the state, or tendencies that cause the church to be tempted to do the work of God using coercive power.

These disparities between O'Donovan and Yoder are not merely theoretical matters. Thus, in the fourth chapter, I will argue that their respective ethical positions on war and violence are logically intrinsic to their political theologies. O'Donovan is an influential expositor and supporter of the Just War tradition, while Yoder has bequeathed a lasting legacy of Christian pacifism in theological ethics. This deep disparity will be an explicit focus for further analysis since the marked divergence in position regarding the legitimate use of force by the state clearly illustrates the differing social instantiations of the two theopolitical visions being discussed.

To explore the attempts by these theologians to challenge the liberal suspicion of political theology is to understand better the shape of our society, and the relationship of religion and politics. The work of O'Donovan and Yoder provides a fitting way into this discussion, and to compare their efforts will contribute to the further development of constructive political theology as part of the ongoing historical, theological, and political conversations that make up the Western religious tradition.

Some scholarship has already been done which brings particular aspects of

---

[18] Yoder, *For the Nations: Essays Public and Evangelical* (Grand Rapids: Eerdmans Publishing, 1997), 6.

[19] Yoder, *The Royal Priesthood: Essays Ecclesiological and Ecumenical*, ed. Michael Cartwright (Grand Rapids: Eerdmans Publishing, 1997), 154.

O'Donovan's thought into conversation with Yoder. O'Donovan mentions Yoder several times in *The Desire of the Nations*,[20] once in *The Ways of Judgment*, but these brief references cannot be considered to be a serious engagement with Yoder's thought. However, I have also not discovered any mention of O'Donovan in Yoder's writings. Thus there has not been a significant conversation carried on between Yoder and O'Donovan.[21] Several essay-length publications deal with topics such as a consideration of the role of Christology in O'Donovan and Yoder's political theology,[22] and a discussion of Christendom and voluntariety.[23] However, the task of understanding O'Donovan and Yoder on their own terms in the post-Christendom context, and then working out a full-length critical comparison of their work remains to be done, and is the burden of this project.

Political Theology

Kathryn Tanner maintains that all theology is political for two reasons: Christianity is a way of living in which beliefs are embedded, and theology makes commentary on the political whenever it incorporates social and political imagery such as Lord, Kingdom, and so on.[24] But to assert that Christian theology is by its nature political does not address the use of the somewhat controversial phrase 'political theology.'[25] The contemporary use of the term is contentious because of Carl Schmitt's work and his notorious connection to the Nazi party in the 1930s. Because of Schmitt's use of the term, 'political

---

[20] See *The Desire of the Nations*, 151-2, 223-4.

[21] It is interesting to note that O'Donovan engages much more specifically and extensively with Stanley Hauerwas's thought than Yoder's, despite the marked similarities between Hauerwas and Yoder, and the extensive influence of Yoder on Hauerwas. Further, Hauerwas engages in conversation with O'Donovan's thought in a number of places, some of which will appear in discussions below.

[22] See my article, "Christology in the Political Theology of Oliver O'Donovan," *Mennonite Quarterly Review* 78 no 3 (July 2004): 433-447.

[23] P. Travis Kroeker, "Why O'Donovan's Christendom is not Constantinian and Yoder's Voluntariety is not Hobbesian: A Debate in Theological Politics Re-defined," in *The Annual of the Society of Christian Ethics* 20 (2000): 41-64.

[24] Kathryn Tanner, "Trinity," in William Cavanaugh and Peter Scott, eds. *Blackwell Companion to Political Theology*, 319-320.

[25] Alistair Kee suggests that even though the phrase 'political theology' has only been used recently, there has always been an interaction of theology and politics. Kee, ed. *A Reader in Political Theology* (London: SCM Press, 1974), ix. Duncan Forrester has a similarly broad definition: "political theology as a theological interpretation of what is happening in the realm of politics and an attempt to relate to the varied forms of political religion which emerge in every age is inevitable, and has been there from the beginning in diverse forms." Duncan Forrester, *Theology and Politics* (Oxford: Blackwell Publishers, 1988), 20.

theology' came to be understood for a time as something that provides theological underpinning for totalitarian government.

Schmitt's use of 'political theology' made the term suspect because at least some of his thought defended and legitimated the Nazi regime in which he lived and worked.[26] Schmitt had been a constitutional advisor to the Weimar Republic, but moved quickly to position himself as a supporter of the Nazis following Hitler's rise to power in 1933. Writing in 1934, Schmitt already describes the German theory of public law in the Weimar Republic as "a deteriorated and therefore self-contradictory normativism," which when blended with positivism, became a "degenerate decisionism, blind to the law, clinging to the 'normative power of the factual' and not to a genuine decision. This formless mixture, unsuitable for any structure, was no match for any serious problem concerning state and constitution."[27] In the same preface to the second edition of *Political Theology*, Schmitt puts forward the notion that the political is the total. Schmitt notes that despite Protestant theology's reference to a supposedly unpolitical doctrine of God as 'wholly other,' any decision about whether something is unpolitical is always political – an idea that also holds for the question of whether some theology is political or not.[28] Schmitt is searching here for some basis on which to (re)establish and protect the authority of the state. Thus he begins the first essay in *Political Theology* with his dramatic assertion, "sovereign is he who decides on the exception."[29] It is not enough that a state have a normative system of law or constitution, but it must also be able to deal with the exception. A general norm can never encompass a total exception. By exception, Schmitt means any case of extreme peril, any danger to the state that cannot be circumscribed factually or made to conform to a preformed law. For Schmitt, the exception, which defies general codification and cannot be subsumed, is much more interesting than the rule, since the rule proves nothing, while the exception proves everything. "In the exception the power of real life breaks through the crust of a mechanism that has become torpid by repetition."[30] Schmitt's concern in this discussion of the exception within an essay regarding sovereignty is that the state must have the authority to suspend the law in the exception on the basis of its right to self-preservation – the norm is destroyed in the exception, but authority is established.

---

[26] It is not my intention here to sort out the extent to which Schmitt was a cynical opportunist or a convinced, intentional promoter of the Nazi regime. He has his defenders and detractors. My intent is much more modest in that I want to show how his political theology became associated with support of totalitarianism on theological grounds.

[27] Carl Schmitt, *Political Theology*, trans. George Schwab (Cambridge: MIT Press, 1985), 3.

[28] Schmitt, *Political Theology*, 2.

[29] Schmitt, *Political Theology*, 5.

[30] Schmitt, *Political Theology*, 15.

It was precisely the pervasive concern regarding the authority of the state that made Schmitt hostile to liberalism of all kinds.[31] The state must be more than some liberal body that reflects the liberal assumption that conflict should be transformed into matters of opinion, and thus be resolved by free and rational discussion. Rather, the political system must have the power to protect itself. Schmitt understood the state as a "body which must make decisions and defend the interests of its 'friends' against assaults from the 'enemy,'" which led him to reject any ideas of state neutrality. Therefore, against political pluralism, the state is the body that makes decisions and wields the authority to protect its subjects.[32]

Schmitt turns, at least in part, to political theology to find a way to support the authority of the state. In the title essay of *Political Theology*, Schmitt famously asserts, "all significant concepts of the modern theory of the state are secularized theological concepts not only because of their historical development – in which they were transferred from theology to the theory of the state, whereby, for example, the omnipotent God became the omnipotent lawgiver – but also because of their systematic structure, the recognition of which is necessary for a sociological consideration of these concepts."[33] This politicization of theological concepts is not some easy equation in which a theological concept has its political equivalent, but rather works by way of analogy, or what Schmitt calls the 'sociology of a concept.' Such sociology "aims to discover the basic, radically systematic structure and to compare this conceptual structure with the conceptually represented social structure of a certain epoch."[34] Another way that Schmitt describes what he is attempting to explain is to suggest that he is concerned with displaying 'general states of consciousness,' whereby, for example, we can understand the monarchy of a certain epoch to correspond not with a direct reflection of God, but with a general state of consciousness that is prevalent in the epoch.[35] Schmitt points out, for example, that the concept of a miracle is analogous to that of the exception. With the replacement of theism by deism, the general state of consciousness was such that the possibility of miracles was rejected, which corresponded with the rejection of the exception. Deism thus allows the modern state to triumph – decisionism and personalistic elements in the concept of sovereignty are lost, and thus the important dimension of authority is also missing. Schmitt finds that several counterrevolutionary Catholic philosophers

---

[31] Michael Hollerich, "Carl Schmitt," in Cavanaugh and Scott, eds. *Blackwell Companion to Political Theology,* 108.

[32] David Nicholls, *Deity and Domination: Images of God and the State in the Nineteenth and Twentieth Centuries* (London and New York: Routledge, 1989), 101-105. The specific quotation is found on 104.

[33] Schmitt, *Political Theology,* 36.

[34] Schmitt, *Political Theology,* 45.

[35] Schmitt, *Political Theology,* 45, 46.

apply the right kinds of analogies – theistic analogies that could support authority.[36] So Schmitt declares that the declining belief in transcendence was being replaced either with positivist indifference to all metaphysics or what he terms as immanence-pantheism, an atheistic Hegelianism, in which mankind had to be substituted for God.[37] Schmitt's search for the possibility of re-establishing authoritarianism on the foundation of political theology was to him a project of "salvaging decisionism in an age of universal suffrage."[38] If the general state of consciousness could be restored to include the possibility of authority, then the state would be restored to its proper place as the protector of its subjects, and take up again the responsibility of dealing with the exception. Schmitt believed that political theology could provide this resource, and so the church becomes important in order to make the state viable in his terms. This 'instrumentalizing of the church,' the presenting of the Catholic Church as the bulwark of authority in an unsteady social world[39] under the term 'political theology' has made the term suspect.[40]

The phrase 'political theology' took on a different association beginning in the 1960s, when it was widely used to describe a development in European and Latin American theology whose principle methodological principle was the primacy of criticism.[41] The term now indicated a specific relationship between politics and theology – one in which political theology does not choose its own agenda, but addresses issues of importance in the world; theology finds common concern with other organizations and movements, and shows a bias for the poor. Political theology here is seen as having a prophetic, critical, and

---

[36] Schmitt, *Political Theology*, 48.

[37] Schmitt, *Political Theology*, 49, 50.

[38] Nicholls, *Deity and Domination*, 108.

[39] See Hollerich, "Carl Schmitt," 110-111, 119.

[40] Erik Peterson viewed the term so suspiciously that he made the sweeping assertion that Nicene trinitarianism and Augustinian eschatology had made a break with every political theology that misuses Christian proclamation as a justification for a political situation. Apparently Schmitt believed that this statement by Peterson was aimed at him. See Hollerich, "Carl Schmitt," 111. See also Rudy Siebert, "From Conservative to Critical Political Theology," in A. James Reimer, ed., *The Influence of the Frankfurt School on Contemporary Theology: Critical Theory and the Future of Religion: Dubrovnik Papers in Honour of Rudolf J. Siebert* (Lewiston: Edwin Mellen Press, 1992), 147-219.

[41] This is how Herbert Richardson describes the essays in *Religion and Political Society*. The preface to the book suggests "Christian and Enlightenment conceptions of criticism and freedom should be systematically interrelated in order to create a *theology of politics*." Italics in original. Jürgen Moltmann, Herbert Richardson, Johann Baptist Metz, Willi Oelmüller, and M. Darrol Bryant, preface to *Religion and Political Society* (New York: Harper and Row, 1974), x.

politicized role.[42] This political theology in its European form is associated primarily with the work of Jürgen Moltmann and Johann Baptist Metz, while in its Latin American manifestation as liberation theology it is associated with theologians such as Gustavo Gutiérrez, Paulo Freire, Jon Sobrino, and Leonardo Boff.

It is the primary dimension of criticism that has brought this use of the term into question, since Christian thought here did not wish to develop a theology of politics, but to articulate the political implications of whatever issue was under consideration. In a critical study of Jürgen Moltmann's theology in particular, Arne Rasmusson describes the political theology exemplified by Moltmann as "an attempt to positively meet the challenges of modernity, characterized by industrialization, urbanization, science, technology, market economy and a growing state and its various ideological backbones in liberalism and socialism, with their common beliefs in progress and in politics as a mean for consciously forming the future."[43] Therefore, politics becomes the basic horizon, and since the issues that theology must deal with are given in the world, the job of the church is to decide which side of a given issue to position itself. Political theology in this guise becomes a mediating project between Christianity and modernity.[44]

'Political theology' as used by Schmitt, or as used to delineate the primarily critical work of the latter half of the twentieth century does not correspond to the work done in this field by O'Donovan or Yoder. However, O'Donovan describes his own work in *The Desire of the Nations* as political theology, although he is explicitly doing so in order to rehabilitate the term and tradition, as he understands it. He mentions Carl Schmitt, but does not address his thought, rather dealing with the more current mode of liberation theology, complaining that it is too critical without being constructive.[45]

O'Donovan describes *The Desire of the Nations* as political theology, which he understands to be part of a larger task, that of "a historico-theological exploration of themes surrounding the proclamation of God's kingdom, preparing the way for a more deliberatively oriented exploration of the tasks of politics," an enterprise that will require two parts – political theology and political ethics, which are but two moments in one train of thought.[46] This is not some new task given to the contemporary church, but one of the retrieval of a

---

[42] Kee, ed., *A Reader in Political Theology*, x-xii. The reader includes essays from Christian-Marxist dialogue, theology of hope, theology of revolution, theology of development, theology of liberation, black theology, violence, and Christian resistance.
[43] Arne Rasmusson, *The Church as Polis: From Political Theology to Theological Politics as Exemplified by Jürgen Moltmann and Stanley Hauerwas* (Notre Dame: University of Notre Dame Press, 1995), 11.
[44] Rasmusson, *The Church as Polis*, 14, 187, 331, 375.
[45] O'Donovan, *The Desire of the Nations*, 2-5.
[46] O'Donovan, *The Desire of the Nations*, ix.

tradition that has been abdicated – the moment of abdication marked by Thomas Hobbes. Thus O'Donovan sees himself as 'rediscovering the roots of political theology,' a task in which his intention is to "push back the horizon of commonplace politics and open it up to the activity of God,"[47] and therefore is not hesitant to use the phrase 'political theology' to describe his project in *The Desire of the Nations*. He acknowledges in passing that Schmitt's use has made the term virtually unusable, but since political theology itself has a long history, albeit one that has been eclipsed, the term can happily be retrieved and rehabilitated. However, while O'Donovan is willing to recognize a fairly broad scope of political theology, he is careful to set his political theology apart from several other forms. That is, on the one hand, political theology "does not suppose a literal synonymity between the political vocabulary of salvation and the secular use of the same terms," and on the other hand, should not be restricted to programmes that "conceive theologico-political discourse as critical, even subversive, of other political discourses."[48] Clearly O'Donovan's understanding of political theology is quite broad, and amounts to an inclusive genre of theology that includes civil religion, those who combine theology with other political discourses such as Marxism, programmes of an 'Anabaptist' slant, and any attempts to combine critical and constructive elements (O'Donovan classifies himself in the latter category). Only one example is given where the term political theology is overextended – the approach which has no interest in political questions as such, "but merely professes an ecclesial anti-foundationalism, the political content reduced to the banal reminder that theology must relate to some community of discourse."[49] By his own description then, O'Donovan engages in retrieval, a rediscovery of theology that assumes a prophet's task, and "accepting history as the matrix in which politics and ethics takes form, affirm[s] that it is the history of God's action, not sheer contingency but purpose."[50] As O'Donovan has put it, 'theology' is the noun in 'political theology', and thus our search for true political concepts, which do not come from secular political philosophy, are authorized from the Bible, and therefore political theology begins as an exegetical task.[51] This is an important move to note, since it enables O'Donovan to address any criticism that might suggest that politics provides the primary horizon for his work.

O'Donovan's cryptic definition of political theology as 'the pushing back of the horizon of commonplace politics to open it up to the activity of God' can generally be applied to Yoder's work, but it is important to recognize that

---

[47] O'Donovan, *The Desire of the Nations*, 2.

[48] O'Donovan, *The Desire of the Nations*, 2, 4.

[49] O'Donovan, *The Desire of the Nations*, 4. O'Donovan's example of a political theology with an 'anabaptist' slant refers to Stanley Hauerwas, not John Howard Yoder, who is actually an Anabaptist theologian writing about theopolitical matters.

[50] O'Donovan, *The Desire of the Nations*, 12.

[51] O'Donovan, *The Desire of the Nations*, 15.

Yoder works quite differently than does O'Donovan, as will become obvious throughout the course of this project.[52] Yoder does not refer to any of his theological work as political theology, even when he is addressing explicitly political issues such as democracy, the role of the state and so on. At first glance, then, it appears that the kind of distinction between political theology and theological politics made by Arne Rasmusson may have some merit. Briefly put, Rasmusson defines *political theology* as that which makes politics of the world primary, in which the issues discussed are given by the world, and the church decides what side to be on. *Theological politics* is that which makes the church the primary locus for its politics, and therefore the church has its own agenda that challenges the way the world's politics is understood.[53] While it is primarily Hauerwas's work that Rasmusson categorizes as theological politics, the term also encompasses Yoder. Rasmusson's primary rationale for the distinction is that someone doing theological politics changes the discussion that occurs in political theology. That is, the church is here seen as the primary locus for a new politics – Christians are called to embody an alternative politics, a contrast society that challenges the way the world's politics is understood.[54] Put another way, Yoder claims that the church is not fundamentally a source of moral stimulus to encourage the development of a better society – it is for the sake of the church's own work that the society continues to function. The church is itself a society, a demonstration of what suffering love means in social relations. But in modern usage the application of the term 'political' to the state rather than the church has become so entrenched that it is nearly impossible to resist. However, Yoder's work shows him attempting to resist the conventional understanding of politics as statecraft.[55]

---

[52] Daniel Bell, Jr., lumps together Yoder, O'Donovan, Hauerwas, and John Milbank into what he calls the 'emergent postliberal tradition.' He specifically puts O'Donovan and Yoder into the same category when he claims "the heart of the emergent tradition is not simply the replacement of the sovereign state with a hegemonic church, but the political rendering of the claim that Christ is Lord." Daniel Bell, Jr., "State and Civil Society," in Cavanaugh and Scott, eds. *Blackwell Companion to Political Theology,* 436. I agree with Bell's drawing out of certain similarities here, but he casts his net so wide as to ignore important distinctions within the 'emergent tradition' category.
[53] Rasmusson, *The Church as Polis,* 331.
[54] Rasmusson, *The Church as Polis,* 187, 188, 331. Hauerwas likes Rasmusson's distinction, and even uses it, although not in a fully consistent manner. See for example Hauerwas's recent essays concerning Dietrich Bonhoeffer, in which the title of the first essay is "Dietrich Bonhoeffer's Political Theology," but the essay itself uses the term 'theological politics' with specific reference to Rasmusson's categories. Stanley Hauerwas, *Performing the Faith: Bonhoeffer and the Practice of Nonviolence* (Grand Rapids: Brazos Press, 2004), 33-54. Daniel Bell also uses the term 'theological politics' instead of 'political theology.' Bell, "State and Civil Society," 436.
[55] Yoder, *The Christian Witness to the State* (Newton: Faith and Life Press, 1964), 13-18. Bell, "State and Civil Society," 433.

But even prior to any assertions concerning the church as politics, Yoder insists that any examination of these questions cannot take place in the abstract. Thus he remains skeptical about the possibility that the exercise of laying some kind of groundwork can come first logically, chronologically, or developmentally, and rejects the option of defining a normative vocabulary prior to a theopolitical discussion.[56] Yoder opts instead to read the Bible to see if there is a political dimension to be found there. In an important passage in which democracy is the topic of discussion, Yoder suggests, "it is the usage of governmental language within the people of God which is the norm. The governmental logic used within the wider culture is then only a pale reflection, analogy, dilution, perversion of 'true politics.' Only the politics of Jesus is politics according to the will of God."[57] Yoder attempts to apply this kind of norm in *The Politics of Jesus,* where he argues that Jesus is a model of radical political action who offers us a particular social-historical-political option.[58]

While it is important to recognize the different ways in which O'Donovan and Yoder proceed, the kind of distinction made by Rasmusson is not adequate as a template to capture that distinction. O'Donovan does not fit Rasmusson's too-narrow use of 'political theology,' while Yoder would resist the prior category of 'theological politics' apart from the working out in detail of what he calls 'true politics.' Therefore, the best way to proceed in a comparative critical analysis is to resist the designation of descriptive or theoretical categories for O'Donovan and Yoder's work prior to proceeding with the analysis itself. In other words, the emphasis here will be the investigation of the various theological issues that are politically important.[59] That is, it is in the investigation of the theopolitical dimensions and particularities of their thought that important differences and similarities will come to view, not in placing them in designated categories and then trying to show that this is indeed where they belong. Thus this project will proceed as an investigation of theopolitical thought of O'Donovan and Yoder, and not an exercise in the analysis of political theology or theological politics.

---

[56] Yoder, *The Christian Witness to the State,* 83; Yoder, *The Priestly Kingdom: Social Ethics as Gospel* (Notre Dame: University of Notre Dame Press, 1984), 7, 172.
[57] Yoder, *The Priestly Kingdom,* 163.
[58] Yoder, *The Politics of Jesus,* 2,11.
[59] In the introduction to the *Blackwell Companion to Political Theology,* William Cavanaugh and Peter Scott suggest that political theology is any explicit attempt to relate discourse about God to the organization of bodies in space and time. Cavanaugh and Scott, editors' introduction to *Blackwell Companion to Political Theology,* 2.

Chapter 1

"God is King": The Hebrew Scriptures in the Theopolitical Thought of John Howard Yoder and Oliver O'Donovan

Introduction

A comparative critical study of the theopolitical visions developed by John Howard Yoder and Oliver O'Donovan must be grounded in an analysis of their respective readings of the Bible, since both thinkers claim to be fundamentally Biblical in their approach to political theology. This chapter will attend briefly to the general approach to reading the Bible taken by Yoder and O'Donovan, but the analysis will focus primarily on their respective readings of the Hebrew Scriptures[1] and the prominent role given to Israel in their Christian political visions. While significant differences will be brought to view, three areas of thematic commonality will guide the analysis provided here. That is, the kingly rule of God, the role of the monarchy in Israel, and the prophetic tradition, especially as represented by Jeremiah, are the shared points of reference that form the structure of the discussion of Yoder's and O'Donovan's Christian theopolitical reading of the Hebrew Scriptures.

My central claim will be that despite the thematic commonalities that can be identified, the visions of Yoder and O'Donovan begin to diverge in significant ways precisely at those points at which they draw upon similar themes in the Hebrew Scriptures. For O'Donovan, an interpretation of the kingship of God provides the resources necessary for recovering the ground traditionally held by the notion of authority. That is, his royalist reading of the texts, while not a defense of monarchy, nonetheless dominates his discussion, since he sees the experience of Israel as the display of God's rule from which it is possible to derive important political concepts and theorems needed for a political theology. Yoder is also adamant that an important dimension of the Hebrew Scriptures is the cry that 'God is King,' with the attendant implication that therefore human monarchy is at best unnecessary, but potentially (and probably) idolatrous – hence Yoder's antiroyal reading of the Hebrew Scriptures. Yoder takes it as a given that human monarchy cannot represent God, and he is wary of the possible misuses of any monarchical analogy. While

---

[1] O'Donovan uses terms such as 'Hebrew Scriptures' or 'Old Testament' to refer to the Jewish Bible, while Yoder's tendency is to use terms such as "Jewish Scriptures' or 'Hebrew Bible.' I will use the term 'Hebrew Scriptures.'

both O'Donovan and Yoder focus on the importance of God as King, their understanding of the content, shape and impact of that kingship differs considerably. Yoder's focus on God as warrior (as opposed to humans taking up that role) enables him to set the stage for a pacifist reading of war accounts in the Hebrew Scriptures, and his focus on the nature of kingship as suffering service brings to view a significant divergence from O'Donovan's treatment of the implications of divine kingship. The kingship of God, for Yoder, does not so much provide the resources for recovering the ground traditionally held by the notion of authority as inaugurate an ever-refined understanding of peoplehood in covenant with God. This emphasis of Yoder's stands at the heart of his focus on the church within his theopolitical thought, to the frustration of his critics, who see Yoder as restricting Christian understandings of politics to a sectarian mode, as promoting an understanding of engagement with politics that cannot be constructive. However, my analysis will show throughout that Yoder seeks constructive political engagements, albeit in ways that differ considerably from O'Donovan.

O'Donovan and Yoder also share common ground in their analysis of the pivotal prophetic role, which takes explicit priority over the monarchy in Israel, beginning with the ministry of Jeremiah. O'Donovan describes Israel's prophets as sharing "the task of tradition-bearing with the monarch; and, indeed, theirs was the more significant part, since it was through their words that Yhwh himself defined and redefined in each new circumstance the moral content of the tradition to which the kings were answerable. That content was the law."[2] This move to the juridical dimension of political theology marks a key moment for O'Donovan, one that allows him to develop an argument for the centrality of law as the form in which God's authority over the whole earth may be realized. The prophetic ministry in Israel draws attention to any unfaithfulness to God's law on the part of the monarchy, and prevents the monarchy from claiming inappropriate authority for itself.

O'Donovan's insistence that each member of the community has to make a choice between listening to the prophet and submitting to the unfaithful authority of the institutions under which they find themselves,[3] shows that "an element of confessional voluntarism enters into Israel's sense of itself."[4] This confessional voluntarism (not to be mistaken for the individualism of the West), along with the emphasis on the priority of the prophetic tradition and on diaspora, bears a close resemblance to Yoder's treatment of the Jeremian shift, although Yoder does not make the move to a focus on law and international order in the same way as O'Donovan. Yoder's focus on the Jeremian shift moves instead toward showing that Jeremiah retrieved a heritage that has always existed among the people of God. Thus, for Yoder, confessional

---

[2] O'Donovan, *The Desire of the Nations*, 62.
[3] O'Donovan, *The Desire of the Nations*, 77.
[4] O'Donovan, *The Desire of the Nations*, 79.

voluntarism, the priority of the prophetic tradition, and diaspora, lead to the creation of a faith community that is called out to represent the way of God in the world. Yoder's move is toward the communal in terms of ethos and practices rather than the juridical rule of law – a very different move that will have significant implications for the envisioned theopolitical role of the Christian church.

Reading the Bible: Yoder's Ecclesial Epistemology

John Howard Yoder's theopolitical thought is based on the reading of the Bible as a normative source, rooted in the revelation of God.[5] However, Yoder is loathe to accept any predetermined method for reading Scripture, since he claims that the New Testament writers, for example, have different ways of proceeding in various contexts.[6] Running throughout Yoder's work is a thread that seeks to warn against and avoid the dangers inherent to imposing any kind of a system upon the interpretation of Scripture. That is, Yoder is extremely skeptical about the adequacy either of any systematic method of reading the Bible or the building of a system that claims to arise out of such readings.[7]

Yoder's suspicions regarding the value of any overarching concept for the reading of Scripture concern possible readings that might be artificially forced into pre-ordained categories, or made to serve the system that is in place prior to an engagement with the text itself. Yoder fears that the imposition of a particular pattern of utter consistency on one's own thoughts, or on someone else's, can quickly become oppressive. Yoder suggests six specific ways in which systematizing may be oppressive: a) it may be assumed that concepts are timeless, which would do violence to the organic historical flexibility that

---

[5] Yoder, *The Priestly Kingdom,* 7. Elsewhere, Yoder simply describes the Bible as the ground floor of all theology. Yoder, "The Use of the Bible in Theology," in *To Hear the Word* (Wipf and Stock: Eugene, Oregon, 2001), 71. This essay first appeared in Robert Johnston, ed. *The Use of the Bible in Theology*, (Atlanta: John Knox Press, 1984), 103-120.

[6] Yoder, *Preface to Theology: Christology and Theological Method,* eds. Stanley Hauerwas and Alex Sider (Grand Rapids: Brazos Press, 2002), 110. This book consists of a series of lectures used by Yoder in a theology course. These lectures have been available in mimeographed form since 1968. The introduction by Hauerwas and Sider provides an important context for the publication of these course lectures.

[7] "The reason for this flexibility of method is not a desire to be 'liberal' either in the sense of an optimistic vision of human nature in general or in the more restrictive methodological sense of being optimistic about the power of one's critical tools. The reason is, rather, modesty about the power of our human instruments of interpretation, which leads rather appropriately, in the face of the choice which God obviously made to become manifest through a multiplicity of literary forms that are mostly narrative on framework and doxological in tone, to skepticism about the adequacy of any system-building of our own." Yoder, "Use of the Bible in Theology," 80.

marks the Bible; b) what counts as 'consistent' may be tilted in favour of certain models of communication specific to some class, gender, or culture; c) it may be assumed that all reasons for being systematic call for the same system, or that one should reign over the others; d) it may be unclear how to validate the choice of which foundational concepts give order to the others; e) it may be wrongly thought that the maker of a system should also be the ruler of the church; and f) any system may hamper the flexibility that the Gospel communicator needs.[8]

Yoder's suspicion of any form of system-building or predetermined systematic approach to reading Scripture does not require that he come to his own reading with some 'pure' precritical naiveté. Some kind of grid is clearly at work when Yoder reads Scripture, a fact that he does not seek to disguise. However, whatever grid may be at work ought to be constantly subjected to testing in what he refers to as "an unending spiral of new learnings and self-correction."[9] Put another way, Yoder's approach to Scripture is more accurately characterized as a 'stance' or 'posture' than as a position or system.[10]

'STANCE'

Yoder's use of the concept of 'stance' or 'posture' is his way of opposing the notion of necessity of some system or architectonic to which a reading is

---

[8] Yoder, "Thinking Theologically From a Free-Church Perspective," in John Woodbridge, Thomas McComiskey, eds. *Doing Theology in Today's World: Essays in Honor of Kenneth S. Kantzer* (Grand Rapids: Zondervan Publishing House, 1991), 253-254. The free-church perspective Yoder refers to here is related to but not equal to his denominational Mennonite home. Yoder is careful in this essay to show a connection to the Radical Reformation of the sixteenth century without restricting the designation to any one theological notion or Reformer, describing instead a "set of shared experiences and a common *stance*," which entails a desire to reform Christianity where it has gone wrong, to take account of why things have gone wrong in the first place (radical), to refuse to be governed by worldly authorities, and to form communities based on adult confession of faith. Ibid., 251-252.

[9] Yoder, "Thinking Theologically From a Free-Church Perspective," 257.

[10] An important dimension of this stance includes the possibility of what Yoder refers to as 'looping back,' a reference to the notion that the wholesome growth of a tradition is for Yoder like a vine rather than a tree. That is, growth takes place by way of pruning, or a "glance over the shoulder to enable a midcourse correction, a rediscovery of something from the past whose pertinence was not seen before, because only a new question or challenge enables us to see it speaking to us." Yoder, *The Royal Priesthood*, 69. Romand Coles makes extensive use of Yoder's notion of 'looping back' in a recent essay entitled "The Wild Patience of John Howard Yoder," in *Beyond Gated Politics: Reflections for the Possibility of Democracy* (Minneapolis: University of Minnesota Press, 2005), 109-138.

subject.[11] He claims that 'stance' is a better term than 'system' to describe the "coherence, such as there is," to his "various concerns."[12] This seemingly casual approach to coherence does not signal a lack of hermeneutical rigour in reading the Scriptures, but functions as an attempt to place the reader before the text in such a way that there can be perpetual openness to renewed understandings and the reshaping of attitudes and the very shape of her life.[13] This 'free church' stance *vis a vis* the Bible includes a central emphasis on the role of the community in the interpretation of the Bible. That is, Yoder argues that the interpretation of the Bible is not primarily the task of the university scholar, the spiritual elite, or the hierarchy of the church. Instead, a community of believers takes on the task of perpetually interpreting the Bible with a view to embodying in the life of that community the truth of the Scripture, a process Yoder refers to as the "hermeneutics of peoplehood."[14] Interpretation as a communal process "makes central (in Anabaptist thought, for instance) a fringe concern in magisterial Protestantism. There must be a believing, obeying, and worshipping community if the meaning of a text is to be properly understood."[15] Yoder's stance might be referred as an ecclesial epistemology in which the "church precedes the world epistemologically. We know more fully from Jesus Christ and in the context of the confessed faith than we know in other ways."[16] For Yoder, it is significant that the people who interpret Scripture are performatively faithful in the interpretive task, since it is precisely in that performative interpretation that an understanding of God becomes possible. It is important to make this point, since it signals Yoder's belief that God revealed himself in a particular historical context, and therefore the Bible as a whole provides various accounts of the attempt to work out what it means

---

[11] Yoder makes use of the notion of stance in several contexts other than the reading of Scripture. See for example, his description of the cross as a stance in the world, his understanding of the Beatitudes as postures in which people find themselves when the kingdom of God comes, and the understanding of the relationship of the church and the world. See Yoder, *Preface to Theology*, 105; Yoder, *He Came Preaching Peace* (Scottdale: Herald Press, 1985), 49; and Yoder, *The Royal Priesthood*, 71, 72 respectively.

[12] Yoder, *For the Nations*, 10. Yoder describes the entire theme of *For the Nations* as a "tone, style, stance of the people of God."

[13] Yoder, "Thinking Theologically From a Free-Church Perspective," 257.

[14] This phrase is the title of the first chapter of Yoder, *The Priestly Kingdom*. A fuller treatment of Yoder's ecclesiology is necessary in order to develop the significance of the role of the church in hermeneutics, ethics, and political theology, a treatment that will unfold in the following chapters. My point here is simply to signal Yoder's insistence that the church community is a vital part of interpreting Scripture.

[15] Yoder, *Preface to Theology*, 372.

[16] Yoder, *The Priestly Kingdom*, 11.

to be a follower of God.[17]

Yoder's refusal of system in favor of stance nevertheless allows for the description of the characteristics of his readings of Scripture that follow from the stance he displays throughout his work. That is, the "permanently fragmentary quality"[18] of his work does not prevent the identification of recurring fragments that play a significant role in Yoder's reading of the Bible.

BIBLE AS STORY

One of the defining characteristics of Yoder's stance toward the Bible is his understanding of the Bible as a "story and not simply a flat collection of instructions and models."[19] While it would be difficult (and perhaps misleading) to classify Yoder as a narrative theologian, since to be committed to narrative as some kind of prior approach to reading would already violate his stance,[20] Yoder does suggest that taking account of the narrative quality of Scripture is more likely to encompass and situate the task of reading than some more timeless or concept-driven mode.[21] For example, it is precisely this narrative quality that Yoder approves of in his commentary on Karl Barth's political theology, namely that Barth prefers to focus on narrative as opposed to some deductive treatment of the Biblical text.[22] However, as noted, to suggest that narrative in itself is a category adequate for encompassing Yoder's work is misleading. The narrative quality that Yoder identifies in the Bible is closely connected to what may be called "organic historical development under

---

[17] Grady Scott Davis, "Tradition and Truth in Christian Ethics: John Yoder and the Bases of Biblical Realism," in Stanley Hauerwas, Chris Huebner, Harry Huebner, and Mark Thiessen Nation, eds. *The Wisdom of the Cross: Essays in Honor of John Howard Yoder* (Grand Rapids: Eerdmans, 1999), 301- 302.

[18] Yoder, *The Royal Priesthood*, 121.

[19] Yoder, *Christian Attitudes to War, Peace, and Revolution: A Companion to Bainton* (Elkhart: Co-op Bookstore, 1983), 443.

[20] I take this point from Chris Huebner's discussion of Yoder and narrative theology in "Mennonites and Narrative Theology," *The Conrad Grebel Review* 16 no 2 (1998): 15-38.

[21] Yoder, "Thinking Theologically From a Free-Church Perspective," 257-258. Yoder insists, "the Bible as a whole corpus of literature is narrative in its framework, although some of its fragments are not. That framework itself dictates the priority of the historical quality over levels of interpretation which would be less historical by being more abstract (ontology, systematic dogma) or individualistic." Yoder, "Use of the Bible in Theology," 77-78.

[22] Yoder, *The Royal Priesthood*, 110. Yoder points out in this context that it is the emphasis on narrative that allows Barth to affirm the scandal of particularity that is embodied in the incarnation of Jesus Christ, a move that is important for Barth's view of the relationship between the church community and the civil community.

guidance."[23] Yoder sees this notion as particularly important, for example, when trying to understand war in the Old Testament. In an introduction to a book written by Old Testament scholar Millard Lind, Yoder claims that war in the Old Testament has been misunderstood in several ways, in part because of "the failure to see in the Hebrew Scriptures the evolution from Joshua to Jeremiah."[24] Yoder's point is that the ancient wars of Israel have been used to justify wars and crusades, as well as to scold Jews for blessing violence. Such negative readings can be forestalled in part by taking note of the development that can be seen in the entirety of both testaments. Yoder notes that if Lind is right, even Jesus brings not some mid-course correction or disavowal of what went before, but a fulfillment of God's shalom-bringing power that was all along an alternative to nationhood as conventionally understood. From the very birth of Israel and even in the young nation's wars this was the case.[25]

Yoder's stance toward the Bible is perhaps most fully on display in his *Preface to Theology,* in his own teaching regarding the nature of the discipline of theology. He argues that the theological task must begin with the biblical material, an approach that he sees as itself true to the historical experience of the church. Therefore to develop readings inductively and historically is to carry on in the pluralistic ways that the Scripture writers and the early church themselves proceeded.[26] The Bible for Yoder is historically conditioned, like all of human history, and therefore demands that it be read as history, thus allowing the reader to retain the "organic historical flexibility" that marks the Bible itself.[27] Yoder sees himself as trying to think the way the Bible thinks when he reads it and when he attempts to take the appropriate stance toward it.

'BIBLICAL REALISM'

In thinking the way the Bible thinks, Yoder seeks to remain free of oppressive system-building tendencies and an epistemological captivity to theory. His own

---

[23] Yoder uses this phrase in a discussion of Millard Lind's reading of the Hebrew Scriptures, a reading with which Yoder is sympathetic, and which is appropriate to describe his understanding of the Bible. Yoder, *Christian Attitudes to War, Peace, and Revolution,* 447.

[24] Yoder, introduction to Millard Lind, *Yahweh is a Warrior: The Theology of Warfare in Ancient Israel* (Scottdale: Herald Press, 1980), 18.

[25] Yoder, introduction to Millard Lind, *Yahweh is a Warrior,* 19. My point here is not to comment on the content of Yoder's (or Lind's) Old Testament reading, but simply show Yoder's understanding of the historical development that he observes in the Bible. Yoder elsewhere sees the Bible as containing "a coherent thread from Miriam's song to Gideon's trust in miracle, from Jeremiah's quietism to the rejection of zealotry by both Jochanan ben Zakkai and Jesus..." Yoder, "Texts That Serve or Texts That Summon?: A Response to Michael Walzer," *Journal of Religious Ethics* 20 no 2 (1992): 234.

[26] Yoder, *Preface to Theology,* 35, 36, 39, 113.

[27] Yoder, "Thinking Theologically From a Free-Church Perspective," 253, 257.

resistance to putatively stultifying typological schemes has no doubt made it difficult for interpreters of Yoder's thought to categorize the way he reads Scripture, or to capture him within the confines of a typology. However, one exception to this general situation is Yoder's own connection with a school of thought known as 'biblical realism' – an association that Yoder finally did not embrace fully.

The prefaces to the two editions of *The Politics of Jesus* display Yoder's skittishness about being aligned with any identifiable 'school.' In the preface to the first edition of *The Politics of Jesus* (1972), Yoder acknowledges that his book is an attempt "to apply in the area of the life of the Christian community the insights with regard to the distinct biblical worldview which have previously been promoted under the name of 'biblical realism.'"[28] Yoder returns to the phrase in the preface of the second edition to clarify what 'biblical realism' was trying to do – it "sought to take full account of all the tools of literary and historical criticism, without any traditional scholasticism, yet without letting the Scriptures be taken away from the church." And yet, Yoder maintains that "If I had known the book would be put on review as a prototype of something methodologically ambitious or profound, I might have gone further into the discussion of theoretical prolegomena – or I might have refused to do so, since one can very soon come to a point, in the abstract discussions of method, where that very discussion gets in the way of letting the text play its role as the documentary spine of the church's identity."[29]

Yet Yoder does use the term 'biblical realism' as an appropriate phrase to describe his reading of the Bible that seeks to take seriously its practical and pastoral thrust. So Yoder is keen both to assert 'biblical realism' as a way to read the Bible and yet deny that it is anything like a 'school,' but more like a tendency which tries to make more of the Bible itself as a model. Therefore, the tendency tries to reflect in its own structure the qualities of the text, incorporating pluralistic styles and formulations since that is the nature of the Biblical text.[30]

In Yoder's view, the endless task of interpretation, with the Bible as the ground floor, is oriented by the revelation of God in Jesus Christ. Yoder maintains that apart from this revelation, it is impossible to know what kind of God is being talked about. The center of Yoder's work then is the historic

---

[28] Yoder, *The Politics of Jesus*, x.
[29] Yoder, *The Politics of Jesus*, viii, ix.
[30] Yoder, "Use of the Bible in Theology," 79-81. See also Yoder, *Preface to Theology*, 390. When asked in a Mennonite context by a student to comment on 'biblical realism,' Yoder claimed that it was not something Mennonites stressed, but he saw it as something like a usable slogan that described a current of thought trying to understand the Bible on its own terms, to use its thought patterns rather than our modern patterns, and to ask the questions the Bible asks rather than take our contemporary questions straight to the Bible. Yoder, *Christian Attitudes to War, Peace, and Revolution*, 438.

reality of Jesus Christ, who functions as a sort of canon within a canon. "The ultimate canon within the canon must in the end, however, be the person of Jesus and, in a broader sense, the narration of the saving acts of God."[31] Attention to these saving acts of God helps Yoder to identify the continuity between the Hebrew Scriptures and the New Testament. That is, he seeks to articulate a "sympathetic understanding of the Torah as a vehicle of grace within Jewish tradition."[32] As contained in the Hebrew Scriptures, the Hebrew heritage of the Christian Scriptures forms "a set of assumptions and prerequisites, cultural backgrounds, and definitions of terms"[33] which are necessary to come to any kind of understanding of Jesus as Christ. Yoder's resistance to setting aside the Hebrew Scriptures is on full display in *The Politics of Jesus,* where he not only refers to the Hebrew Scriptures frequently, but also develops several central themes as part of his Christian argument for the kind of politics brought to view in Jesus Christ.[34] Yoder therefore tries consistently to reach back to the Hebrew Scriptures as part of the Christian story, just as he sees the early church following in a similar historical movement from promise to fulfillment.[35]

Yoder summarizes his stance as one that takes seriously the narrative, historically conditioned quality of the Bible, which continually calls into being a community that intends to obey what it comes to understand as God's call within its particular time and place.

The Bible, then, is not best taken as a repository of infallible propositions, better understood when lifted from their particular settings, which God would have been better advised to give us in a less narrative, more "systematic" mode. The Bible is the document produced by the formative and thereby normative generations of God's working with us.... It is historically conditioned like all human reality and thereby demands that it be read as history. It is written demanding to be read like any other text. It is the record, then, of God's calling men and women into obedience and praise and will most aptly be read as

---

[31] Yoder, "Use of the Bible in Theology," 73, 77.

[32] Richard Hays, *The Moral Vision of The New Testament: A Contemporary Introduction to New Testament Ethics* (San Francisco: Harper Collins, 1996), 245. Yoder puts the point negatively when he points out what he describes as the great apostasy – the loss of the way of faith that he sees perpetrated by the early apologetes who tried to make the message palatable to the philosophers by reducing Jewish particularity, whereby the faith becomes a moral monotheism with no particular peoplehood. As a result, Christianity lost its understanding of the Torah as grace and privilege and capacity for decentralized congregationalism. Yoder, *The Jewish-Christian Schism Revisited,* 107.

[33] Yoder, "Use of the Bible in Theology," 74.

[34] Yoder makes the point specifically that readers have to be careful of setting aside the Old Testament simply by suggesting that Jesus now says "But I say to you." Yoder, *The Politics of Jesus,* 87.

[35] Yoder, *Preface to Theology,* 112, 373.

calling us now into the same obedience and praise. A mode of systematizing that takes account of this narrative quality will be more likely to encompass and situate our task than would a more timeless or concept-centered mode.[36]

Yoder favors a non-systematic, narrative reading of the Scriptures in which the practicing community of faith is seen as the rightful interpreter of the history of revelation from divine promise to fulfillment.

Yoder's reading of the Bible generally and his use of the Hebrew Scriptures in political thought raises a number of issues, beginning with his resistance to systematization. It is difficult for readers to take seriously Yoder's insistence that systematization carries with it an inherent temptation of oppression and the imposition of structures foreign to the Biblical material itself. In several cases readers have attempted to show that despite Yoder's disavowals, he is systematic after all. For example, Craig Carter, in his monograph on Yoder's social ethics, observes that one has to read a lot of Yoder's essays before it is possible to realize the consistency of his overall system. Carter acknowledges the inherent danger that he will turn Yoder's thought into a system, and undertakes to avoid just that problem. However, despite a nuanced reading of Yoder's thought, Carter in the end does not heed his own warning, criticizing Yoder for being too unsystematic.[37] As part of his concluding chapter, Carter isolates three weaknesses in Yoder's work, the first being Yoder's rejection of system. Carter concludes that Yoder's critique of methodologism "has a point, but he probably pushes it too far," in that the refusal to write some sort of major systematic book on Christian ethics leaves Yoder open to misinterpretation and caricature. Carter contends that Yoder simply cannot avoid systematic questions, and indeed that Yoder undeniably has a system, one that has a high degree of logical consistency. Carter concedes that the refusal of the systematic challenge opens the way for theology to be done in a more *ad hoc* and dialogical manner, but nonetheless argues for some kind of a "better balance" in which Yoder might forego a search for a neutral, scientific method that expects a universally accessible truth while still overtly acknowledging the systematic theological task. But Carter's concern and call for Yoder to do

---

[36] Yoder, "Thinking Theologically From a Free-Church Perspective," 257, 258. Grady Scott Davis describes Yoder's reading of the Bible as follows: "It is important to be faithful in interpreting Scripture because it is there that the Christian claims to learn most clearly what God is like. This signals the belief that the Lord revealed himself most clearly in a particular historical context, that the Bible read as a whole provides various accounts of the attempt to work out what it means to be a follower of the Lord, and that an important component of faithfulness to that enterprise lies in according these accounts a privileged place in contemporary Christian attempts to continue the project of faithful living. Grady Scott Davis, "Tradition and Truth in Christian Ethics," 301, 302.

[37] Craig Carter, *The Politics of the Cross: The Theology and Social Ethics of John Howard Yoder* (Grand Rapids: Brazos Press, 2001), 18, 19; 235-239. See Travis Kroeker, review of *The Politics of the Cross*, by Craig Carter, *Journal of Mennonite Studies*, 20 (2002): 268-270.

systematically what he has done dialogically misses at least in part the point that Carter acknowledges and that Yoder seems to see precisely *as* the point – that theology should be authentically dialogical, a conversation that never closes. As noted above, Yoder is open to systematizing that takes into account the narrative quality of the Bible, and so Carter's comments are not without merit. However, Carter seemingly cannot accept Yoder's stance as being fully authentic or effective even on its own terms. Carter, at the last moment, turns back to systematic theological categories, and apparently cannot believe that Yoder's intention was at bottom not part of a greater attempt at systematization. Carter speculates that perhaps Yoder simply intended to work out the social-ethical implications of the systematic work done by Karl Barth. This assessment of Yoder's work suggests two things - Carter does not accept Yoder's intention of refusing systematization as being fully serious. He also does not give appropriate credence to Yoder's free church stance, a posture that suggests that Yoder was doing theology, and not just applying Barth's system, which is perhaps most obvious in Yoder's disagreement with Barth concerning pacifism.[38] Presumably, then, according to Carter's line of thinking, had Yoder ever finished unfolding the social-ethical implications of Barth's system, the real work of avoiding possible misunderstanding (that which happens in the

---

[38] It must be said that Carter nevertheless does a fine job of showing Yoder's debt to Barth. What is much less clear in Carter is the deep influence of historical Anabaptism on the way Yoder worked. For an early example of how crucial the dialogical nature of theology is to Yoder's work, see John Howard Yoder, *Anabaptism and Reformation in Switzerland: An Historical and Theological Analysis of the Dialogues Between Anabaptist and Reformers,* ed. C. Arnold Snyder, trans. David Carl Stassen and C. Arnold Synder (Kitchener: Pandora Press, 2004). This book includes the English translation of two of Yoder's books previously only published in German. The second part of the English translation is the theological analysis of a historical study done by Yoder, and it is here that Yoder's focus on the theological importance of dialogical theology comes to view. The focus comes from a reading of Anabaptist-Reform dialogues, and the research was done during a time that Yoder would also have taken classes from Barth at the University of Basel. Mark Thiessen Nation has recently edited and introduced a collection of Yoder's essays on Barth, in which it is clear that Barth was influential on Yoder, but to suggest as Carter does, that Yoder was simply drawing out the implications of Barth's work seems to be a misreading which ignores Yoder's specific historical/theological research, his denominational history, and his constructive theological work. See Yoder, *Karl Barth and the Problem of War and Other Essays on Barth,* ed. Mark Thiessen Nation (Eugene: Cascade Books, 2003) for Yoder's lengthy criticism of what he considers to be Barth's ultimately incoherent view of war. Neal Blough documents the relationship between Yoder's historical scholarship and the major theological themes he subsequently developed. Blough begins by noting that for Yoder, the doing of church history was a way of entering ecumenical dialogue. Thus for Yoder, being a church historian and being in dialogue was precisely the same thing – as was doing theology and being in dialogue. Neal Blough "The Historical Roots of John Howard Yoder's Theology," in *Anabaptism and Reformation in Switzerland,* xliii.

dialogical mode) through systematization could finally have begun. In some way, Carter seems compelled to see Yoder as systematic, no matter what kind of disavowals and counter-evidence have been encountered.[39]

While Yoder may have resisted such attempts at systematization of his genuinely dialogical work, even an interlocutor as sympathetic as Gerald Schlabach has insightfully pointed out that despite Yoder's resistance to system-building, and his favoring of ecumenical conversation in the free-church style, it is the case that "eventually, however, one does accumulate a repertoire of responses."[40] Schlabach points out, for example, that Michael Cartwright sensed some kind of need for an anthology of Yoder's essays (published as *The Royal Priesthood*). The usefulness of such a collection seems to indicate "certain limitations in Yoder's 'fragmentary' and 'ad hoc' approach to theology – limitations for example in extra-community accountability and intra-community catechesis."[41] Extra-community accountability suggests that accountability is possible in showing consistency that emerges as fragments are exposed on an issue-by-issue basis and seen to fit together within a basic coherence. Intra-community catechesis presumes at least some sequence of teachings, in part for the sake of ease of learning, but more importantly as reminders of teachings that may be important but neglected because of other urgencies. For example, Schlabach points out that anthologizing Yoder's work makes it easier to see there an emphasis on grace, God's initiative in the Christian life, the need for personal conversion, the place of the ancient creeds and so on – topics that Yoder sometimes seems to avoid.[42] But unlike Carter, Schlabach does not try to do Yoder the unwanted favor of either suggesting that he really should create a theological system, or that he already has done so.

---

[39] Similarly, Nancey Murphy argues that Yoder's writings constitute a systematic defense of Christian theology, something she sees as important to back up his claims for pacifism. In order to show the systematic structure of Yoder's theology, Murphy draws on the work of philosopher of science Imre Lakatos. Yoder would not be sympathetic to Murphy's attempt to show that "Yoder's theology fits the form of a scientific research program," complete with a core theory and network of auxiliary hypotheses, with the Bible providing the necessary data for this 'research program.' Murphy is offering a gift Yoder would not be eager to accept, since in her zeal to systematize Yoder's thought, Murphy seems rather to be imposing a structure on that thought which Yoder sees as foreign both to the Biblical text and certainly to his own attempt to embody a stance rather than promote some system. Nancey Murphy, "John Howard Yoder's Systematic Defense of Christian Pacifism," in Stanley Hauerwas et al., eds., *The Wisdom of the Cross,* 46-47.

[40] Gerald Schlabach, "Anthology in Lieu of System: John H. Yoder's Ecumenical Conversations as Systematic Theology," *Mennonite Quarterly Review* 71 (April 1997): 307. Schlabach emphasizes the fact that Yoder engages in theology itself in a conversational mode.

[41] Schlabach, "Anthology in Lieu of System," 307.

[42] Schlabach, "Anthology in Lieu of System," 307, 308.

Instead, Schlabach acknowledges that Yoder's work allows theologians to continue to ask whether systematic theology is an attempt to control and oppress, and even may offer the opportunity to offer "confessionally, narratively or biblically derived truth-claims in systematically ordered presentations."[43]

It is also important to note that Yoder's reading of the Bible is guilty at times of what might be called 'lumping.' That is, since he is nearly always writing relatively short essays to deal with specific questions in particular situations, time is often not taken to give precise accounts of the concepts being put forward.[44] This kind of lumping can be seen in Yoder's discussion of Israel's ambivalence toward kingship, when he moves quickly from Isaiah to Jeremiah, to Ezra and Nehemiah to make his point about Jewish diaspora.[45] Yoder's sweeping statements intend to further whatever argument he is making, and he seems to be fully aware that leaping about from one historical figure and era to another may be frustrating to readers who are trained to expect a systematic account that can qualify as legitimate warrant for an argument. For example, Yoder presses this point in an essay entitled "On Not Being in Charge," where, in making a historically rooted argument, he claims to "renounce any vision of stopping in every century along the way."[46] Yoder's explanatory note is telling – he claims that Donald Durnbaugh also leaps across centuries in the course of following a historical theme. Yoder goes on to say that "Durnbaugh has also used the image of 'hop, skip, and jump' as a description of the way spiritual continuity occurs in non-established communities; this might well characterize my selective presentation here."[47] Yoder's sentence is a curious one - to suggest that what he "might" be doing is providing a selective presentation of historical events in order to support his argument and that this mode of arguing is related to the shape of spiritual continuity in non-established communities comes dangerously close to

---

[43] Schlabach, "Anthology in Lieu of System," 309.

[44] Yoder is also guilty of 'lumping' is some of his historical interpretation. For example, he locates the 'fall of the church' "at the point of that fusion of church and society in which Constantine was the architect, Eusebius the priest, Augustine the apologete, and the Crusades and Inquisition the culmination."Yoder, *The Royal Priesthood*, 89. Travis Kroeker suggests that such lumping can only make responsible historians cringe in the face of such crudities. See Kroeker, "Why O'Donovan's Christendom is not Constantinian and Yoder's Voluntariety is not Hobbesian," 61. Kroeker registers a similar complaint when he draws attention to Yoder's tendency to "lump together the Platonic Christianity of classical theologians such as Augustine with Constantinian political theology in some unfortunate ways." Kroeker, "The War of the Lamb: Postmodernity and John Howard Yoder's Eschatological Genealogy of Morals," *Mennonite Quarterly Review* 74 (April 2000): 307.

[45] Yoder, *The Jewish-Christian Schism Revisited*, 162.

[46] Yoder, *The Jewish-Christian Schism Revisited*, 172.

[47] Yoder, *The Jewish-Christian Schism Revisited*, 178, note 27.

excusing shoddy historical work on the basis of a commitment to resisting systematization. In some of Yoder's work, fuller, more sustained treatments, rather than imprecise lumping together of disparate elements, are on display, but even these discussions often come in the form of published class lectures.[48] Yoder evidently intended to do more extensive historical work, as when he promises a fuller text on Constantine and the 4th century.[49] In the case of his doctoral work, he provides an extensive historical treatment of a series of disputations that form the basis of an in-depth theological analysis. Here Yoder apparently does not see the need to use the kind of 'hop, skip, and jump' method that appears more frequently in some his later work. Yoder's tendency to indulge in 'lumping' events, people, or ideas in ways that are sometimes unfortunate, and perhaps at times even irresponsible, is nevertheless not entirely unrelated to the way he works. Given his resistance to systematization and the dangers he saw in trying to dominate others through the presentation of complete systems that have to be accepted whole, Yoder may have been seeking to subvert more conventional readings and ways of presenting arguments. In other words, whether or not Yoder's accounts met some kind of conventional standard of a given scholarly guild, he nonetheless wanted his readers to have to confront the large issues that his 'generalizations' pointed toward.

If Yoder rejects the unwanted gifts offered by systematizers of his thought, even when his work is anthologized (by sympathetic interpreters, by himself as in *For the Nations*, or posthumously as in *The Jewish-Christian Schism Revisited*), and if he is guilty of lumping, it remains the case that Yoder's reading of the Bible opens up possibilities for conversations and for returning to the text for new readings, and resists the temptation to have the text pressed into service of a system foreign to the ways the Bible thinks. In any case, Yoder's avoidance of system or commitment to concepts is different than O'Donovan's search for political concepts that can be fit into an architectonic structure, which plays a substantive role within his pursuit of political theology.

Reading the Bible: O'Donovan's Theological Epistemology

Yoder and O'Donovan both claim to have as their starting point an exegetical reading of the Scriptures, and indeed, they engage in close reading of Biblical texts, often of the same passages. However, where we have observed Yoder's reading of the Scriptures proceeding within an ecclesial epistemology, with an attendant refusal of systematization, O'Donovan embarks on his reading of Scripture from what he terms as a theological epistemology. When he turns to Scripture to pursue political theology, O'Donovan searches for political

---

[48] See for example, Yoder, *Preface to Theology*, and Yoder, *Christian Attitudes to War, Peace, and Revolution*.

[49] Yoder, *For the Nations*, 6.

concepts that will help to recover the ground traditionally held by the notion of authority. As he proceeds, he moves toward putting into place an architectonic hermeneutic and unifying conceptual structure[50] that will provide the political concepts necessary to pursue political theology. He does not attempt to read moral order off of the face of creation or nature. That is, he describes himself as agreeing with Stanley Hauerwas regarding the "non-self-evidence of the creation order."[51] Human fallenness is seen as a persistent rejection of the created order, and thus there is an inescapable confusion in the perception of that order. Therefore, we can only know how or when or where the natural order is violated *theologically,* since our knowledge depends on God's disclosure.[52]

THINKING FROM SCRIPTURE

O'Donovan's thought is unabashedly theological in nature, based as it is in his attempt to think out of Scripture, a way of reading that O'Donovan refers to as 'theological epistemology.' In discussing the Thirty-Nine Articles of Anglican Christianity, O'Donovan suggests that theological epistemology is the proper approach to the Holy Scriptures, as described in Articles 6-8. The authority of Scripture must be considered prior to its interpretation. That is, the Scriptures are considered authoritative by the church, and thus provide a way of knowing for the church.

The problem encountered by the modern reader, according to O'Donovan, is to conceive of a way of knowing that is not defined entirely in terms of the knowing subject. This is not some fideistic claim, but an exposition of the way the Anglican Church traditionally has understood Scripture, a view itself based on the tradition of the church in its belief that the Scriptures testify to the historical event of the incarnation of Christ. O'Donovan uses the term "biblical epistemology" as part of his view that it is possible and necessary for Christian thought to develop beyond Scripture as a way of elucidating the faith, and also to speculate in order to draw out the implications of faith for matters not directly addressed there. As part of this discussion, O'Donovan suggests that "biblical epistemology does not mean that thought must stand still."[53] O'Donovan seems to use "biblical epistemology" in the same way as the previous reference to theological epistemology. That is, O'Donovan seeks knowledge by thinking from Scripture, which he considers as authoritative for the Christian church as it seeks to discharge its God-given tasks, including a

---

[50] O'Donovan, *The Desire of the Nations,* 22.
[51] O'Donovan, *Resurrection and Moral Order: An Outline for Evangelical Ethics,* 2d ed. (Grand Rapids, Mich.: Eerdmans Publishing, 1994), xv.
[52] O'Donovan, *Resurrection and Moral Order,* 19.
[53] O'Donovan, *On the 39 Articles: A Conversation with Tudor Christianity* (Carlisle: The Paternoster Press, 1986), 49-54, 115.

faithful understanding of political concepts. The connection between biblical and theological thinking in O'Donovan's work is that Scripture has a determinative shape that is authoritative for theology.[54]

Given O'Donovan's commitment to theological epistemology, it comes as no surprise that when he turns to a reading of the Hebrew Scriptures for political theology, he does so in a self-consciously Christian way. His view of the authority of Scripture presupposes the possibility of a harmonious reading of both Testaments, and therefore any notion of contradiction within the Scriptures should be banished, since it "bespeaks an ahistorical, two-dimensional understanding of the Scriptural texts that conceives of them all as synchronous and competing propositions, rather than dialectically successive and mutually implicating testimonies of God's unfolding self-disclosure."[55] In other words, the Bible is the unfolding of the theological idea of God in relationship with humanity, concretized and lived out in a specific society.

THE SEARCH FOR POLITICAL CONCEPTS IN SCRIPTURE

According to O'Donovan, the reading of the Scriptures as sacred history can never be some naïve or conceptually innocent (pure) process, especially in the search for usable political concepts. Therefore, his reading of the Bible in search of political concepts proceeds in an exegetically thick manner, pursued as part of a carefully worked-out conceptual framework. The concepts O'Donovan searches for are required for organized theory, since "concepts disclose the elementary structures of reality in relation to which we can begin to identify questions for theoretical development."[56] But true political concepts for political theology must be authorized from Scripture itself, and so O'Donovan is careful not to plunder the text willy-nilly for concepts that address whatever topic he may be addressing, but he attempts to read the Bible in a way that is consistent with itself. In this stance toward Scripture, there is a significant congruence with Yoder's approach to reading the Bible. However, O'Donovan's reading is more explicitly a search for concepts that will mediate between the reader and the theologian, between reading the text and constructing a theory. This is an important observation, since it gestures toward the power both of the individual concepts and the conceptual framework O'Donovan claims to need in order to do political theology in a way that seeks to treat the Scriptures in their entirety,[57] a conceptual framework of the sort that

---

[54] I take this way of putting it from Craig Bartholomew, "Introduction" in Craig Bartholomew et al., eds., *A Royal Priesthood?,* 37. Bartholomew is generally impressed with O'Donovan's biblical work.

[55] O'Donovan, *On the 39 Articles,* 60.

[56] O'Donovan, *The Desire of the Nations,* 15.

[57] A similar observation is made in Victor Austin, "Method in Oliver O'Donovan's Political Theology," *Anglican Theological Review* 79 (Fall 1997): 586.

Yoder claims not to need. For O'Donovan, if the concepts that serve as the building blocks of the structure are brought into dispute, the structure itself may be compromised, or so it would seem. Just as he reads the Bible to guide Christian thought toward a comprehensive *moral* viewpoint, and not merely to articulate disconnected moral claims, so O'Donovan reads the Bible to guide Christian thought toward a comprehensive *political* vision, and not just to articulate disconnected political claims.[58]

At its heart, O'Donovan's theological work is conceived as an exegetical task. In the case of political thought, he suggests that the search for and identification of political concepts in Scripture calls for a process in which identifying concepts comes before constructing theory, but comes *after* reading the text.[59] However, *before* embarking on a reading of the Hebrew Scriptures, O'Donovan makes an important interpretive move when he declares that the central thesis in *The Desire of Nations* is that theology, by developing its account of the reign of God, may recover the ground traditionally held by the notion of authority. After praising the Southern school of theology (often referred to as Liberation theology) for taking Scriptural concepts seriously, O'Donovan complains that the Southern school has lacked a concept of authority in its investigations of the relations of Scripture, society, and social scientific guidance. O'Donovan is quick to have the reader notice that he says "'a' concept, because it would be inauthentic to make advance stipulations for what kind of concept of authority it might derive from reading Holy Scripture."[60] Nonetheless, it is authority that must be found, since it is "the nuclear core, the all-present if unclarified source of rational energy that motivates the democratic bureaucratic organizations of the Northern hemisphere; but it is also a central theme of the pre-modern political theology, which sought to find criteria from the apostolic proclamation to test every claim to authority made by those who possessed, or wished to possess, power." Indeed, authority has either been viewed with suspicion or simply ignored in silence, with a resultant "*political* incoherence at the heart of contemporary politico-theological aspirations."[61] Therefore, when O'Donovan turns to the political theological task as an exegetical exercise that will bring true political concepts to view, which will in turn provide the material for construction of theory, he gains purchase on this task by seeking to recover the lost notion of authority, which he believes can be recovered theologically by developing an account of the reign of God in Israel, which is to be read as sacred history, as a

---

[58] "... it is not a matter of simply emphasizing key words in the text, 'judgment', 'love', or whatever, and even if key words may sometimes be used (as we shall use them) to identify the concepts, the words themselves are not the concepts but are like flags on a map which signal their presence." O'Donovan, *The Desire of the Nations*, 15-16.

[59] O'Donovan, *The Desire of the Nations*, 15-16.

[60] O'Donovan, *The Desire of the Nations*, 16.

[61] O'Donovan, *The Desire of the Nations*, 16-17. Italics in original.

display of God's rule over a particular nation.

To talk of politics within the category of history, even if it is the history of one particular nation, carries the modern danger of arbitrariness that can be part of historicism, wherein nothing outside of historical contingencies can be taken into account, a danger that is to be avoided. Placing political history within the history of God's reign adds three elements that serve to address the danger O'Donovan has identified. First, the history of divine rule safeguards and redeems the goods of creation, and thus politics can be seen as having a world-affirming and humane character. Second, we are forced to strip away the institutional fashions within which the Western tradition has clothed the idea of authority and focus on the political act instead of institution. Third, a history of divine rule is a revealed history that takes place as the history of Israel, which means that our understanding of general and universal history must be measured against this canonical history. A political theology of the kind O'Donovan attempts to develop will seek to understand how and why God's rule confers authority on political acts, something that can only be understood through the history of divine rule that is displayed in the canonical account of the history of Israel.[62] This history of Israel is a record of God's action and is thus revelatory of God's purposes, and is useable for political theology.[63] The shape of this usability is not straightforward, however, and therefore O'Donovan argues that it cannot be something like a choosing of an isolated theme from the Hebrew Scriptures, no matter how dominant such a theme may be, as can be seen in the use of the Exodus account as political paradigm. The problem is that such a theme is not integrated into the whole story, and so O'Donovan argues that "an architectonic hermeneutic which would locate political reflection within an undertaking that had its centre of gravity in the Gospel" is needed.[64] He finds that unifying hermeneutic in Israel, that unique political entity through which God made his purposes known to the world. In other words, "the governing principle is the kingly rule of God, expressed in Israel's corporate existence and brought to final effect in the life, death, and resurrection of Jesus."[65] But not everything about Israel is equally

---

[62] O'Donovan, *The Desire of the Nations,* 19-21. O'Donovan defines the political act as that "which, performed by one or few on behalf of the many, witnesses faithfully to the presence and future of what God has undertaken for all. The political act is the divinely authorized act." Ibid., 20. O'Donovan claims to have learned the particular understanding of the political act from Paul Ramsey.

[63] Austin, "Method in Oliver O'Donovan's Political Theology," 588, 593.

[64] O'Donovan, *The Desire of the Nations,* 22.

[65] O'Donovan, *The Desire of the Nations,* 27. O'Donovan uses a number of descriptors for Israel in the few pages in which he works out the usability of Israel's history for political theology. Israel is the hermeneutic *principle* that governs a Christian appeal to political categories within the Hebrew Scriptures; Israel's political categories were a *paradigm* in the church's understanding of other political categories; the future of the one nation Israel was a *prism* through which the faithful looked to see the future of all

paradigmatic, and here O'Donovan is insistent that "it is the authoritative *Christian* hermeneutic of Israel that finds the announcement of Yhwh's kingship determinative."[66] Therefore, since the kingly rule of God is central for political theology both in the life of Israel and in an appropriate understanding of Jesus, when O'Donovan's exegetical work begins, he will 'use' the Jewish cry of "Yhwh is King" as a point of purchase for political theology.

O'Donovan's approach to the reading of Scriptures has been criticized from several directions. William Schweiker suggests that O'Donovan provides too little guidance regarding underlying methodological and theological judgments, resulting in a reading of the Bible that is inadequate for its intended task of funding a political theology. Schweiker maintains that the Bible as the revealed history of a particular nation is not up to the task of explicating the knowledge of the political, and he does "not believe that all valid and politically relevant knowledge of ourselves, the world, and the divine must be derived from Scripture."[67] But according to Schweiker, O'Donovan structures his argument so that in the end he has to "fold his entire political theology within a specific reading of the biblical witness."[68] This 'revelationalism,' to use Schweiker's term, means that O'Donovan's unnecessarily truncated and therefore misleading primary dependence on Scripture leads to several problems. First, we are presented with a dyadic view of social reality, in which we only know the secular through its opposition, where the 'world' is lumped into one abstract category. Second, a homogeneous religious conception with Protestantism providing the ground rules is at play here, one which cannot confront diversity,

---

nations; and Israel leaves a political *legacy* for the evangelists. Ibid., 21-26. Connecting the reading of the Bible to a unifying conceptual structure leads O'Donovan to make four comments regarding the right and wrong ways of using the Hebrew Scriptures in political theology: a) the Hebrew Scriptures must be treated as history and not plundered for the manufacture of theological artefact; it is the disclosure of a succession of political developments; b) the reader cannot do justice to the Hebrew Scriptures as history by constructing a subversive counter-history that would challenge the "official history" of Israel; c) Israel's history cannot be rewritten in such a way that the normative principle is simply the emergence of rationality from barbarism, since to do so would be historicist, not historical; d) Israel's history is a history of redemption, so attention must be given to the logic of Israel's faith, finding truth in the unfolding patterns of history. Ibid., 27-29.

[66] O'Donovan, "Deliberation, History and Reading: A Response to Schweiker and Wolterstorff," *Scottish Journal of Theology* 54 no 1 (2001): 140. Italics in original.

[67] William Schweiker, "Freedom and Authority in Political Theology: A Response to Oliver O'Donovan's 'The Desire of the Nations,'" *Scottish Journal of Theology* 54 no 1 (2001): 122. Schweiker puts it even more provocatively, when he argues that "exclusive reliance on 'revealed history,' – seen not only in O'Donovan's work but also so-called narrative and postliberal theologies – funds forms of theological reflection below the complexity of the actual world in which we live." Ibid., 123.

[68] Schweiker, "Freedom and Authority in Political Theology," 115.

since there is no room to debate the validity of comprehensive beliefs. Third, O'Donovan's work results in semantic reduction, in which the churches control the semantic dispersion of scripture in order to combat heretical readings, and therefore 'dogmatic' readings promoted by O'Donovan are problematic for Schweiker. Fourth, despite O'Donovan's discussions of the status of persons, there is just not a strong enough case made for the individual.[69] So Schweiker wants O'Donovan to move considerably beyond the Bible to address political theology, and also insists that the methodological and theological structure should be more clearly on display.

O'Donovan defends himself against the charge of revelationalism, but not by some simple reassertion of authority. Rather, his response affirms the importance of experience in the task of envisaging political action. However, O'Donovan is adamant that experience cannot serve as a starting point. Since political theology is a deliberative task, and not a theoretical one, it is crucial to learn how to understand what it is that we are experiencing as we live in the world. This is precisely why, according to O'Donovan, concepts are so important, since it is only through concepts that experience can be processed. So experience counts for O'Donovan, but the point at which it counts is where he identifies the rift between himself and Schweiker. That is, Schweiker has embarked on a correlationalist programme, one that insists on treating Scripture and experience as a 'both/and' set, where the theologian is seen as a peacemaker between the two. But O'Donovan insists that his theology is deliberative reasoning, which encounters experience not as a source, but as a puzzle that insists on being addressed.[70] O'Donovan remains consistent in his theological epistemology, but adds that the reading of historical texts requires something he believes is often missing, i.e. historical diastasis, an appropriate critical distance that allows the reader to learn from the past and not dismiss it as entirely alien and unuseable, nor simply to act as a scavenger of ancient texts without regard for the human face one might find there. "It requires distance and suspension of moral judgment to allow an ancient society constructed on different terms from any we know to express its own moral priorities without our wanting to reprove it."[71] It is in reading Scripture that O'Donovan hopes to find such historical diastasis.

O'Donovan's reading of the Hebrew Scriptures for political theology, with its emphasis on architectonic hermeneutic and unifying conceptual structure,[72]

---

[69] Schweiker, "Freedom and Authority in Political Theology," 122-126. O'Donovan includes an extensive discussion of the ways in which the Christian understanding of the individual is fundamentally different than the modern notion of the individual in *The Ways of Judgment* (Grand Rapids: Eerdmans Publishing, 2006), 293ff.

[70] O'Donovan, "Deliberation, History and Reading: A Response to Schweiker and Wolterstorff," *Scottish Journal of Theology* 54 no 1 (2001): 128-130.

[71] O'Donovan, "Deliberation, History and Reading," 142-143.

[72] O'Donovan, *The Desire of the Nations*, 22.

leaves him open to several other lines of criticism from those who are more willing than Schweiker to accept O'Donovan's theological approach to the Bible. The concepts that O'Donovan uses mediate between the reader and the theologian, between reading the text and constructing a theory. The questions related to specific concepts used by O'Donovan have been a significant part of the discussion surrounding *The Desire of the Nations*. In one of the most penetrating critiques of O'Donovan's conceptual structure, offered within an appreciative and positive reading of his exegetical work, Stanley Hauerwas and James Fodor make the observation that many of O'Donovan's theologico-political insights are fully intelligible *without* the conceptual framework within which these insights appear. Hauerwas and Fodor claim to find it difficult to identify the difference between the exegesis and theory in *The Desire of the Nations*, which leads them to question the relation between the value of the formal outline and the material specifications of the narrative. In other words, it is not readily apparent how the exegesis itself informs the hermeneutic architectonic.[73]

The danger in O'Donovan's work, on this account, is that his rich exegetical work may ironically be subordinated to the conceptual structure he is so keen to construct. It is instructive to note that O'Donovan, at the end of the chapter in which he has discussed the revelation of God's kingship, uses a mechanical metaphor to describe what he is attempting. That is, he claims that "we have, as it were, examined the design of the vehicle; now we must see it move."[74] If one is responsible for a vehicle, then a significant amount of time and energy has to be given over to the operation and maintenance of that machine. Further, if that is the vehicle that is available for use, it stands to reason that it will be used in every instance in which transportation is needed, thus potentially reducing the flexibility that comes with not being committed beforehand to using only one vehicle to reach some important destination. In other words, O'Donovan is in danger of trapping himself within the structure that he believes to be necessary to the task of political theology.

---

[73] For the Hauerwas and Fodor critique, see Stanley Hauerwas and Jim Fodor, "Remaining in Babylon: Oliver O'Donovan's Defense of Christendom," *Studies in Christian Ethics*, 11 no 2 (1998): 37-48. Bernd Wannenwetsch concurs with Hauerwas and Fodor when he suggests that O'Donovan's work, while explicitly committed to methodological conceptualization, offers "a wide array of fascinating insights and splendid analyses ...not dependent upon the degree to which the reader is able or willing to follow O'Donovan's systematic construals." Wannenwetsch wonders "whether the normative political concepts O'Donovan analyses will be rendered to function as principles ready for application to political questions of the day, thereby reducing the hermeneutic thirst that should be intrinsic in every single one of those questions." See Wannenwetsch, review of *The Desire of the Nations: Rediscovering the Roots of Political Theology* by Oliver O'Donovan, *Modern Theology* 14 (July 1998): 465.

[74] O'Donovan, *The Desire of the Nations*, 81.

The Hebrew Scriptures in Yoder's Theopolitical Thought

Yoder and O'Donovan both claim to think the way the Bible thinks, and seek to find the shape of their theopolitical projects from Scripture, and when they turn to the actual task of reading the Hebrew Scriptures, they focus on the kingship of God, human monarchy, and the importance of the prophetic tradition. However, as noted above, their respective understandings of these themes differ in significant ways. In order to bring these differences to view, it is important to examine closely in turn the development of these themes in both Yoder and O'Donovan's projects.

Yoder's stance toward the reading of the Bible is displayed in his theopolitical use of the Hebrew Scriptures. Whereas O'Donovan sees in the Hebrew Scriptures the importance of the monarchy in Israel as a showcase of God's ordering of society, Yoder's focus is on the antiroyal strand of the Hebrew Scriptures, especially in the writings of the deuteronomic historian(s).[75] This antiroyal strand in turn gives way to what Yoder calls the Jeremian shift, in which a positive rendering of Israel's diasporic existence as obedience and mission is central. The key text in Yoder's understanding of the significance of diaspora is Jeremiah 29:7, "Seek the peace of the city where I have sent you."

GOD AS KING

Yoder acknowledges that the Hebrew Scriptures celebrate the kingship of God, which is displayed in the historical experience of Israel. Divine kingship precludes the need for human royalty, however, and therefore the establishment of a monarchy can only be seen as a move that is idolatrous at its base, which helps to explain the deep ambivalence to human monarchy in the Hebrew Scriptures.[76] Yoder argues that to acknowledge God as king entails the ever-refined understanding and formation of a community in covenant with a God whose kingship comes in servant form. Yoder's argument becomes clear in his

---

[75] Yoder seems to accept the notion that the deuteronomic narratives were produced after the exile to Babylon of 587, although he does not address the scholarly discussion as such at any length. In a footnote, he says that the "general understanding, held by scholars today, of the editorial slant of the 'deuteronomic historian(s)' is that those narrators' reasons for retelling the whole history of royal Israel was to show who was to blame for the exile. But the fact that there was unfaithfulness along the way does not make the mission to Babylon any less a mission." Yoder's use of scare quotes in this quotation is not explained - his interpretive point has to do with a positive reading of exile, and a negative understanding of the monarchy in Israel. Yoder, *For the Nations,* 65, footnote 30.

[76] Yoder insists that in spite of the central role played by the king in history and theology, ancient Israel never fully embraced the royal ideal in its standard ancient Near Eastern form. This ambivalence will be dealt with more fully below. See Yoder, Douglas Gwyn, George Hunsinger, and Eugene Roop, *A Declaration on Peace: In God's People the World's Renewal Has Begun* (Scottdale: Herald Press, 1991), 41.

understanding of God's kingly role in the war narratives of the Hebrew Scriptures.[77]

Yoder relies heavily on the work of Millard Lind for an argument that refuses to allow the wars in the Hebrew Scriptures to act as a model for just wars, for a crusader spirit, or to underwrite any use of violence for nationalistic purposes. Following Lind, Yoder resists the notion that Jesus represents an entirely novel approach to warfare, one that opens the door to negative judgment on Jewish life as inherently violent.[78] Yoder frequently returns to this issue, underlining the importance of understanding that the accounts of warfare are historical narratives that reveal the historical work of God, and are not rooted in a general command to build strong armies or to develop military strategies to invade foreign powers. The key note struck by Yoder is that the war narratives show that it is God as king who fights for Israel, thereby calling for a rejection of the institution of human kingship. Thus an account that focuses on any sort of nationalism, but especially Jewish nationalism, with reference to the memory of the ancient wars of God is simply wrong, according to Yoder.[79]

Yoder argues in *The Original Revolution* that it is easy to see the story in the Hebrew Scriptures as one that tolerates, fosters and even glorifies violence – as may be seen in the holy warfare in the age of Moses, Joshua, and the Judges. Civil legislation in the Pentateuch seems to breathe a spirit other than forgiveness. The national existence of Israel and Judah seems to depend on the fate of a kingly house, and the imprecatory Psalms and prophetic visions sometimes rejoice at the prospect of the destruction of enemies. Such a tolerant view of violence can cause difficulties for a nonviolent, nonresistant reading of the New Testament. The modern question in Christian ethics is always one that asks how a Christian who rejects all war can reconcile his position with the Hebrew Scriptures. Yoder argues that the reading of war narratives must also take into account the historical situations in which they occurred, and that Israelites would not ask the modern question. Rather, they would look at the text as their own story, with particular attention given to the identification of YHWH as the God who saves his people without their needing to act.

Yoder outlines and rejects several possible explanations for reconciling nonresistance with war narratives - dispensationalism, God's concession to disobedience, the pedagogical concession (Israel needs to be taught as part of the maturation process), and the Lutheran division of realms. Instead, Yoder believes the more important question concerns how the narrative of the Hebrew

---

[77] The interpretive move Yoder makes here in explaining the war narratives also plays an important role in discussions of pacifism, which, in conversation with the Just War tradition as displayed in O'Donovan's thought, will be the primary focus of chapter 4 of this book.

[78] Yoder, introduction to Millard Lind, *Yahweh is a Warrior*, 18.

[79] Yoder, *The Jewish-Christian Schism Revisited*, 70.

Scriptures might be different from what preceded and followed it, i.e., how was holy war distinctive or original in its own context? So he asks how Jesus and his listeners would have conceived of the action of God against the background of their people's way of telling their history.

Yoder identifies several differences in how war might be seen in Israel as opposed to the modern setting, beginning with his contention that Israel's holy wars were not related to commands of God. They were religious or ritual wars, in which Canaanite cities, for example, would be dedicated to God, and bloodshed was part of ritual sacrifice, which also included the destruction of flocks and other goods, thus ensuring that there were no spoils. A holy war was not to be an opportunity for plunder, or for economic development. These wars were not primarily strategic in nature but *ad hoc* charismatic events that occurred as the result of God's call, not by the preparation of standing armies or military strategies. In other words, Yoder's point is that all victories in holy wars were miracles – which came to an end once Israel demanded a king like the other nations. Holy war, then, was a concrete experience of needing only trust in God as King as the basis of identity and community. Such a view of God's work suggests to Yoder that there was indeed a progression within the history of Israel, but the progression is one of an increasingly precise definition of the nature of peoplehood. That is, throughout the history of Israel, what has been "fundamentally at stake is an understanding of the covenant community and its relationship to God who has called it and promised it his care."[80] Yoder's discussion of the so-called holy war enables him to argue that such war is "the concrete experience of not needing any other crutches for one's identity and community as a people than trust in Jahweh as king, who makes it unnecessary to have earthly kings like the neighboring nations."[81]

Yoder's view depends largely on the work of Millard Lind, whose discussion of political power in ancient Israel concludes that Isaiah, for example, saw other ancient Near Eastern nations as human attempts to control history. Such attempts, undergirded by political self-interest, revealed the arrogance of these nations against God. Lind argues that dependence on God as opposed to the human exercise of violent power is not a withdrawal from political concerns but leadership that has to do with political order, both internal and external to the covenant community's life. That is, to depend on a

---

[80] Yoder, *The Original Revolution: Essays on Christian Pacifism* (Scottdale: Herald Press, 1971), 94. The larger argument is taken from *The Original Revolution*, 85-100, and *The Politics of Jesus*, 76-84.

[81] Yoder, *The Original Revolution*, p. 101. Various questions and criticisms can and have been raised concerning this kind of reading of the war narratives. For example, is Yoder offering a naïve historical argument? Were swords used in these wars? Is elimination of another tribe and conquering arable land strategic? The point here is to bring to view the way Yoder reads the Hebrew Scriptures, not to solve these kinds of issues.

covenant with God sets God as the political leader and places issues such as land tenure, military leadership, power, authority and so on under the prerogative of the deity.[82]

Yoder's understanding of holy war, and the notion that God is a warrior, leads him to argue that the dismantling of the applicability of the concept of the holy war takes place not by promulgation of the new ethical demand but by a restructuring of the Israelite perception of community under God.

Through the incorporation of non-Israelite blood into the tribe, through the expansion of the world vision to include other nations, through the prophets' criticism of and history's destruction of kingship and territorial sovereignty as definitions of peoplehood, the movement continued through the centuries which was ultimately to culminate at the point where John the Baptist opened the door for Jesus.[83]

The kingship of God, especially as displayed in the context of holy war, thus compels an ever-refined understanding of peoplehood in covenant with God. Furthermore, the nature of divine and human kingship as displayed in the Hebrew Scriptures (however ambivalent they may be concerning human kingship) comes primarily in the shape of a servant. Yoder draws primarily on the "Servant Songs" of the prophet Isaiah to show that the notion of a godly king is given the shape of a servant – "the kind of king God wants is a servant," and the kind of person God wants to represent God's people is the Suffering Servant.[84] Yoder clearly sees in Isaiah's writings a foreshadowing of Jesus' form of kingship, although this identification does not preclude the identification of some person or group (such as the Jewish nation) with the image. "Whoever he be, the intent of the Spirit of God in calling and sending the Servant is that justice shall be brought to the nations."[85] Therefore, if

---

[82] Millard Lind, "The Concept of Political Power in Ancient Israel," *Annual of the Swedish Theological Institute* 7 (1970): 18-20.

[83] Yoder, *The Original Revolution*, 102-103. Yoder goes on to conclude: "To be the son of Abraham means to share the faith of Abraham. Thus the relativizing of the given ethnic-political peoplehood is completed in both directions. There is no one in any nation who is not a potential son of Abraham since that Sonship is a miraculous gift which God can open up to Gentiles. On the other hand there is no given peoplehood which can defend itself against others as bearers of the Abrahamic covenant, since those who were born into that unity can and in fact already did jeopardize their claim to it by their unbelief. Thus the very willingness to trust God for security and identity of one's peoplehood, which was the original concrete meaning of the sacrament of holy warfare, is now translated to become the willingness or readiness to renounce those definitions of one's own people and of the enemy which gave the original sacrament its meaning." Yoder, *The Original Revolution*, 103-104.

[84] Yoder notes that the term 'servant of the Lord' is a technical term that refers to a kingly figure. Yoder, *Preface to Theology*, 243-244.

[85] Yoder, "The Spirit of God and the Politics of Men," *Journal of Theology for South Africa* 29 (December 1979), 63-64. In addition to Yoder's use of the Suffering Servant

kingship of any kind is to be seen as representing the rule of God, it can only be so with the refined understanding that to rule is to serve. However, Yoder is reticent to see anything but an ambivalent embrace of human kingship in Israel.

AMBIVALENCE TO THE HUMAN MONARCHY IN ISRAEL

In *A Declaration on Peace,* Yoder and several co-authors argue that despite the central role played by the king in history and theology, ancient Israel never fully embraced the royal ideal in its standard ancient Near Eastern form.[86] Yoder privileges the antiroyal strand of the Hebrew Scriptures that narrates Israel's story from an exilic point of view. The exile of Israel is to be understood as mission, and Yoder insists therefore that any notion of human kingship in Israel is seen ambivalently by the Jewish people themselves, by the deuteronomic historians, and even more so by the prophetic traditions. Yoder generalizes his reading of kingship in Israel by noting that "...the adoption by ancient Israel of models of kingship 'like the other nations,' was seen quite ambivalently even at the time, by the earliest historians, and even more so by the prophets. Isaiah condemned his king's 'realistic' foreign alliances, Jeremiah accepted the loss of national sovereignty, and Ezra and Nehemiah restored the worshipping community without political sovereignty."[87] It is important to trace and elaborate this rather cryptic assertion of Yoder's because of the central role it plays in his political reading of the Hebrew Scriptures.

The general ambivalence toward kingship is especially focused on a strongly negative view of the Davidic monarchy, which Yoder refers to as "the error of the age of Samuel."[88] The rise of the Davidic dynasty is described as a disappointment to Samuel and to God. The Northern kingdom fell first, but both Northern and Southern kingdoms eventually fell because God finally gave up on both of them. The 'deuteronomic' historiography retold the history, correlating the ups and downs of the royal houses with their rising and falling faithlessness to the law, "but when we remember that that retelling was done and committed to writing in the setting of the diaspora, it constitutes a document of the acceptance of the Jeremianic turn; there is in the multiple strata and versions of the entire narrative no irredentism."[89] The story goes on like that – nothing like 'kingship' or 'statehood' is advocated by any party as desirable for the honor of God or the dignity of the people. The prophets to whom Jesus appealed were rereading their history in light of the Hebrew story

---

material of Isaiah in *Preface* and "The Spirit of God and the Politics of Men," see also Yoder, *He Came Preaching Peace* (Scottdale: Herald Press, 1985), especially chapters 1 and 11.

[86] Yoder, et al., *A Declaration on Peace,* 41.
[87] Yoder, *The Jewish-Christian Schism Revisited,* 162.
[88] Yoder, *The Jewish-Christian Schism Revisited,* 163.
[89] Yoder, *For the Nations,* 60.

of the exodus and they were especially rereading in its light the "long, failed history of kingship and statehood into which Israel had made such a tragic detour from Saul to Zedekiah."[90]

Yoder is aware that the king is often seen as an expression and personification of Israel's identity, but he seems especially concerned that the tendency toward accommodation and even idolatry can be too easily missed if the deep ambivalence of the Hebrew Scriptures toward kingship is not highlighted. So instead of a narration that focuses on the fact of Israel's kingship, or any kind of praise of royalty in Israel (both themes can be found in the Old Testament literature), Yoder is at pains to point out that Israel had no king from Moses through Gideon, largely because a covenant relationship with God seemed to imply that no king but God was needed. Yoder reads Israel's longing for a king simply as a desire for conformity to pagan nations, and suggests that kingship is only then accepted under the conditions of charismatic leadership (Northern kingdom), or a dynastic succession (Southern kingdom). But even these conditional acceptances of kingship are given a negative verdict by God in favor of the recovery of God as King, with a developing understanding of the king as suffering servant, as seen especially in the words of the prophet Isaiah. The principled negative judgment of God on human monarchy is seen most fully expressed in Jeremiah's writings.[91]

It might be said that Yoder is providing a counter-narrative to one that sees in Israel's history a monarchical pattern to be emulated.

> It is being said with special clarity by a few Old Testament scholars that we need to stop seeing Hebrew origins through the lens of the Davidic tradition according to which what God ultimately wanted and would have liked to keep forever would be the succession of Solomon. Hebrew *origins,* they show, were an anti-imperial movement. Even the word "Hebrew" might mean "insurgent" or "outsider." The original covenant experience was an anti-royal kind of empowerment of people with no power. From George Mendenhall to Norman Gottwald and Walter Brueggeman, the most interesting scholarship is finding in the Old Testament more and more a liberation message, not only at the point of the exodus event but also at the point of what it meant to become Israel in Canaan.[92]

Yoder's take on God as warrior, the emphasis on the anti-royal strand of the

---

[90] Yoder, *For the Nations,* 60, 140.
[91] Yoder, *Preface to Theology,* 242-245. Yoder goes on to show how the redefinition of kingship as suffering servant is given full expression in Jesus Christ, a theme that will be elaborated below.
[92] Yoder, "Biblical Roots of Liberation Theology," *Grail* 1 no1 (September 1985): 67. Michael Cartwright suggests that Yoder believed that the 'Davidic Project' to constitute a monarchy in Jerusalem was prototypical of Christian faithlessness. Cartwright, editors' introduction in *The Jewish-Christian Schism Revisited,* 20.

Hebrew Scriptures, his strong ambivalence specifically regarding the Davidic monarchy, and his understanding of king as Suffering Servant combine to form the basis of a focus on the prophetic critique of kingship in Israel specifically and on the primary role of the prophet generally. Yoder points out that the Hebrew Scriptures often shows the prophets chastening the kings, especially the denunciation of idolatry and clarification of the shape of God's working with Israel.[93] But Yoder is not satisfied with bringing the role of prophet more clearly to view; he insists that the role of the prophet was more fundamental than the priest or the king of the Hebrew Scriptures. The prophet had a crucial sociological role in that he was called upon to interpret the events of Israel's history, as well as a theological role in communicating the word of the Lord. Thus Israel could be Israel without priests and without a king, but not without prophets, since it was the word of God spoken through the prophets that made Israel what it was.[94]

This move to favoring the prophetic critique over kingship is crucial to Yoder's treatment of the Hebrew Scriptures, since the prophet Jeremiah plays an increasingly important role in Yoder's thought. The so-called Jeremian shift might be described as the hinge upon which Yoder's theopolitical thought swings.

THE SAD, TRAGIC PROPHET: THE JEREMIAN SHIFT

In the last book published before his death, *For the Nations,* Yoder offers a defense of sorts of his work, seeking to clarify that his thought should not be construed in any way as being sectarian. The theme of the book is described by Yoder as a "tone of voice, a style, or a stance of the people of God in the dispersion," a stance that Yoder takes in large part from the experience of Israel. "When the people of God who had taken Jeremiah seriously began to settle into Babylon as a place where they would maintain their community, raise their children and grandchildren, and thereby testify to the supranational authority of their God, they needed to decide whether to talk the local language. That was part of the larger question of whether to make themselves at home there or to constitute an alien enclave."[95] Thus the basis of Yoder's diaspora emphasis is God's command, through Jeremiah, to "Seek the peace of the city where I have sent you," which gave the Jews the imperative to live *for the nations.*[96] Yoder had previously discussed Jeremiah and the importance of exile, and had been working on this set of ideas for some time as becomes obvious in the posthumous publication of *The Jewish-Christian Schism Revisited.* However, *For the Nations* is where Yoder develops the most

---

[93] Yoder, *The Christian Witness to the State,* 15-16.
[94] Yoder, *Preface to Theology,* 330-332.
[95] Yoder, *For the Nations,* 1.
[96] Yoder, *For the Nations,* 3. Italics in original.

extensive interpretation of the Jeremian shift. Yoder contends that the two ancient turning points represented by Jeremiah and Constantine have become "the two most important landmarks outside the New Testament itself for clarifying what is at stake in the Christian faith."[97] As will become clear below, while Yoder sees a kind of turn or shift with Jeremiah, he also identifies continuity within the Hebrew Scriptures. The Babylonian captivity, or to be scattered via exile, is *not* a hiatus, after which normalcy will resume. That is, a Palestinocentric reading of Israel's history is a mistake.[98]

The call to seek the welfare of the foreign city is part of Yoder's present point – "The move to Babylon was not a two-generation parenthesis, after which the Davidic or Solomonic project was supposed to take up again where it had left off. It was rather the beginning, under a firm, fresh prophetic mandate, of a new phase of the Mosaic project."[99] Thus Yoder provides what might be called a revisionist counter-narrative of God's gracious dispersal of his people, who place their trust radically in God alone, not in some embrace of sovereign kingship or violent conquest of the land.[100] It is important, therefore, to trace the highlights of Yoder's counter-narrative to show both the centrality of the Jeremian shift in his thought, and his construal of the continuity of that theme in the rest of the Hebrew Scriptures.

Yoder's counter-narrative goes back to the first chapters of Genesis, where he sees something of a diasporic/exilic notion at work even in the Cain and Abel confrontation. The slaying of Abel by Cain has the puzzling result of the founding of a city by Cain. Yoder concludes from this incident that this first city is not the product of some 'natural' process of growth, expansion or planned development, but is founded by a fugitive, although God's ultimate choice is to work on the model of Abel, i.e. the model of weakness. Both the founding of a city through the fugitive, Cain, and Abel's way of weakness fit Yoder's reading of the central idea of gracious dispersion, something he identifies as even more clearly evident in the Genesis 11 account of the Tower of Babel.

Yoder's interpretation of the Babel story is most clearly displayed in an

---

[97] Yoder, *For the Nations,* 8. The subject of the Constantinian turn will be discussed below in detail, as part of the comparison between O'Donovan and Yoder's views of Christendom. Yoder remarks in a footnote that he has already discussed Constantine in previous writings, but that "this book *adds* an interpretation of the Jeremian shift." *For the Nations,* 9, italics added. Michael Cartwright suggests that Constantine is overshadowed by Jeremiah in Yoder's later writings. Cartwright, "Editors' Introduction," in *The Jewish-Christian Schism Revisited,* 21.
[98] Yoder, *The Jewish-Christian Schism Revisited,* 186.
[99] Yoder, *For the Nations,* 52-53.
[100] Alain Epp Weaver, "On Exile: Yoder, Said, and a Theology of Land and Return," *Cross Currents* 52 no 4 (2003): 441-442 provides a helpful summation of the Jeremian turn.

extensive conversation with Jeffrey Stout,[101] for whom 'Babel' stands for multiplicity of voices, the mythic metaphor for lost unity. However, what Stout regrets losing 'after Babel,' according to Yoder, is what God in the Genesis story says his creatures should not have been trying to protect. "The intention of the people at Babel was to resist the diversification which God had long beforehand ordained and initiated, and to maintain a common discourse by building their own unprecedentedly centralized city. They were the first foundationalists, trying to absolutize themselves."[102] Instead, Yoder argues,

Babel in the myth of Genesis places the multiplicity of cultures under the sign of the divine will. Scattering had been commanded and had begun in chapters 9 and 10. It was rebellious humankind, proud and probably fearful, who wanted to live all in one place, seeking to escape their dependence on divine benevolence by pulling back from the dispersion and reaching heaven on their own. It was JHWH who scattered them, for their own good, restoring his original plan. This scattering is still seen as divine benevolence in the missionary preaching of the Paul of Acts (14:16-17, 17:26-27). It appears as 'confusion' only when measured pejoratively against the simplicity of imperially forced uniformity, or when forced by considerations beyond the text into the picture of an angry, controlling, and retributive God.[103]

Yoder goes on to argue that it was the generations of Jewry living around Babylon who told the Babel story as the immediate background to the call of Abraham.[104] In Yoder's view, then, the Biblical story really begins with Abraham, the Father of those who believe. If it can be said that some idea is 'basic' to Yoder's thought, he comes close to admitting that his understanding

---

[101] The book referred to by Yoder is Jeffrey Stout, *Ethics After Babel: The Languages of Morals and Their Discontents* (Boston: Beacon Press, 1988). Babel makes only a fleeting appearance in O'Donovan's political theology as a warning against imperial pretensions. O'Donovan, *The Desire of the Nations*, 70. Further, O'Donovan sees the plurality of Babel as providing a necessary restraint on evil to which unity had given free reign. O'Donovan, *Common Objects of Love: Moral Reflection and the Shaping of Community* (Grand Rapids: Eerdmans Publishing, 2002), 40.

[102] Yoder, *For the Nations*, 62-63.

[103] Yoder, "Meaning After Babble: With Jeffrey Stout beyond Relativism," *Journal of Religious Ethics* 24 no 1 (1996): 127. In the same article, Yoder clarifies his point further by comparing 'Babel' to 'babble'. "'Babel' is to be accepted as the human condition under God, as a good thing. Genesis 11 narrates a gracious act of JHWH, saving humankind from its presumptuous and premature effort at divination. For every tribe to speak its own language, for all meaningful discourse to be community-dependent, is not a mistake. Neither is it the Fall nor the expulsion from Paradise. It is the way things ought to be. Only 'babble' is a mistake – that is, the denial that trans-communal communication is possible or desirable." Yoder, "Meaning After Babble," 132.

[104] Yoder, *For the Nations*, 65.

of Abraham is one of these basics.[105] That is, Yoder wants to highlight the creation of a new definition of peoplehood. The original revolution begun in Abraham, the formation of a new community based on faith in God, is picked up, extended and developed by the prophet Jeremiah in the Babylonian exile, after the failed Davidic kingship experiment. The Jeremianic model prefigured the Christian attitude to the Gentile world, insofar as Christian moral standards are derived from and therefore illuminated by Jewish models of how to relate to the world's powers. For example, it is possible to see in Jewish attitudes to pagan empires several models - a) since God is sovereign over history, there is no reason to take charge; b) to establish ultimate righteous social order among the nations is the work of the Messiah; c) revolts were not blessed by God; d) if God wants to punish us for our sins, then self-defense is at cross-purposes; and e) the possibility of martyrdom.[106]

Thus Yoder claims to take seriously the "Babylonian basis of continuing Jewish identity," which means that he must also take into account the story of too-early returns to the land. Ezra and Nehemiah should be seen as "inappropriate deviations from the Jeremiah line, since each reconstituted a cult and a polity as a branch of the pagan imperial government."[107] The Jews not only kept their culture alive, they contributed greatly to making the Gentile world viable. There was enormous flexibility and creativity, but the one truth remained - there is no other God.[108]

Yoder's revisionist narrative of Jewish history, centered in exile, suggests that the faith community is marked by characteristics other than kingship or conventional nationalistic characteristics.

- The primary vehicle of identity definition is a text which can be copied, and can be read anywhere. Decentralization and fidelity are therefore not alternatives, as they are with any religious forms which need a priesthood in a temple.
- The ground floor of 'worship' (if that is the word for it) is reading and singing the texts.
- A valid local cell of the world Jewish community, qualified to be in that place the concretion of the people of God, can exist wherever there are ten households. No priesthood, no hierarchy is needed. If they can afford a rabbi, his role is that of a scribe, rather than that of

---

[105] The essay entitled "The Original Revolution" is included in the book of that title, and also reprinted in *For the Nations,* where it is grouped with two other essays under the rubric 'basics.' Yoder explains this use of the term 'basic' as being valid in at least two ways – " a) their themes are the simplest logical foundations of my position; b) friends have told me they are the best introduction to my thought." *For the Nations,* 11.
[106] Yoder, *For the Nations,* 66-68.
[107] Yoder, *For the Nations,* 71.
[108] Yoder, *For the Nations,* 76.

prophet, priest, or prince.
- The international unity of the people is sustained by intervisitation, by intermarriage, by commerce and by rabbinic consultation, needing no High Priest or Pope or King to hang together. When, some time later, a central senior Jewish spokesman, the *resh galut,* 'ethnarch' or 'exilarch', was called forth by the Babylonian power structure, he was intermediary, co-coordinator, culture broker between the community and the Gentiles. He was not a Jewish emperor.
- Although there is plenty of material, and plenty of freedom, with which thinkers over the centuries can develop Jewish philosophical systems (cosmological, mystical, linguistic, scientific), the ground floor of identity is the common life itself, the walk, *halakah,* and the shared remembering of the story behind it.[109]

Yoder sees these marks of the faith community as evolving throughout the history of Israel, both before and after the exile. "A theology for diaspora existence was thus not, as some would have us believe, developed as a merely pragmatic expedient, out of the collapse of Jewish nationhood after the year 70 or 135. Those vital tragedies only settled and restated what had existed already in the messages of Jeremiah and Ezekiel, and in the ministries of Ezra and Nehemiah. The defeats of 70 and 135 only clarified and made sense of what most of world Jewry had already been living for seven centuries."[110] A theologically and sociologically coherent strategy for renouncing civil kingship as the instrument for the renewal of the people of God was already present in that heritage.

Yoder's reading of the Hebrew Scriptures, with his emphasis on diaspora as obedience, opens him to the criticism of simply being too selective. In his effort to provide a counter-narrative that resists any heroic reading of the kingly tradition in Israel, Yoder has swept aside without proper regard other dimensions of the Hebrew Scriptures. For example, Yoder seems to brush aside Ezra and Nehemiah because these stories do not fit his reading; he largely ignores the centralist tradition in Israel; he marginalizes the Noachide epoch and its more global vision, and generally ignores the wider world, which is brought to view in Genesis 1-11. So goes the sharp criticism of A. James Reimer, who concludes that Yoder is just too preoccupied with tracing a messianic ethic back into the Hebrew narrative and has virtually no vision for ultimate unity and reconciliation of the wider world, since it is never clear to Reimer how Yoder can account for God's work outside of participation in the

---

[109] Yoder, *The Jewish-Christian Schism Revisited,* 187.
[110] Yoder, *The Jewish-Christian Schism Revisited,* 79.

chosen community of God in exile.[111]

But perhaps most interestingly, Reimer accuses Yoder of being ahistorical in his reading of the Hebrew Scriptures due to Yoder's perceived univocal identification of Reformation Radicals with a 'free church' movement of Messianic Judaism.[112] However, upon closer examination, Reimer's complaint is not really about ahistoricism as much as it is a theological disagreement with Yoder. That is, to identify a thematic thread that can be traced throughout history as Yoder does is at its base *historical* investigation. Reimer admits as much when he approves Yoder's identification of "sociological and ethical parallels between the Radicals of the Reformation and early Jewish Christians (really Messianic Jews, according to Yoder), and between later Mennonites and Jews."[113] Reimer's real criticism entails the notion that Yoder's work is reductionistic in its emphasis on political-ethical themes at the expense of "critical theological insights central to the Christian tradition," insights that can only be found in classical orthodoxy, according to Reimer.[114]

Reimer's criticisms, especially those regarding Yoder's selective reading of the Hebrew Scriptures, can be answered in part by Yoder's admission that he must be selective in his work, but that this is unavoidable. And yet, claims Yoder, he is not advocating some form of pervasive relativity. Instead, "we need then to resolve the problem of how to read the story fairly from within relativism, with no claim to have escaped subjectivism in principle."[115] Yoder's attempt to read in this way leads him to acknowledge that "we cannot not be selective; we can ask that the selectivity should contribute to reciprocal recognition, finding in the other what one needs, for the sake of one's own integrity, to esteem." Therefore, says Yoder, "I am not co-opting Jews to enlist them in my cause. It is that I am finding a story, which is really there, coming all the way down from Abraham, that has the grace to adopt me."[116] The kind of selectivity practiced by Yoder, then, is open to at least some more objective

---

[111] A. James Reimer, "Theological Orthodoxy and Jewish Unity: A Personal Tribute to John Howard Yoder," in Stanley Hauerwas, et al., eds. *The Wisdom of the Cross*, 444-447. Reimer is drawing on the work of Old Testament scholar John Miller.

[112] Reimer, "Theological Orthodoxy and Jewish Unity," 448.

[113] Reimer, "Theological Orthodoxy and Jewish Unity," 448.

[114] Reimer, "Theological Orthodoxy and Jewish Unity," 448. This line of criticism remains a constant in Reimer's analysis of Yoder's work over the years. See for example, Reimer, "The Nature and Possibility of a Mennonite Theology," *The Conrad Grebel Review* 1 (Winter 1983): 33-55, where Reimer argues that Yoder's emphasis on the historical-ethical (horizontal) dimension of faith, comes at the expense of the experiential (vertical) dimension. Reimer's complaint here varies from the essay referred to above, but his basic argument is consistent – Yoder needs classical orthodoxy to undergird his moral and ethical claims.

[115] Yoder, *The Jewish-Christian Schism Revisited*, 114.

[116] Yoder, *The Jewish-Christian Schism Revisited*, 115.

ways to verify that selectivity in a fair and empathetic way.[117] Alain Epp-Weaver attempts to help Yoder defend this kind of selectivity by suggesting that Yoder need not even claim that the motif of a Jeremianic embrace of exile was necessarily dominant, but merely a) that this strand continued both within scriptural witness and within the history of post-biblical Judaism in the Diaspora and b) that this strand is the one most in continuity with the Gospel message.[118] For Epp Weaver, Yoder's identification of the exilic strand as normative allows one to "highlight the continuity between YHWH the God of Israel and the Triune God incarnate in the non-violent Messiah."[119] The point being made by Epp Weaver is that Yoder's selectivity is at bottom a Christian selection that reads Scripture through the lens of God incarnate in Jesus Christ, which is a selectivity defensible at least on Christian grounds.[120]

The Jewish scholar Peter Ochs, while often sympathetic to Yoder's work, suggests that Yoder has a tendency to reify the exilic paradigm. Jeremiah

> the sad, tragic prophet dominates Yoder's book in the end.... For both Zweig and Yoder, chapter 29 of Jeremiah's prophecy offers a scriptural warrant for their desire to join the fate of the people Israel directly to the universal goal of redeeming humanity and, thereby, to avoid the embarrassment, burden, and unreasonable complexity of Israel's landedness... But for Yoder there is no middle between exilic separation from the land and the Maccabean strategy for retaining it... It is an ethically moving yet still late-modern effort to over-generalize one chapter of Jeremiah's long prophecy, as if it were the only prophetic alternative to what remains Israel's late-modern practice of landedness...Yoder has made a beautiful monument of one chapter of Jeremiah's ministry. But there are many chapters.[121]

---

[117] Yoder cites six 'modes of verification' in a non-exhaustive list – a) the criteria of literary coherence that confirms that mercy has the last word in prophetic discourse; b) the criteria of socio-historical viability, whereby rabbis outlive Maccabees and martyrs outlive Nazis; c) the mystical, doxological criteria of coherence whereby people involved in God's work are able to discern God's mode of action; d) the criteria of narrative and causative coherence; e) the criteria of connaturality and congruence, whereby our story and their story demonstrate similarities even within their differences; and f) there are modes of clarification through conflict and contrast, whereby such experiences can tell two very different communities something true about themselves and each other. Yoder, *The Jewish-Christian Schism Revisited,* 115-116.

[118] Epp Weaver, "On Exile," 458, endnote 17. Epp Weaver is here attempting to refute James Reimer's critique of Yoder.

[119] Epp Weaver, "On Exile," 442.

[120] Epp Weaver, "On Exile," 457, note 12.

[121] Ochs, in Yoder, *The Jewish-Christian Schism Revisited,* p. 92, 203, 204. Gerald Schlabach also offers a related criticism of Yoder. According to Schlabach, Yoder's emphasis on the problem of Constantinianism may allow (or force) him to ignore the more basic problem of the 'Deuteronomistic temptation.' That is, the "Deuteronomic

Gerald Schlabach also offers a related criticism, suggesting that Yoder's emphasis on the problem of Constantinianism may allow (or force) him to ignore the more basic problem of the 'Deuteronomistic temptation.' That is, the "Deuteronomic problem is the problem of how to receive and celebrate the blessing, the *shalom*, the good, or 'the land' that God desires to give, yet to do so without defensively and violently hoarding God's blessing."[122] Alain Epp Weaver extends Schlabach's criticism as a way of pushing his own criticism of Yoder's seeming ignoring of the issues of land. That is, in Yoder's zeal to draw appropriate implications from his emphasis on the exilic strand of the Hebrew Scriptures, he hardly mentions issues of returning to the land.[123] This exclusion has a distorting effect on the Old Testament message, as well as a Christian reading of the issue, according to Michael Cartwright, who suggests (following Schlabach), "for Christians *neither* the possibility of diaspora *nor* the challenge of landedness can be eliminated (as Yoder does)."[124] Thus Yoder's exilic reading of the Hebrew Scriptures comes under significant critique both from Jewish and Christian commentators as providing a truncated view of the narrative. This is a significant critique, since a truncated view of the narrative potentially draws in its train a distortion of political theology. For example, ignoring issues of land has implications not only for issues surrounding Israel, but for other questions of justice, distribution and so on. One specific instance of such a truncation is exemplified in Yoder's unconvincing reading of the books of Ezra and Nehemiah.

The place of the post-exilic books of Ezra and Nehemiah in Yoder's exilic reading is problematic in that he does not engage in any sustained reading of these texts. Instead, in making the argument that the move to Babylon was a new beginning under a fresh prophetic mandate, Yoder suggests in a footnote that a careful reading of Ezra and Nehemiah would not deny this new start, although Yoder does not undertake such a reading.[125] In the same essay, he suggests that what Ezra and Nehemiah recount stays well within the constraints of submission to the Gentile empire, a situation in which any notion of kingship or statehood is advocated as desirable for the honor of God or the dignity of the people. Thus even if there is a return of sorts under Ezra and Nehemiah, this return has a new quality given by the reorientation of identity created by the Jeremianic shift. But Yoder also argues that Ezra and Nehemiah need to be

---

problem is the problem of how to receive and celebrate the blessing, the *shalom*, the good, or 'the land' that God desires to give, yet to do so without defensively and violently hoarding God's blessing." Gerald W. Schlabach, "Deuteronomic or Constantinian: What is the Most Basic Problem for Christian Social Ethics?" in Stanley Hauerwas et al., eds., *The Wisdom of the Cross*, 451.

[122] Schlabach, "Deuteronomic or Constantinian," 451.

[123] This is part of Alain Epp Weaver's larger argument in "On Exile."

[124] Cartwright, "If Abraham is Our Father..," in Yoder, *The Jewish-Christian Schism Revisited*, 221. Italics in original.

[125] Yoder, *For the Nations*, 53, note 6.

seen as inappropriate deviations from the Jeremiah line, since what is reconstituted is a cult and polity as a branch of the pagan imperial government; most of Ezra's story is an account of politicking for imperial authorization to rebuild the temple.[126] Thus in order to save his diasporic argument, Yoder largely avoids discussion of Ezra and Nehemiah.

For Yoder, then, the reading of the Hebrew Scriptures is one that is best pursued in a communal context, a reading that itself brings to view "an increasingly precise definition of the nature of peoplehood. Yoder sees the Old Testament as moving upward in the call of Abraham and the exodus, downward in the development of the monarchy, upward in the exilic vision of Jeremiah, and downward in the return under Ezra and Nehemiah."[127] In Yoder's words, it is crucial to "appropriate as did Jesus the full and patent ambivalence of the Jewish experience with the usability of majesty, whether Canaanite kingdoms or Mesopotamian empires, as instruments of divine rule."[128] Therefore, while "'Yahweh is King' is the central Hebrew doxology," it is important to see such an analogy as dismantling instead of supporting powerful oppression.[129] Yoder's antiroyal reading of the Hebrew Scriptures allows him to call for the rejection of the institution of human kingship, focusing as he does on the ambivalence toward human monarchy, especially regarding the Davidide dynasty, that error of the age of Samuel. Along with this antiroyal reading comes a sustained focus on the Jeremian shift, a move to embrace a prophetic understanding of the diasporic/exilic notion, whereby the community of God, as part of an ever-increasingly refined understanding of peoplehood, seeks the peace of the city in which that community finds itself. Thus Yoder finds in the Hebrew Scriptures a redefinition of rule that centers on engagement with the wider world through the suffering service of an exilic community of faith, which while creative and challenging, leaves many wanting more positive understandings of civil institutions within his thought.

The Hebrew Scriptures in O'Donovan's Theopolitical Thought

O'Donovan hints at the identification of God's kingly rule displayed in Israel as the hermeneutical principle for political theology a decade prior to the publication of *The Desire of Nations*. Embedded in a discussion concerning the authority of Scripture is O'Donovan's illustration that an understanding of Jesus as the Christ forces the reader to confront the history of the Messianic idea in the Hebrew Scriptures. Coming to grips with the history of the messianic idea in the Hebrew Scriptures requires a comprehension of the

---

[126] Yoder, *For the Nations*, 60, 74.
[127] Carter, *The Politics of the Cross*, 152.
[128] Yoder, "To Serve our God and to Rule the World," in Yoder, *The Royal Priesthood*, 133.
[129] Yoder, "Thinking Theologically From a Free-Church Perspective," 260.

history of kingship displayed there, which reveals some ambivalence about the origins of the monarchy, e.g. the tussle between theocratic and monarchic ideals.[130] Although O'Donovan raises the Messianic idea in this context to illustrate a point about reading the Bible, it is possible to see here the seeds of his more fully developed position in *The Desire of Nations,* where the phrase 'Yhwh reigns' is the central proclamation on which a political reading of the Hebrew Scriptures turns.

GOD'S KINGSHIP AS THE BASIS OF AUTHORITY

To take up the concept of divine kingship is an attempt to recover the ground traditionally held by the notion of authority. O'Donovan's focus on authority in *The Desire of Nations,* and subsequently in *The Ways of Judgment,* is intended to be broad enough to include moral, epistemological, and political authority. Such a wide notion of authority, which O'Donovan describes as the objective correlate of freedom, evokes free action and makes free action intelligible.[131] This description is expanded by O'Donovan's assertion that "authority in society is *one* form in which the intelligible ends or grounds of action, the created goods to which our action is oriented, lay claim on us."[132] Authority construed in this way is to be distinguished from power (the most general term for an ability to get things done by any means) or persuasion (the rhetorical exercise of presenting the grounds of action to the mind). O'Donovan refers the reader to his earlier work on authority in *Resurrection and Moral Order,* where his discussion, beginning with authority in general and then moving on to divine authority and then the authority of Christ, argues that while it is the case that all authority comes from God, that authority is fully real and really given. There is such a thing as political authority, which can be defined as "a concurrence of the natural authorities of might and tradition with that other 'relatively natural' authority, the authority of injured right," which are "exercised together when the first two are put at the disposal of the third; that is, when one whose possession of *might* is in accord with the *established order* of a society takes responsibility for the *righting of wrongs* within that society."[133] Put another way, since authority is not displayed in any one given

---

[130] O'Donovan, *On the 39 Articles,* 59.

[131] O'Donovan repeats, clarifies and extends this relationship of authority and freedom described in *The Desire of the Nations* in *The Ways of Judgment*. Freedom is power to act, but to give it moral significance, we must understand it in terms of the orientation of the individual to social communications. So freedom is the realization of individual powers within social forms, while authority is the objective correlate of freedom. Authority attaches to those structures of communication in which we engage in order to realize freedom. No society is free that cannot sustain the forms that make for its members' freedom. O'Donovan, *The Ways of Judgment,* 67-68.

[132] O'Donovan, *The Desire of the Nations,* 30.

[133] O'Donovan, *Resurrection and Moral Order,* 128. Italics in original.

institutional form, but in the performance of the political act of judgment, "political authority arises as judgment is done."[134] Institutions may be devised to channel political authority, but no single form of institution is to be considered as having divine origin as such. Rather, O'Donovan argues for an understanding of political authority that is a "*general* provision of non-reciprocal relations under which we may flourish."[135] However, it would be wrong to mistake such authority for the absoluteness of truth and goodness. Rather, "the exercise of political authority is the search for a compromise which, while bearing the fullest witness to the truth that can be in the circumstances to be borne, will, nevertheless, lie within the scope of possible public action in the particular community of fallen men which it has to serve."[136] It seems that O'Donovan's central burden in his discussion of authority is to show that political authority, properly understood, has an inadequate basis if grounded solely in the assertion of human will (as in humanist social contract theory). Political authority is also poorly understood if the focus is entirely on divine will with no clear view of "how to present the otherness of God as propitious to mankind."[137] In O'Donovan's view, the Jewish cry of "Yhwh is king" is precisely the kind of act that fused political and religious meaning in a way that avoids the inadequate positions he has described. The cry of the Jews acknowledges divine authority that nonetheless "evokes free human action because it holds out to the worshippers a fulfillment of their agency within the created order in which their agency has a place and a meaning."[138] Thus an investigation of the meaning of the revelation of God's kingship is the exegetical starting point for O'Donovan's political theology.[139]

In a brief excursus, O'Donovan reveals that the Scriptures from which he unfolds his understanding of 'Yhwh is king' are a small group of Psalms – Psalm 93, 97, and 99. In the references to God's kingship in these Psalms, and in other supplementary texts used by O'Donovan to support the enthronement Psalms, he notices a reluctance to make a direct connection to any concrete form of political order, since Israel always aspired to remain free of images of God. Because God's kingship cannot be seen in or identified with any particular government or king, another way must be found to explore the idea on a national and international scale. Here O'Donovan makes what amounts to a pivotal interpretive move – he suggests that the exploration of God's kingship

---

[134] O'Donovan, *The Ways of Judgment*, 128.

[135] O'Donovan, *The Ways of Judgment*, 129. Italics in original.

[136] O'Donovan, *The Ways of Judgment*, 130.

[137] O'Donovan, *The Desire of the Nations*, 32.

[138] O'Donovan, *The Desire of the Nations*, 32.

[139] The cry "Yhwh is King" has 3 kinds of association: a) geophysical reassurance about stability in the natural order; b) reassurance about the international political order, that God was in control of all nations; and c) reassurance about the national order by justice and law. O'Donovan, *The Desire of the Nations*, 32.

must be pursued by way of identifying leading political terms or themes that are habitually grouped with the claim that God is king. These themes are salvation, judgment, possession, and praise.[140]

POLITICAL THEMES DRAWN FROM THE CLAIM THAT GOD IS KING

The first political theme that is grouped with the kingly rule of God is *salvation*, which includes triumphs that go beyond a narrow human military sense, and focus instead on the victory of God over the enemies of His people. Salvation has subsidiary parallels such as God's favour and righteousness, which serve to display the meaning of God's victories.[141]

The second political term developed here is *judgment*, which is to say that God's judgment brings to light the distinction that already exists between the just and the unjust. O'Donovan takes pains to stress the importance of this theme. "It is impossible to overestimate the importance of this concept for a study of biblical political ideas. It is often obscured by the influence of a quite different conception of justice, classical and Aristotelian in inspiration, built on the twin notions of appropriateness and proportionate equality – justice as receiving one's own and being in social equilibrium. *Mishpat* is primarily a judicial performance."[142] This message of equitable judgment applies also on an international scale, and so Israel is charged with telling the nations that God is king and will judge the people with equity. This judgment is a performance with lasting validity, in that right juridical activity carries on from generation to generation, a stream that never dries up.

The third political term identified and developed by O'Donovan is

---

[140] O'Donovan describes these political concepts such as salvation, judgment, possession, and praise as words that serve only as indicators of trains of thought that could in each case be exchanged for other words. One could use a term such as 'mighty deeds' instead of 'salvation,' for example, but the ideas indicated by these terms are not exchangeable for others. So, "if someone says that the judicial idea as such is not central to Israel's political life, or that the praise of the community is irrelevant to Yhwh's rule, then we have a disagreement. And since this exegetical framework is to play an organizing role in our exposition of political theology, the disagreement may turn out to be a serious one that will touch on the very nature of the political act itself." O'Donovan, *The Desire of the Nations*, 36. O'Donovan does display a willingness to abandon his structure if necessary. For example, In *The Ways of Judgment*, he disavows an attempt made in *The Desire of the Nations* to extend a tetrad of church-signs to corresponding ministries, claiming that this attempt "had more ingenuity than strength." O'Donovan, *The Ways of Judgment*, 266. Nonetheless, his tetrad of concepts extends from the Hebrew Scriptures to Jesus' ministry, the moments of the Christ-event, marks of the church's identity, practices of worship, positive marks of liberal society, and parodic practices of liberal society. See Appendix 1.

[141] O'Donovan, *The Desire of the Nations*, 36-37.

[142] O'Donovan, *The Desire of the Nations*, 39.

possession of land and the law. "Possessing the land was a matter of observing that the order of life which was established by God's judgments; possessing the law was a matter of enjoying that purchase on the conditions of life which was Yhwh's gift."[143] Possession has to do with community identity, where the land is the material cause, the law is the formal cause, and victories are the efficient cause of God's kingly rule. According to O'Donovan, there was never a pure nomad ideal in Israel's history, even in the days of Abraham, when the stories were already organized around the promise of settlement. However, this notion of possession does not lead O'Donovan to suggest that Israel must possess some particular piece of land. Instead, he shows that Israel itself is God's possession, and that the landless status of the Levite tribe provides a model for the faithful when all of Israel becomes landless.[144]

O'Donovan adds the fourth political theme of the *praise* of God's people, in which God's rule receives its answering recognition. Therefore the community of Israel is a political community by virtue of being a worshipping community. Praise proves/demonstrates the fact of God's kingly rule. Indeed, within every political society there occurs implicitly an act of worship of the divine rule. According to O'Donovan, the doctrine that *we* set up political authority to secure our own purposes has left Western democracies in a state of pervasive moral debilitation that inevitably throws up idolatrous and authoritarian reactions, since without the act of worship, political authority is unbelievable.[145] While praise serves as the fourth political theme for O'Donovan's structure, it is set apart from the other three, which are descriptions of what God has done. Thus kingly rule takes effect in the praises of his people, and in that sense is the final cause of God's kingdom.

The four political themes that O'Donovan draws from an investigation of God's rule in Israel provide the pieces of the framework that he is constructing for political theology, and he further contends that this kind of reading of the Hebrew Scriptures is continuous both with the New Testament and with the Western tradition. He admits that this analysis of concepts cannot claim to be directly authorized from Scripture, but, "like all exegetical structures it can only claim to comprehend the text and illuminate it by allowing one aspect to shed light upon another."[146] However, that claim can be sustained and provide an important clue for the affirmation of God's kingship in the New Testament. But O'Donovan stretches this even further to argue that this framework will provide a way to explore the major questions about authority posed by the Western tradition.

The unique covenant of God and Israel can be seen as a point of disclosure from which the nature of all political authority comes to view. Out of the self-

---

[143] O'Donovan, *The Desire of the Nations*, 41.
[144] O'Donovan, *The Desire of the Nations*, 41-45.
[145] O'Donovan, *The Desire of the Nations*, 46-49.
[146] O'Donovan, *The Desire of the Nations*, 45.

possession of this people in their relation to God springs the possibility of other peoples possessing themselves in God. In this hermeneutic assumption lay the actual continuity between Israel's experience and the Western tradition.[147]

Therefore, by identifying the kingship of God as central to Israel's life, and by bringing into relief the four political themes that accompany descriptions of God's kingship as displayed in Israel, O'Donovan gains purchase for giving an account of the reign of God and thereby recover ground traditionally held by authority. The purchase that these concepts give O'Donovan is that he can now say that political authority comes from God, not from humans, and has been historically instantiated in the life of Israel, and so political theology can proceed from within a theological understanding of that history.

The authority O'Donovan claims to have brought to view comes in a historically mediated form, with the attendant problem of mediating authority in human form without producing idolatrous images of any kind, given Israel's strong prohibition of idolatry in any form. This is the problem of imageless mediation – the authority of God must be mediated without the mediator becoming an image, and so O'Donovan turns to a discussion of how it can be that the authority of God can be mediated without making an image of God out of the monarch. Several things are flagged as important ways of constraining the monarchy as a divine image: the rejection of absolutism, the permitting of a unitary government, and an independent prophetic voice that might be able to subject a unitary government to the independent authority of God's law.[148]

O'Donovan asserts that the authority of God cannot be represented, and as such is imageless, yet not unmediated. Nonetheless that authority is shown in events both natural and political, whereby "immediacy and human mediation complemented each other in delicate balance."[149] This balance is explored by O'Donovan in a lengthy treatment of Exodus 33 and 34, where "Yhwh is immediately present in conquest; his presence is mediated in judgment; and he is present in a kind of concealed immediacy in the law."[150] The meeting of God and Moses on Mount Sinai, and Moses' role in the Book of Exodus more generally are seen as corresponding to the pattern that has already been lifted out of the discussion of the Hebrew Scriptures – Moses leads the people out of Egypt to victory (salvation), he judges their cases in the wilderness (judgment), and he lays before them the pattern of their new life as possessors of the land (possession). However, even if Moses can be conceived as the mediator of all three of these aspects, a problem arises with the passing of Moses, in that "the

---

[147] O'Donovan, *The Desire of the Nations*, 45-46. Part of the burden of my second chapter will be to follow O'Donovan's argument through to his analysis of Christ as king.

[148] O'Donovan, *The Desire of the Nations*, 65.

[149] O'Donovan, *The Desire of the Nations*, 49.

[150] O'Donovan, *The Desire of the Nations*, 50.

prospect for the future is a diffused and differentiated mediation."[151] The search for a true successor of Moses raises a tension in Israel, since the institution of a monarchy to lead Israel is controversial. The question to be answered about any monarchy is how the imageless faith of Israel can become reconciled to the institution of the monarchy. O'Donovan suggests that it is possible to see that the claims of the monarchy were to hold together military, judicial, and tradition-bearing functions in one pair of hands.

While these claims were not without controversy, O'Donovan argues that "*in the end* nobody opposed the monarchy."[152] O'Donovan's conclusion about the lack of opposition to the monarchy in the end does not preclude opposition along the way. For example, while the monarch in Israel could mediate God's military victories, opponents of monarchy found it especially offensive that a military function was institutionalized. Not only was it very expensive, but to assume permanent military leadership was to challenge the supreme sign of God's leadership. However, O'Donovan deals with the mediating relation of the monarch in a way that can conceive of victories as won by God and granted as a favor to the king. Thus *God* gives victory to kings, suggesting an understanding of warfare as a sacral performance by God.[153] The important point regarding the king, according to O'Donovan, is that "if there is any figure who is allowed to mediate Yhwh's victories, it is he."[154] However, the kind of mediation O'Donovan sees here is not to be equated with the king being understood as an image of God.

Also important in the monarch's position as God's representative was the exercise of judicial functions. Other levels of judgment are present in the life of Israel, such as judges, prophets, priests, and so on, but "great stress is laid on the principle that all judgment is Yhwh's, especially that of the king's judges … the king, by asserting his jurisdiction over all others, establishes his role as the unique mediator of Yhwh's judgments."[155]

The most important thing the monarchy offered Israel was the function of continuity, which was to ensure an unbroken tradition in the occupation of territory and the perpetuation of national identity. The king thus took on a role of double representation in that he represented God's rule to the people, ensuring their obedience, and he represented the people to God, ensuring his favor.[156] O'Donovan sees as conclusive the principle that the monarch could provide the unitary representation of God's rule through the elements of

---

[151] O'Donovan, *The Desire of the Nations*, 52.

[152] O'Donovan, *The Desire of the Nations*, 53. Italics added.

[153] O'Donovan, *The Desire of the Nations*, 53-56. O'Donovan includes a discussion of war as a sacral performance initiated by God, and the absence of the ideal of the warrior-hero in Israel.

[154] O'Donovan, *The Desire of the Nations*, 56.

[155] O'Donovan, *The Desire of the Nations*, 60-61.

[156] O'Donovan, *The Desire of the Nations*, 53-61.

military victory given by God (salvation), the jurisdiction over judicial matters (judgment), and the ensuring of continuity in land and law (possession). But the king could never intrude himself between the people and God; there was no room for definition or determination by the monarch, but rather a safeguarding of what was God's on God's behalf.[157] O'Donovan asserts that "there are no anti-monarchist voices among the scriptural witnesses,"[158] and therefore the kingly rule of God as displayed by the monarchy in Israel can be used to fund political theology.

JURIDICAL AUTHORITY AND PROPHETIC TRADITION

O'Donovan recognizes that in addition to monarchy, another important dimension of the discussion of the mediation of God's rule is the prophetic tradition. He sees Israel's prophets as sharing "the task of tradition-bearing with the monarch; and, indeed, theirs was the more significant part, since it was through their words that Yhwh himself defined and redefined in each new circumstance the moral content of the tradition to which the kings were answerable. That content was the law."[159] Prophets do what kings cannot do, since there was a part of Moses' authority that the monarchy could not absorb, the form of which was the law, and the social voice that of the prophet. That is, the problem of an imageless representation that can resist the dangers of absolutism nonetheless permits a unitary government that remains subject to the independent authority of God's law, which is voiced through the prophetic movement. The danger that accompanies this added dimension of the discussion is that of individualism – the voice of the prophet is often a lone voice that stands in opposition to that of the tradition of the community. O'Donovan acknowledges that it may be surprising to speak of the individual in a treatment of the theopolitical concepts found in Israel's history, and therefore he is quick to distance the discussion from the individualism of Western thought. According to O'Donovan, the community is always prior to the individual in Hebrew thought, but the significance of the individual, found within the holy community, develops within the history of the First Temple period.

Such a development is analyzed in O'Donovan's lengthy and significant discussion of the prophet Jeremiah, in whom "a combination of interior isolation and moral certainty comes to its fullest expression, often in close interaction with the psalm tradition."[160] Jeremiah becomes a mediatorial representative who expresses God's anger *and* the despair of the people under that anger. In this role as a double representative, Jeremiah is in perilous

---

[157] O'Donovan, *The Desire of the Nations*, 62.
[158] O'Donovan, *The Desire of the Nations*, 61.
[159] O'Donovan, *The Desire of the Nations*, 62.
[160] O'Donovan, *The Desire of the Nations*, 76.

loneliness, isolated as he is because he is too much identified both with the people and with God in their conflict. The prophetic role of Jeremiah in the midst of exile takes over the mediatorial role that had been filled by the monarchy. With the monarchy set aside in this manner, the sole role (obedience) of the people is to heed prophecy. Each member of the community has to make a choice between listening to the prophet and submitting to the unfaithful authority of the institutions under which they find themselves.[161]

However, the life of exile, the wandering of the lonely refugee was not to be the end of the story, since there was the promise of a restored community. But the character of the remnant community was altered from that of life under the monarch – "it had faced the challenge to heed the voice of the prophet against the totality of its national institutions, and had seen the prophet vindicated by events. From that point on an element of confessional voluntarism enters into Israel's sense of itself."[162] Thus the reconstruction of community was grounded on a new covenant that would reach to hidden personal depths of understanding and motivation. But this sense of confessional voluntarism is not to be mistaken for the individualism of the West, as noted above. Rather, it is to be viewed as the memory of hope of faithful individuals that can conserve continuity when national institutions collapse.[163]

O'Donovan assumes that God's law can in principle be extended to other nations besides Israel, since God is understood as being king over the whole earth. Although there is an element of God asserting Israel's superiority over other nations, such an assertion does not encapsulate the entire story. Rather, "Israel's awareness of its own distinctness as Yhwh's chosen is held in careful equilibrium with a hope for co-operation with surrounding peoples."[164] Israel and other nations were to be held responsible in judgment, which implied that the other nations had the same vocation to exercise just judgment as did Israel, and Israel was subject to the same standards of judgment as the nations that offended her.[165]

However, the suggestion that the God of Israel is king over the whole earth is not to be misconstrued as the basis of imperial domination by Israel. The rise of empires such as Babylon serves as a sign of God's judgment on Israel, and in the writings of Jeremiah, leads to the encouragement of exiles. O'Donovan

---

[161] O'Donovan, *The Desire of the Nations*, 77-78.

[162] O'Donovan, *The Desire of the Nations*, 79.

[163] O'Donovan, *The Desire of the Nations*, 79, 80. O'Donovan extends his discussion of the individual in the final chapter of *The Ways of Judgment*. Here he notes that the God the modern subject seeks is the God reduced to absolute will, which is a misguided search. Instead, O'Donovan argues for the notion of "individual reflective judgment," in which the individual seeks to be a conscientious subject by being not an isolated individual, but a social individual who both shapes and is shaped by the community. See the chapter "The Longest Part," 293-319.

[164] O'Donovan, *The Desire of the Nations*, 67.

[165] O'Donovan, *The Desire of the Nations*, 67, 68.

traces a critique of empire from the account of the Tower of Babel (Genesis 11:1-9) through the prophetic writings of Isaiah, Jeremiah, and Daniel, and reiterated by John of Patmos. In place of empire, O'Donovan suggests that the order of the future (post-exile) "will be an internationally plural order, free from the unifying constraints of empire."[166] Israel was a messenger that thought in terms of law that would bind the nations universally, since there would be no unitary mediator at the international level. The world-order constituted by God was to be plural in nature. This leads O'Donovan to assert that if Israel's experience is a model for other societies, then it is the case that other national traditions besides the sacred one will be protected, and that particular societies will be afforded a kind of protection that society as a whole will not receive. "In securing the total tradition of humanity, we are in a context in which it is out of place to invoke the commanding rule of a government; but it is not out of place to invoke the role of law and to conceive relations between particular national communities in terms of a law-structure."[167] This amounts to a significant move for O'Donovan, as it allows him to imagine a political theology that is not limited to action within a particular state.[168] As will be seen below, especially in the fourth chapter, Yoder will insist that it is the church that is a truly international body, and thus forms the way to conceive of relations between particular states, while O'Donovan's complaint about Yoder is that he simply cannot find a way to break free of a much too narrow view of the work of the church, restricted largely to the pastoral arena.

SIX POLITICAL THEOREMS FOR POLITICAL THEOLOGY

Woven throughout O'Donovan's account of the kingship of God in Israel is his attempt to reclaim the "actual continuity between Israel's experience and the Western tradition."[169] In order to advance this reclamation project, O'Donovan adds a series of theorems that can be put forward in "terms adapted for general theoretical use."[170] To recap, O'Donovan's project attempts to recover the ground traditionally held by the notion of authority. In order for this recovery to proceed, he has begun an exegetical task, from which four political themes were drawn, which opens the way for a series of six political theorems that will fund O'Donovan's political theology. While the relationship of these six

---

[166] O'Donovan, *The Desire of the Nations*, 71.

[167] O'Donovan, *The Desire of the Nations*, 73.

[168] O'Donovan suspects that Yoder's emphasis on the church community limits him to what can be done within the state the church finds itself, and therefore unable to say anything about international matters. This criticism comes into especially sharp relief in the disagreement regarding violence and war, which will be dealt with in chapter 4 of this book.

[169] O'Donovan, *The Desire of the Nations*, 45-46.

[170] O'Donovan, *The Desire of the Nations*, 46.

theorems to the four themes and to particular exegetical work is not always clear, O'Donovan's purpose in distilling his exegetical work into these theorems is precisely to show that it is possible to move from reading the Bible to being engaged in the political realm without dropping what has been learned from the history of Israel. It is in abstracting political theorems from Israel's experience that Christian political theology gains the tools, as it were, for the task to which it is called, to recover the ground traditionally held by authority.

The six theorems O'Donovan draws from his exegetical work include:

> Theorem 1: Political authority arises when power, execution of right, and the perpetuation of tradition are assured together in one coordinated agency.[171]
>
> Theorem 2: That any regime should actually come to hold authority and continue to hold it is a work of divine providence in history, not a mere accomplishment of the human task of political service.[172]
>
> Theorem 3: In acknowledging political authority, society proves its political identity.[173]
>
> Theorem 4: The authority of a human regime mediates divine authority in a unitary structure, but it is subject to the authority of law within the community, which bears independent witness to the divine command.[174]
>
> Theorem 5: The appropriate unifying element in international order is law, not government.[175]

---

[171] All three must exist together for authority to be legitimate. O'Donovan, *The Desire of the Nations*, 46.

[172] By this O'Donovan is suggesting that there is a divine regime of history behind every historically successful political regime. O'Donovan, *The Desire of the Nations*, 46. The first two *theorems* arise at the end of O'Donovan's discussion of the first three political *themes* (salvation, judgment, possession).

[173] The term 'proves' here is a reference to acknowledging the relation that exists between a society and its own political authorities. The three political themes and two theorems remain unfinished in this form, claims O'Donovan, and so he connects a third theorem to the discussion of the fourth theme (praise). The identity O'Donovan refers to here entails not "a constitutive sense of conferring existence" on some regime, "but in the much more basic sense of simply acknowledging that they are *there* and that they are *theirs*." O'Donovan, *The Desire of the Nations*, 47. Italics in original.

[174] The fourth theorem arises within O'Donovan's discussion of the possibility of monarchical mediation of God's rule without collapsing into idolatry or absolutism. This theorem corresponds to Western ideas of 'Natural Law.' That is, government is responsible to a political reality within the very society being governed. O'Donovan, *The Desire of the Nations*, 65.

[175] The fifth theorem is important to O'Donovan's move from a discussion of God's rule on a national scale to that same rule on an international scale, a move whereby O'Donovan is keen to avoid the temptations of imperial pretensions, which can be done through a turn to the juridical. Part of this move to the juridical is the heightened role of the prophetic movement, especially in Jeremiah, in which " the distinctive strengths of a

Theorem 6: The conscience of the individual members of a community is a repository of the moral understanding which shaped it, and may serve to perpetuate it in a crisis of collapsing morale or institution.

By abstracting these themes from his exegetical reading of the Old Testament, a reading that is a self-defined search for political concepts, O'Donovan believes he has the purchase he needs for political theology.[176] He has gathered a set of tools, as it were, which enable him to reclaim the ground held by political authority. His concepts and theorems take into account issues of power, the execution of right, and the perpetuation of tradition. He has sought to resist radical voluntarism of the sort that seeks to impose its will on any and all societies. O'Donovan has also provided a sense of legitimate political identity that is nonetheless appropriately modest in remaining subject to the authority of law, which is also a unifying element that functions on a national and international scale. O'Donovan also finds room for the conscience of the individual as a repository of moral understanding, with allowance made for the resistance to government or law that is collapsing.

For O'Donovan, then, "The six general theorems which we have drawn from Israel's political experience provide an outline of what theology may need to put in the place traditionally held by a notion of political authority...What we have done ... is simply abstract from Israel's experience a general understanding of what the divine rule is which is the subject of the proclamation. We have, as it were, examined the design of the vehicle; now we must see it move."[177] Equipped with these six theorems, and the four political themes drawn from exegetical work in the Hebrew Scriptures, O'Donovan has drawn up a framework for understanding the rest of the Bible and a rehabilitation of political theology in the West.

A number of questions arise concerning O'Donovan's choice of themes and concentration on certain Scriptural elements to the exclusion of others. For example, Hauerwas and Fodor wonder what becomes of the theme of covenant in the conceptual structure and where one might find discussion of other themes

---

voluntary community have been grafted on to the racial stock." O'Donovan, *The Desire of the Nations*, 80.

[176] Once O'Donovan has gleaned political concepts from a close reading of Scripture, his theopolitical work seeks to apply these concepts, but often without explicit theological language, presumably as a way to seek a hearing in the wider realm of conventional politics. For example, his book, *The Just War Revisited* (Cambridge: Cambridge University Press, 2003) does not use the kind of theological language found in *The Desire of the Nations*, although surely O'Donovan would argue that his treatment of just war issues calls for political concepts and theorems to be put to proper use without having to reiterate his entire theological underpinning, which nonetheless is clearly still at work.

[177] O'Donovan, *The Desire of the Nations*, 80, 81.

such as God as shepherd, God as servant and so on.[178] The list of suggestions given to O'Donovan about his choice of 'concepts,' in addition to the ones mentioned, is lengthy. Victor Paul Furnish is too general in his suggestion that 'concepts' cannot do justice to the richness and variety of Scripture's witness. Furnish should have pursued the point further in more specific terms.[179] Nicolas Wolterstorff's complaint is more specific. He argues that while kingship entailed victory, judgment, and possession, this does not mean that this is the nature of kingship. Perhaps, Wolterstorff suggests, we are simply being shown a manifestation of kingship that could be an exception to that nature.[180] Gordon McConville, while in basic agreement with O'Donovan's use of a victory-judgment-tradition triad, argues that a different picture would emerge if the Old Testament material would be used in a different way. McConnville's suggestion is that Deuteronomy is the Hebrew Scriptures' supreme political text and therefore should have priority in political theology. If O'Donovan would agree to this, a very different picture of political authority would arise, whose focus would center on a covenant with the people, and thus the focus on kingship would be problematized considerably. O'Donovan's reply to McConnville argues that while his is not a theology of monarchy, he does admit to saying too little about covenant, citing nervousness about discussions of covenant falling prey to modern contractual concepts that he is keen to avoid.[181] Despite this concession, O'Donovan insists that Deuteronomy is not an anti-monarchical book. Instead it is in the promulgation of law (in the form of the Decalogue) that we see the role of the monarch, i.e. the monarch determines the form in which the principles of the Decalogue are to be elaborated as law. Therefore by focusing on the law, O'Donovan in essence claims to cover the territory that his critics want to have addressed through the category of contract.[182]

Despite the weight given to law in national and international order, O'Donovan gives very little account of the content of the law of the Hebrew Scriptures, or how its emphases and priorities demonstrate the nature of God's rule.[183] It seems that for O'Donovan the formal existence of the law, at least in his reading of the Hebrew Scriptures, is more important than the material content of that law. Without this focus on the content of the law, O'Donovan

---

[178] Hauerwas and Jim Fodor, "Remaining in Babylon," 47-48.

[179] Victor Paul Furnish, "How Firm a Foundation? Some Questions About Scripture in *The Desire of the Nations*," *Studies in Christian Ethics* 11 no 2 (1998): 20.

[180] Nicholas Wolterstorff, "A Discussion of Oliver O'Donovan's *The Desire of the Nations*," *Scottish Journal of Theology* 54 no 1 (2001): 101.

[181] J. Gordon McConnville, "Law and Monarchy in the Old Testament," in Craig Bartholemew, et al., eds. *A Royal Priesthood?*, 69-77. O'Donovan, "Response to Gordon McConnville," Bartholemew, et al., eds., *A Royal Priesthood?*, 89.

[182] O'Donovan, "Response to Gordon McConnville," 89-90.

[183] See R.W.L. Moberly, "The Use of Scripture in *The Desire of the Nations*," in Craig Bartholemew, et al., eds., *A Royal Priesthood?*, 54.

runs the danger that the formal concept may be given content in ways that owe less to Scriptural principles than to some other source or priority. Moberly points out that O'Donovan does, however, give a close and extensive reading of Jesus' teaching in the Gospels. O'Donovan describes his own work on law as being more closely connected with discussions of the New Testament than the Hebrew Scriptures.[184]

Comparative Observations

The preceding description and analysis of Yoder and O'Donovan's close readings of the text of the Hebrew Scriptures reveals their use of an approach that takes into account the narrative nature of the Scriptures themselves, in a reading that takes the move from promise to fulfillment seriously. Neither theologian seeks some neutral vantage point from which a reading must begin, seeking instead to read and think out of Scripture, and refusing to be held captive to any demands that they would see as alien to Scripture. The similarities in approach that mark both Yoder's and O'Donovan's projects open up interesting possibilities for the kind of critical comparative study being pursued here, i.e. this is a comparison of two political theologies that use the same fundamental source and approach it in significantly similar ways.

While the similarities in a general approach to Scripture are substantial ones, some distinctions in the use of the Bible for political theology become evident quickly. That is, O'Donovan sets out deliberately to produce a political theology in the Western Christian tradition,[185] a task that for him is separate from but not unrelated to Christian ethics, yet is most closely connected to political ethics, which he develops in *The Ways of Judgment*, a book that O'Donovan claims as the second of "two phases in a single extended train of thought."[186] The fundamental source for all of these projects is Scripture, but each project requires separate exegesis in order to answer the different questions raised by each enterprise.

It is not difficult to imagine Yoderian criticism of O'Donovan's use of the Hebrew Scriptures to search for the kind of architectonic structure O'Donovan develops at length. To be fair to O'Donovan, he tempers his conceptual concerns somewhat in the midst of his presentation of political terms and theorems that he finds in the Old Testament. "This analysis of concepts cannot,

---

[184] Moberly, "The Use of Scripture in *The Desire of the Nations*," 55; O'Donovan, "Response to Gordon McConnville," 89.

[185] O'Donovan recalls spending a sabbatical term "reading Hobbes' *Leviathan* very slowly; since when everything in the idea of this book has been altered except the author's excitement at discovering a Great Tradition of political theology, almost unknown to today's theologians." It is this Great Tradition that O'Donovan is seeking to draw on and extend. O'Donovan, *The Desire of the Nations*, xi.

[186] O'Donovan, *The Ways of Judgment*, x.

of course, claim to be directly authorized by the text of the Hebrew Scriptures. Like all exegetical structures it can only claim to comprehend the text and illuminate it by allowing one aspect to shed light on another.... Our view here, however, stretches beyond this exegetical claim to a theoretical one."[187] That is, when O'Donovan turns to the Hebrew Scriptures he does so with an intent to develop an account of the reign of God, i.e. the Bible must provide what political theory needs, what the political theologian requires to do political theology, and therefore O'Donovan looks for unity within the pluralist voices of the Bible.

Yoder, on the other hand, sees the diversity in the Bible as normative for its reading, and thus claims to avoid a search for a unified voice or system that can be used as the basis for a full-blown architectonic. It might be said that Yoder does not set out to develop a political theology *per se*, and certainly not as something that can or should be separate from discussions of ethics, but instead searches for the appropriate stance called for by taking the diversity of the Scriptures into account. Therefore, it seems that Yoder's approach is more flexible in nature, and committed by its very approach to continuing dialogue. Even if O'Donovan were to argue that the terms for true dialogue could only be established and realized under the coherent rule of divine law, Yoder might respond that even the understanding of the divine rule is accessible only through an 'ecclesial epistemology,' which is itself established not by an epistemological commitment, but an ecclesial one. This flexible approach to continuing dialogue holds considerable potential for ecumenism, which itself is an important dimension of the role of the church in political theology.

Therefore, Yoder's approach focuses more directly on the church as the community that reads the Scripture in order to obey it. This approach, which I have termed a sort of 'ecclesial epistemology,' contrasts with O'Donovan's approach, based on 'theological epistemology,' in which the Christian theologian reads the Bible while drawing on theological tradition to provide orientation and direction. This is not to say that Yoder's ecclesial approach is not also theological. Rather, the more substantive point is that O'Donovan draws distinctions between the church and secular politics in a way that Yoder does not.[188]

Despite the commitment of both Yoder and O'Donovan to take into the account the wider narrative of the Bible and in that way avoid the misleading isolation of some particular theme that would in turn produce a truncated understanding of the Biblical narrative, neither writer is entirely successful in this intention. That is, as seen above, O'Donovan privileges the monarchical themes of the Hebrew Scriptures at the expense of covenant, while Yoder centers on diaspora experience as mission to the exclusion of issues of

---

[187] O'Donovan, *The Desire of the Nations,* 45.

[188] The nature and extent of this difference will be dealt with in a number of contexts in the next three chapters of this book.

"God is King"

authority, land, and irredentism. Nonetheless, given the similarity of approach to the Bible, it is not surprising that several common points of reference have been brought to view within the particular readings of the Hebrew Scriptures provided by Yoder and O'Donovan – the kingly rule of God, the role of the monarchy in Israel, and the prophetic tradition. However, even these common reference points do not operate in identical ways in the respective projects being considered here, as they lead Yoder to interpret the church as a political analogy, while O'Donovan is led to an architectonic heremeneutic.

The centrality of the kingly rule of God as displayed in Israel is brought to view in both theopolitical projects by investigating the implications of the worshipful cry, "God is King," which by implication means that no one else may claim that role. Both O'Donovan and Yoder agree that the war narratives of the Hebrew Scriptures show that it is God who is victorious in Israel's wars, quite apart from conventional military methods and campaigns. God's victory is a kind of sacral performance designed to reveal God's power and mark the necessity of human dependence on God. Yoder and O'Donovan agree on this basic premise, although they again part company when attempting to develop this understanding for Christian political theology. Yoder takes the notion of God's kingship, and his role as warrior in place of human initiative and effort as the inauguration of an ever-refined understanding of peoplehood in covenant with God. Further, the understanding of God's kingship is ever-refined in the direction of king as suffering servant. Therefore, any human who presumes to lead, or rather, is called to lead, will have to lead in the form of a servant. Yoder's focus on the kingly rule of God leads away from discussions of authority and the need for human kingship, no matter how sensitive to the temptations of power such a human king might be. Even analogies of kingship are problematic for Yoder.

O'Donovan's understanding of the kingly rule of God allows him to do what he considers necessary for political theology, i.e. to recover the ground held by authority. O'Donovan's insistence that any war narratives of the Hebrew Scriptures display God's sovereignty leads in a direction that is different than Yoder's. Whereas Yoder makes a move toward peoplehood, O'Donovan takes God's sole initiative in battle as a warning that kings, while legitimate, must acknowledge God's granting of military victory.[189] So authority comes from God, but can be represented by a human king even in a nation that believes in

---

[189] The fact that O'Donovan and Yoder both understand wars in the Old Testament as testimony to God's initiative and power, and not as a call for Christian militarism in any form, does not, however, result in agreement regarding involvement in war. For example, O'Donovan sees even in Deuteronomic law a move in the "direction of an elementary 'just-war' code." O'Donovan, *The Desire of the Nations,* 54. A comparison of Yoder and O'Donovan on the issue of violence and war will be taken up in chapter 4 of this book.

imageless representation. An investigation of the themes that surround God's kingship gives O'Donovan a way to identify political themes necessary for political theology. Yoder's writing and thinking focuses then on church practices that must be 'translated' into the wider world, since the church as community must find ways to act politically, to engage constructively in the political arena as the church.

The common focus on human kingship reveals a stark difference between Yoder and O'Donovan. Yoder's relentless focus on the antiroyal strand of the Hebrew Scriptures urgently seeks to uncover the deep ambivalence to human monarchy, since an embrace of monarchy fails to capture the sense of mission that Yoder connects to the antiroyal reading that includes an embrace of the exilic, of gracious diaspora. He is especially concerned about any tendency toward accommodation and even idolatry, temptations that are treated as inherent to all forms of monarchy except God's. Yoder therefore is suspicious of any political theology that connects the mission of the church to the role of any particular government, or underwrites any such arrangement as being God's plan for the church. It is precisely this kind of suspicion, the kind that O'Donovan wants to move beyond in ways of which Yoder would be even further suspicious, that is at the heart of the complaints about Yoder's tendency to obfuscate the nature of the connections between the church and the wider world.

O'Donovan shares Yoder's concerns regarding the human monarchy, and is more explicit about the dangers of empire, but these concerns do not lead him to reject the notion that human monarchy can mediate God's authority in a way that avoids idolatrous temptations. Kingly authority is useful, according to O'Donovan, in a way that suggests that he is open to at least some form of Christendom, albeit not in any way that would suggest that any particular form of government could embody the image of God. This is important to note, since O'Donovan will in this way avoid connecting the work of the church directly to some governmental regime. However, O'Donovan is more optimistic about the positive possibilities of Christendom than Yoder can be, given their respective readings of the Old Testament.[190]

The third area of commonality in Yoder and O'Donovan is a turn to the prophetic tradition, especially as represented by Jeremiah, as a way of addressing the concerns that are brought to view in their respective discussions of monarchy. O'Donovan's use of the prophetic tradition entails a turn to the juridical, whereby monarchical authority, if it seeks to overstep its legitimate role, is called to faithfulness by the law. The prophets give the community the resources to remain true to their identity and resist any illegitimate grasping for

---

[190] The difference I have marked here will become even more obvious in the comparison of Yoder and O'Donovan's reading of the New Testament, which will be taken up in the next chapter. The respective understandings of Christendom will be the burden of Chapter 3.

excessive power on the part of any given form of government. In this sense the prophetic tradition is more important than the monarchical tradition as a resource for political theology, since it is law rather than government that is the appropriate unifying element on a national and international scale.

Yoder's turn to the prophetic tradition, also centered on Jeremiah, is not a turn to law but a more focused turn to community than is possible in a monarchy toward which the Hebrew Scriptures are deeply ambivalent. So the Jeremian shift in Yoder is merely a continuation of the theme that he picked up in his discussion of the monarchy, and of God as king and warrior. That is, instead of looking to monarchy or law as a way to fund political theology, the narrative from beginning to end is an ever-refined understanding of peoplehood that is on a pilgrimage through this world, and it is this community that sees its gracious dispersion as mission which embodies the politics of the people of God in Yoder's thought.

The two-fold task of this first chapter, to compare the ways in which Yoder and O'Donovan approach the Bible, and then to look at the ways in which they read the Hebrew Scriptures for political theology has brought to view a number of important issues. It has become clear that these thinkers refuse to understand politics as the imposition of the human will on the world, as though that is somehow the essence of politics. In this they are not unique, but they hold in common the belief that political theology has to do with taking the role of God in the world seriously, with the concomitant understanding that politics then has to take history, the Bible, theology, and the church seriously. But it has also become clear that neither Yoder or O'Donovan read history, the Bible, and especially the Hebrew Scriptures as a way to support monarchy, to privilege a single nation or government as *the* embodiment of God's rule. Both signal the importance of the prophetic role in society, calling whatever government or policy to be more just and right. The theological, biblical understanding of God as king does not move Yoder or O'Donovan to find ways of ignoring political engagement, but rather to search for ways of constructively engaging in the world, although this initiative is more difficult to see in Yoder's thought. However, it is simply not the case that Yoder is sectarian – his antiroyal reading of the Hebrew Scriptures, along with his emphasis on the building up of the people of God and the seeking of the peace of the city do not lead him to sectarianism, but to building of and cooperation with certain elements in whatever society God's people find themselves, as will become ever more evident as we follow his work through discussions of the New Testament, Constantinianism and peace. In addition then to resisting some assumption that Yoder's political theology does not result in constructive political engagements, it will also be important to resist any un-nuanced assumption that O'Donovan's work is merely some highly sophisticated theologically systematic attempt to underwrite Christendom. O'Donovan's is not at its heart an accommodationist political theology that is able to constructively engage politics without remaining theologically faithful.

The common focus on God's kingship found in Yoder's and O'Donovan's reading of the Hebrew Scriptures is followed through to their readings of the New Testament. Christian political theology must also give an account of what it means that Christ is King. Therefore, the second chapter will engage in a critical comparative study of Yoder and O'Donovan's reading of the New Testament for their respective theopolitical projects.

Chapter 2

A Political Rendering of the Claim that Jesus is Lord: Yoder and O'Donovan's Theopolitical Reading of the New Testament[1]

Introduction

For both Yoder and O'Donovan, the reading of the Hebrew Scriptures for an understanding of the central phrase 'God reigns' is followed by an exploration of the claim that Jesus Christ is Lord as put forward in the New Testament. The present chapter is a critical, comparative examination of the theopolitical reading of the New Testament in the thought of Yoder and O'Donovan. Christology is central to both theopolitical projects in that an attempt is being made to develop a politically relevant Christological interpretation of the New Testament. I will critically examine the claim that Yoder's Christology constitutes a 'Jesuology,' an assertion which suggests that his is a truncated theological position that does not succeed in moving beyond a too-immediate modeling of political theology on the actions of Jesus, that there is in Yoder's work a tendency toward Christomonism, especially at the expense of paying appropriate attention to the work of the Holy Spirit in the world beyond the church, and a less than robust view of orthodox Trinitarianism. Yoder disavows these claims, despite the fact that he uses the term 'Jesuology' to describe his own work, which for him signals a focus on the incarnation as the full display of the godlikeness of Christ, in contrast to more formalized Christologies, which, while doctrinally orthodox, tend to find the life, teaching, and ministry of Jesus irrelevant for political theology. So-called 'high' Christologies also tend toward triumphalism and the desire to assume control of secular power in the name of Christ.

O'Donovan finds Yoder's sort of focus too depoliticized because of its narrow focus on a too-immediate following of Jesus, and insists that Christian political theology must also give an account of what it means that Christ is King. For O'Donovan, it is only in a full understanding of the triumph of Christ the King, the desire of the nations, that theology is given its full political conceptuality, and politics receives its full theological conceptuality.[2] O'Donovan asserts that a political theology shaped by the Christ-event must undertake notions of public and political that are wide and generous, which is

---

[1] I take the title phrase from Daniel Bell, "State and Civil Society," in Cavanaugh and Scott, eds. *Blackwell Companion to Political Theology,* 436.
[2] O'Donovan, *The Desire of the Nations,* 2.

impossible if political theology stops at a 'Jesuology' that focuses on the message of Jesus in a way that seeks to model itself on Jesus, but does not have the theological depth to account for the work of God in the larger world. A political theology shaped by the entire Christ-event, and not just the life or teachings of Jesus, is what makes wider and more generous notions of public and political possible. It becomes possible to have both a critical and constructive dimension if political theology performs its task Christologically and not just Jesulogically.[3] O'Donovan (along with others) is worried that Yoder can only be critical and not constructive, although in this O'Donovan is wrong, as a careful reading of Yoder's work will bring to view his sustained concern for constructive political engagements.

The Christ-event is important in both projects, with particular focus given to the dialectic between cross and resurrection. Neither O'Donovan nor Yoder denigrate one part of the Christ-event at the expense of another, but their respective understandings of the logic of cross and resurrection differ considerably. O'Donovan asserts that the crucifixion of Jesus signals a defeat of the earthly political action of Jesus. However, his resurrection from the dead reveals the triumph of Christ over death, a triumph that has implications for current political reality, despite the fact that victory is not entirely transparent, awaiting as it does the final consummation of Christ's return. O'Donovan sees the ministry of Jesus as a disclosure of the reign of God which introduced a clash between the passing age of Rome and the kingdom come in Christ.

It is within the time before the final consummation that the church exists as a political entity, authorized by Christ and subject to God's ultimate judgment. The church is differently authorized than secular power, which holds authority that is penultimate and therefore provisional, authorized to assert political authority in the form of judgment.

Yoder also believes that in Christ the kingdom has come, and the old age is therefore passing away. However, the fullness of the kingdom is not complete, but is an eschatological reality that suggests that the church lives in an age of tension between the overlapping passing age and the coming assured kingdom. This existence in an age of eschatological tension leads Yoder to see in the church a paradigm for secular power, offering its own practices as 'body politics' that can also become real in non-religious society. For Yoder, the politics of Jesus instantiated in the church *is* political theology, whereas secular power exists for the sake of the church.

Therefore, while O'Donovan presses a political theology centered on Christology, and Yoder puts forward a Jesuology as the basis of political theology, the claim by these two theologians that Christ is lord nonetheless brings to view a number of commonalities that will form the framework for the critical comparison undertaken here - a focus on the Christ-event (advent,

---

[3] In Yoder's writings, the term 'Jesulogical' serves as the adjectival form of the noun 'Jesuology.'

death, resurrection and exaltation of Jesus), the life, teaching, and ministry of Jesus of Nazareth, the eschatological dimension of the New Testament, the role of the church in political theology, and the authorization of the state in light of the work of Jesus.

The Logic of Cross and Resurrection

Yoder and O'Donovan treat the Christ-event similarly in that they seek to keep all the moments of that event – advent, passion, resurrection, and exaltation – as central. While they can both be described as putting forward a classically orthodox Christology, their respective readings of the *significance* of Christology for political theology cannot be equated, especially in terms of the logic of cross and resurrection. Yoder insists that a close study of the narrative account of the Gospels will reveal a social ethic for Christians today, and not a way of ignoring or relativizing the message and life of Jesus, or allowing a focus on the cross of Jesus to be pushed into the realm of pastoral care, otherworldly irrelevance, or irresponsibility. This, for Yoder, means that it is the cross and not the sword - suffering, and not brute force - that determines the meaning of history. But Yoder does not ignore the power of the resurrection. Instead, he notes that the triumph of right is assured because of the power of the resurrection, and not because of any other calculus. Thus, "the relationship between the obedience of God's people and the triumph of God's cause is not a relationship of cause and effect but one of cross and resurrection."[4] The resurrection vindicates the way of the cross, which itself came about as a result of the politics of Jesus. The resurrection vindicates a politics of the people of God that is inherently cruciform. Further, as will be made clear below, Yoder also sees in the cross the victory over the powers, and in the resurrection the vindication of the cross, which makes intelligible the cruciform community, a logic that has no need for separate space for authorization of secular space – just the ordering of that space. As will become evident, Yoder's notion that secular space is not authorized separately by Christ often appears to feed a tendency in his work to downplay the importance of the reality and complexity of that space, along with the church's responsibility within that sphere, especially when this notion is highlighted in concert with an emphasis on the normativeness of exile/diaspora.

O'Donovan's view is that the cross signals a defeat of Jesus' earthly politics, and indeed any political theology that focuses too intently on the cross is in danger of a radical depoliticization of Jesus, since his death came about in the sphere of an authority that was passing away. The confrontation at the cross was a moment that occurred between the passing orders and the coming kingdom of God. It is in the resurrection that it is possible to see that the vindicated creation is the theater in which political actions become intelligible.

---

[4] Yoder, *The Politics of Jesus*, 232.

The fact that the resurrection vindicates creation, thus making action in the world intelligible, means that O'Donovan's political theology will move toward an authorized secular power within that vindicated creation.

It is tempting to say that O'Donovan and Yoder differ only in emphasis, but this is not entirely true. Just as O'Donovan warns of the dangers of focusing on the cross without the central role of resurrection, Yoder cautions against seeing the cross only as a recipe for the resurrection, as a way of making things turn out right after all. Rather, for Yoder the crucified Jesus is a more adequate key to understanding what God is about.[5] It might seem as though this is an argument between cross and resurrection, but in fact it cannot be reduced to such a conflict. Yoder does not ignore the resurrection, and O'Donovan does not leave out the life and death of Jesus. However, the death of Jesus, for O'Donovan, is treated as a leaving behind of the old in order to get to the resurrection, while Yoder takes the life of Jesus, which leads to the death of Jesus, as paradigmatic for God's people. Indeed, Yoder goes as far as to suggest that the criteria for recognizing normativeness for the church in this world cannot be merely "Christological" in some vague, cosmic sense, but must be "Jesulogical," a focus on the humanity of Jesus that does not seek to be free of the limits of Jesus' earthliness, Jewishness, and cross.[6] It should be noted here then that while Yoder's caricature of "Christology" does not do justice to O'Donovan's Christology, and O'Donovan's characterization of "Jesuology" does not fully circumscribe Yoder's politics of Jesus, there are significant differences here, which will be brought to view by a close reading of Yoder and O'Donovan's respective treatments of the logic of cross and resurrection.

THE VINDICATION OF THE WAY OF THE CROSS: YODER'S LOGIC OF CROSS AND RESURRECTION

Yoder's understanding of the politics of Jesus finds its central focus in the crucifixion of Jesus as a criminal, an execution perpetrated by political authorities.[7] From the early incident of feeding the multitude and his subsequent withdrawal from the crowd's acclamation (Matthew 14:13-33; Mark 6:32-52; John 6:1-16), Jesus is shown making his first statement regarding the nature of his ministry of suffering and cross-bearing which his own disciples would have to share. "The cross is beginning to loom not as a ritually prescribed instrument of propitiation but as the political alternative to both insurrection and quietism."[8] In Yoder's reading of the ministry and teaching of Jesus, the social non-conformity displayed there came with an expected price. The cross was not so much any kind of suffering of anxiety, but

---

[5] Yoder, *The Politics of Jesus*, 238-46.
[6] Yoder, *For the Nations*, 24-42.
[7] Yoder, *Preface to Theology*, 84-85.
[8] Yoder, *The Politics of Jesus*, 36.

the culmination of a political path freely chosen after counting the cost. The way of the cross taken by Jesus, therefore, is also a normative statement about the relation of obedience to Jesus the Messiah, which suggests that Jesus' people will experience the hostility of the old order in the same way that Jesus experienced it.[9] Yoder is careful to specify in what sense the cross of Christ is to be a model for followers, since 'the cross' is a concept that can and has been easily misconstrued as some kind of pastoral assistance in facing suffering, loneliness, and the like, but this must be differentiated from the meaning of the cross for Jesus. The cross is not some inexplicable event such as an accident or illness; it is not an inward experience of the self; it is not the renunciation of pride and self-will. Rather, Yoder seeks to protect the notion of the cross of Christ from Protestant pastoral care, so that it is properly understood as the destiny that was the result of a freely reiterated choice that "was the political, legally-to-be-expected result of a moral clash with the powers ruling his society."[10] The imitation of Jesus for his followers, then, does not mean a mimicking of his rural lifestyle (or some other such dimension of his life). Rather,

> there is thus but one realm in which the concept of imitation holds – but there it holds in every strand of the New Testament literature and all the more strikingly by virtue of the absence of parallels in other realms. This is at the point of the concrete social meaning of the cross in its relation to enmity and power. Servanthood replaces dominion, forgiveness absorbs hostility. Thus – and only thus – are we bound by New Testament thought to 'be like Jesus.'[11]

Put another way, Yoder sees the cross as the effect of the fact that Jesus' new regime was a kingdom: Jesus talked about the kingdom in terms that must be understood as political, since they encompass matters that have to do with how any society is organized – issues such as economics, power, how to deal with offenders and so on. Yet it was non-coercive. The way Jesus lived the life of the kingdom was political, he died for it, and he told his disciples that they would have to do the same.[12]

Yoder's notion of crucifixion expected as the logical conclusion of political choices suggests that what happened to Jesus on the cross in some way reveals the shape of what God is like, and what he does in the total drama of history. The clash with the political powers, and the refusal to choose any of the conventional options before him, means that the New Testament writers affirm in a permanent pattern what in Jesus was a particular event.[13] Yoder finds evidence of the logic of a particular pattern in Jesus that serves as the model for

---

[9] Yoder, *The Politics of Jesus*, 94-96.
[10] Yoder, *The Politics of Jesus*, 129.
[11] Yoder, *The Politics of Jesus*, 131.
[12] Yoder, *Christian Attitudes to War, Peace, and Revolution*, 428.
[13] Yoder, *He Came Preaching Peace*, 83-84.

his followers in Pauline writings, especially in the pre-Pauline hymn found in Philippians 2. Central to this passage is the concept of *kenosis* – the technical term for Christ's condescension, which Yoder understands as signifying that equality with God was still ahead of Jesus and could be seized, or 'robbed.' Here *kenosis* does not consist in Jesus divesting himself of divinity, but refusing to seize that which was not yet his, refusing to disobey. That is, Jesus' *kenosis* is a matter of accepting the position of creatureliness. As a result, two affirmations can be made: a) Jesus' life was the acceptance of humiliation, renunciation, b) Jesus displayed genuine humanity – not just in the metaphysical sense. Yoder concludes that Jesus' way of being godlike was to be humanlike. Jesus' genuine humanity included the choice not to rule the world violently. His godlike humanity was the surfacing of a divine eternal decision to enter the world of humanity, not as a conventionally understood political leader, but as a servant who loves his enemies, and as one who provides a paradigm for the stance of faith that is to be instantiated in the church.[14]

In Yoder's view, the cross is not the defeat of Jesus' earthly politics,[15] but the logical outcome of challenging the powers of the day. Such an understanding of the cross in the account of the Christ-event means that it is not the case that Jesus is a superior victim primarily because he is divine, but rather he is a better priest because he gives *himself* up. As Yoder makes plain in a discussion of the theological themes of the epistle to the Hebrews, the resurrection is not at the center of this epistle since it is the image of the priesthood that is the theme. In this reading of Hebrews, death is the victory, not the way, not the prerequisite, not something the people did and to which God then reacted. "Now it is the suffering of death that is itself what he did. *It* is the victory. One could follow this theme throughout Hebrews... The victory of Christ is therefore not only at the point of the resurrection and ascension. It is already part of the quality with which he accepts humiliation, with which he

---

[14] The material for Yoder's reading of Philippians 2 is taken from *Preface to Theology*, 81-87 and *He Came Preaching Peace*, 91-95. Yoder has obviously moved from the Gospel accounts of Jesus' life to the Pauline writings, a move that he explains and supports in his chapter "Trial Balance" in *The Politics of Jesus*. Yoder asserts that "the early apostolic church made that political humanness normative for their life." Yoder, *The Politics of Jesus*, 98-99. Doug Harink describes "Trial Balance" as forming a crucial bridge from Yoder's explication of the politics of Jesus to the rest of the New Testament. "Yoder's thesis that the political stance of Paul's Gentile churches recapitulates the politics of Jesus thus finds strong confirmation in Paul's letter to the Philippians." Harink, *Paul Among the Postliberals: Pauline Theology Beyond Christendom and Modernity* (Grand Rapids: Brazos Press, 2003), 114.

[15] "But the cross is not defeat. Christ's obedience unto death was crowned by the miracle of the resurrection and the exaltation at the right hand of God." Yoder, *The Original Revolution*, 56.

obeys and suffers."[16] The cross is therefore not merely a recipe for resurrection,[17] as though *that* Jesus died is somehow more important than *how* he died. This is not to say that suffering is intrinsically redemptive, but that cross-bearing, as practiced by Jesus and called for in his followers, is "the inevitable suffering of those whose only goal is to be faithful to that love which puts one at the mercy of one's neighbor, which abandons claims to justice for oneself and for one's own in an overriding concern for the reconciling of the adversary and the estranged."[18] The seeming defeat of Jesus brings into sharp relief a strategy that is no strategy, a breaking of any calculating link between any action that seeks to control the efficacy of any given plan of action. That is, to die on the cross, or to take up the cross as a follower of Jesus, is not to be construed as simply another method of gaining control or assuring the efficacy of one's action.[19]

The way Yoder highlights the cruciform pattern in the New Testament comes close to neglecting the resurrection of Jesus, given that discussions of the cross in Yoder's work are seen as the locus of identification with humanity, as pattern and as victory. But to read Yoder as denigrating the role and power of resurrection in Christian political theology is to miss an important dimension of his work. The resurrection is never far removed from discussion of the cross in Yoder's work. Rather, what Yoder seems to be working out in his political reading of the New Testament texts is a logic of cross and resurrection that is inherent in those texts. In a well-known statement, Yoder claims that

> The triumph of the right is assured not by the might that comes to the aid of the right, which is of course justification of the use of violence and other kinds of power in every human conflict. The triumph of the right, although it is assured, is sure because of the power of the resurrection and not because of any calculation of causes and effects, nor because of the inherently greater strength of the good guys. The relationship between the obedience of God's people and the triumph of God's cause is not a relationship of cause and effect but one of cross and resurrection.[20]

Yoder's claim shows clearly that while the cross is central in his understanding, this can only be the case in a post-Easter context.[21] Thus while

---

[16] Yoder, *Preface to Theology*, 119. Italics in original.
[17] Yoder, *The Politics of Jesus*, 238.
[18] Yoder, *The Politics of Jesus*, 236.
[19] Yoder, *The Politics of Jesus*, 237-239.
[20] Yoder, *The Politics of Jesus*, 232.
[21] Craig Carter, *The Politics of the Cross*, p. 109. Carter believes that the resurrection of Jesus is downplayed too much in *The Politics of Jesus*, but that this lacuna is corrected in other contexts of Yoder's writings, as for example, when Yoder states that "the cross becomes meaningful in the New Testament only in relation to the resurrection and to Pentecost." Carter is quoting an early Yoder essay entitled "The Anabaptist Dissent: The

the pattern of life which followers of Jesus are called to is cruciform, it is nonetheless the resurrection that *vindicates* the way of the cross. This notion, that it is only through the resurrection that the cruciform pattern of life becomes intelligible, is so important to Yoder that he occasionally uses the language of guarantee in his discussions of the resurrection.[22] However, it is the concept of vindication that is more prevalent, as can be seen when it appears within Yoder's grappling with an understanding of the doctrine of the atonement, where the logic of cross and resurrection again comes into view. Yoder's discussion of the atonement resists the embrace of any single understanding of the doctrine, especially if the doctrine is reduced to the notion that Jesus' death was only meant to solve the problem of the spiritual lostness of humanity. Rather, God sent Jesus to reveal exactly what God intended humans to be, which is most fully obvious in the comprehensive way of the cross. Jesus therefore offered his own sinlessness and obedience to God, and it was precisely that sinlessness and utter faithfulness to love that cost the life of Jesus in a sinful world. It is at this point in the explication of the doctrine of the atonement that Yoder brings the resurrection of Jesus to bear in several distinctive ways. The resurrection is ontologically a simple necessity, says Yoder - death could not hold Jesus down (Acts 2:24). The resurrection also proves that even when humanity does its worst, the love of God cannot be destroyed. The point that is crucial for the present discussion is Yoder's notion that the resurrection is fundamental for discipleship. The rationale provided for this statement is that the resurrection "vindicates the rightness, the possibility, and the effectiveness of the way of the cross."[23]

This notion of the resurrection as vindication also appears in O'Donovan's work, but there the resurrection vindicates creation, thus providing a rationale for understanding creation and history as the theater of God's work, and the appropriate basis for rendering the work of humanity intelligible. Yoder's move is quite different, in that the resurrection's vindication of the way of the cross renders that way of the cross intelligible both for Jesus' life and the pattern of life for disciples of Jesus. While Yoder's move to find vindication of the way of the cross in the resurrection does not take the discussion of ethics or politics out of the created world, the shape of the relationship between the community of believers and the wider world is understood differently that it is in

---

Logic of the Place of the Disciple in Society," *Concern* 1 (June 1954): 60. Quoted in Carter, *The Politics of the Cross,* 109.

[22] For example, "We confuse the kind of 'triumph of the good', whose sole *guarantee* is the resurrection and the promise of the eternal glory of the Lamb, with an immediately accessible triumph which can be manipulated, just past the next social action campaign, by getting hold of society as whole on top." Yoder, *The Politics of Jesus,* 238. Emphasis added.

[23] Yoder, *Preface to Theology,* 311. The discussion of the atonement is found from 281-327.

O'Donovan's project. For Yoder, the true meaning of history is carried by that community of believers acting in the world, following the way of the cross because that way was vindicated by the resurrection and exaltation of Jesus.[24]

The conclusion of the logic of cross and resurrection is the exaltation of Christ, as Philippians 2 shows. The exaltation is the proclamation that Jesus is Lord. God's exaltation of Jesus subjects all creation to him. Jesus as Lord is a reference to his relation with the world. Yoder takes the view that something really happened on the cross, and something really happened at the resurrection, which was not simply an unfolding of what already was the case. Christ's death is the culminating point of his humble identification with humanity, and this leads to the logic of cross and resurrection, which creates a pattern that is not just death and resurrection, but "a *pattern* of humiliation that results in death, a *pattern* of exaltation that takes off from resurrection … Although the pattern of humiliation *unto death* is unique (none of us have yet died), and although the exaltation and title of Lord is unique (none of us have yet ascended), the pattern is still a norm for us."[25]

Therefore, while the resurrection serves as the point from which Yoder reasons, it is the pattern of the cross that reveals the grain of the universe.[26] Yoder makes use of the concept of 'the grain' in several ways. For example, it can refer to the way things are conventionally understood, but which needs to be corrected. Thus Yoder can say that God's message runs across the grain of our sense-making reflexes, because those reflexes are titled in our own favour, a response that is challenged by the pattern set by Jesus.[27] Such a concept of 'the grain' is also visible in many of the characteristics of political systems that are found in the world, characteristics such as nationalism, racism, and coercive power. So Yoder sees in movements such as the arms race simply an exposure of the grain that runs right through such systems. The problem according to

---

[24] Yoder reiterates the basics of this 'resurrection vindicates the cross' argument in *The Original Revolution,* where he notes that the cross is not defeat, but rather, Christ's obedience unto death was crowned by the miracle of the resurrection and the exaltation at the right hand of God. Options representing conventionally understood effectiveness and success had been sacrificed for the sake of love, but God turned this sacrifice into a victory that vindicated to the utmost the apparent impotence of love. Yoder, *The Original Revolution,* 56-61.

[25] Yoder, *Preface to Theology,* 87-88. Italics in original.

[26] The phrase 'with the grain of the universe' has been given currency especially by Stanley Hauerwas's use of it as the title of his recent Gifford lectures. Hauerwas, *With the Grain of the Universe* (Grand Rapids: Brazos Press, 2001). The phrase is taken from Yoder "Armaments and Eschatology," *Studies in Christian Ethics* 1 no1 (1988): 58, where Yoder asserts that "people who bear crosses are working with the grain of the universe." The same concept is used extensively in David Toole, *Waiting for Godot in Sarajevo: Theological Reflections on Nihilism, Tragedy, and Apocalypse* (Boulder: Westview Press, 1998).

[27] Yoder, *He Came Preaching Peace,* 42.

Yoder is that the grain thus revealed is not in fact the grain of the universe, the way things are meant to be, and ultimately will be. The true grain of the universe is exposed only in the cruciform pattern that is fully revealed in Jesus. In this sense the cross is to be considered 'natural,' not foolish or weak.[28] However, "only from within the community of *resurrection* confession is the cruciformity of the cosmos a key rather than a scandal."[29]

THE VINDICATION OF CREATION: O'DONOVAN'S LOGIC OF CROSS AND RESURRECTION

O'Donovan's account of the logic of cross and resurrection is embedded within his concern that Christian political theology must give an account of what it means that Christ is king. O'Donovan's focus on the importance of Christology for political theology should be seen as a continuation of his emphasis on the centrality of Christology for ethics which is on full display in his earlier book, *Resurrection and Moral Order*. The relationship between *Resurrection and Moral Order* and *The Desire of the Nations* is important, since there is a sense in which the earlier book sets the stage for the latter, especially in the case of the centrality of Christology.

In the preface to the second edition of *Resurrection and Moral Order*, O'Donovan makes clear that theological ethics, if it is to provide evangelical content to moral reasoning, must follow the linkage between evangelical proclamation and moral inferences, a move possible within the belief that "a distinct behavior is demanded by the resurrection of Jesus."[30] This specific linking of resurrection and moral action is not some arbitrary choice of a most important "moment" in the Christ-event, or even some analysis of a concatenation of moments. The reason O'Donovan refuses any such pattern is that he sees no self-evident principle for arranging the specific subject areas of ethics so that they can be fit into a particular moment of the Christ-event.[31] O'Donovan seeks to avoid both the difficulties found in a monothematic program and any other structure based on multiple moments that apply to specific issues. He quickly moves to point out that his focus on the resurrection is *not* an example of a monothematic scheme. Indeed, his prologue in the second edition of *Resurrection and Moral Order* is in part an attempt to show

---

[28] Yoder, *For the Nations*, 212.
[29] Yoder, *The Priestly Kingdom*, 36.
[30] O'Donovan, *Resurrection and Moral Order*, xi.
[31] O'Donovan observes that James McClendon and Barth both suffer from the problem of trying to fit specific issues into certain moments of the Christ-event. O'Donovan, *Resurrection and Moral Order*, xvii.

his recognition (inspired in part by Hauerwas's critique[32] and the publication of Barth's *Ethics*) that he may not have said enough about how resurrection ought to relate to the other Christological moments.[33] For O'Donovan, then,

> Christian thought will be concerned with *all* the moments of the Christ-event and *all* the moments will shape the lives of Christians . . . yet when we think quite specifically about Christian *action* we have to single out the resurrection moment which vindicates the creation into which our actions can be ventured with intelligibility.[34]

O'Donovan's focus on the resurrection of Jesus as the basis of the vindication of creation allows him to critique any ethic that is only natural, which he describes as voluntarist at its heart—a morality that is a creation of man's will by which order is imposed on the world.[35] This voluntarism fails to take into account the reality of a divinely given order of things in which human nature itself is located. It is only in Christ that we can apprehend that order in which we stand, and the knowledge of it with which we have been endowed.[36]

Similarly, O'Donovan argues that God has conferred authority on Jesus at the resurrection. This means, among other things, that while God's authority may oppose natural authority in its fallenness, it is not opposed to created order as such. Rather, the teaching and life of Jesus are morally authoritative in that the particularity of Jesus has assumed universal significance. O'Donovan concludes, therefore, that Jesus' authority is irreplaceable, because in his resurrection the moral order was publicly and cosmically vindicated by God—Jesus does not just teach: he reveals - all this to conclude that Jesus is precisely the one in whom the order has come to be,[37] the meaning of which can only be understood by taking account of the entire Christ-event.

In a chapter entitled "The Triumph of the Kingdom," O'Donovan shows how it is possible to express the continuity and discontinuity of Jesus' message

---

[32] The critique O'Donovan refers to is found in Hauerwas, *Dispatches From the Front: Theological Engagements With the Secular* (Durham: Duke University Press, 1994), 175.

[33] O'Donovan follows through with this recognition with the publication of *The Desire of the Nations*. Here he continues to insist on the importance of the resurrection as basic to Christian moral action, but he includes resurrection as one of four moments of the Christ-event—advent, passion, resurrection, and exaltation. The significance of the four moments of the Christ-event for political theology will be dealt with at some length below.

[34] O'Donovan, *Resurrection and Moral Order*, xvii, xviii. Italics are included in the original.

[35] This recurring concern of O'Donovan's has already been brought to view on chapter 1 above.

[36] O'Donovan, *Resurrection and Moral Order*, 16, 20.

[37] O'Donovan, *Resurrection and Moral Order*, 140-162.

with that of the apostles. Jesus proclaimed the coming of the kingdom of God as the disclosure of God's reign, while the apostolic church told the story of what happened when the kingdom had come, with the decisive resurrection of Jesus between the two. A variety of attempts have been made to express the balance of continuity and discontinuity adequately.[38]

The key to this move is Christology, in that there are in Christ two roles — he is the mediator of God's rule, and the representative individual or, put another way, Christ is the decisive presence of God and is the decisive presence of God's people.[39] The dying, rising, and future disclosing of Jesus is where the divine authority is irreplaceably immediate, more fully transparent than it has been possible to discern in the tasks of angels, kings, or the Davidide line of kings.[40] O'Donovan argues that the role of representation has to keep in balance two "complementary and mutually necessary statements: (a) the representative *alone* constitutes the presence of the represented; (b) the represented are *really present* in what the representative does and experiences on their behalf."[41] O'Donovan takes pains to clarify the fact that Jesus' representation consists not in replacement of the represented but as co-presence, since "Christ is not first alone and then together with his brothers, first representing them and then handing back the representative function; he is at one and the same time alone and unaccompanied, always representing, always together with those he represents."[42] This mediatorial representation of Christ is to be understood as entailing the whole drama of the coming of the kingdom in Christ, the conflict of that kingdom with the passing age, and the triumph of the kingdom as seen in the resurrection and exaltation of Jesus, not just his death on the cross, since to focus primarily on the death of Christ would be a radical depoliticising of the central saving event of the Gospel.

O'Donovan's point is that the events of Good Friday and Easter must be seen as a double event, with the two events of death and resurrection acting as complementary, not isomorphic moments. "Jesus' death was the overthrow of God's cause at the hands of rebellious Israel; his resurrection was the reassertion of God's triumph over Israel."[43] But the church has not replaced Israel, though it is the case that after Christ's resurrection the Gentiles have been grafted onto Israel's root, suggesting to O'Donovan that, until the final reconciliation, the communities of Israel and the Gentile must coexist as the community of circumcision and the community of baptism. Therefore, the Christ-event is one in which God's rule is mediated, but the event is one that

---

[38] O'Donovan gives several examples, such as those of Schweitzer, Tolstoy, and liberation theology. O'Donovan, *The Desire of the Nations*, 120-22.
[39] O'Donovan, *The Desire of the Nations*, 123-24.
[40] O'Donovan, *The Desire of the Nations*, 124.
[41] O'Donovan, *The Desire of the Nations*, 125.
[42] O'Donovan, *The Desire of the Nations*, 127.
[43] O'Donovan, *The Desire of the Nations*, 129.

Jesus is Lord 81

must be seen as going beyond an assertion of divine sovereignty or divine intervention. It is the narrative display of the Christ-event that gives O'Donovan the basis for the Christology that is needed in order to make the move from Christ's victory to the subjection of the nations to the vindicated Christ, the desire of the nations. O'Donovan displays this narrative according to a four-fold division – the 'moments' of Christ's advent, passion, restoration, and exaltation, which can be aligned with the political themes discovered in the reading of the Old Testament.[44] As part of this discussion, O'Donovan points

---

[44] The four-fold division is "purely an exegetical schema; it has no theoretical function and adds nothing that is not in the story itself – unlike the analysis of the kingdom in terms of power, judgment and possession, which, although intended provisionally, does propose an interpretation of political authority not simply given in the concept." So the structure here is used simply as a way to "achieve an optimum balance of economy and fidelity." O'Donovan, *The Desire of the Nations*, 133. Despite this disavowal of theoretical function for the present schema, O'Donovan does present it as parallel to, and thus guided by his interpretive structure of the kingdom. O'Donovan has dealt with the moment of the **Advent** in his discussion of the coming of the kingdom in the ministry of Jesus, but he adds here a brief discussion of Christ's baptism which alerts us to his divine authorization. That is, in submitting to the baptism of John the Baptist, Jesus represents mankind, and specifically Israel, before God, and then also takes on the role of Israel's Savior. The second moment of the Christ-event is the **Passion,** the crucifixion of Jesus which while an act of judgment, cannot be restricted to that moment alone, but must include the resurrection as well. O'Donovan points therefore to the sequence of cross and resurrection as that place where Christ is set in opposition to guilty Israel, and then is vindicated against guilty Israel. It might be said that the resurrection is the sole moment of judgment whereby God intervenes to overthrow Israel's false judgment on Christ, but O'Donovan insists that the judgment of God is already obvious in the confrontation between Jesus and the established authorities. O'Donovan describes this confrontation as a 'moment' that occurred when the existing orders of government from a passing age stand poised against the kingdom of God. The Passion moment for O'Donovan is the setting of Christ in opposition to Israel, not the vindication or victory over those powers but the defeat which sets the stage for the restoration of Christ in the resurrection. Ibid., 136-141. It is in the **restoration** of Christ that the full judgment both for and against Israel comes to view. The resurrection of Christ, according to O'Donovan's account, restores the life of humanity, reverses the effects of sin, and "reorders the disorder of which death is the emblem, and vindicates God's original order of creation." Ibid. 142. The restoration of life by Christ has endowed that life with authority and power. The resurrection also leads to a moment of transition from the restored life to the empowered life, or from resurrection to Ascension. To attend to the restoration of Christ in two elements serves as a defense against two mistakes – first, the temptation to think of Christ's triumph as a doctrine of history and not redemption, but more importantly for O'Donovan's political theology, the connection between resurrection and ascension "is a bridge between the time of Christ's life and the time of the world's future," or put another way, though the Christ-event is accomplished, it is "still an event for the future." Ibid., 143-144. The fourth moment of the Christ-event, **exaltation,** is the fulfillment of the political promise Jesus

out that it is possible to focus not only on the dawning of the kingdom of God in the moment of Advent, but also on the pre-existing Christ as God's Word. An emphasis on the latter in classical Christology caused the focus on the dawning of the kingdom to be lost, a choice that O'Donovan is keen to avoid. Rather, he salvages both emphases so that he can assert that "Jesus wholly mediates the Kingdom in his personal being, and that the Kingdom has its origins in God's eternal purpose."[45] In this way, Christ's action in time, the dateable coming of the kingdom, does not give ground to a singular emphasis on its source outside this world. O'Donovan clearly keeps these two emphases together in order to be able to assert a Christology that is not a Jesuology, and at the same time does not slip into an abstract, otherworldly category myth.

O'Donovan's use of the New Testament in his political theology carries forward both the focus (God is king) and the four-fold structure established by his reading of the Hebrew Scriptures. God's rule is fully present in the Christ-event,

> presented in the narrative account of a decisive act, an act in which God's rule was mediated and his people reconstituted in Christ . . . We cannot discuss the question of 'secular' government, the question from which Western political theology has too often been content to start, unless we approach it historically, from a Christology that has been displayed in narrative form as Gospel.[46]

However, O'Donovan's recounting of the narrative of the Christ-event leaves him open to the criticism that he does not take the politics of Jesus seriously enough. While he has moved considerably in *The Desire of Nations* from an earlier focus on the resurrection—as shown in his dealing with the Christ-event as four moments —O'Donovan is still concerned about the danger of *not* focusing on the resurrection. As noted above, to abstract the death of Jesus from the resurrection or to interpret death on its own is to radically depoliticize the central saving event of the Gospel, according to O'Donovan. The death of Jesus should be understood as a severance from the old, destroyed authority, and the resurrection the establishment of the authority of the new life.

---

had come to bring, and acts as his own authorization as the representative of the Kingdom of God in two ways. First, the Ascension is the conclusion of the story of Christ – that is, it expresses the meaning of the single story in four parts (the Christ-event) in a climactic way, and so could be said to confirm what the whole story has been about. Secondly, the logic of the Ascension leads from Christ's absence at the Mount of Olives to his appearance at the Parousia. The time that lies between the Ascension and the point at which the Kingdom appears universally is the time that is determined by the Christ-event, which means that the public existence of the church as well as the provisional public life of the world with a limited authorization are also determined by the Christ-event. Ibid., 144-146.

[45] O'Donovan, *The Desire of the Nations,* 136.
[46] O'Donovan, *The Desire of the Nations*, 133.

That is, Christ's death takes place under the old authority—his death was the overthrow of God's cause at the hands of rebellious Israel, while the resurrection was the reassertion of God's triumph over Israel.[47]

But what is missing from this account of things is the notion that the kind of a life led by Jesus, which resulted in his execution by *political* authorities, can also be seen as a display of what it might mean to be political in a certain kind of way, especially as might be displayed by a community called into being by the slain Lamb. O'Donovan's account of Christ's death sees it as an exit from the old authority and the resurrection as an entrance into the new—but all of this in a way that is more formal than concrete. That is to say, the four "moments" are treated as important primarily because of the fact that they happened, without sufficient attention to the way in which they happened. One can see further evidence of this dimension in O'Donovan's work by noting his repeated concern, voiced especially in *Resurrection and Moral Order*, that if the resurrection is not understood as the center of the Christ-event, then other aspects of it can be interpreted in a destructive manner. For example, O'Donovan notes that a misconstrued focus on the cross of Christ runs the danger of becoming a symbol of Gnostic other-worldliness.[48] If the resurrection is not central, then even a focus on Jesus can be destructive, when it collapses into what O'Donovan refers to as "Jesuology," in which the life of Jesus is seen as analogical to creative political opportunities. But O'Donovan complains that such a political Jesuology, to model action on Jesus, is only a hopeful illusion that fails to take into account the defeat of Jesus' program, or for that matter, the vindication of it by resurrection.[49]

Yoder, for his part, lodges a complaint about Anglican notions of the Incarnation when he insists that the Incarnation does not mean (as in some Anglican theology) that God took all of human nature as it was, put his seal of approval on it and thereby ratified nature as revelation. Rather, Jesus broke through the standard definition of what it means to be human and gave it a new formative definition in Christ.[50] Unfortunately, Yoder does not engage in any reading of a specific text, or interact with any Anglican thinker on the topic as a way of substantiating his claim. If he engaged O'Donovan's theology of the Incarnation on this point, Yoder's claim could not be substantiated, since O'Donovan's political theology, and his ethics more generally, is centered on a fully-conceptualized Christology.[51]

---

[47] O'Donovan, *The Desire of the Nations*, 128-29.
[48] O'Donovan, *Resurrection and Moral Order*, 15.
[49] O'Donovan, *The Desire of the Nations*, 121.
[50] Yoder, *The Politics of Jesus*, 99.
[51] For just one example of an Anglican theologian whose work could be used as an example to refute Yoder's criticism of Anglican views of the Incarnation, see Rowan Williams, "Incarnation and the Renewal of Community," in Williams, *On Christian Theology* (Oxford: Blackwell, 2000), 225-238.

However, it need not be the case that a focus on the cross of Christ becomes Gnostic other-worldliness, or that finding political pattern in Jesus Christ is naïve. O'Donovan has been questioned precisely at this point by Victor Paul Furnish, who argues that Jesus' exaltation is a far less prominent theme in the New Testament than it is in O'Donovan's work. Rather, we have the resurrected, crucified Christ who is definitive for the church's developing Christological traditions. This emphasis leads Furnish to ask how a political theology principally oriented to Christ being lifted up on the cross would have to be configured.[52] Furnish's line of questioning brings into sharp relief O'Donovan's wariness regarding Jesuology, which he sees as a simplistic discovery of immediately political content in the words of Jesus. Such a discovery amounts to a 'helpful illusion,' which, combined with a focus on the death of Christ in isolation, results in the radical depoliticizing of the central event of the Gospel.[53] Furnish counters with his own fear that O'Donovan's treatment of the Christ-event is misleading, in that the account of the crucifixion put forward in *The Desire of the Nations* is seen only as the negative work of divine judgment when it is the case that the biblical writers (especially Paul and John) "view the cross not just as confronting and condemning the old but also as affirming and establishing the new... For Paul, the cross is the decisive saving event for the whole of humankind, and Christ is resurrected precisely *as* the Crucified One."[54] In contrast, O'Donovan's analysis of the crucifixion focuses on the importance of the confrontation with the authorities, but it is only a 'moment' when two claimants (Rome and the kingdom of God) stood poised against each other.[55] But that moment of Christ's death, "takes place within the sphere of the old authority; it represents the point at which the old is confronted and challenged; in the resurrection the challenge issues in the assertion of the new."[56] In other words, as O'Donovan makes clear, the Pauline view of authority includes "a more positive affirmation of the government's role than there could be at the moment of the Kingdom's challenge to all settled authorities."[57] The effect of O'Donovan's analysis of the crucifixion is to relativize it for the purposes of political theology. While Christ's ministry and death are taken seriously, there is a sense in which their real role is to provide the conditions necessary for the resurrection and ascension of Christ.[58] It is this sense of taking Christ's ministry and death

---

[52] Victor Paul Furnish, "How Firm a Foundation?," 23.
[53] O'Donovan, *The Desire of the Nations*, 120, 121, 128.
[54] Furnish, "How Firm a Foundation?," 23. Italics in original.
[55] O'Donovan, *The Desire of the Nations*, 137.
[56] O'Donovan, *The Desire of the Nations*, 129.
[57] O'Donovan, *The Desire of the Nations*, 149.
[58] "From Jesus' resurrection as the 'centre' of Christian ethics, a strand reaches back to the crucifixion as the negating aspect which pronounces God's 'No' to life in the flesh and serves as the condition for the 'Yes' of Easter to life in the Spirit." W. Clyde Tilley, "World-affirmation and the Resurrection of Jesus Christ," *Perspectives in Religious*

seriously that differs from Yoder, whose understanding of these matters leads him to use the language of imitation much more explicitly than does O'Donovan.

The Life, Teaching, and Ministry of Jesus

Both Yoder and O'Donovan see the earthly life, teaching and ministry of Jesus as morally authoritative, fulfilling, but not replacing the story of Israel. That is, their work brings into bold relief the messianic dimension of Jesus of Nazareth, and takes from the Gospel accounts the notion that in Jesus the kingdom has come, albeit in such a way that the fullness of the kingdom has not yet fully been realized, and is therefore not entirely transparent. But as messiah, as the bearer of the kingdom, Jesus in the very particulars of his life, ministry and teachings assumes universal significance, a fact that enables followers of Jesus to see the contours of a political theology. In this sense, it is the case that the politics of Jesus are central to both O'Donovan and Yoder, despite the fact that such a term ('politics of Jesus') is most closely associated with Yoder's work. In other words, it is inaccurate to say that for O'Donovan the life of Jesus has no political implications. Indeed, the longest section of his exposition of Jesus' ministry has to do with Jesus' exposition of the law, which, as O'Donovan sees it, is key to the communal identity of God's people, and gives purchase to the judicial dimension of politics, whereby the kingship of Jesus is given expression in the world. For O'Donovan the politics of Jesus take the shape of the political themes that have already been discovered in the Old Testament. Teachings central to Jesus' ministry, such as the Sermon on the Mount, are given significant attention by O'Donovan as a way of explicating the content of the law that is to guide the community of God's law, which does not need litigation, for example, since it is a law that is written on the hearts of the people. However, this reserve about litigation is not reserve about the law as such, but a signal that while the people of God abide by his judgment in their community, judgment is also required outside of the church.[59]

Yoder's understanding of the earthly life, ministry and teachings of Jesus lead him to what he calls 'the politics of Jesus.' He is not unique in this, although his notion of the politics of Jesus is not to be equated with the notion seen in O'Donovan. His focus on the Sermon on the Mount also refers to how the life of the community of God is to be shaped by following the ethics described there. But Yoder's reading of the Gospels includes a focus on the temptations of Jesus that is not seen in O'Donovan. This is a significant difference, in that Yoder sees here a key political move by Jesus, whereby he rejects available political options in favor of a life of suffering service, a move

---

Studies 15 (Summer 1988): 166. Tilley's comment is a reference to *Resurrection and Moral Order*, which applies equally well to *The Desire of the Nations*.

[59] O'Donovan, *The Desire of the Nations*, 112-113.

that Yoder believes is to be replicated in the life of the community that follows Christ, and which as such represents a political option in the world for Christians. That is, the politics of Jesus for Yoder are themselves a political theology as they are embodied in the church, while for O'Donovan such practices belong in the church, but then do not function in the same way in the political realm, where the activity of judgment is the focus of political theology. It is to the contours of these differing accounts of the earthly life, teaching, and ministry of Jesus that we now turn.

THE POLITICS OF JESUS: YODER ON JESUS' EARTHLY LIFE, TEACHING, AND MINISTRY

Yoder's understanding of Jesus as Lord begins with the basic claim that Jesus proclaims by way of his life and ministry that a new kingdom is at hand, that he has brought a whole new order of things, that God's rule is visible in Jesus' life. Among the names and titles used of Jesus in his earthly ministry is that of Messiah, a reference to his anointed status[60] as the one who is to come, the desire of the nations. This messianic claim is also clearly a political one, since it proclaims that he represents the rule of God. The humanity of Jesus is a revelation of the divine purpose of God, and it is that human career that was politically relevant, insofar as Jesus reformulated what it means to be the people of God in the world.[61] Yoder highlights the difference between the actual shape of Jesus' ministry and common expectations of the promised kingdom with references to the poignant question posed by his precursor, John the Baptist. In response to the challenge "Are you the one who is to come, or do we wait for another?" Jesus points to his activities (such as healings) rather than some projected takeover of the palace or conventional political program. That is, Yoder interprets Jesus' answer to John as the proclamation of a new social possibility for the human story, in which "the Gospel account affirms a sequence of historic projects in which precursor and successor both understand God to be working in the real world to establish justice... Both of them affirmed the real alternatives of first-century Palestine as the place where, thanks to a renewed transcendent intervention, God's will is known and achieved."[62] Put another way, the major landmarks of the recorded ministry of Jesus are public events that relate to the socio-political concerns of the people, which means that "power in the simplest sense of the word was Jesus' agenda."[63]

---

[60] Yoder, *Preface*, 69.

[61] Yoder, *Preface*, 69-76, and Yoder, *The Original Revolution*, 128-130; *For the Nations*, 201.

[62] Yoder, *For the Nations*, 204.

[63] Yoder, "Jesus and Power," in Donald Durnbaugh, ed., *On Earth Peace* (Elgin: The Brethren Press, 1978), 366.

It is the display of the socio-political agenda of Jesus that is the burden of the central argument of Yoder's seminal work, *The Politics of Jesus*. Yoder "claims not only that Jesus is, according to the biblical witness, a model of radical political action, but that this issue is now generally visible throughout New Testament studies, even though the biblical scholars have not stated it in such a way that the ethicists across the way have had to notice it." Further, says Yoder, "I shall ... be testing the hypothesis that runs counter to the prevalent assumptions: the hypothesis that the ministry and claims of Jesus are best understood as presenting to hearers and readers not the avoidance of political options, but one particular social-political-ethical option."[64] That hypothesis is tested through a close reading of the ministry of Jesus as found in the Gospel of Luke.[65] Yoder admits that his account of Jesus' ministry according to Luke leaves major gaps, but insists that more thoroughness would only have reinforced his interpretation, which is summarized here:

> Without the reinforcement which careful analysis of all this material would have brought, the conclusion is already clear enough to bring the answer to the question with which we began. Jesus was not just a moralist whose teachings had some political implications; he was not primarily a teacher of spirituality whose public ministry unfortunately was seen in a political light; he was not just a sacrificial lamb preparing for his immolation, or a God-man whose divine status calls us to disregard his humanity. Jesus was, in his divinely mandated (i.e., promised, anointed, messianic) prophethood, priesthood, and kingship, the bearer of a new possibility of human, social, and therefore *political* relationships. His baptism is the inauguration and his cross the culmination of that new regime in which his disciples are called to share.[66]

A crucial dimension of Luke's account of the career of Jesus for Yoder is the account of the temptations in the desert. Jesus's confrontation with the tempter consists of a series of temptations best understood as economic, socio-political, and revolutionary in nature, and serve to bring to view the political options that Jesus deliberately and pointedly rejects. At his baptism by John, "Jesus is commissioned to be, in history, in Palestine, the messianic son and servant, the bearer of the goodwill and the promise of God. This mission is then further defined by the testing into which Jesus moves immediately."[67] The tempter's goal seems to be to lay various options before Jesus, all of which are ways of being king. The economic option of providing food offers the chance to act like

---

[64] Yoder, *The Politics of Jesus*, 2, 11.

[65] Yoder claims that there is not much at stake in the choice of Luke as opposed to the other Evangelists. Rather, it is the case that Luke is often seen as having an editorial slant the concern of which it is to deny that the Christian movement afforded any kind of danger of Mediterranean society to Roman rule. Yoder, *The Politics of Jesus*, 11, 53-54.

[66] Yoder, *The Politics of Jesus*, 52. Italics added.

[67] Yoder, *The Politics of Jesus*, 24.

a certain kind of messiah who provides a banquet for his followers, a scenario that Jesus will confront in the feeding of the crowd that follows him, only to reject the conventional response of worship from that satiated crowd. The second temptation in which Jesus is offered control of all the kingdoms of this world seems most obviously socio-political in nature, and includes the notion of the idolatrous character of the desire for political power and nationalism. The third temptation, framed as a question about surviving a fall from the pinnacle of the temple, is a reference to Jesus' contemplation of the role of the religious reformer who comes unheralded from above to set things right. All three of these temptations are given a socio-political reading by Yoder, thereby denying some personal or spiritual understanding that might blunt the political force of the confrontation with the tempter in the desert.[68]

The three temptations of the desert are related to other options that Jesus confronted during his earthly ministry. For example, Jesus rejected the option of 'realism,' if realism is understood to describe the acceptance of whatever situation Jesus found himself in, without attempting to challenge it in any significant way. Also available was the option of righteous revolutionary violence as represented by the Zealots, whereby those in power would be overthrown by violent means, after which power would be controlled by the revolutionaries, suggesting that violence or at least the threat of violence would be used to remain in power in order to challenge any future righteous revolutionaries willing to use similar means. A third option was that of quietism, or withdrawal into the desert. Fourth, the option of living a separately 'pure' religious life after the model of the Pharisees was also possible. The one possibility that seems attractive to many in today's world but which was not an option for Jesus, according to Yoder, was infiltrating the establishment, since such a stance, "the critic-from-within-the-establishment, the house prophet, will, if he stays inside when the crunch comes, be with Herod after all."[69]

It is Jesus' confrontation and rejection of these available options, along with the one he chooses - suffering servanthood - that becomes the key to understanding the politics of Jesus. In addition, his teachings can also be read politically in the sense that they serve as political axioms for the people who are part of the community that embraces the politics of Jesus. For example, when Jesus delivers teachings such as the Beatitudes in the Sermon on the Mount (Matthew 5), he is not announcing a set of moral demands for which rewards are distributed, but is describing postures or attitudes that people can embody already because the rule of God has come.[70] Yoder understands the Sermon on the Mount, along with other of Jesus' specific teachings, to describe a way of life that is made possible because of the appearance of the rule of God

---

[68] Yoder, *The Politics of Jesus*, 24-27.
[69] Yoder, *The Original Revolution*, 21. The description of these four available options is taken from 18-27.
[70] Yoder, *He Came Preaching Peace*, 49.

in the earthly life and ministry of Jesus. While the teachings of the Sermon on the Mount are often seen as dictums of personal spiritual guidance, or as necessary though unrealistic utopianism, Yoder interprets them as prescribing an ethic that should mark the lives of those who seek to follow Jesus, but not only because of a command ethic. Rather, Jesus' moral teaching here and in other places depends on "the coming of the kingdom in His person and work; its expectation of novelty, of miracle, of visible witness; its derivation from the unqualified love of God; its unity of motive and deed."[71] Any following of the ethic found in the Sermon on the Mount is seen as the most appropriate reflection of and witness to God's love and His kingdom. Therefore, says, Yoder, "We do not, ultimately, love our neighbor because Jesus told us to. We love our neighbor because God is like that. It is not because Jesus told us to that we love even beyond the limits of reason and justice, even to the point of refusing to kill and being willing to suffer – but because God is like that too."[72] The Sermon on the Mount is not primarily a law around which the identity of God is founded. Rather, it is a description of the kind of life led by people who can see what God is like because of the life path taken by Jesus. So Yoder sees the life and teaching of Jesus as fully political, made obvious by what he rejected, by what he taught, by the option he chose, and by the fact that his life displayed what God is like. Yoder's identification of political axioms within the context of imitating Jesus here in the Sermon on the Mount stands in contrast to O'Donovan's reading of the Bible as a way to identify political theorems, as we have seen in his understanding of the Hebrew Scriptures.

A strong criticism of Yoder's 'politics of Jesus' has centered on the question of whether such a reading is reductionist in scope, i.e. does his self-described Jesuology in fact reduce the Christian understanding of Jesus primarily to the role of ethical exemplar, and thus the following of Jesus to politics? A. James Reimer has put forward the most sustained and consistent criticism of Yoder in this regard. In a series of articles concerning various dimensions of Anabaptist theology, Yoder has often functioned as a kind of foil for Reimer's own theological concerns.[73] While Reimer applauds Yoder's retrieval of the

---

[71] Yoder, *The Original Revolution*, 51. The argument is found in the chapter "The Political Axioms of the Sermon on the Mount," in Yoder, *The Original Revolution*, 34-51.

[72] Yoder, *The Original Revolution*, 51.

[73] Many of Reimer's essays have been published recently in A. James Reimer, *Mennonites and Classical Theology: Dogmatic Foundations for Christian Ethics* (Kitchener: Pandora Press, 2001). Reimer's constructive project includes the retrieval of what he calls the "classical imagination," by which he means the "imagination of the biblical and post-biblical 'patristic' realm of thought in which the Christian doctrine of God, Christ, and the Holy Spirit evolved in the matrix of the encounter between the Jewish and the Greco-Roman world," 14. Within his own Anabaptist context, Reimer sees himself as calling Mennonites not to understand themselves as "developing an alternative theology which better suits their non-conformist history, but as situating

normativeness of Jesus for social ethics, much less convincing to him is Yoder's politicization of that message at the expense of metaphysical and ontological language. Reimer repeatedly asserts that Yoder's work is at its heart a modern project in that it is based on historicist assumptions, evident, for example, in the basically historical approach taken by Yoder in *Preface to Theology*. According to Reimer, Yoder's emphasis on the social-political-ethical dimension of the New Testament message, rooted in a theological method that is fundamentally historical-eschatological in nature reduces or is biased against the metaphysical and ontological understanding of the Christ event. Reimer acknowledges that there are places where Yoder shows sympathy toward Trinitarian and Christological creedal formulations, for example, but he refuses to concede that Yoder ever overcomes the reductionistic reinterpretation of many Biblical passages and the creeds primarily on ethical and moral bases.[74]

Reimer's main concern, it seems, is that Christian ethics needs to be grounded in an orthodox Trinitarian framework, and if this grounding is somehow truncated, the possibility arises that ethics can be a form of human ideology, or as he puts it, "unless our Christology is understood in relation to the larger Trinitarian life of God, our Jesus ethic will be Promethean and

---

themselves at the center of classical Trinitarian and Christological orthodoxy..." 15. The references to Reimer's essays are taken from their publication in *Mennonites and Classical Theology*, not in their original location of publication.

[74] Reimer, *Mennonites and Classical Theology*, 161-181. Craig Carter defends Yoder against Reimer's charges of reductionism, claiming that it is a mistake to see Yoder as reductionist since his is a project of retrieval, not reduction. Carter offers a series of reasons for this characterization of Yoder's Christology: a) Yoder's conversational style, which means that he addresses what is not being addressed adequately by others: "Rather, what was not being said in all of these contexts, and needed to be said, was that life of discipleship means following Jesus rather than merely living up to the best moral wisdom of the pagan world."; b) Yoder's own claims not to be intentionally reductionistic; c) Yoder's criticism of reductionism in others; d) the logic of Yoder's position – i.e. the logic of his position collapses if Jesus is not Lord; e) Yoder's view of the authority of Scripture – the creeds can never supersede the Biblical texts themselves; f) Yoder's Barthian Christocentrism: Yoder was applying Barth's theology to social ethics and in doing so was working out Barth's Christocentric trinitarianism; g) Yoder's radical 'catholicity.' Carter, *The Politics of the Cross*, 126-136. Yoder's own description of his work is that it is neither reduction, retrieval, nor restoration, but restitution. By this Yoder means to take history seriously, not as progress, or as something which only begins in the present. Instead, restitutionism identifies the locus for understanding history within Scripture, whereby the claims of Christ make it possible to interpret faithfulness (or not) of the church. Yoder admits that this is historicist in that it affirms the character of the human as a being that makes real decisions, and also in the sense that the very particular story of the Bible is the source to which the church must return to understand history. Yoder, *The Priestly Kingdom*, 125-130. Yoder seems to use historicism as a way to get beyond historicism.

idolatrous."[75] Thus for Reimer, the dangers inherent in Yoder's work run deep. However, Yoder would no doubt respond that the kind of work being done in *Preface to Theology* for example, is an attempt to trace the development of the church's theology. This reading is an attempt to narrate how the biblical material, historically understood, has been communicated in various new contexts without losing its meaning. As Yoder 'watches' the theological activity of the church, he does so in order to draw conclusions about how the church can do theology in new situations. The choice of attending to Christology in *Preface to Theology* is not arbitrary, says Yoder, since the earliest Christians thought about Christology the most.[76] That is, Yoder attempts to discern faithfulness over against unfaithfulness to the biblical tradition.[77] His defense against Reimer might be to argue that so-called historicism, especially in sources such as *Preface,* is not a reduction of things to the historical process, but an acknowledgement that the way to become (and remain) orthodox is to take history seriously.

While he does not mention Yoder specifically as one who is guilty of championing a Jesuology, O'Donovan cautions against any attempt to move too quickly in Christian political thought to the immediately political message of Jesus, a move that he warns may lead to a "helpful illusion," where Jesus serves as a model that can help to achieve something but that cannot deal with the "defeat of Jesus' programme, nor of its vindication."[78] That is, to move too quickly toward one's interest in the political dimension of the message of Jesus is to be naïve, because one then avoids both the complexity of the world as well as the wider implications of the Christ-event. In other words, Jesuology, as construed by O'Donovan, must give way to Christology. "If political theology cannot perform its task by striking out on its own into Jesuology, it must learn how to perform it Christologically, making its way along that stream which flows from the apostles' proclamation of Christ as 'Lord' to the later, ontologically developed definitions of the ecumenical creeds."[79] Yoder follows that same stream, and is willing to express his respect for the creeds, which are attempts to continue the task of theology (remaining faithful to the biblical tradition in new situations) – creeds are helpful as fences, but not as expressions of the faith that are parallel to the biblical account.[80]

But Yoder is not Jesulogical in the sense that O'Donovan cautions against,

---

[75] Reimer, *Mennonites and Classical Theology,* 273. In his own work, Reimer has not developed in detail what a Christology understood in relation to the larger Trinitarian life of God might look like. To this point, it often seems as though Reimer's Trinitarianism serves a formal function in his work.
[76] Yoder, *Preface to Theology,* 39.
[77] Yoder, *The Priestly Kingdom,* 67-71.
[78] O'Donovan, *The Desire of the Nations,* 121.
[79] O'Donovan, *The Desire of the Nations,* 123.
[80] Yoder, *Preface to Theology,* 223.

nor in the way that Reimer interprets him. Yoder admits that he did not give enough emphasis to the fact that writing *The Politics of Jesus* was in part his attempt to correct what has been ignored:

> My presentation, in order to correct for the one-sided social ethic which has been dominant in the past, emphasizes what was denied before: Jesus as teacher and example, not only as sacrifice; God as the shaker of the foundations, not only as the guarantor of the orders of creation; faith as discipleship, not only as subjectivity. The element of debate in the presentation may make it seem that the "other" or "traditional" element in each case – Jesus as sacrifice, God as creator, faith as subjectivity – is being rejected. It should therefore be restated that – as perusal of the structure of our presentation will confirm – no such disjunction is intended. I am rather defending the New Testament against the exclusion of the "messianic" element. The disjunction must be laid to the account of the traditional view, not of mine. It is those other views that say that because Jesus is seen as sacrifice he may not be seen as sovereign, or that because he is seen as Word made flesh he cannot be seen as normative person.[81]

In the brief epilogue included in the second edition of *The Politics of Jesus,* Yoder remarks that perhaps the above paragraph should have been given a more prominent place in the book, since there were readers who missed its significance, and therefore interpreted the book as "reductionistic or materialistic,"[82] which might well be a response to critiques such as Reimer's that do not acknowledge Yoder's selective restitution of often neglected dimensions of the biblical account of Jesus.

Alain Epp Weaver also focuses on Yoder's radical catholicity as a way to defend Yoder against charges of having a low Christology. That is, Epp Weaver understands Yoder to be pursuing ecumenical conversation precisely with reference to the orthodox Christology found in the ecumenical creeds. Again Reimer is the main interlocutor for this discussion, as Epp Weaver resists the contours of Reimer's arguments, insisting instead that Yoder had a two-pronged strategy in his use of the creeds – he appealed to them in ecumenical conversations, while at the same time relativizing their centrality for theological work. "Yoder's own presentation of the politics of Jesus can be viewed as a missionary attempt to make the gospel comprehensible to a world guided by historicist assumptions while at the same time subverting historicism by identifying Jesus with the God of creation and the apocalypse."[83]

It might be said that for Yoder, Christology is Jesuology. He is not afraid to say that Christology should not be frozen in some way by creedal formulations.

---

[81] Yoder, *The Politics of Jesus,* 226.
[82] Yoder, *The Politics of Jesus,* 227.
[83] Alain Epp Weaver, "Missionary Christology: John Howard Yoder and the Creeds," *Mennonite Quarterly Review,* 74 no 3 (July 2000): 425.

Yoder concludes that his view of Jesus is in fact more orthodox than other views based on the classical (Nicene, Chalcedon) creeds, but that the burden of his work, especially as found in *The Politics of Jesus* is an attempt to understand the "implications of what the church has always said about Jesus as Word of the Father, as true God, and true Human…"[84]

In fact, Yoder promotes the idea of reformulations in every generation and every setting as part of the mission of the church. But each reformulation must remain tied to "the Jewishness of those first-century events which we celebrate as Easter and Pentecost, which made people apply the titles of Messiah and Lord to a rebel rabbi whom the Sanhedrin had hounded and the Romans had killed. The proper ground of mission is a proper Jesuology. If we begin there the Christology should be able to take care of itself."[85] This focus on the particularity of the incarnation of Jesus serves not only as a way to 'take care of' Christology,' but also as a way to address the question of universality. In grappling with the question of how the particularity of the Jesus story must encounter the call of believers for a higher level of generality, Yoder looks at five New Testament passages (John's Prologue [John 1:1-14], the Epistle to the Hebrews, Colossians, Revelation 4:1-5:4, and Philippians 2) and finds there what he calls a deep structure which involves a series of moves claiming that the Hebrew story had widened out to include everyone. The moves that Yoder discerns in these five biblical passages, which respond to the challenge of a previously formed cosmic vision which encounters the claim that Jesus is Lord, are: 1) the writer uses the language, questions of the new linguistic world; 2) instead of placing the Jesus message in the slots prepared for it by the newly encountered vision, the writer places Jesus above that cosmos; 3) there is a concentration on suffering and rejection in human form, beneath the cosmic hierarchy as that which 'qualifies' Christ for his lordship; 4) we are not called to enter into a salvation system through ritual or initiation, but are called to enter the self-emptying and death of the Son; 5) behind the cosmic victory, enabling it, is the preexistence of the Son, co-essentiality with the Father, possession of the image of God, and the participation of the Son in creation and providence; 6) the writer and readers share by faith in all the victory means.[86]

---

[84] Yoder, *The Politics of Jesus,* 102. Yoder is not specific about what other views he has in mind.

[85] Yoder, "Confessing Jesus in Mission." This article was published in the Dutch journal *Wereld en Zending,* 24 (1996). The English translation was accessed at http://www.nd.edu/~theo/jhy/writings/christology/confessing.htm.

[86] Yoder, *The Priestly Kingdom,* 53. Yoder's compressed description of these moves is on much fuller display in *Preface to Theology,* where he traces the 'widening' of the Jesus story from the 'kerygma,' through the Gospels, other New Testament writers, and the patristic period. Stanley Hauerwas and Alex Sider register concern regarding this notion of 'kerygma,' if by this Yoder means some core message that is not already embedded in a rich theological matrix. Hauerwas and Sider, introduction to *Preface to Theology,* 24. This is a valid concern, since Yoder moves from the message of the

For Yoder, regarding the church's mission to the world, it is neither the world nor anything else that is the definitional category the church then proceeds to join up with, approve, or improve in some way. Rather, it is the rule of God as displayed in Christ that is the basic category, since the "rebellious but already (in principle) defeated cosmos is being brought to its knees by the Lamb. The development of a high Christology is the natural cultural ricochet of a missionary ecclesiology when it collides, as it must, with whatever cosmology explains and governs the world it invades."[87] In other words, for Yoder the particularity of incarnation is the universality of the good.[88] In terms of political theology, then, Yoder makes a move that is parallel to his argument for the relationship of particularity and universality, or perhaps better put, it is part of the same argument. In order for the church to be involved in politics, followers of Christ will not be shaped by the definitional categories of conventional secular politics, or whatever regime they find themselves in, but will continue as part of the church to seize the categories of surrounding culture and hammer them into new shapes formed by Christology. In this sense, the particularity of the church is the universality of politics for Yoder. Here again Yoder's concern for constructive political engagement is made explicit, although it is often not recognized as such, perhaps because the shape of those engagements remain so closely connected to his understanding of the church's mission and his refusal to accept conventional notions of the world or state in which these entities determine the shape of engagement. That is, when Yoder refers to constructive political engagements, his ecclesiological concerns and even his theological language do not drop from view, making it difficult for some interlocuters to recognize the extent to which Yoder pushes the church to engage in the world.

GOD'S RULE DISPLAYED IN CHRIST: O'DONOVAN ON JESUS' EARTHLY LIFE, TEACHING, AND MINISTRY

O'Donovan turns to his discussion of Jesus' earthly life, teaching and ministry in relation to political theology in a chapter entitled "Dual Authority and the Fulfilling of Time." He shows that the terms "spiritual" and "political," which are often the basis of discussion regarding the nature of political theology,

---

apostles to the Gospel writers, whom he describes as developing the simple first message of the apostles in the book of Acts. He does not deny that some sifting or interpreting is going on, but claims that the Gospel writers simply reflect the faith of the church in which they live. Yoder, *Preface to Theology,* 60-63.

[87] Yoder, *The Priestly Kingdom,* 54. The essay being drawn on here is entitled "'But We Do See Jesus': The Particularity and the Universality of Truth." Yoder covers somewhat similar territory albeit in a more formally philosophical mode in "On Not Being Ashamed of the Gospel: Particularity, Pluralism, and Validation," *Faith and Philosophy* 9 no 3 (July, 1992): 285-300.

[88] Yoder, *The Priestly Kingdom,* 61.

instead take us to the very substance of the proclamation of the kingdom of God, *which spans the two*.[89] That is to say, God's rule in Christ spans both political and spiritual, and the task of Christian witness is to proclaim the unity of the kingdom. Nonetheless, it still remains the task of Christian reflection to understand the duality of these two concepts, since understanding that duality properly is key to understanding political theology. It is important here to note that O'Donovan posits a duality, but not a dualism, by taking an Augustinian line in interpreting the experience of Israel as the archetype of the duality of this-worldly and divine rule. Jeremiah 29 provides a key to Augustine's understanding of the concept of two cities, whereby two political entities can coexist at one time and place, but the duality can be interpreted either as the two social entities of Babylon and Israel that live side by side, or the two "rules" under which Israel finds itself—God and Babylon. This duality makes it "flexible as a model, capable of illuminating not only the situation in which Israel shared social space with others, but also the situation at home where it sensed its own provisional political institutions as alien to its true calling."[90] The Babylonian experience became a paradigm of Jewish existence thereafter, with attendant warnings concerning the dangers of life within empire. Subjection to the foreign sword gave Israel an opportunity for separation from its own idolatrous power, but also for influence with imperial power. Therefore, to arm itself against the temptation of accommodation, Israel had to be alert to prophecy, for in the culmination of God's purposes he will entrust his kingdom to the son of man, who comes in Jesus Christ.[91] Thus the diaspora experience as seen in Jeremiah's prophetic ministry functions both as paradigm for Israel's life and as connection to the ministry and life of Jesus, according to O'Donovan's way of connecting the Old and New Testaments.

The coming of the Kingdom of God was announced in Jesus' teaching ministry, which is a disclosure of the reign of God, and therefore a carrying forward of God's authority both epistemically and politically. That is, O'Donovan understands there to be a connection between 'word' and 'power,' as seen for example in the Gospel of Mark. While the capacity to give instruction (epistemic) is a kind of authority, it is parallel but different than the capacity to give effective commands (political), but both mediate the rule of God, where word and the act are one. Despite the historical context in which Roman imperial oppression motivated a fundamental orientation to look for the intervention of God's rule to rectify Israel's political and social situation, Jesus "did not recognize a permanently twofold locus of authority. He recognised only a transitory duality which belonged to the climax of Israel's history, a duality between the coming and passing order."[92] The secular power of Rome

---

[89] O'Donovan, *The Desire of the Nations,* 82. Italics added.
[90] O'Donovan, *The Desire of the Nations,* 83.
[91] O'Donovan, *The Desire of the Nations,* 82-88.
[92] O'Donovan, *The Desire of the Nations,* 93.

was not to be understood as an uncontested sphere of secular right, but rather as an anachronistic power that was on its way out, since the "coming era of God's rule held the passing era in suspension."⁹³

O'Donovan's description of Jesus' ministry during this period of dual authority carries forward the same structure used to analyze God's rule over Israel, i.e. salvation, judgment, possession of identity, and praise. The salvation demonstrated in Jesus' ministry included works of power such as exorcism and healing, suggesting a focus on spiritual liberation rather than colonial oppression, which may seem at first glance to be apolitical salvation. Yet O'Donovan insists that Jesus' departure from the zealot option shows his theological understanding of power, not his lack of interest in it, in that empowerment of Israel was more important than disempowerment of Rome. The power of Jesus was directed against spiritual and natural weaknesses that hindered Israel from living effectively as a community under God's rule, weaknesses that would not necessarily be addressed by the disempowerment of Rome. Jesus' works of power were to indicate a demonstration of God's rule, pointing to the existence and reality of the Kingdom of God.⁹⁴

Jesus also proclaimed the coming judgment of Israel, both against the governing classes and in support for the poor. The judgment of Jesus on the governing classes and their misdirection of Israel's life is harsh, but not finally the closing of the door on them; while the support for the poor includes not only an economic dimension but also a spiritual one.⁹⁵

The bulk of O'Donovan's attention to Jesus' ministry is given over to what he considers the characteristic concern of Jesus' age to put Israel in possession of its national identity. Jesus' work was taken up in a context whereby national self-consciousness should be poured into the construction of a law-culture, not armed resistance, since national restoration had to come through the reappropriation of the law. "If the law is Israel's national possession, those who possessed it were Israel. Jesus' decisive account of God's law had as its corollary the formation of a decisive Israel, a community which would be the spiritual centre of the restored people."⁹⁶ The community that Jesus gathers around himself in the form of a group of twelve disciples will "focus representatively the life of the restored Israel living under the authorization of

---

⁹³ O'Donovan, *The Desire of the Nations*, 93.

⁹⁴ O'Donovan, *The Desire of the Nations*, 93-96.

⁹⁵ O'Donovan, *The Desire of the Nations*, 96-100.

⁹⁶ O'Donovan, *The Desire of the Nations*, 104. It is important to note that O'Donovan's discussion of Jesus' emphasis on the law as the focus of national self-identity is significantly longer than those of salvation, judgment, or praise. This signals the importance that O'Donovan places on the law over against government as the unifying element in international order. This lifting up of law is a key move for Christian political theology in O'Donovan's view. Unlike his discussion of the Hebrew Scriptures, in which the material content of the law is given short shrift, Jesus' handling of the law is given detailed attention.

the coming Kingdom."[97] These disciples then take on an authority structure of sorts, according to O'Donovan, because "in the combination of power, judgment and the continuity of Israel's identity the authority of the coming kingdom resided, and the Kingdom's representatives bore that authority in a representative form."[98] That authority is not the same as authority commonly understood as some exercise of power. Rather, Jesus redescribes authority as being dynamically disposed into the place of need; that is, authority spends itself in action for those who need it. Therefore the notion of authority has not been abolished, but it has been refashioned on the model of how God exercises his own. To gain purchase on the controlling features of Jesus' teaching of the law as the basis of authority within the community under the rule of God, O'Donovan turns to an extended discussion of the Sermon on the Mount as recorded in Matthew's Gospel. Jesus displays an approach to the law that provides a way for the community of God's law to give expression to that law without the necessity of human law courts. The community has not lost confidence in judgment, but exercises judgment in light of God's judgment within the community. That is, within the community of God's people, law can be expressed without secular litigation, since this is the community promised by the prophets in which the law would be written on their hearts.[99] It is important to observe that O'Donovan's treatment of Jesus' exposition of the law as the basis of community identity sets the stage for a subsequent discussion of the role of law outside of that community. O'Donovan's focus on the refashioning of the law by Jesus, and the attendant refusal of litigation within the community of God does not preclude the legitimacy of litigation outside of that community. In other words, O'Donovan has left the door open for members of the community of God's rule to proceed quite differently within the community than might be the case outside, even while the space inside and outside the community of faith are both under God's rule, albeit in different ways.

Corresponding to the praise of the people, which demonstrated God's kingly rule over Israel, is the faith with which Jesus was received. This reception does not confer authority, but authority proves itself by eliciting faith. O'Donovan draws on the account of Jesus' triumphal entry into Jerusalem to show that "Jesus placed himself at the centre of socio-political and religious authority in Israel."[100] The entry into Jerusalem should be understood as Jesus' claim to the legacy of Davidic expectation, but in this restoration, the unity of political and religious spheres under God was made possible by the appearance of true authority. That is, Jesus was the one who satisfied the hopes and expectations based on the reappearance of traditional kingly leadership, but his appearance

---

[97] O'Donovan, *The Desire of the Nations*, 105.
[98] O'Donovan, *The Desire of the Nations*, 106.
[99] O'Donovan, *The Desire of the Nations*, 100-113.
[100] O'Donovan, *The Desire of the Nations*, 117.

as king presupposed the recognition of the coming of the Kingdom in his ministry, with the very political concern regarding the reauthorization of Israel, not the deauthorization of Rome. So Jesus' ministry as the disclosure of the reign of God is political, even if not in a conventional sense. O'Donovan insists that the ministry of Jesus makes it possible and necessary to find an analogy from the categories of salvation, judgment, community identity, and political recognition as displayed in Israel and in Jesus to 'core' political concepts. "The first assumption of political theology must be that these analogies are valid, and that through them the Gospel of the Kingdom offers liberation to an imprisoned political culture."[101]

O'Donovan's understanding of Jesus' ministry as the disclosure of God's reign shows that here too is a 'politics of Jesus,' albeit in a way that is significantly different than Yoder. The locus of the difference is found in the fact that O'Donovan finds in the ministry of Jesus the basis of core political concepts that find life in the wider world outside of the church, whereas Yoder finds in Jesus' ministry the pattern for the church, which acts as the paradigm for the wider world, a move that O'Donovan simply finds to be naïve, an illusion that not only does not take the world seriously enough, but also operates with an unnecessarily truncated view of Jesus.

Eschatology

The form of the reign of Christ in the world is closely connected to the role of eschatology within the theopolitical visions of O'Donovan and Yoder. Yoder puts forward an 'apocalyptic stance' which dictates that the church must refuse any form of 'grabbing the handles of history' in order to control its direction. While Christ's lordship has visible consequences in history, and the church lives in hope of the ultimate consummation of Christ's victory, it also lives in tension until such a time. Thus Yoder's partially realized eschatology[102] calls for the church to embody as fully as it can the life modeled after the example of Jesus in light of the future fulfillment of the kingdom, but at the same time cautions against all attempts to make claims that suggest it is possible to bring about God's kingdom either in the church or in the world. To make such a claim would be to move too far toward a realized eschatology.

O'Donovan's political theology takes eschatology seriously, in that he sees the final victory of God, which is assured by the resurrection and exaltation of Christ, as not yet fully transparent, creating eschatological tension in the current age. Any political theology must take this tension into account, and doing so allows O'Donovan to give theological and political conceptuality both to the church as a place where God's people live under God's judgments, and to

---

[101] O'Donovan, *The Desire of the Nations*, 119.

[102] I am using Craig Carter's descriptive term here. See Carter, *The Politics of the Cross*, 150.

secular power, where believers and unbelievers alike live under penultimate judgments. On O'Donovan's reading, the church plays a less significant role in the consummation of Christ's victory, since in the Apocalypse of John, the focus is not on the church, but on the Great City where all nations will ultimately be gathered. This downplaying of the church allows O'Donovan to warn the church of becoming too inward-looking and making the error of equating the kingdom that is to come with the church.

YODER: ESCHATOLOGY AND THE POWERS

Yoder's view of eschatology is closely connected to the death and resurrection of Jesus, and to a particular understanding of the powers and principalities. In an extensive discussion of principalities and powers in the Pauline writings, Yoder argues that the powers generally understood are sociopolitical realities.[103] These powers, or structures of creaturely existence, while created good, have fallen, and continue to exist in a fallen state and exercise an ordering function within the created world. Despite their fallenness, the powers nonetheless remain under the providential sovereignty of God, who can use them for good. When these created powers do good, or are used for good, they fulfill an ordering function in the world. However, being fallen, these powers often fail to serve the world as they should. As Yoder sees things, humanity, even though it is in a fallen condition, needs to be able to live in this world even while awaiting the redemption of God. It is in such a world, fallen, attempting to survive, and awaiting redemption that the fallen powers exist.[104]

It is precisely these fallen but active powers that hold lost humanity in a struggle for survival, and must have their sovereignty broken if God is to save his creatures in their humanity, according to Yoder. Jesus did that by living a genuinely free and human existence, a life that led to the cross and showed that he is a slave to no power. His cross is a victory, the confirmation that he was free from the rebellious pretensions of the creaturely condition; Jesus was not a slave to any kind of power on any terms. Drawing on Philippians 2 and Colossians 2, Yoder argues that Jesus' death on the cross led to him being exalted above all other powers, thus disarming and making a public example of and triumphing over the powers that be.[105]

---

[103] See Yoder's chapter, "Christ and Power" in *The Politics of Jesus*, 134-161. Yoder's work on the powers in the New Testament is based largely on that of Hendrik Berkhof. Yoder served as the translator of Berkhof, *Christ and the Powers* (Scottdale: Herald Press, 1962). See also Harink, *Paul Among the Postliberals*, 115ff.

[104] Yoder, *The Politics of Jesus*, 142-144. See also Yoder, "Jesus and Power," in *On Earth Peace*, 141 for a brief version of the same argument.

[105] Yoder, *The Politics of Jesus*, 144-145. Yoder draws out the implication of 'making a public example of the powers,' 'triumphing over the powers,' and 'disarming the powers' by including a direct quotation from Berkhof that runs for more than an entire page of text. The conclusion that Berkhof reaches, which goes without comment from

Given the triumph of Jesus over the powers by the way of the cross, it then becomes the message of the church to proclaim Christ's victory, since the church is rightly understood as a gift of God, created by the cross and not by the sword. According to Yoder, the very existence of the church is its primary task. It is in itself a proclamation of the lordship of Christ to the powers from whose dominion the church has begun to be liberated, and therefore the church concentrates on not being seduced by the powers. By existing as the body of Christ, the church demonstrates that their rebellion has been vanquished. The primary social structure through which the gospel works to change other structures is the church, which recognizes that certain kinds of power may have to be rejected/refused. Nonetheless, the church is called to contribute to the creation of structures that contribute to the good of human society. That Christ is Lord is a social, political and structural fact that constitutes a challenge to the powers.[106] Yoder's explicit concern for constructive political engagement is again brought to view in this context. That is, while Yoder resists the advocating of less than discriminating involvement with any number of institutions, he goes beyond the involvement and cooperation here to the suggestion that the church may in certain instances be called to *create* structures that have not been constructed by or within secular space. He is attempting to push the church further than the embrace of or cooperation with worldly powers, or even the transformation of such structures to the more radical view that the church can and should, for the world outside the church as well as the church, create new initiatives for the so-called common good.

Closely connected to this view of Christ and the powers is Yoder's understanding of eschatology. Yoder reads Paul's language of the powers as consistently apocalyptic in the sense that it always points to the cosmic scope of the conquest of Christ on the cross, whereby the cross is an event of cosmic reordering, which by faith awaits its full consummation. According to Yoder, the eschaton as end-event imparts to life a meaningfulness which it would not otherwise have; a hope, which by defying present frustration, defines a present position in terms of the yet unseen goal which gives it meaning.[107]

While the cross is a victory over the fallen powers, a robust eschatology is necessary to see in what sense the powers have been defeated but are still active. Yoder makes a distinction between eschatology (whose concern is the meaning of the eschaton for present history) and apocalyptics (the effort to obtain precise information as to the date and shape of things to come). To make

---

Yoder, is that "we are called to a higher destiny: we have higher orders to follow and we stand under a greater protector. No powers can separate us from God's love in Christ. Unmasked, revealed in their true nature, they have lost their mighty grip on us. The cross has disarmed them: wherever it is preached, the unmasking and the disarming of the Powers takes place." Yoder, 147, taken from Berkhof, *Christ and the Powers,* 30-31.
[106] Yoder, *The Politics of Jesus,* 147-159.
[107] Yoder, *The Original Revolution,* 53.

sense of the meaning of the end for present history, Yoder describes two overlapping aeons that differ in nature or direction; one points backwards to human history outside of Christ and is manifested in the world; the other points forward to the fullness of the kingdom of God, of which it is a foretaste – manifested in the body of Christ. The new aeon is a radical break with the old.[108] The gospel, even though expressed in terms borrowed from politics, proclaimed the institution of a new kind of life, not a new kind of government.[109]

What interests Yoder about eschatology is what he alternatively calls a

---

[108] Yoder uses the term "political" in this context to designate the structures of the human community under the old aeon. The term is later used to speak of the work and will of Christ as "political" in the most proper sense of the term – as having to do with the *polis*, the common life of humanity. Yoder, *The Original Revolution*, footnote 3, 179.

[109] Yoder, *The Original Revolution*, 53-55. Yoder's argument in this chapter "If Christ is Truly Lord" is recapitulated and published as "Peace Without Eschatology?" in *The Royal Priesthood*, 143-167. The particular issue in those essays is the relation of pacifism and eschatology. My interest here is the role of eschatology on a broader scale in Yoder's thought. It is interesting to note that writers such as Doug Harink and David Toole prefer to use the term 'apocalyptic' in reference to Yoder's work. Harink explains that he uses the term 'apocalyptic' as shorthand for Jesus Christ, in the sense that in the New Testament, and especially in Paul, all apocalyptic reflection and hope comes to this, that God has acted critically, decisively, and finally for Israel, all the peoples of the earth, and the entire cosmos, in the life, death, resurrection, and coming again of Jesus, in such a way that God's purpose for Israel, all humanity, and all creation is critically, decisively, and finally disclosed on the history of Jesus Christ." Harink, *Paul Among the Postliberals*, 68. The emphasis for Harink is on God's action in Jesus Christ, especially as both determining and revealing the grain of the universe, which is obviously a Yoder reference, as Harink acknowledges. However, Harink uses the term 'apocalyptic theology without reserve' to describe "theology which leaves no reserve of space or time or concept or aspect of creation outside of or beyond or undetermined by the critical, decisive and final action of God in Jesus Christ." Ibid., 69. David Toole, drawing almost uncritically on Yoder's work, prefers to use the term "apocalyptic style" to refer to the style or way of life that follows from what he claims is the 'strange view of the Bible.' Toole, *Waiting for Godot in Sarajevo*, 210. Toole's chapter title is "Toward a Metaphysics of Apocalypse." Yoder is not entirely consistent with his language, as when in discussions of eschatology, he will also use the language of 'apocalyptic style,' for example. In fact, the distinction between terms such as 'prophecy,' 'apocalypse,' or 'eschatology' seem not to interest Yoder much in his article "Ethics and Eschatology," where he refuses to adjudicate any of these issues within such literature, preferring instead to use what he refers to as "the still coarser metaphor of 'vision.'" Yoder also uses the term 'apocalyptic style' in the same article. Yoder, "Ethics and Eschatology," 119. However, Yoder uses 'eschatology' when referring to issues of the meaning of the end for present history, as is evident even in the titles of chapters and articles such as "Peace without Eschatology?," "Ethics and Eschatology," "Armaments and Eschatology."

stance,[110] or a vision[111] that has to do with the meaningfulness of history. That is, the slain Lamb in the Apocalypse of St. John is worthy to receive power, as against the conventional assumptions concerning the meaningfulness of history. Yoder observes that social ethical concern is motivated most often by a deep desire to make things move in the right direction, and therefore part of social concern has to do with looking for the right 'handle' by which one can 'get hold on' the course of history and move it in the right direction. Yoder sees in this way of thinking at least three distinguishable assumptions which he wants to disavow: a) the relationship of cause and effect is transparent; b) we are well informed enough to make decisions about social and political realities; and c) effectiveness in moving toward these goals is itself a moral yardstick.[112] He finds a response to these kinds of assumptions in the eschatological literature of the Bible. For example, the liturgical literature that is embedded in the Revelation of St. John relates a vision in Rev. 4-5 in which the seer is presented with a sealed scroll, and the question that is posed – who is worthy to open the seal? – is precisely the question of the meaningfulness of history.[113] The answer

---

[110] Yoder, *The Politics of Jesus,* 228. Yoder claims here that the Apocalypse of St. John has a stance that can be contrasted to a worldly stance that seeks to take hold of history and move it in some direction.

[111] Yoder, "Ethics and Eschatology," 119.

[112] Yoder, *The Politics of Jesus,* 229-230. Yoder pursues a similar argument in "Ethics and Eschatology," where he claims that we take for granted a deterministic world view – one that assumes a massive causal nexus with no loopholes. But the ancient seers assumed divine agency. Since Constantine, some broad assumptions have been operative which represent a kind of 'fulfilled apocalyptic.' The role of the ruler himself is part of the changing history of Christian eschatology. That is, the new era is seen as the new millennium when the great serpent has been chained. "This providentially transformed social setting makes fundamental differences for ethics." The new way of seeing things has several components: 1) the frame of reference of ethical deliberation has to do with the person in power, and what the best possible outcomes can be. This in turn has several assumptions – a) that the social system of causation is a transparent nexus of connections, comparable to a machine whose shafts and cogwheels interact in reliable ways, so that the results of one's decision and action can be calculated; and b) that the actor whose decision we are evaluating has power; 2) information can be known – this is of course not possible; 3) rulers are prototypical moral agents. Yoder, "Ethics and Eschatology," 121.

[113] Yoder is explicit about the fact that the church is central to the point made here by John - "Revelation 4 and 5, the first vision of John, is of the gathering church. The scroll represents the meaning of history that can be opened only by the Lamb. The Lamb is praised because of his worthiness to ransom persons for God from every tribe, nation, or kingdom, and make them a priestly kingdom to reign on earth. *To reign. To share in his kingship."* Yoder, *Preface to Theology,* 247. Italics in original. It is clear that the question of history, and especially the meaningfulness of history and the exertion of control is important to this discussion. While this issue will not be ignored here, it will

to the question is "The lamb that was slain is worthy to receive power." John is saying here that suffering and not brute power determines the meaning of history, and the key to participation in the meaningfulness of history is patience:

> The triumph of the right is assured not by the might that comes to the aid of the right, which is of course justification of the use of violence and other kinds of power in every human conflict. The triumph of the right, although it is assured, is sure because of the power of the resurrection and not because of any calculation of causes and effects, nor because of the inherently greater strength of the good guys. The relationship between the obedience of God's people and the triumph of God's cause is not a relationship of cause and effect but one of cross and resurrection.[114]

This is what Yoder calls a biblical 'philosophy of history,' a position that "is nothing more than a logical unfolding of the meaning of the work of Jesus Christ himself, whose choice of suffering Servanthood rather than violent lordship, of love to the point of death rather than righteousness backed by power, was itself the fundamental direction of his life. Jesus was so faithful to the enemy-love of God that it cost him all his effectiveness; he gave up every handle on history."[115] In other words, Jesus excluded any normative concern for the capacity to make things come out right, having renounced the claim to govern history, the compulsiveness of purpose that leads the strong to violate the weak. "The point is not that one can attain all of one's legitimate ends without using violent means. It is rather that our readiness to renounce our legitimate ends whenever they cannot be attained by legitimate means itself constitutes our participation in the triumphant suffering of the Lamb."[116] The church is not called to be the guardian of history, but rather, once "freed from compulsiveness and from the urge to manage the world [the church] might then find ways and words to suggest as well to those outside its bounds the invitation to a servant stance in society."[117]

In Yoder's view, apocalyptic and prophetic literature serve to strike down our confidence in system-immanent causal explanations for the past, and, in system-immanent causal descriptions of how the future is to unfold based on our decisions.

---

be dealt with more fully in the following chapter where the burden taken up will be to clarify the stance that Yoder and O'Donovan take in relation to Christendom.

[114] Yoder, *The Politics of Jesus*, 232.

[115] Yoder, *The Politics of Jesus*, 233.

[116] Yoder, *The Politics of Jesus*, 237.

[117] Yoder, *The Politics of Jesus*, 240, 241. The discourse of the church may be called 'apocalyptic' if by that "we designate a portrayal of the way the world is being efficaciously called to do that does not let present empirical readings of possibility have the last word." Yoder, *For the Nations*, 216.

Such an apocalyptic stance also provides the basis of hope which, according to the biblical seers, was not merely compensating for desperation. The seers were engaged in doxology, restating in a new setting their proclamation of the resurrection. They were testifying that the powers of oppression were swallowed up in God's larger story, whereas modern explanations try to do it the other way around, by subsuming God-talk within visions of human dignity and therapy.[118]

Yoder concludes that "when read carefully, none of the biblical apocalypses, from Ezekiel through Daniel to Mark 13 and John of Patmos, is about either pie in the sky or the Russians in Mesopotamia. They are about how the crucified Jesus is a more adequate key to understanding what God is about in the real world of empires and armies and markets than is the ruler in Rome, with all his supporting military, commercial, and sacerdotal networks."[119] Yoder is careful to warn that this sense of eschatology must not be seen as fulfilled, which would lead to a misreading of the present situation without appropriate weight being given to the not yet fully transparent coming reign of Christ.[120] Jesus introduced an eschatological tension of the already/not-yet that is embodied in an eschatological community of disciples who both reject violence and live in tension with the old social order, just as Jesus did. Therefore, Yoder's eschatology is characterized by a theological realism that undergirds a view of Christ's lordship as having visible consequences in history. But his eschatology is only partially realized – the kingdom has come in the person of Jesus, but not in its fullness.[121]

O'DONOVAN: ESCHATOLOGY AND THE POWERS

There is a marked common eschatological emphasis in both Yoder and O'Donovan, with agreement that the full display of Christ's victory is yet to come. However, according to O'Donovan, the Pauline view of the time between the Ascension and the Parousia should be compared to that presented by St. John in the Apocalypse. Pauline literature agrees with the Apocalypse in that Christ's crucifixion was the decisive achievement of God's purposes,[122] and full display of that victory is yet to come. In this sense, there is a common marked eschatological emphasis in Paul's writings and the Apocalypse of St.

---

[118] Yoder, "Ethics and Eschatology," 122-123.

[119] Yoder, *The Politics of Jesus*, 246.

[120] Yoder does not refer to his own eschatological views as partially fulfilled, but warns explicitly against the danger of Constantinianism, which is precisely a mistake of assuming a fulfilled apocalyptic. Yoder, "Ethics and Eschatology," 121. This connection between eschatology and Constantinianism will also be dealt with more fully as part of my next chapter, which deals with Christendom.

[121] Carter, *The Politics of the Cross*, 139, 150.

[122] Carter, *The Politics of the Cross*, 151.

John.[123] O'Donovan's focus, however, lies in the contrast between the Pauline approach to politics and that of the Apocalypse, a contrast summarized by naming the Pauline strand 'secular' and St. John's approach 'apocalyptic.' That is, "Pauline believers pray for 'a quiet and peaceable life' under their authorities (1 Tim. 2:2), whereas John expects those same prayers to let loose an idolatrous empire."[124] John's emphasis is on the final conflict of the idolatrous imperial pretensions of world empire with the crucified, resurrected Christ. The Apocalypse thus displays a disciplined theology in which Christian believers, through prayer, prophecy, and worship of God resist the empire that, through military and economic means, serves as a parodic mirror image of the kingdom of God, which seeks to demand allegiance to its religious absolutization of political doctrine. O'Donovan suggests that at this point, mainstream Christianity has traditionally turned to the church as a balancing factor to the demand for allegiance by the empire of the Antichrist, whereby the church functions as "a form of social life in which the predominance of truth and love is maintained, imperfectly but really, in a form of social organization which points beyond itself to the city of God. Strikingly John refuses to take this path."[125] O'Donovan argues that in the confrontation between Christ and the powers of evil, in which it becomes possible to see the eschatological triumph of the church, the present form of the church loses its social 'solidity.' The churches described in the first chapters of the Apocalypse are only "ambiguously faithful," but in "the heat of persecution the gap between appearance and reality within the church has opened up. The faithful are as scattered, isolated witnesses before the massive solidity of the idolatrous empire… For the majority of voices in the apostolic generation the church is the primary reality in the Messianic age; but here its social existence seems to have become attenuated."[126] The attenuated social existence of the church in the Apocalypse does not mean that the church disappears – it still gathers, worships, suffers, and prays – but John's emphasis is on the Great City that is ruled by God, on the ultimate choices between two governments, "the creative government of the Word of God and the predatory self-destructive government of human self-rule."[127] The church is not the guarantor of a society with a true order given by God; rather the scattered believers in exile rely on the Great City that displays the rule of God, a holy city that is founded through true divine speech that enters into conflict with the false orders of human society.[128]

---

[123] O'Donovan, "History and Politics in the Book of Revelation," in Oliver O'Donovan and Joan Lockwood O'Donovan, *Bonds of Imperfection: Christian Politics, Past and Present* (Grand Rapids: Eerdmans Publishing, 2004), 35.
[124] O'Donovan, "History and Politics in the Book of Revelation," 35.
[125] O'Donovan, "History and Politics in the Book of Revelation," 42.
[126] O'Donovan, *The Desire of the Nations*, 155.
[127] O'Donovan, *The Desire of the Nations*, 157.
[128] O'Donovan, "History and Politics in the Book of Revelation," 47.

O'Donovan does not want to denigrate the importance of the church, but to point the challenge contained in the Apocalypse at "an inward-looking preoccupation with ecclesial matters, or the comfortable assumption that to be part of the church is to be part of, or on the way to, the kingdom of God...Readers (and hearers) of the Apocalypse are offered the resources, in their own circumstances, to work out what faithfulness to the testimony might mean."[129]

O'Donovan's reading of the New Testament for political theology, especially the highlighting of the resurrection and exaltation of Jesus Christ, gives his theopolitical thought an eschatological dimension that has been applauded by some,[130] but nevertheless contains some ambiguity. The primary role of eschatology for O'Donovan concerns the assertion that the authorities which govern the world have been made subject to the sovereignty of God, and that this subjection awaits the final universal appearance of Christ in order to become fully apparent.[131] That is, without this eschatological dimension there would be no space at all for secular authority. However, such a view of secular authority resists any notion of it being self-posited, or that its existence depends on its own authority. The judgments of secular authority are therefore provisional and penultimate since the church reckons with the final judgment of God, and thus with matters of ultimate judgment. However, the presence of the secular judgments "is an important witness to those to whom the word of final judgment has yet to come."[132] Christ's triumph in the resurrection and exaltation thus provides the place both for the church and secular authority.[133]

O'Donovan's recovery of eschatology for political theology has been criticized for harboring an inordinate focus on the 'already' rather than the 'not yet' of the eschatological. For example, in the view of Stanley Hauerwas and James Fodor, O'Donovan thinks he knows more about how the story comes out than can be justified. Their view, by contrast, is that Scripture is best read as an aid for the church to 'muddle through' rather than the basis for an architectonic of rule. Hauerwas and Fodor instead find hope in the prospects of rule under God which must be tempered more by the eschatological 'not yet' than encouraged by the eschatological 'already.'[134] This suggests that O'Donovan's eschatology is too 'realized,' granting too much authority to secular power,

---

[129] Christopher Rowland, "The Apocalypse and Political Theology," in Craig Bartholomew, et al., eds., *A Royal Priesthood?*, 243-244.

[130] See for example, Christopher Rowland, "The Apocalypse and Political Theology," 241-254; and Jonathan Chaplin, "Political Eschatology and Responsible Government," in Craig Bartholomew, et al., eds., *A Royal Priesthood?*, 265-308.

[131] O'Donovan, *The Desire of the Nations*, 147.

[132] O'Donovan, *The Desire of the Nations*, 151.

[133] "The coming of Christ, then, functions as an eschatological turning point for the political authorities." Chaplin, "Political Eschatology and Responsible Government," 277.

[134] Hauerwas and Fodor, "Remaining in Babylon," 40, 42.

suggesting that a surplus of desire for rule or official status is granted to or sought by the church. Put another way, O'Donovan's focus on the exaltation, which is compatible with concepts of divine rule, pushes his thought in a direction that does not relativize the role and value of every social institution nearly enough. So argues Victor Paul Furnish in an attempt to move O'Donovan's focus from the exaltation to the crucifixion, which Furnish believes to be, by far, the more prominent theme in the New Testament.[135] William Cavanaugh is in basic agreement with Furnish's point of view, suggesting that O'Donovan's recovery of eschatology is one that has a strong accent on the 'already' of Christ's victory, and therefore a great deal of emphasis on biblical images of rule instead of exile, resident alien, and so on. Therefore, while O'Donovan challenges Christian accommodation to liberal orders, he nevertheless locates himself within an established national church and depends on the state to be the police department of the church.[136]

O'Donovan's recovery of eschatology, then, is vulnerable to criticism that it is too 'realized,' that he knows too much of how secular power receives authorization from God, and especially that the church is too focused on questions of rule. Another way of understanding the role of eschatology in political theology would be to agree with O'Donovan that the existence of the church in the world relativizes all the politics of the age, even in the eyes of the practitioners of those politics, thus making secular politics penultimate, but then extending that argument to say that the first political calling of the church is to itself be a sign of the eschaton. Put another way, the church is a gateway to eschatological polity, and in that way, relativizes all other polities, which is not merely a negative assertion. Rather, "to relativize something is to relate it to something else; in this case to relativize the kingdoms of this world is to relate them to the kingdom of God."[137]

It is O'Donovan's reticence in relativizing all other polities fully enough that leads to his being criticized for having an eschatology that is not 'realized' enough.[138] It is especially the case that the judicial function of secular

---

[135] Victor Paul Furnish, "How Firm a Foundation?," 19-23.

[136] William Cavanaugh, "Church" in Cavanaugh and Scott, eds. *Blackwell Companion to Political Theology,* 403. Daniel Carroll agrees as well, noting that in O'Donovan's work the eschatological reality of the inauguration of the kingdom determines the provisional nature of human government and its limited judicial obligations and exposes the rebellious nature of the nations as part of a cosmic struggle, but that no sustained exposition of the 'not yet' of eschatology is on offer. Instead, Carroll argues, O'Donovan focuses too much on future judgment. M. Daniel Carroll R., "The Power of the Future in the Present: Eschatology and Ethics in O'Donovan and Beyond," in Craig Bartholemew, et al., eds., *A Royal Priesthood?,* 123-125.

[137] Robert Jenson, "Eschatology," in Cavanaugh and Scott, eds. *Blackwell Companion to Political Theology,* 417.

[138] P. Travis Kroeker, "Why O'Donovan's Christendom is not Constantinian and Yoder's Voluntariety is not Hobbesian," 58.

government, which serves a mediating role for the rule of Christ, is not relativized to the extent that a more robust eschatology might entail. On Yoder's account, responsibility can be pursued on the basis of the servant church, not primarily through the exercise of public juridical activity. The church for O'Donovan, however, has an essentially hidden political character, since "its essential nature as a governed society, is hidden, to be discerned by faith as the ascended Christ who governs it is to be discerned by faith."[139] This assertion suggests that

O'Donovan refuses to allow that the church constitutes a new political order or alternative society, since it serves a hidden Lord whose rule cannot yet be made visibly public. This refusal causes him to limit formally the meaning of Christian political witness to addressing the judicial acts and authority of the secular state, even while suggesting that the visible practical form of the church offers substantive prophetic content to political society through obedience to the divinely authorized rule of Christ.[140]

When O'Donovan's eschatology is contextualized by his understanding of the political nature of the church, it is clear that he can be understood as having either an eschatology that is too 'realized', or not 'realized' enough. Therefore, his construal of authorization of the provisional judicial activity of secular government, and his attendant view of the authorization and political presence of the church are contentious, especially considering O'Donovan's reading of the Apocalypse, where the scattered, isolated faithful witnesses do *not* constitute much of a social witness "before the massive solidity of the idolatrous empire."[141] To read the church in the Apocalypse as experiencing a loss of a distinct political presence is to deny the possibility that it is precisely the diasporic community that is the social presence of the church. Further, to understand the church as ever having anything more than such a presence is to overstate the case and move toward a 'realized' eschatology in the sense that too much is taken for granted (that is, that what the shape of that social presence should be can be known). On the other hand, such an eschatology may not be realized enough in that the social presence of God's people is always a witness through prayer, worship, and prophetic witness, albeit in a suffering diasporic community.

Ecclesiology

The importance of ecclesiology in Yoder and O'Donovan's theopolitical projects is already obvious in the way discussions are related to the life of the church. It might be said that both projects proceed on the basis that a

---

[139] O'Donovan, *The Desire of the Nations*, 166.
[140] P. Travis Kroeker, "Why O'Donovan's Christendom is not Constantinian and Yoder's Voluntariety is not Hobbesian," 58.
[141] O'Donovan, *The Desire of the Nations*, 155.

theological account of how this world is ruled must proceed from and through an account of the church,[142] which in turn is closely connected to their respective accounts of secular power. However, the agreement on the importance of the church for political theology does not imply concurrence on that role.

Yoder's logic of cross and resurrection moves him toward the view that it is a mistake to believe that the church can or should attempt to grab the handles of history as a way of making things turn out 'right.' In Christ the kingdom has come, and the old age is therefore passing away. However, the crucifixion is understood as the defeat of worldly powers, while the resurrection vindicates the way of the cross taken by Jesus, which therefore acts as the exemplar for the cruciform life of the church. The fullness of the kingdom is not complete, but is an eschatological reality that suggests that the church lives in an age of tension between the overlapping passing age and the coming assured kingdom. The church is called to witness to the state, and it does so by acting as a paradigm for secular power, offering its own practices as 'body politics' that can also become real in non-religious society. For Yoder, the politics of Jesus instantiated in the church is political theology. Secular power is not given any kind of separate authorization as a result of Christ's triumph, but simply exists as one of the worldly powers that serves the ends of the church, not the other way around.

According to O'Donovan, the church is a political entity in its own right, a place where God's judgment holds sway in a way that is different than in the secular sphere. The Christian's submission to God's ultimate authority in the church does not entail freedom from the authority wielded in the secular realm. That is, secular power is called by God to enact judgment to which the church is required to submit, in keeping with the recognition that such authority is provisional and penultimate. The church, the body of Christ, the result of Christ's triumph, is also authorized, albeit differently than secular power. Christ's triumph then created a situation in which the end of the passing kingdom is assured, as is the coming of God's kingdom in its fullness. The result is that time when the passing and coming kingdoms need the presence of secular power, which is authorized in a penultimate, provisional way to assert political authority in the form of judgment.

YODER: BODY POLITICS

The fact that Yoder has no doctrine of the state as such, as will be made clear below, is directly related to his robust ecclesiology, in which the church is seen as that new peoplehood brought into being by Jesus Christ, which is also a new way of living together, a new social phenomenon that, if faithful to the example

---

[142]See O'Donovan's self-description in *The Desire of the Nations*, 158-59.

of suffering love set by Jesus, is a most powerful agent of social change.[143] The church is for Yoder the primary category in any discussion of Christian social strategy, since the very existence of the church is its primary task. It is in itself a proclamation of the lordship of Christ to the powers. By existing *as* the church, the church demonstrates that the rebellion of the fallen powers has been vanquished. According to Yoder, it is often assumed that the forces which really determine the march of history are in the hands of leaders of armies and markets, and in turn Christians will want to become lords of state and market to use their power for their desirable ends. However, what needs to be seen is that the primary social structure through which the gospel works to change other structures is the church, which is called to contribute to the creation of structures which shape human society in a manner that is evermore congruent with the rule of God.[144] This suggests that withdrawal from the larger world is simply not an option for Yoder, since the ethic of Jesus was transmitted and transmuted into the stance of the servant church within society. "Since in the resurrection and in Pentecost the reign which was immanent has now in part come into our history, the church can now live out, within the structures of society, the newness of the life of that reign."[145] Thus the political novelty God brings into the world is a community of those who serve instead of ruling, who suffer instead of inflicting suffering, a body that *is* the good news, the mission, and not just an agent of it.[146] The line of thinking that sees the visibility of the church as the primary political category for Christians is evident throughout Yoder's body of work, going back to his doctoral dissertation, where in his historical analysis of the dialogues between Zwingli and the Anabaptists, and a companion work in which he subjects his historical work to theological analysis, Yoder already understands the church as being both for and against the world, joining in initiatives where it can, and rejecting partnerships that would be unfaithful to the Lordship of Christ. But central is the notion of the visibility of the church. In fact, Yoder argues that this visibility is the central

---

[143] Yoder, *The Original Revolution*, 31.

[144] Yoder, *The Politics of Jesus*, 150-155.

[145] Yoder, *The Politics of Jesus*, 187. According to Doug Harink's reading of Yoder, it is in the church that religious, cultural, social, economic, political structures that make human community possible at all are reordered to their proper function under the rule of Christ. In turn, the church, as redeemed and reordered humanity, presents to the wider world and its structures a picture of the world's own redemptive promise, should it submit to the lordship of Christ. Further, "Precisely as one polis among many, or rather as the polis among others, the people of God engage in practices which are in some sense recognizable by the other cities and nations of the world – recognizable as ways of social and political life. The strangeness or otherness of the ecclesial polis is not that it engages on sociopolitical practices of another order or kind (say, religious or spiritual) but that it engages on sociopolitical practices in the new way of Jesus Christ." Harink, *Paul Among the Postliberals*, 117, 132.

[146] Yoder, *The Royal Priesthood*, 91.

concept of Anabaptism - if one seeks to find the breaking point between Anabaptism and Reformers, the first concern is for the community, its visibility, and its capacity for action.[147]

The fundamental notion that the church is always a visible entity grounds Yoder's contention that rather than being irrelevant or perhaps a useful symbolic gadfly, the church is called to witness to secular power in whatever form that power appears. If the reign of Christ means that the state has the obligation to serve by encouraging good and restraining evil, to provide social cohesion, "it is possible for the Christian or the Christian church to address the social order at large or to the state criticisms and suggestions concerning the way in which the state fulfills its responsibility for the maintenance of order."[148] This witness to the state finds its ground in Jesus' lordship, accomplished by the power of the cross, resurrection, ascension, and the Holy Spirit, with the effect of triumphing over the powers of this world. The resultant co-existence of two ages, one which is passing and one which has come but is not fully here, means that the new community called by God cannot be identified by way of solidarity with any power that is part of the passing age. At any rate, God charges any such power with the responsibility of preserving the fabric of the community as the context within which the church's work can be carried out. That is, Christ is Lord over the world and the church, but it is for the sake of the church's own work that society continues to function. Yoder thus is able to acknowledge that the state has a function within an ordered society that is part of God's plan without having a separate (and different) authorization than the church, in comparison to the way O'Donovan construes these matters. Because the state exists, and is given a task under the Lordship of Jesus, the church is assigned the task of witnessing to the state, as part of the primary task of existing as the church.

The form of the church's existence is important, and is based primarily in the church's obedience to the standards of discipleship. By being a society in its own right, the church, in some aspects, can be an instructive example to the conscience of society. This example is not necessarily mediated through the use of religious language, but in a way that is derivative of the gospel and is also concerned about the moral integrity of the society being addressed. "The Christian speaks not of how to describe, and then to seek to create the ideal society, but of how the state can best fulfill its responsibilities in a fallen society."[149] That is, Yoder recognizes that society at large is not necessarily committed to the lordship of Christ, and so he argues that the church's witness must take into account the duality of response to the lordship of Christ. Yoder firmly rejects any notion of a dualism of realms, but insists on this duality of

---

[147] Yoder, *Anabaptism and Reformation in Switzerland*, 280-299.

[148] Yoder, *The Christian Witness to the State*, 5. The following material is taken largely from this book, especially the first four chapters.

[149] Yoder, *The Christian Witness to the State*, 32.

response. He sees it as necessary to deny a dualism, since to accept the splitting apart of territories would falsely separate the political from the nonpolitical. The duality which is real is a difference of responses separating obedience from rebellion, and so there is no special realm of politics which Christians or the church can avoid and leave to its own resources, or leave to run by its own rules. The community of faith does not live unto itself, scattered as it is among myriad other systems such as the state, the nation, the economy, media, and so on. No one of these systems is identical either with the believing community or the fallen world.[150]

How then can the church witness to a state, to a society or to any individual for that matter, whose response to Jesus is not one of obedient discipleship? The church's speech must take the form of 'middle axioms,' which are concepts that "will translate into meaningful and concrete terms the general relevance of the lordship of Christ for a given social ethical issue. They mediate between the general principles of Christological ethics and the concrete problems of political application. They claim no metaphysical status, but serve usefully as rules of thumb to make meaningful the impact of Christian social thought."[151] Therefore, according to Yoder, the church's existence as a visible alternative politics does not preclude it from involvement in the affairs of the state, but means that the engagement will be on an *ad hoc* basis, always seeking to remain obedient even while it calls the state to its own best impulses of ordering society in a peaceful and just manner. Even the Anabaptist notion of the state's use of the sword as being 'outside of the perfection of Christ,' as indicated in the Schleitheim confession,[152] does not preclude involvement in or concern for public life. Yoder notes that the feudal lordship of the time in Switzerland concentrated on issues such as social control, punishment of crimes, and persecution of Anabaptists, and it was that kind of government in which there was no place for the disciple of Christ. However, there was still significant room for involvement in issues such as taxation, usury, the death penalty, civil wars, and potential wars against the Turks. "Thus renunciation of 'the sword' by no means meant avoiding involvement in public life."[153] For Yoder, there is never a question of whether or not to be political, but only what shape that politics will take.

The shape of the visible community of the church that acts as an alternative

---

[150] Yoder, *For the Nations,* 233-235.

[151] Yoder, *The Christian Witness to the State,* 32-33. Alain Epp Weaver notes that Yoder's view allows the church to speak of its own practices in religious terms, and can use the pagan language of the state as the basis of appeals to the state. Alain Epp Weaver, "After Politics: John Howard Yoder, Body Politics, and the Witnessing Church," *Review of Politics* 61 no 4 (Fall 1999): 670.

[152] The Schleitheim Confession is an early Anabaptist confession of faith written by Michael Sattler in conjunction with other Anabaptist leaders. See Yoder, *The Legacy of Michael Sattler* (Scottdale: Herald Press, 1973), 27ff.

[153] Yoder, *The Jewish-Christian Schism Revisited,* 128.

politics is given a significant amount of descriptive attention in Yoder's writing, often in liturgical terms. That is, he asserts that the life of the church's character is at its base doxological; the church is not interested in the engineering of society, but in doxology, by which Yoder means a recognition, a seeing of things the way they really are. In that sense, the choice of Jesus to reject certain available political options in favor of suffering service was ontological, i.e. it risks an option in favor of the restored vision of how things really are. If Christian disciples confess the world as the ontological locus of God's sovereign intentions, and the believing community as its epistemological locus, the imperative is not first to stoke up motivational devotedness, nor to develop more powerful sociological tools of persuasion or coercion, but to nurture the organic integrity of the community charged with the task of insight.[154] The Christian church is therefore charged with serving God, which is a way to live in the world the way it is, which means that it is crucial to see the world and history doxologically - to describe the cosmos in terms dictated by the knowledge that a once-slaughtered Lamb is now living.

Yoder aims for even more specificity in giving an account of how the life of the church is political, and how that kind of politics is not withdrawal from society but witness to it when he offers an analysis of a number of church practices that serve as a paradigm for the state.[155] In *Body Politics*,[156] which has come to serve as the standard source in Yoder's oeuvre in terms of the practices of the church that act as paradigm for the state, he begins by rejecting both liberal and pietistic methods for bridging the gap between church and politics – liberal Christianity because it believes that certain concepts such as justice, a set of insights concerning human nature and the world, must be properly understood and then acted on. This view claims that worship helps understand those concepts, and then the Christian can be usefully active in public affairs as they stand. Yoder understands pietism as arguing that worship primarily

---

[154] Yoder, *For the Nations*, 212-215.

[155] I say 'a number' because at various places in his writings, Yoder offers lists of practices that function as paradigms. While there is a significant amount of overlap in these lists, they are not identical, presumably not because of inconsistency on Yoder's part, but because these lists are always samplings of what could be longer, more detailed descriptions of the practices of the church. Yoder clearly gives little weight to providing a definitive list that might take on the permanent status of something like a template for evaluating the effectiveness of a church. Rather, what is consistent about these lists is that they are drawn from reading the New Testament with a view to finding there the shape of church life that is required from the obedient community of disciples. See Yoder, *The Jewish-Christian Schism*, "The Forms of Possible Obedience," 121-131; *For the Nations*, 29-36; 43-50; *The Priestly Kingdom*, 92-94; *The Royal Priesthood*, 203-207.

[156] John Howard Yoder, *Body Politics: Five Practices of the Christian Community Before the Watching World*, (Scottdale: Herald Press, 1992). The following material is drawn from this source unless otherwise noted.

modifies the individual, through whom society is changed. The problem for Yoder is that both suggest that the 'spiritual' is prior to the 'political.' But at the same time, the values of 'politics' are considered autonomous, and therefore worship does not actually effect our understanding of them, which suggests that the world and history are not being understood doxologically. The church community as political reality, a structured social body, has its way of making decisions, defining membership, and carrying out common tasks. In this community "the will of God for human socialness as a whole is prefigured by the shape to which the body of Christ is called. Church and world are not two separate compartments under separate legislation or two institutions with contradictory assignments, but two levels of pertinence of the same Lordship. The people of God are called to be today what the world is called to be ultimately."[157] So "the difference between church and state or between a faithful and an unfaithful church is not that one is political and the other not, but that they are political in different ways."[158] Therefore, Yoder describes in some detail five practices, in which he sees "there is a social practice lived out by the early Christians, under divine mandate, which at the same time offers a paradigm for the life of the larger society."[159]

---

[157] Yoder, *Body Politics,* ix.

[158] Yoder, *Body Politics,* endnote 5, 81.

[159] Yoder, *Body Politics,* x. In the first of these practices, binding and loosing, the confrontation of people in the church who have sinned (based on Matthew 18:15-18), Yoder sees the church practice as an activity that entails two dimensions – moral discernment and reconciliation, a mode of practice whereby the community's standards are clarified and if need be, modified. At stake for Yoder is the guidance that the church receives from this practice, guidance that is constitutional or procedural, and so the church can meet new situations by exercising the resources of a valid community process that also includes substantial prescriptions. At its best, the practice of binding and loosing can unite substantial moral concern for people with redemptive confidential admonition. If this is the case, the church's facing of conflict in redemptive dialogue demonstrates a process which shows that "conflict is not merely a palliative strategy for tolerable survival or psychic hygiene, but a mode of truth-finding and community-building. That is true in the gospel; it is also true, *mutatis mutandis,* in the world (13)."

The second practice Yoder focuses on is that of disciples breaking bread together. The act of communion in the apostolic church included a focus on meal fellowship and thanksgiving, as well as the memory of the celebration of the Passover. Yoder sees here a basic economic fact that entails some kind of sharing of resources, as well as rank and status, all of which reflect the good news of Christ, the inauguration of the messianic age, whereby the church acts as both the specimen and symbol of the responsibility to display the beginning of the fulfillment of the promises of the messianic age. Breaking bread together, the Eucharist, is a sign of the new world in the ruins of the old, but so is feeding the hungry, and Yoder insists that one is no more a 'real presence' than the other.

Yoder begins his discussion of the practice of baptism with a reading of 2 Corinthians 5:17 in which he concludes that the concrete, social-functional meaning of

Yoder concludes that each of these practices can be thought of in terms of

that passage is that the inherited social definitions of class and category are no longer basic. Baptism celebrates and effects the merging of the Jewish and Gentile stories, melding the legacies of both. Yoder sees there a new inter-ethnic social reality into which the individual is inducted rather than the social reality being the sum of individuals. "Thus the primary narrative meaning of baptism is the new society it creates, by inducting all kinds of people into the same people. The church is the new society, it is therefore also the model for the world's moving in the same direction (32)." Paul's equalization message is rooted in redemption, and so Yoder asserts that the politics of baptism displays inter-ethnic inclusiveness, repentance and cleansing, nonviolent conflict, and religious liberty – all of which can be communicated beyond the church.

After discussing the three practices of binding and loosing, breaking bread together, and baptism, Yoder then pulls together a series of threads to reveal what he sees as a common pattern that is emerging, a pattern with six dimensions: a) these practices are 'sacramental' in the sense that when humans do these practices, God does them; b) these practices are ordinary observable human behavior, not esoteric rituals; c) doing these practices is what makes the group doing them a group; d) all three practices are derived from the work of Jesus Christ; e) all three have a social meaning at the outset. "They are not only political in that they describe the church as a body with a concrete social shape; they are also political in the wider sense that they can be commended to any society as a healthy way to organize (46)." f) all three have more to do with a style of approaching any question than with particular choices, and are all good news, marks of the new world that has already begun.

The fourth practice, which Yoder identifies as 'the fullness of Christ,' denotes "a new mode of group relationships, in which every member of a body has a distinctly identifiable, divinely validated and empowered role (47)." In addition to this chapter in *Body Politics,* Yoder develops this theme at much greater length in his book *The Fullness of Christ: Paul's Revolutionary Vision of Universal Ministry* (Elgin: Brethren Press, 1987). Within the church, this multiplicity of gifts comes about as the result of the work of the Holy Spirit within the pattern of a particular social process. Yoder acknowledges that this distribution of gifts may have contributed to modern notions of human dignity and individualism, but he is quick to point out that the Christian view is not to be equated with that modern notion, in that within the Christian church, each part of the body is unique and irreplaceable, but can only exercise its dignity within the bondedness to other members of the community. This vision can be translated into terms that outsiders can understand, so that groups other than the church can deal with role relationships, drawing on ideas of interdependence with peers and so on.

The fifth practice of the church before the watching world is what Yoder refers to as 'the rule of Paul.' The focus here is on the process of congregational decision-making through open conversation, a commitment to listening openly, even to the voice of the underdog or the opposition, with a view to arriving at an uncoerced consensus through open conversation. The conversation itself is a search for truth, which Yoder hopes can be true in local and wider assemblies of the church, and also act as a paradigm in non-religious groups.

social process, and more importantly, "they can be translated into non-religious terms. The multiplicity of gifts is a model for the empowerment of the humble and the end of hierarchy in social process. Dialogue under the Holy Spirit is the ground floor of the notion of democracy. Admonition to bind or loose at the point of offense is the foundation for conflict resolution and consciousness-raising. Baptism enacts interethnic social acceptance, and breaking bread celebrates economic solidarity." All of these practices are worship, ministry, doxology, and celebratory, and are mandatory. "They are actions of God, in and with, through and under what men and women do. Where they are happening, the people of God is real in the world."[160]

The body politics of the church form the shape of political faithfulness, from which Yoder draws the following general political lessons - a) we are called to a believing view of world history. "The modern world is a subset of the world vision of the gospel, not the other way around. That means we can afford to begin with the gospel notions themselves and then work out from there, as our study has done, rather than beginning with the 'real world' out there (someone else's definition of 'the nature of things') and then trying to place the call of God within it;"[161] b) respect the world's unbelief; c) there is a real common agenda, a concrete historical presence among neighbors as believers in Jesus who do ordinary things differently. "They fraternize trans-ethnically; they share their bread; they forgive one another. These activities are visible; they are not opaque rituals. They lend themselves to being observed, imitated, and extrapolated;"[162] d) there is no dichotomy of substance, and therefore firm dualism, separating Christ from culture or creation from redemption must be rejected; e) disciples are called not to rule but to serve; f) the good news derived from the redemption of Christ is good news for the whole world; g) the believing community, not the individual is the pivot of change; h) Jesus' fundamental political choice was one of suffering Servanthood; i) since Jesus told people to do these things, they are authoritative; j) these practices are spoken of in social process terms and as such serve as a paradigm, and so people who do not share the faith can learn from them. Therefore, the church is both present in and foreign to the world at the same time, which are two sides of the same coin.[163] Briefly put, where O'Donovan searches for political theorems and architectonic structures, Yoder looks to the practices of the church to shape political theology, a move that is not without its dangers.

Yoder's confidence that the church's practices can be translated into non-religious terms puts him in danger of slipping into the "common tendency of functionalizing religious practice as the source for political vision and action,"

---

[160] Yoder, *Body Politics*, 72.
[161] Yoder, *Body Politics*, 72.
[162] Yoder, *Body Politics*, 75.
[163] Yoder, *Body Politics*, 71-80.

or so argues Bernd Wannenwetsch,[164] who is concerned that Yoder wants more than he can get from church practices as models for secular society. That is, particular church practices such as eucharistic celebration and baptism, which Yoder wants to be more than just church practices, are of course about sharing and egalitarianism, but these practices, when stripped of their Christian specificity, become less than they were meant to be. For example, the sharing in the eucharistic celebration is not a case of "generous condescension" but a "sharing together *in* the goods that God has provided for us." Likewise baptismal egalitarianism may well be scandalous if the differences overcome are political and economic ones. Wannenwetsch warns Yoder that a too direct line is being drawn between civil imperatives to church practices, which "buys too readily into the idea of translatability for one language to another without loss."[165]

O'DONOVAN: THE CHURCH AS POLITICAL SOCIETY

In O'Donovan's account of the authorization of the church, Jesus stands at the transition between the ages where the passing and coming authorities confront one another, and, in the form of the church, the future age has a social and political presence. Therefore, the dual authority tradition, in which two powerful and authorized political communities (although differently powerful and unequally authorized) are seen, is essentially sound, according to O'Donovan. A theological account of how this world is ruled must proceed from and through an account of the church.[166] O'Donovan fleshes out his account of the church in considerable detail via two assertions about Christ's rule in the church, a discussion of some positive criteria for ecclesiology and a description of the recapitulation of the four moments of the Christ-event within the life of the church.

The first of these assertions describes the church as having the true character of a political society, by which O'Donovan means that the church

> is brought into being and held in being, not by a special function it has to fulfill, but by a government that it obeys in everything. It is ruled and authorized by the ascended Christ alone and supremely; it therefore has its own authority; and it is not answerable to any other authority that may attempt to subsume it.[167]

The key point O'Donovan makes here is that Israel does not represent the

---

[164] Bernd Wannenwetsch, "Liturgy," in Cavanaugh and Scott, eds. *Blackwell Companion to Political Theology*, 88.
[165] Wannenwetsch, "Liturgy," 88. See also Wannenwetsch, *Political Worship: Ethics for Christian Citizens*, trans. Margaret Kohl (Oxford: Oxford University Press, 2004).
[166] O'Donovan, *The Desire of the Nations*, 158-59.
[167] O'Donovan, *The Desire of the Nations*, 159.

church. To lose sight of the church's rooting in the Christ-event is to cease to understand it as a society ruled by another king, which opens the church to the danger of becoming accommodationist and territorial.[168]

The second of O'Donovan's assertions is that the political character of the church, its essential nature as a governed society, is hidden, to be discerned by faith. From within, the church is a community of freedom and obedience, a society formed by Christ; from the outside, the church presents the appearance of a functional religious organism rather than a political one. This results in the "paradoxical combination of independence and conformity to local law and custom."[169] That is, the church may function internally by way of forgiveness, reconciliation and so on, but the God-authorized secular space works according to judgment, extending mercy, but not forgiveness. O'Donovan devotes an entire chapter in *The Ways of Judgment* to an extended discussion of the notion of mercy as a legitimate dimension of public judgment. The extension of mercy is based on "a reflective self-transcendence evoked by the recognition that judgment is imperfect."[170] Mercy based on such "partial and conditioned reflections that we may from time to time be given to display" is not the same as the forgiveness displayed in the church.[171] Even the embodiment of forgiveness within the church must be acknowledged as provisional, since the counter-politics of the church are themselves constrained by the eschatological 'not yet.' That is to say, while the church may model the coming eschatological community in which full forgiveness and reconciliation will be realized, the church is not identical to that eschatological community.[172] Therefore, political theology does not simply consist in ecclesial self-description, but rather is a reckoning with the difference between ecclesiology and that which leads out to the missionary horizon, "where the church encounters the 'other' that is summoned into the church, the world that God is redeeming."[173]

Nonetheless, the self-description of the church remains an important element of church life. The positive criteria for ecclesiology put forward by O'Donovan have to do with the sacramental order of the church's ministry prior to any other order of ministry. The sacraments bind the church together, and give some institutional form and order. From here O'Donovan shows how the life of the church recapitulates the four moments of the Christ-event that he is working

---

[168] O'Donovan, *The Desire of the Nations*, 162.
[169] O'Donovan, *The Desire of the Nations*, 166.
[170] O'Donovan, *The Ways of Judgment*, 95.
[171] O'Donovan, *The Ways of Judgment*, 100. The extension of mercy within the conventional political arena might be seen as an example of the exercise of absolute power, given that the decision to extend mercy (or not) remains in the hands of those in power, in terms of who is to receive mercy, and what the nature of such an exception might be. Thus the one who controls the exception is the absolute ruler even in the case of showing mercy.
[172] O'Donovan, *The Ways of Judgment*, 261.
[173] O'Donovan, *The Ways of Judgment*, 239.

with—in response to the Advent of Christ, the church is a gathering community that is both given and aspires to unity, a process expressed by the practice of baptism; in response to the Passion of Christ, the church is a suffering community that imitates the suffering of Christ in its double representation of the righteous God and sinful humanity, a process displayed in the Eucharist; in response to the Restoration of Christ the church is a joyful community that practices worship, confession and mutual forgiveness, processes marked by the keeping of the Lord's Day;[174] and in response to the Exaltation of Christ, the church is a proclaiming community that speaks the words of God in prophecy and prayer, as seen in the practice of the laying on of hands in confirmation, ordination and the anointing of the sick.

Political Authority and the State

A key distinction between the theopolitical projects of Yoder and O'Donovan is brought to view in their respective positions regarding the authorization (or not) of secular power. O'Donovan's view holds that the nations are subject to Christ's rule, which is also visible in secular authority, albeit with the understanding that the defeat of any worldly powers is to be understood as true only eschatologically, presumes that if the mission of the church needs a certain social space for men and women of every nation to be drawn into the governed community of God's kingdom, then secular authority is authorized to provide and ensure that space.[175] This authorization of secular space by Jesus opens the way to become involved in that realm as an expression of obedience to Jesus Christ, and, since this space is differently authorized than the church, suggests that action taken in secular space may be different than that taken in the church.

Yoder's 'apocalyptic stance' dictates that the church must refuse any form of 'grabbing the handles of history' in order to control its direction. While Christ's lordship has visible consequences in history, and the church lives in hope of the ultimate consummation of Christ's victory, it also lives in tension until such a time. Thus Yoder's partially realized eschatology calls for the church to embody as fully as it can the life modeled after the example of Jesus in light of the future fulfillment of the kingdom, but at the same time cautions against all attempts to make claims that suggest it is possible to bring about God's kingdom either in the church or in the world. To make such a claim would be to move too far toward a realized eschatology.

---

[174] O'Donovan, *The Desire of the Nations*, 174-92. There is a typographical error in the text on 181, where the *third* moment is named as Christ's exaltation—O'Donovan means "restoration."

[175] O'Donovan, *The Desire of the Nations*, 146.

YODER: 'NO STATE AS SUCH'

Whereas O'Donovan's understanding of secular power includes separate authorization for the state, a rump authority expressed especially in its juridical role, in which the government is called to exercise judgment, Yoder's account of the secular government calls for a much more modest role, whereby the state is simply one of the powers which is necessary for the ordering of society, but has no separate authorization of its own. Because the rule of God is displayed in Christ and lived out in the church, Yoder sees no reason for having a doctrine of the state as such, but sees the state as another entity that seeks to establish order by an appeal to force.[176] Nevertheless, the reign of Christ means for the state the obligation to serve by encouraging good and restraining evil, in other words to provide social cohesion. The witness to the state has never been based on a theory about what the state is and should be in itself – nor rendered for the sake of the state 'in itself.'[177] Thus Yoder finds no particular space for the state, but "the cross of Christ together with the community which takes up that cross as the shape of its own mandate are thus found in the sociopolitical space where the new creation is in conflict with the old."[178] Where O'Donovan specifically finds theological space for the authorization of secular power, albeit differently authorized than the church, Yoder finds space only for the authorization of the church.

If a fixed notion of the state as such is unnecessary, the question is what remains for any kind of secular power, and does the church then have anything to say to secular power. Basically Yoder claims that the state has to be accepted because it can provide order to society - we need it, yet it is fallen. He clearly wants to challenge the idea that by virtue of some divine institution of government by God's good creation, the state's mandate (sword) and the Christian duty to obey the state place on the Christian a moral duty to participate in legal killing, which Yoder claims is the traditional reading of Romans 13:1-7. Yoder challenges such a reading in a series of affirmations that derive from his own understanding of Romans 13:1-7.[179]

---

[176] Yoder says that there is no state as such in *Christian Attitudes to War and Peace,* 452. According to Yoder, this is a position drawn from early Anabaptist sources, whose rejection of the church-state tie was a reflection or deduction from their concept of the nature of Christian discipleship and community, not a topic in its own right. Therefore, the free church denies that the course of secular history and the structures of society are the most significant measures of whether people are doing the will of God. Yoder, *The Royal Priesthood,* 68. See also Craig Carter's comments in *The Politics of the Cross,* 150.

[177] Yoder, *The Christian Witness to the State,* 5, 77.

[178] Harink, *Paul Among the Postliberals,* 110.

[179] Yoder develops this reading of Romans 13:1-7, and delineates his series of affirmations in *The Politics of Jesus* in his chapter "Let Every Soul Be Subject." **First, the New Testament speaks in many ways about the problem of the state; and Romans 13 is not the center of this teaching.** For example, a strong strand of Gospel

teaching sees secular government as the province of the sovereignty of Satan, as can be seen in the account of the temptation of Christ in the desert, and in Revelation 13, where the powers persecute the true believers. Romans 13, at most, calls for acquiescence to a pagan government, not the accrediting of a given state by God – not a "state as such." Here is a statement of the church's view of government that is strikingly less simple and affirmative than the traditional interpretation of Romans 13.

Second, in the structure of the epistle, chapters 12 and 13 in their entirety form one literary unit. Therefore, the text 13:1-7 cannot be understood alone. Chapter 12 constitutes a call to non-conformity, suffering, and 13:8-10 deals with the concept of love. Therefore any interpretation of Romans 13:1-7 must also be an expression a suffering and serving love. Indeed, the entire text of Romans 12 and 13 sees Christian nonconformity and suffering love as driven and drawn by a sense of God's triumphant movement from the merciful past into a triumphant future, which implies that there nothing static or conservative here, and neither is there a notion that Christians are called to execute vengeance and wrath on anyone, since that is God's role, but nevertheless is one that is executed by the secular power. At any rate, the function exercised by government is not the function to be exercised by Christians. But God can 'use' Assyria, for example, which creates a possible scenario in which such action can take place without declaring that the destructive action by pagan powers which God thus 'uses' is morally good or that participation in it is required by God's people. Therefore vengeance/wrath is within providential control and is not to be exercised by Christians.

Third, the subordination that is called for recognizes whatever power exists, accepts whatever structures of sovereignty happen to prevail. The text does not affirm, as the tradition has it, a divine act of institution or ordination of a particular government. Yoder here resists both what he terms the 'positivistic' view, that government exists by revelation, and the "normative" view, which suggests that the principle of government is ordained, so that when government lives up to expectations it can claim the sanction of divine institution, but if it does not, it loses its authority, a view that opens up the possibility of participation in 'just rebellion.' One expression of this 'normative' view is the juxtaposition of Romans 13 with Revelation 13, wherein the Romans passage depicts the 'good' state, while the Revelations passage reveals the 'evil' state which glorifies itself religiously and therefore must be resisted by Christians. However, it is better to say that these two passages "represent the two dimensions of the life of any state." According to Yoder then, neither text calls for active moral support or religious approval of the state; but both texts call for subordination to whatever powers that be. Put another way, "God is not said to *create* or *institute* or *ordain* the powers that be, but only to *order* them, to put them in order, sovereignly to tell them where they belong, what is their place...What the text says is that God orders them, brings them into line, providentially and permissively lines them up with divine purposes." Paul is not making a metaphysical, but a moral statement about the God and the state: God orders powers.

Fourth, the Romans are instructed to be subject to a government in whose administration they had no voice. The text cannot mean that Christians are called to do military or police service. Military and police service were hereditary professions or citizen's privileges, but not required of all citizens. The important point for Yoder is that the government did not ask of its citizens participation in bearing the sword of government.

Yoder concludes that Romans (along with other New Testament teaching) calls for subordination but not obedience to the state, a stance that may well include suffering, which is logical, given Yoder's emphasis on what the larger call to discipleship entails. Yoder sees no contradiction between the demands of discipleship outlined in the Sermon on the Mount and the discussion of the state in Romans 13. "They *both* call Christians to respect and be subject to the historical process in which the sword continues to be wielded and to bring about a kind of order under fire, but not to perceive in the wielding of the sword their own reconciling ministry."[180] While Yoder does focus on Romans 13 in his discussion of the Christian view of the state, there is a sense in which his concern is to read that passage correctly, but perhaps even more so to show that this single brief passage is in fact not the centerpiece of that view. The state itself is not central to the Christian view of the state. Rather, the center is the Christian disciple who lives out a faithful life within a community of suffering love. Yoder deals with some of these issues in two early essays - "The State in the New Testament," and "Following Christ as a Form of Political Responsibility." These essays show Yoder working out the material that later becomes part of his *Christian Witness to the State* and *The Politics of Jesus*. For example, he shows that Christians believers are often inclined to think of political involvement as somehow attempting to work within given governmental structures – the attempt to control who is elected, get things done by wielding political power as conventionally understood. Yoder argues that the ultimate justification for the mandate of the state is to be found within the mandate of the church. The church is often seen as a support system for the state, but Yoder insists that "the Christian faith inverted this relationship and viewed the world-embracing empire as merely a support system, subservient to the real work God is accomplishing in the world." Put another way, the state is there for the sake of the church. In contrast to the notion that in order to have

---

Fifth, the function of bearing the sword to which Christians are called to be subject is the judicial and police function; it does not refer to the death penalty or to war. The sword referred to in this passage is a symbol of judicial authority, not a weapon of war or capital punishment, a description which is not meant to deny that the Roman government had those weapons and was committed to using them. What interests Yoder here is the structural difference between war and policing in areas such as the object of the application of force, the review of action by higher authorities, and so on. When the appropriate distinctions are not made, then it becomes possible to extend the logic of 'just war' to what should be the logic of the limited violence of police authority.

Sixth, the Christian who accepts subjection to the government retains moral independence and judgment. The authority of government is not self-justifying. Whatever government exists is ordered by God; but the text does not say that whatever government does or asks of its citizens is good. Yoder, *The Politics of Jesus,* 193-211.

[180] Yoder, *The Politics of Jesus,* 210.

Jesus is Lord 123

any effect in this world, standards foreign to the Christian way might have to be adopted, Yoder points to the priority of the church.[181]

O'DONOVAN: SEPARATE AUTHORIZATION OF SECULAR POWER

O'Donovan's theopolitical project reaches a turning point with the completion of his description of the display of God's rule in Israel, in the coming of the Kingdom in Jesus' ministry, and in the four moments of the Christ-event. Now it is possible to see that the "kingly rule of Christ is God's own rule exercised over the whole world."[182] The nations are subjected to this rule in that Christ, the desire of the nations, has come. This rule is visible in the church, which is an important element in O'Donovan's political theology, but Christ's rule is also visible in secular authority, albeit with the understanding that the defeat of any worldly powers is to be understood as true eschatologically. That is, the powers are subject to Christ's exaltation, but this subjection awaits Christ's final universal presence to become fully apparent. Between the assertion of the reality of Christ's victory and the future display, "there opens up an account of secular authority which presumes neither that the Christ-event never occurred nor that the sovereignty of Christ is now transparent and uncontested."[183]

The description of secular authority in the New Testament follows from the understanding that the authority of the risen Christ is present in the church's mission. If the mission of the church needs a certain social space for men and women of every nation to be drawn into the governed community of God's kingdom, then secular authority is authorized to provide and ensure that space.[184]

An appropriate understanding of the authorization of both church and secular authority (although differently powerful and unequally authorized)[185] is the burden of much of the remainder of O'Donovan's project. Regarding

---

[181] Yoder, *Discipleship as Political Responsibility*. According to Doug Harink's analysis of Yoder, the social and political order of God's new *polis* in Jesus Christ is always being enacted in the midst of other societies and policies. The logic of *The Politics of Jesus* is one "that leads from the politics of Jesus in Israel to the politics of Paul and the Pauline churches. Yoder explicates the way in which Romans 13 is also the good news of Jesus' nonviolent victory over the powers and structures which hold humankind in bondage." Harink, *Paul Among the Postliberals,* 142. Harink claims that Yoder is not interested in providing a 'theology of the state;' nevertheless the state exists, and the church exists in a relationship to the governing authorities as it does to other authorities. The church is in no sense indebted to nor does it receive any mandate from the ruling powers – the church is simply subordinate to the powers. Harink, *Paul Among the Postliberals,* 142-145.

[182] O'Donovan, *The Desire of the Nations*, 146.
[183] O'Donovan, *The Desire of the Nations*, 146.
[184] O'Donovan, *The Desire of the Nations*, 146.
[185] O'Donovan, *The Desire of the Nations*, 158.

authorized secular authority, O'Donovan especially presses the point that an appropriate concept of political authority in the Gospel era must recognize that the "rationale of secular government is seen to rest on the capacity to effect the judicial task."[186] Drawing on Pauline writings (especially Romans 13:1-7), O'Donovan sees the political element of possession of the law as privileged over other themes of salvation, judgment, or praise. No form of government ought to be the locus of collective identity, but the judicial principle that serves the general needs of the world must be respected by all people, including Christian believers.[187] Put another way, the principalities and powers, although overcome by Christ in his death and resurrection, still hold sway, but in a way that serves the church's mission. It is this remaining authority, which includes "a more positive affirmation of the government's role than there could be at the moment of the Kingdom's challenge to all settled authorities,"[188] that forms the foundation of secular authority, an authority which can deal only in provisional and penultimate judgments. Thus while secular authorities are not mediators of the rule of God in a full sense, but only the mediator of judgments, there is nonetheless a "rump of political authority which cannot be dispensed with yet...the theme of Romans 13 is the authority which remains to secular government in the aftermath of Christ's triumph." [189]

This separate authorization of both church and secular authority recognizes that the rationale of secular government is seen to rest primarily on the capacity to effect the judicial task, and asserts that while no form of government ought to be the locus of collective identity, the judicial principle that serves the general needs of the world must be respected by all people, including Christian believers. The political authority displayed in acts of judgment is not specific to any one institution. Rather, authority, according to O'Donovan, is an occurrence that arises as judgment is performed.[190] In this sense, we stumble on political authority, and may devise institutions to channel that authority, institutions provided by God for the flourishing of humanity.[191] Any legitimate bearer of such authority is one who defends the common good,[192] which "arises where power, the execution of right, and the perpetuation of tradition are

---

[186] O'Donovan, *The Desire of the Nations*, 148.

[187] The Christian community is called to practices of its own, such as love, forgiveness and so on, which mark the life of the church that submits to the ultimate judgments of God, and which is important for political theology as well.

[188] O'Donovan, *The Desire of the Nations*, 149.

[189] O'Donovan, *The Desire of the Nations*, 151.

[190] O'Donovan, *The Ways of Judgment*, 128.

[191] O'Donovan, *The Ways of Judgment*, 128.

[192] O'Donovan understands common good as: a) right; and b) the flourishing of a particular society with a particular identity (that is, tradition). O'Donovan, *The Ways of Judgment*, 139-140.

assured together in one coordinated agency."[193]

This rump of political authority that remains to secular government in the aftermath of Christ's triumph, according to O'Donovan is the theme of Romans 13:1-7, and thus he finds Yoder's reading of this passage to be misleading in several ways. First, O'Donovan admits that he could be comfortable with Yoder's statement made in *The Original Revolution* (1971), where Yoder understands the text of Romans 13 to "give criteria for judging to what extent a state's activities (since the state incarnates this semisubdued evil) are subject to Christ's reign. If the use of force is such as to protect the innocent and punish the evildoer, then the state may be considered as fitting within God's plan as subject to the reign of Christ," since here Yoder allows for Christ's triumph and the state's subjection, or at least semisubjection.[194] But O'Donovan understands Yoder to make a major break with this line of interpretation in *The Christian Witness to the State* (1964) and in chapter 10 of *The Politics of Jesus* (1972), where Yoder ostensibly uses language of principalities and powers to "point up the demonic character of the state, requiring 'at best acquiescence,' and the whole text was a call to 'a nonresistant attitude towards a tyrannical government... with which I find it impossible to reconcile Paul's statements that the authorities praise those who do good, and that obedience is due 'as a matter of principled conviction.'"[195] O'Donovan is also critical of Yoder's notion that Romans 13 refers not to war or capital punishment but to police function. This O'Donovan sees as an anachronism, since the text "knew of no civil order that was not maintained by soldiers. This distinction, like the question of whether Christians are permitted to engage in military service, is simply not envisaged by the text."[196] Further, O'Donovan dismisses Yoder's characterization of the difference between a law-state and a totalitarian state as two dimensions in the life of any state.[197]

But O'Donovan's glancing comments regarding Yoder's treatment of Romans 13 specifically and the state more generally are not entirely fair to Yoder's work, and the charge of inconsistency must be attenuated considerably. It would seem odd that Yoder would assert one thing in 1971, and break with that position both in 1964 and in 1972, as O'Donovan suggests. Yoder's statement in *The Original Revolution*, quoted approvingly by O'Donovan, is also quoted inaccurately. Whereas O'Donovan quotes Yoder as saying that "*the*

---

[193] O'Donovan, *The Ways of Judgment*, 142. This statement is a reiteration of O'Donovan's first of the 6 political theorems which he put forward early in *The Desire of the Nations*, 46.

[194] O'Donovan's complaints about Yoder are found in *The Desire of the Nations*, 151-152. He is quoting Yoder, *The Original Revolution*, 59ff.

[195] O'Donovan, *The Desire of the Nations*, 151.

[196] O'Donovan, *The Desire of the Nations*, 152.

[197] O'Donovan's reference is to Yoder, *The Christian Witness to the State*, 77, where he suggests that Romans 13 and Revelation 13 are the two faces of the state in the New Testament.

state may be considered as fitting within God's plan as subject to the reign of Christ," Yoder actually refers not to *the* state, but claims that "If the use of force is such as to protect the innocent and punish the evildoers, to preserve peace so that 'all men might come to the knowledge of the truth,' then *that* state may be considered as fitting within God's plan, as subject to the reign of Christ."[198] As is the case in Yoder's other works, he is not here suggesting any notion of the state as such, an entity that is given some status because of Christ's triumph. Yoder of course does not deny the significance of Christ's triumph, but is arguing that the lordship of Christ means that the new aeon revealed in Christ takes primacy over the old, and will finally vanquish that old aeon, of which the state is a part, and which is given no new authorization because of the triumph of Christ, a position that is consistent with Yoder's work in *The Christian Witness to the State* and *The Politics of Jesus*.

Further, O'Donovan's critique of Yoder' putative anachronism regarding the police function of the state must be examined closely. Yoder does not so much say that the reference to the sword in Romans 13 is to someone other than soldiers, but rather he makes the point that the Roman military did not serve only as executors of criminals or as a war machine, but that it also filled a police function, and interestingly for the conversation with O'Donovan, a judicial function.[199] That is, it is just when the Roman state functions *as* police and judiciary that the Christian is to be subject, a point with which O'Donovan would be sympathetic, although his is a much more robust view of the judicial function of the state as part of the reign of Christ in the world. Nonetheless, it would be misleading to suggest that Yoder is dismissive of the work of the state, or the church's constructive political engagement

Jesuology and Christology in Political Theology

O'Donovan's pressing of a political theology centered on Christology, and Yoder's putting forward of a Jesuology as the basis of political theology have brought to view a number of commonalities - a focus on the Christ-event (advent, death, resurrection and exaltation of Jesus), the life, teaching, and ministry of Jesus of Nazareth, the eschatological dimension of the New Testament, the role of the church in political theology, and the authorization of the state in light of the work of Jesus.

Yoder's reading of Jesus' ministry and teaching, the logic of cross and resurrection, Jesus' defeat of the powers, and the apocalyptic stance lead to 'Jesulogical' criteria for the meaningfulness of human experience under God. That is, the particularity of Jesus in the incarnation is basic to understanding what things mean, what is to be spoken, things that must be tested at the bar not so much of relevance as of resonance with the person of Jesus, and Yoder

---

[198] Yoder, *The Original Revolution*, 59-60. Italics added.
[199] Yoder, *The Politics of Jesus*, 203.

seems willing to risk accusations of reductionism in order to mark this point, to the extent of using the language of 'Jesuology' instead of the more conventional 'Christology.'[200] Therefore, says Yoder, our criteria must be not merely "Christological" in some vague, cosmic sense, but "Jesulogical," namely, concrete deeds of suffering servanthood, a cruciform pattern vindicated by the resurrection and that awaits eschatological consummation. Therefore, while some may appeal to the Father, others to the Spirit, others to the Cosmic Christ or to the Trinity as a whole as warrants for learning from 'creation' or 'nature' or 'history' other lessons than those of the incarnation, the apostolic witness insisted that any 'larger' claims for Christ as preexistent, as creator or cosmic victor, must not be disengaged from the man Jesus and the cross.[201] This way of the cross, the logical outcome of challenging the powers of the day, provides the pattern Yoder calls the 'politics of Jesus,' which the church is called to recapitulate as the way to be political in the world. In addition, Yoder's apocalyptic stance leads him to reject attempts to take control of the secular political realm, since to do so would be to reject the politics of Jesus. Secular power, which exists for the sake of the church to provide order, not authorized by God separately from the church, is not to be ignored by the church, but the church is called to witness to that secular power.

O'Donovan's reading of Jesus' life and ministry, the logic of cross and resurrection, and his eschatologically-charged understanding of the triumph of Christ lead him to political conceptualizations that are fully Christological. In order to avoid a naïve and illusory notion of following Jesus that cannot extend beyond the church, O'Donovan insists that the triumph of Christ authorizes not only the church, but also secular power. This enables O'Donovan to make a critical move whereby he understands the political realities of the secular realm to be of a provisional, penultimate nature, which in the final consummation will give way to the ultimate judgments of God. But to misunderstand or ignore the provisional realm of the secular, that world vindicated by the resurrection of Christ, is to be unfaithful to Christ.

Yoder and O'Donovan understand the shape and nature of Christian political theology as it might be instantiated in the world quite differently. This is brought into relief not only in direct comparison of their reading of the Bible, but in their respective interpretations of the Christian experience during the historical era of Christendom, as well as the legitimacy of and church's participation in (or not) the use of violence in the secular realm.

---

[200] Craig Carter, in trying to defend Yoder against charges of a reductionist Christology, refuses to use Yoder's own term (Jesuology), believing that it distracts the reader from recognizing Yoder's fully orthodox Christology. Carter, *The Politics of the Cross*, chapters 3 and 4, especially page 93.

[201] Yoder, *For the Nations*, 241-242.

Chapter 3

The Secular and the Eternal:
A Contested Reading of Christendom

Introduction

Yoder and O'Donovan's biblically-based theopolitical projects are both extended into readings of historical instantiation of Christian political thought into specific cultural forms. The variegated experiences of the Christian church from periods of intense persecution to the exercise of virtually total temporal power come under the theological scrutiny of Yoder and O'Donovan, as they attempt to trace and learn from the development of Christian political thought, and to discern the faithfulness or unfaithfulness of the Christian church to the message of the Bible. Central to their respective readings of church history for political theology is an understanding of Christendom. Yoder and O'Donovan disagree in significant ways regarding Christendom, and it is in uncovering these differences that it will become possible to see more clearly the implications of a theological reading of the Bible for political theology. Briefly put, O'Donovan believes Christendom to be a legitimate Christian tradition, from which much positive guidance can be taken for contemporary political theology, while Yoder sees Christendom as an era of the church's unfaithful acquiescence to the various temptations of secular power, a time of formation of a specious symbiotic relationship between the church and secular power - a phenomenon he labels as 'Constantinianism.' I will argue that Yoder conflates Christendom and Constantianism and criticizes them both as a simple type, that O'Donovan's view of Christendom is not Constantinian, and that these disparate readings of Christendom are based in large part on differing theologies of history, which in turn leads to disparate views of the political responsibility of the church.

O'Donovan's account of Christendom cannot be reduced to a Yoderian caricature of Constantinianism, since O'Donovan's contested history of this Christian tradition takes the church seriously, seeks to be aware of temptations to civil religion and illegitimate use of coercion by the state on behalf of religion, and is careful to keep the appropriate distinctions between the age that is passing away and the age that has come but is not yet present in its fullness. Nonetheless, even if O'Donovan's retrieval of Christendom is not

Constantinian, his understanding does not coincide with Yoder's view. That is, they do not share some sort of fundamental agreement regarding the nature of Christendom with only nuances of meaning to separate their views, and the differences between them here are important for the shaping of their respective conceptions of constructive political engagement. For O'Donovan, Christendom is the process of an alien power becoming attentive to the mission of the church; for Yoder, Christendom is the process of the church making an unfaithful agreement with an alien power. O'Donovan warns that once Christendom is in place, the church must exercise great care not to yield to temptations of power that might compromise the church's mission; Yoder warns the church not to yield to the temptation of Christendom itself. O'Donovan affirms an analogy between the church and the order of early modern liberalism insofar as it acknowledges the triumph of Christ; Yoder agrees that church practices can have social instantiations in any society, but these are not necessarily connected to liberalism, and certainly not to Christendom, which is largely captured by Constantinianism. Nonetheless, according to Yoder, a great variety of involvements in society are possible for Christians – often by way of analogy to Christian practices - even if those believers do not assume that the sword is necessary. [1]

These views of Christendom are related to differing understandings of history. Since O'Donovan's Christendom is not by nature Constantinian, his historical project is one of retrieval of the Christian tradition, with the attendant disclaimer that this is a contested history. Nevertheless, it takes seriously the notion that history is the theater of God's activity, and so O'Donovan can fully embrace the task of drawing on the sources of Christendom to retrieve for Christian political theology a tradition that moves beyond the suspicious stance of modernity, which is precisely the stance that O'Donovan seeks to oppose,[2] a stance which he suspects Yoder holds.

Since Yoder sees Christendom as Constantinian, his reading of history becomes a re-reading of history, not searching for retrieval or reformation, but restitution of the church to faithfulness to Jesus Christ. He believes reformation to be impossible in the case of Christendom, since efforts to reform it are themselves captured by the very things they hope to change. Instead, restitution, which is possible, or rather, required, can only take place with the appropriate view of history informed by eschatology. "An ahistorical bias is incompatible with restitutionism; historiography is theologically necessary. By standing in judgment on particular fruits of historical development such as the state/church linkage, episcopacy, and pedobaptism, restitutionism accepts the challenge to be critical of history and thereby to take it more seriously than do those for whom some other criterion than the New Testament determines the

---

[1] Yoder, *The Priestly Kingdom*, 165-166.
[2] O'Donovan, *The Desire of the Nations*, 6-12.

faithfulness of the church."[3] Therefore, much of Yoder's discussion of Christendom centers on his view of what might constitute an appropriate theology of history.

An important distinction between O'Donovan and Yoder on Christendom concerns eschatological understanding. While they share the view that it is important to distinguish between the passing age and the coming age, O'Donovan's focus on the triumph of Christ leaves him vulnerable to the charge that the coming age is too scrutable, that there is not enough eschatological tension in his political theology. For example, O'Donovan's insistence that the state is minimally representative and coercive includes a view of responsibility which assumes that if the triumph of Christ is visible, then Christians must assume at least provisional and penultimate responsibility which includes coercion – not to defend or promote the church (as in Constantinianism), but coercion nonetheless. Christian political responsibility therefore includes taking at least some control of secular power in judicial form.

Yoder's rejection of Christendom is based on his apocalyptic historiography, which assumes that the church must live in light of a future that is in God's hands. Since this is the case, the church cannot presume to take control of secular power as a way to do the work of God, but instead is called to be faithful to the call of God. Yoder therefore assumes that the church has responsibility, but not primarily to control or shape the judgments of government – or at any rate, it is not those judgments that display the triumph of Christ. Rather it is the church that is representative of the triumph of Christ, and therefore responsible in the world. The practices of the body of Christ are translated into societal norms, so the responsibility of the church to the risen Lord is the exercise of responsibility to society.

Christendom: Great Reversal or Great Tradition?

In its simplest terms, there is a fundamental disagreement between Yoder and O'Donovan concerning Christendom, in which Yoder argues that it is a 'great reversal,' while O'Donovan understands it as part of a 'great tradition.' Yoder's theopolitical reading of the Old Testament as the account of God's faithful people on pilgrimage in the world, seeking the peace of the city in which they find themselves, and of the New Testament as the calling out of a cruciform servant community practicing the politics of Jesus lead him to be wary of any notion that would see a symbiotic relationship between the church and the secular state. Despite the vigilance that marks this particular kind of separation of church and state, Yoder is nonetheless insistent that the church serves the world, and that secular power has a legitimate role to play, namely, providing an orderly structure within which the church can discharge her mission, which

---

[3] Yoder, *The Priestly Kingdom,* 127.

is fatally compromised if the church succumbs to the temptations that he believes to be inherent within Christendom. Yoder's views do not preclude constructive political engagement, provided such engagement is not unfaithful, or in his terms, Constantinian.

Yoder's understanding of Christendom cannot be separated from his reading of Constantinianism, which is simultaneously perhaps his most contested and most influential concept.[4] Whereas O'Donovan is keen to have political theology learn as much as possible from the Christian tradition of Christendom, understood as an historical era, Yoder finds in Christendom almost exclusively a turning away of the church from faithfulness. That is, Christendom is by its nature intrinsically Constantinian, with only minimal (and almost exclusively theoretical) constructive possibilities for the church that has 'fallen' into the various temptations on offer in Christendom. Yoder has garnered criticism that suggests there is not enough appreciation for God's work in the wider world or appropriate acknowledgement of the church's many intersections with society.[5] Yet Yoder's theopolitical thought does not in fact ignore the wider world. Rather, in a statement that sounds remarkably like O'Donovan, Yoder asserts that the world is God's theatre of divinely purposeful action,[6] although their respective understandings of how that action is to be understood are not identical. Yoder's recognition and acknowledgement of divinely purposeful action calls for appropriate discernment to ensure that the church does not pursue faithfulness to God in the theatre of the world via illegitimate worldly means. The most powerful symbol of precisely this temptation to embrace worldly means is Constantine, whose name Yoder turns into a noun that stands as a symbol for what must be understood as the 'fall' of the church – namely, 'Constantinianism', which briefly put, "is the identification of church and world in the mutual approval and support exchanged by Constantine and the bishops."[7] Put another way, "the Roman emperor who began to tolerate, then supported, then administered, then finally joined the church, soon became and has remained until our time the symbol of a sweeping shift in the nature of the empirical church and its relation to the world."[8] Constantinianism continues in the form of Christendom, and thus, "for a millennium and a half, European Christians have been identifying faith in Jesus Christ, for themselves and for

---

[4] Alain Epp Weaver calls Constantinianism "Yoder's most notorious analytical category," unsurpassed in influence and contestation. Alain Epp Weaver, "After Politics," 649.

[5] A. James Reimer is one of the Yoder's Mennonite interlocutors who has come to just this kind of conclusion. Reimer, "Mennonites, Christ, and Culture: The Yoder Legacy," *The Conrad Grebel Review* Volume 16 no 2 (Spring 1998): 9-11.

[6] Yoder, *Preface to Theology*, 256. O'Donovan's similar phrase, "… one public history which is the theatre of God's saving purposes and mankind's social undertakings," is found in *The Desire of the Nations*, 2.

[7] Yoder, *The Royal Priesthood*, 154.

[8] Yoder, *The Royal Priesthood*, 245.

others whom they meet, with an all-encompassing set of ideas and practices largely of Greek, Roman, and Germanic origins. This is 'Christendom' as a total religious-cultural package, in many ways marked more by those other religious cultures than by the Bible."⁹

It is precisely this kind of reading of Christendom that seems to have motivated O'Donovan to address the issue in his own work. His inclusion in *The Desire of the Nations* of a lengthy and richly detailed discussion of Christendom was, by his own description, an "afterthought," without which the formal structure of the book runs quite naturally.¹⁰ O'Donovan makes an important assertion here, namely, that his sympathetic reading of Christendom is not in fact a defence of Christendom but of the formal analogy between the church and the liberal order, a move that he is able to make precisely by taking Christendom seriously, by making it clear that the relation between churchly and secular authority was dictated by the mission of the church. In other words, the formal analogy between the church and the liberal order that O'Donovan expounds finds its justification in the core notion of Christendom, which is the relationship between secular and churchly authority.¹¹

---

⁹ Yoder, *The Royal Priesthood*, 248. Yoder goes as far as to say that "'Christendom' is the word for Europe. It is a geographic expression." Yoder, *Preface to Theology*, 233.

¹⁰ Oliver O'Donovan, "Response to Respondents: Behold the Lamb!" *Studies in Christian Ethics*, 11 no 2 (1998): 103. O'Donovan notes that "the four moments of the Christ-event in chapter 4 are followed by four moments of the church and its sacraments in chapter 5, which lead in turn to four moments of the liberal society which the church produced, first in its true form and then in its corrupt version, in chapter 7." O'Donovan, "Response to Respondents," 7.

¹¹ O'Donovan, "Response to Respondents," 104. Put another way, "O'Donovan's project, then, is an attempt to articulate – via the idea of 'Christendom' – the qualitative changes that resulted with the dawning of the Christian regime over against the former pagan political regimes." Hauerwas and Fodor, "Remaining in Babylon," 40. Despite O'Donovan's disclaimers, he has had to fend off accusations that he is in fact engaged in a spirited defense of Christendom. In addition to the telling subtitle used by Hauerwas and Fodor, others have also assumed that O'Donovan's point is defence. For just one example, see Gilbert Meilaender, "Recovering Christendom," *First Things* 77 (November 1997): 36-42. In a somewhat exasperated tone, O'Donovan disavows such a goal for his project, insisting that "the important thing is not to be *for* Christendom or *against* it – what earthly point could there be in either of these postures, if Christendom is, as everybody seems to agree, not only dead, but quite decomposed? – but to have such a sympathetic understanding of it that we profit from its politico-theological gains and avoid repeating its politico-theological mistakes." O'Donovan, "Response to Respondents: Behold the Lamb!" 103. Italics in original. It is interesting to notice that this passage, embedded within a longer paragraph, appears later as the preface to the paperback edition of *The Desire of the Nations*, followed by a reworked sentence in which he states that "discussion of Christendom should be read, perhaps, not so much as a defence, but as a word of advice to its would-be critics." O'Donovan, *The Desire of the Nations*, ix. Perhaps the placement of this passage in the preface serves to forestall

The particular occasion of O'Donovan's decision to include an entire chapter dealing with Christendom was a rainy walk on the Cotswold escarpment during which he was occupied with Hauerwas's *After Christendom* and Yoder's *The Priestly Kingdom*, and realized that he "could not ask anyone to accept *on trust* that there was a formal analogy between church and liberal order."[12] O'Donovan does not explain clearly what it is about these two books that creates a reaction strong enough to have an additional chapter's worth of argument intrude itself into his previously developed sequence.[13] The present chapter of this book could be seen as an attempt at such an explanation. That is, O'Donovan does not agree that Christendom is by its very nature tainted by unfaithfulness to God. However, he has felt it necessary to deal with Christendom in detail as a way of responding to suspicious readings such as the one put forward by Yoder. O'Donovan is keen to set his work apart from those that are in some way 'for' or 'against' Christendom.

Christendom plays a crucial part in O'Donovan's move from biblical exegesis to discussions of wider society. As he moves beyond an exegetical consideration of the Biblical text to engage a Christian understanding of political and theological realities after the death, resurrection and exaltation of Christ, O'Donovan is careful to note that the political theology he espouses "does not suppose a literal synonymity between the political vocabulary of salvation and the secular use of the same terms."[14] Rather, O'Donovan understands history to be the matrix in which ethics and politics take their shape, and affirms that this matrix is a history of God's purposeful action. History is the theater of God's purposes and the social undertakings of humanity in which we are provided with partial indications of what God is doing, particularly within events of liberation, rule, and community foundation. In order to grasp the full meaning of political events, "we must look to the horizon of God's redemptive purposes."[15] O'Donovan resists speaking

---

further putative misunderstandings of the intentions of O'Donovan's ruminations regarding Christendom.

[12] O'Donovan, "Response to Respondents" 104. Italics in original.

[13] Indeed, Jonathan Chaplin claims that O'Donovan's explanation leaves him "in a fog." Chaplin, "Political Eschatology and Responsible Government," 268. One of the implications of the inclusion of a separate chapter regarding Christendom is that O'Donovan treats society and its rulers separately. That is, he distinguishes between societies and rulers on the basis of their respective destinies: "The former is to be transformed, shaped in conformity to God's purpose; the latter are to disappear, renouncing their sovereignty in the face of his." O'Donovan, *The Desire of the Nations*, 193. The distinction pursued here is not absolute, as seen in the eschatological truth that communities will be incorporated into God's kingdom and rulers will resign all of their pretensions – both being the result of the one conquest contained in Christ's triumph. O'Donovan, *The Desire of the Nations*, 243.

[14] O'Donovan, *The Desire of the Nations*, 2.

[15] O'Donovan, *The Desire of the Nations*, 2, 12.

primarily of political institutions, but focuses insistently on the political act, which he sees as the divinely authorized act, one which, if truthfully described, will establish its conditions, purpose, and mode of execution, and thereby also shed light on political institutions.[16] In an extended treatment of the political act, O'Donovan clarifies his understanding of the coinherence of judgment with the political act. Briefly put, "judgment is an act of moral discrimination that pronounces upon a preceding act or existing state of affairs to establish a new public context."[17] He explains further that the political act of judgment is one in which right is divided from wrong, and is reactive in that it speaks about what is already the case, establishing a public context in which succeeding acts can be performed. This retrospective and prospective act of judgment has as its object a new public context and in this way is distinct from all actions that have as their object private or restricted good.[18] Thus the political act includes the realm of influencing judgment in public, which is why the historical era of Christendom is such an important resource for Christians. That is, as a way of examining the authenticity and authority of the political act, O'Donovan claims that political theology has as a primary resource the historical era of Christendom, to which he turns in order to think about the relationship of Gospel, society and rule.

However, O'Donovan is aware that his justification of the analogy between the church and liberal political order via Christendom has to be "an inconclusive history, a history open to contest," one which, while necessarily contested, nonetheless has "plausible fruitfulness" and which includes the possibility of acknowledging temptations and weaknesses of the church within the historical era of Christendom.[19]

O'Donovan uses the term 'Christendom' to refer to a historical idea: "that is to say, the idea of a professedly Christian secular political order, and the history of that idea in practice. Christendom is an *era,* an era in which the truth of Christianity was taken to be a truth of secular politics… it is the idea of a confessionally Christian government, at once 'secular' (in the proper sense of that word, confined to the present age) and obedient to Christ, a promise of the age of his unhindered rule."[20] The historical parameters of this era lie between AD 313, the date of the promulgation of the Edict of Milan, and 1791, the date of the First Amendment to the American Constitution. O'Donovan subsequently explains more fully that the First Amendment serves as the most

---

[16] O'Donovan, *The Desire of the Nations,* 20. O'Donovan attributes the learning of the term 'political act' to his teacher Paul Ramsey, who taught that the form of the act was decisive for everything else in political theory, and bound together all of politics into one moral field.

[17] O'Donovan, *The Ways of Judgment,* 7.

[18] O'Donovan, *The Ways of Judgment,* 8-10.

[19] O'Donovan, "Response to Respondents," 104, 105.

[20] O'Donovan, *The Desire of the Nations,* 195.

suitable symbolic end of Christendom: "since it propounds a doctrine meant to replace the church-state relations which Christendom had maintained, it was formulated largely by Christians who thought they had the interests of the church at heart, and it was argued for, as it still is, on ostensibly theological grounds."[21] On the basis of this rationale, O'Donovan rejects the French Revolution and World War One as suitable symbolic ends of Christendom, although he does admit that other dates could be found that would do as well as the First Amendment.[22]

YODER AND THE 'CONSTANTINIAN SHIFTS' OF CHRISTENDOM

It is important to clarify further why Yoder sees the historical era of Christendom as a great reversal while O'Donovan sees it as part of a great tradition. In part, this comes to view in discussions of the effects of the conversion of Constantine in the fourth century, along with the attendant political changes such as the end of persecution, and the eventual adoption of the Christian religion as an official religion of the Roman Empire. Where Yoder sees in the Constantinian era a series of actual (unfaithful) shifts from the practices and beliefs of the early church, O'Donovan identifies dangers that the church can avoid if it remains faithful to its mission. Indeed, in

---

[21] O'Donovan, *The Desire of the Nations*, 244.

[22] O'Donovan is challenged several times on just this point. For example, Arne Rasmusson pointedly wonders why 1532, the occasion of Henry VIII's acknowledgement by the English clergy as Supreme Head of the Church, should not serve as the end of Christendom, seeing as this signals the division of the church along state lines. Rasmusson, "Not All Justifications of Christendom Are Created Equal: A Response to Oliver O'Donovan," *Studies in Christian Ethics*, 11 no 2 (1998): 74-75. Colin Greene suggests that the so-called religious wars of the seventeenth century should be seen as the symbolic and historical end of Christendom, since "the unstable conflagration of political and religious interests proves unsustainable," and this series of wars "undermines the theological and political conviction that it could be the one, holy, catholic and apostolic church that guaranteed the political stability of Europe." Colin J.D. Greene, "Revisiting Christendom: A Crisis of Legitimation," in Craig Bartholomew et al., eds., 335. On the question of the religious significance of the First Amendment, using richly detailed historical argument, legal scholar Philip Hamburger shows that the notion of disestablishment as included in the First Amendment was interpreted, especially by Thomas Jefferson, to signify a wall of separation between church and state. Hamburger argues that such a notion was not part of the Amendment itself, which sought instead to differentiate between church and state, and "denote a freedom from laws instituting, supporting, or otherwise establishing religion." However, the Amendment was not designed to create a wall of separation between church and state, as it is so often understood. That is, while differentiation between church and state as well as disestablishment were desired, the religious freedom sought in the constitution was not of the sort that isolated religion from politics. Philip Hamburger, *Separation of Church and State* (Cambridge: Harvard University Press, 2002), 2-3.

O'Donovan's view, it is precisely the church on mission that led to the conversion of the Emperor, and therefore the new developments of that era cannot be defined as unfaithful by nature. To do so would be to deny the triumph of Christ.

Yoder's analysis of ecclesial unfaithfulness can be found scattered throughout numerous listings of critiques he makes of Constantinianism, whether labeled as differences, shifts or compromises. The fundamental point elaborated in these critiques is that the Constantinian approach is constitutionally incapable of making Christ's lordship visible over the church and the world,[23] so that when embraced by the church, Constantinianism ushers in a series of changes for the church, especially in its relation to the secular world.

Yoder argues that one of these changes is the inauguration of a new ecclesiology. Whereas previously it had taken great conviction to be a Christian, in part because of a minority status that sometimes invited official persecution, now it would take great conviction *not* to be one, since the government took up the role of punishing heresies, outlawing paganism, and so forth. So the term 'Christian' changed in meaning to refer to almost everybody, whereas the doctrine of the invisibility of the true church was developed to account for 'true' Christians, who were still a minority. The definitions of the faith could no longer take the visible gathering of worshipping Christians as basic. Instead, those looking for the church had to look for a formalized church hierarchy more than for a people whose lives are patterned after the way of the cross.[24]

Yoder identifies another shift that occurs when attempts at contextual theology become examples of capitulation to loyalties other than the church's basic confession that Jesus is Lord. Yoder does not deny the need for contextual theology, but is adamant that the church must constantly remain committed to contextual theology precisely as part of its missionary stance in the world, which presumes that the church is perpetually crossing new frontiers, and learning new ways of incarnating and expressing its message and mission. Thus as the church crosses new frontiers in time and space, it faces historical and cultural developments that necessarily leave the church vulnerable to changes of many kinds, suggesting that the church has to constantly resist the temptation to capitulate to thought forms or cultural expressions that compromise or warp the faithfulness of the church.[25] The establishment of the

---

[23] Yoder, *The Royal Priesthood*, 61.

[24] Yoder, *The Priestly Kingdom*, 135-136.

[25] A book-length example of Yoder attempting to trace theological development across time and space with an eye to the church's attempts (successful and failing) at faithful contextual theology can be found in his *Preface to Theology*. Regarding developments in theology, Yoder suggests that the more frontiers the church crosses, the greater the need for testing words used by their relationship to the original confession, which he

church under the leadership of Augustine, for example, leads to unfaithful contextual theology in that, while the church still continued to worship, its attempt to provide a form of worship for everyone, not just believers, in effect took over the religious functions of pagan religion that had previously provided for the needs of the larger Roman population. Other changes in ethics, Christian thought, holy celebrations, and so on were all part of the larger attempt to put everything into a single Christian framework in service of Christendom.[26] For example, Yoder uses the move from pacifism to legitimation of war as an example of a model of unfaithfulness within the continuing attempt at faithful contextualization of the gospel. He shows how the move passes through various phases such as rejecting the privileged place of the enemy as the test of whether one loves the neighbor, rejecting the norm of the cross, and assigning to civil government an illegitimate role in carrying out God's will. While the church must always remain open to discovery or retrieval of new or rediscovered expressions of faith, Yoder does not see a Just War undercurrent during the first few centuries waiting to be uncovered. Instead, while Augustine did the best he could, in the end he borrowed far too much from Cicero, and therefore, in providing the Christian undergirding of just war theory, he initiated a reversal and not a faithful contextualization of the Christian faith. The Christian just war thinkers early on were still thinking from a minority position, so they were not underwriting a simple embrace of just war theory, but were basically dragging their feet as they saw Christianity being drawn into administering a corrupt order. Thus, according to Yoder, the early church view that war is wrong was changed into a simple affirmation that war is acceptable if it meets certain requirements that are drawn not so much from the gospel as they are interpretations of Christian beliefs transmuted into Roman and Hellenistic juridical forms.[27]

Yoder also points out that when Christians began to ask questions concerning what the best form of government might be, it is possible to see another example of contextual theology gone awry. Such a question is representative of an already established social posture made possible by the Constantinian moral paradigm. This posture's assumptions about the generalizability of Christian moral thought would not have made any sense to the earliest Christians. To generalize in such a way is to think in terms of the

---

understands as "a procedure that continues to go back to the course and test again when new questions arise and new answers have been proposed." Yoder, *Preface to Theology,* 379. The picture Yoder invokes is that of a stream – within the historical stream, the theologian looks back and forward when pursuing contemporary tasks. Yoder, *Preface to Theology,* 381ff. Similarly, Yoder's treatment of theopolitical questions often takes the form of testing the church's changing relationship to secular power in terms of faithfulness or unfaithfulness.
[26] Yoder, *Preface to Theology,* 231–233.
[27] Yoder, *The Priestly Kingdom,* 74-79.

social whole as an agent; assuming that when one asks what is right for Christians, the answer would be right for the whole of society; believing that putting oneself in the place of the ruler is the appropriate way of asking what is right; focusing on "everyman," testing moral statements by whether they can be applied to everyone.[28]

Where O'Donovan identifies in Christendom (admittedly mixed) evidence of the church pursuing its mission, Yoder sees instead a severely if not fatally compromised mission. That is, if the mission of the church is reconciliation of all races and people, then the sacralization of any one people or of one bearer of sovereignty or the identification of the Kingdom of God with any imperial society is the denial of the church's mission. Entailed in the larger compromise of mission are more specific compromises in evangelism, in history and in an understanding of the congregation.[29] Even if the church believes itself to be true to its mission within Christendom, or sees Christendom as the fruit of that mission, it is altogether too easy to found that optimism on a mix of "coercive beneficence with claimed theological modesty."[30] Rather, according to Yoder, any such optimism can only be based on the servant role of the church in society. Yoder disavows any facile equation between the faithful church in mission and the triumph of God in history, since these realities are not linked by cause and effect; that is, "we do not sight down the line of our faithfulness to his (Christ's) triumph."[31] Yoder claims that once Christians come to reject a causal connection between faithfulness and triumph, they will be able to see that it is not the job of the church to be the soul of society. That is, Yoder calls for the disestablishment of the soul of the church. Since the time of Constantine, the church has become convinced that it must be the soul of the existing society, which in turn has moved Christians to believe that they need to provide religious resources for the morality of all people. "It was assumed that if Christians did not take management responsibility for society, there was no one else who could do it and the world would fall apart."[32] However, Yoder overstates his historical case when he argues that it is only since Constantine that the church thought of itself as the soul of society. For example, the *Letter to Diognetus*, believed to have been written in the second or third century, makes just that point.

> What the soul is in the body, that Christians are in the world. The soul is

---

[28] Yoder, *The Priestly Kingdom*, 154-155.

[29] The compromise in evangelism can take the form of the social gospel on the one hand or an inordinate focus on the individual soul on the other; the compromise regarding history finds the church beginning to identify the structures of secular society as the locus of meaning; the compromise concerning the congregation is a denigration of the inherent missionary structure of the church body. Yoder, *The Royal Priesthood*, 89-101.

[30] Yoder, *The Priestly Kingdom*, 167.

[31] Yoder, *The Royal Priesthood*, 177.

[32] Yoder, *The Royal Priesthood*, 178.

dispersed through all the members of the body, and Christians are scattered through all the cities of the world. The soul dwells in the body, but does not belong to the body, and Christians dwell in the world, but do not belong to the world. The soul, which is invisible, is kept under guard in the visible body; in the same way, Christians are recognized when they are in the world, but their religion remains unseen... The soul is shut up in the body, and yet itself holds the body together; while Christians are restrained in the world as in a prison, and yet themselves hold the world together. [33]

Yoder's point is clear enough - the church must recognize that it must be visible by *being* the church, not by casting its lot with some political structure. But in his zeal to make his theological (ecclesiological) point, historical accuracy is sacrificed at this point.[34]

O'DONOVAN AND THE TEMPTATIONS OF CHRISTENDOM

O'Donovan's protestations that his is not a defence of Christendom, and his assertion that Christendom is poorly understood when interpreted primarily as an instance of Constantinianism are well-taken in that he shows deep concern for the temptations that exist within Christendom, and is keen to alert the Christian church to the problems that are visible in a close study of the history of Christendom. The perpetual problem besetting the church is that of abandoning its mission, which would amount to leaving the church in a Babylonian captivity to its own Christian rulers. That is, "the temptation was precisely to see the conversion of the rulers as achieved and complete, and to abandon mission," a problem that extends into the post-Christendom era as "negative collusion: the pretence that there was now no further challenge to be issued to the rulers in the name of the ruling Christ."[35]

Further, O'Donovan understands it as a mistake to speak of the state's duty to defend the church or reinforce church discipline, since the state cannot

---

[33] "The So-Called Letter to Diognetus," in Cyril Richardson, trans. and ed. *Early Christian Fathers* (New York: Collier Books, 1970), 218. The author of this letter seems to be saying that 'the world' is in need of being held together, and that Christians somehow hold it together, in part by way of the moral lives they lead.

[34] C. Arnold Snyder points out that "it is strange but true that critiques of specific parts of Yoder's early historical work seem to leave his work as a whole unchallenged." The issue of the when the church began to think of itself as the soul of society is a good example of this dynamic. That is, his point that the church is not called to be the soul of society, and that this notion itself is Constantinian is carried forward despite historical evidence that points in a somewhat different direction. C. Arnold Snyder, "Editor's Preface," in John Howard Yoder, *Anabaptism and Reformation in Switzerland: An Historical and Theological Analysis of the Dialogues Between Anabaptist and Reformers,* ed. C. Arnold Snyder; transl. by David Carl Stassen and C. Arnold Synder (Kitchener: Pandora Press, 2004), xxxviii.

[35] O'Donovan, *The Desire of the Nations,* 197, 213.

pursue the mission of the church, as the state is not consecrated and its weapons of coercion are not fitted for such a task. Any conceptions justifying the state's coercion in church matters were among the false steps of Christendom, which helped to create ambiguity about the church's identity, which does not count compulsion among its tools.[36] William Cavanaugh thinks that O'Donovan locates himself in an established national church and depends on the state to be the police department of the church.[37] Given O'Donovan's disavowal of coercion as one of the church's tools for the fulfillment of mission, it seems that Cavanaugh is wrong here. That is, O'Donovan believes that the church does not need the state to police ecclesiastical matters, nor does the church rely on the state for establishment as a necessity. If Cavanaugh means that O'Donovan relies on the state to inculcate characteristics of liberal society that correspond to church practices, then his statement may be basically accurate. However, to describe O'Donovan's position as dependent on the state to be the police department of the church is misleading. While the same historical record that allows for a positive reading of Christendom reveals a record of persecutions and compulsion, this "does not resolve the question whether it was a *necessary* entailment of the Christendom ideal."[38] Human judgment, according to O'Donovan, has no ultimate power at its disposal, as does the divine judgment of God. Instead, the force available to human judgment is the kind of force given a new rational and moral framework in judgment.[39] But in O'Donovan's view, such force is not to be understood in a way that construes violence as constitutive of the state. Instead, the state's claim to legitimate force "derives from the harnessing of power to the service of right and tradition."[40] The founding rationale of the state is the monopoly of the community's right, not a monopoly of violence.[41] In this way, O'Donovan seeks to establish an important point for the possibility of a positive reading of Christendom, since even if force is used within Christendom, such force is not simply violence, and at any rate is not constitutive of the legitimate state of which Christianity is an integral part. However, such a view of legitimate state force serves to open the way for a robust view of the Just War tradition.

More dangerous even than coercion, in O'Donovan's view, is civil religion. Whereas "coercion violates the openness of unbelief to come to belief freely

---

[36] O'Donovan, *The Desire of the Nations*, 217-220.

[37] Cavanaugh, "Church," 403.

[38] O'Donovan, *The Desire of the Nations*, 221, emphasis added. In a reply to Colin Greene, O'Donovan reiterates the point, insisting that while Christendom's record is mixed, he has never argued that coercion is not endemic to Christendom, simply that it was "not logically implied by the concept of a Christian state." O'Donovan, "Response to Colin Greene," 343.

[39] O'Donovan, *The Ways of Judgment*, 28-29.

[40] O'Donovan, *The Ways of Judgment*, 141.

[41] O'Donovan, *The Ways of Judgment*, 141. O'Donovan also argues here that 'violence' and 'legitimate force' are exclusive alternatives.

while God's patience waits on it; civil religion violates the freedom of belief to believe truly. But civil religion wears the form of the Antichrist, drawing the faith and obedience due to the Lord's Anointed away to the political orders which should only have provisional authority under him."[42] Civil religion is only one manifestation of a more general temptation, i.e. accommodating the demands of the Gospel to the expectations of society. Any successful mission will leave the church inculturated, and at the same time, any inculturated church is liable to lose its critical distance to society. O'Donovan argues that "to the extent that the Christian community is possessed by its Gospel, it will be protected against social conformity,"[43] suggesting that the church needs to keep some critical distance *vis a vis* secular power. Further, the presence of the church can be a disturbing factor in political society even while it renders assistance to political functions by forwarding the social good. The disturbing factor becomes possible when the church points beyond the boundaries of exclusively political identity, or utters truths that question unchallenged political doctrines. In such ways, the church can be counter-political, although O'Donovan does not want the effect of the church in society to be only counter-political.[44]

YODER'S CONFLATION OF CONSTANTINIANISM AND CHRISTENDOM

While Yoder and O'Donovan agree that new difficulties arise for the church when Constantine embraces Christianity, they diverge significantly regarding the nature of those difficulties. Briefly put, Yoder in essence conflates Christendom and Constantinianism and criticizes them both as a display of Christian unfaithfulness to the gospel of Jesus Christ. O'Donovan, on the other hand, without acquiescing to a compromised view of the church's faithfulness, nevertheless believes that Christendom is a display of the faithful church on mission. This distinction is based on very different readings both of the historical events of the fourth century, as well as their implications.

While the 'fall' of the church in the fourth century hinges on the historical era of the man Constantine,[45] Yoder sees "creeping empire loyalty" prior to the church's rise from minority status to political power and wide cultural influence. That is, he sees a shift beginning fairly early within Christian history. For example, some Christians begin to serve in the army; there is an increased emphasis on apologetics; Christians begin to see themselves as one religion among many; and more generally, "space is opening up to be less polarized in relation to the authority system and still be Christian, without any abandoning

---

[42] O'Donovan, *The Desire of the Nations*, 224.
[43] O'Donovan, *The Desire of the Nations*, 226.
[44] O'Donovan, *The Ways of Judgment*, 291-292.
[45] Yoder uses the term 'historical hinge' to refer to Constantine in *The Jewish-Christian Schism*, 171, for example.

of the places in which they were firm."[46] The drift Yoder identifies develops into full-blown betrayal of ecclesial faithfulness within Christendom, which on this account, "identifies an epoch, an arrangement, as well as a territory, when/where the adjustment between the political and the ecclesiastical elites of the Mediterranean and European world was such that no other world view was permitted."[47] Therefore, Christendom, in Yoder's thought, is not something that simply needs to be approached carefully, or perhaps renovated, but an arrangement that is disobedient at its heart – a stance which is exemplified by Constantine the historical figure and captured in Constantinianism as a symbol. Christendom, for Yoder, never had a chance to be a faithful expression of Christian political discipleship, since it was Constantinianism that *created* Christendom.[48] In the historical era of Constantine, a deep shift occurs of which Constantine is the architect, Eusebius the priest, Augustine the apologete, and the Crusades and Inquisition the culmination.[49] For all intents and purposes, then, Yoder collapses Christendom into Constantinianism and criticizes them both at the same time. It is this kind of sweeping generalization that O'Donovan no doubt has in mind when he complains,

> It is impossible for anyone interested in the ideology of the Constantinian revolution not to take notice of Eusebius' two speeches and of his biographical sketch of the emperor; among the texts of that period they are exceptional for the thoroughgoing theological way in which they uphold the political settlement. But that poses a temptation to theologians who as moderns dislike Constantine, as Westerners dislike Eusebius' Origenism, and as free-churchmen dislike the Nicene Creed. What a fine story the Council of Nicaea offers, wrapping everything unlikable about the fourth century into one package! Constantine promotes his political control, adopts Eusebius' theology and personally propounds a 'strictly monarchical' doctrine of the divinity of Christ. This event becomes an icon of Christendom itself.[50]

O'Donovan does not specifically single out Yoder with this complaint, and in any case would need to show how Yoder as a modern dislikes Constantine and as a Westerner dislikes Origenism. Yoder clearly would also disavow any accusation that describes him as disliking the Nicene Creed simply because he

---

[46] Yoder, *Christian Attitudes to War, Peace, and Revolution*, 30-33. Part of the creeping empire loyalty that Yoder discerns is the development of the just war theory. Yoder, *The Priestly Kingdom*, 74. The disagreement between just war thinking and pacifism as developed by O'Donovan and Yoder respectively will be the focus of the next chapter.

[47] Yoder, "On Not Being Ashamed of the Gospel," 299, note 10.

[48] John Howard Yoder, "Cult and Culture in and After Eden: On Generating Alternative Paradigms," in *Human Values and the Environment: Conference Proceedings. Report 140* by the University of Wisconsin Academy of Sciences, Arts, and Letters, (University of Wisconsin, 1992), 56.

[49] Yoder, *The Royal Priesthood*, 89.

[50] O'Donovan, "Response to Colin Greene," 342.

is a free-churchman. However, Yoder tends to treat the fourth century as one package. The Mennonite theologian, A. James Reimer, offers a similar criticism of Yoder on this point.

> There is no denying the power of Yoder's critique of Constantinianism and the 'fall of the church.' It is message that is not original with Yoder, and one that the church caught in civil religion needs to hear over and over again. But there is an injustice to history, including the Constantinian era, that is committed by Yoder and others for whom 'Constantinianism' is a shibboleth for all that is bad. The third and fourth centuries were a time of great upheaval and diversity. There were many serious Christians, including theologians, clerics, and statesmen, who were attempting to address the profound issues raised by their cultures in the light of the gospel. One cannot dismiss the working of the divine in the movements of history, even in its most unlikely places and persons (like Constantine).[51]

It is of course the case that Yoder would never deny that God works in the strangest places and persons, but his point is that the church needs to be capable of recognizing the meaningfulness of history by being aware of both apostasy and faithfulness wherever it happens, and that the church is the body of Christ that represents the in-breaking kingdom. Nevertheless, O'Donovan's complaints, if applied to Yoder's work, along with Reimer's direct criticisms, are difficult to refute, since Yoder is guilty of treating the Constantinian era as monolithic.

In several instances Yoder pays lip service to the possibility that Christendom could be non-Constantinian, but he almost begrudgingly grants these scenarios as formal, logical possibilities that are not actually viable. For example, Yoder ends his most important essay on Constantinianism, "The Constantinian Sources of Western Ethics," by entertaining the question of what might have happened had there been a stronger faith in the time of Constantine. Yoder notes that there has been a consistent stream of Christian thinkers who have assumed that a Caesar simply must follow moral assumptions that run counter to the gospel, and so it is in fact impossible for the Christian to become a leader of the secular state. Yoder disavows such an absolute position, and asserts that "it would however be *logically* possible to argue the other way around."[52] That is, given a number of disclaimers (the society is authentically imperial, there is respect for the monarchy, and so on), the political leader would be "perfectly free *(for a while)* to bring to bear upon the exercise of his office the ordinary meaning of the Christian faith."[53] Yoder points out a number of things that might happen to such a leader (he might be defeated by enemies, be voted out of office, be assassinated, and so on), but these kinds of things

---

[51] A. James Reimer, "Mennonites, Christ, and Culture," 10-11.
[52] Yoder, *The Priestly Kingdom,* 146.
[53] Yoder, *The Priestly Kingdom,* 146.

often happen anyway. Yoder suggests therefore that "there *could* have been in *some* times and in *some* places the *possibility* that good *could* be done, that creative social alternatives *could* be discovered, that problems *could* be solved, enemies loved and justice fostered...To assert a systematic pessimism would be to deny the Christian belief in Providence and the lessons of social experience which have shown some progress in the direction of greater humanity and justice."[54] So while Yoder cannot deny the logical possibility of Christendom being something that *could* be an example of Christian political discipleship, the language he uses in describing such possibilities, and the fact that he assumes that Christendom is intrinsically unfaithful since it represents the Constantinian reversal, reveals that he could never read Christendom as a Christian tradition from which Christians have much to learn, as does O'Donovan. Yoder does not take constructive advice from Christendom era, just as he is careful to resist any kind of normative pattern from any era of history that displays the marks of unfaithfulness that are so clearly evident to him in Constantinianism. Any credit for the kind of progress that he acknowledges in the direction of greater humanity and justice is not to be given to Christendom, but to the church, precisely to the degree to which it has provided the embodied biblical moral pattern and paradigm for the world in which it exists.

Craig Carter attempts to deflect the critique that Yoder conflates Christendom and Constantinianism, arguing that "while it is true that Constantinianism has been prevalent within Christendom, it would not be quite accurate to say that Yoder simply and completely equates the two concepts."[55] Carter makes reference here to O'Donovan's criticism of Hauerwas's work on Christendom and Constantinianism. While willing to follow O'Donovan when he accuses Hauerwas of conflating them and then attacking both, Carter insists that such a critique would not be fair in Yoder's case, since in his work is found the possibility of the ruler being converted and ruling as a Christian.[56] Carter fails to see that the fundamental disagreement between O'Donovan and Hauerwas regarding Christendom encompasses Yoder's view as well. O'Donovan directly contradicts Hauerwas's assertion that Christendom is an

---

[54] Yoder, *The Priestly Kingdom*, 146-147. Italics added to emphasize the tone of this passage. Yoder makes many of the same points in *Christian Attitudes*, p. 53-54. Yoder also is careful to assert that his critique of Constantinianism "does not deny the good faith of the possible salvation by grace though faith of persons within Christendom who despite its intrinsic bias nonetheless live in Christ and in Christian fellowship." He refers to the radical reformation use of the picture of the rose among the thorns (Song of Songs 2:2) to support his point. Yoder, *The Jewish-Christian Schism Revisited*, 141.
[55] Carter, *The Politics of the Cross*, 156.
[56] Carter, *The Politics of the Cross*, 156.

attempt by Christians to further the kingdom through the power of this world.[57] O'Donovan's response is firm, "No historical justification is offered for this claim, and I am afraid that I think it simply wrong. That is not what Christians were attempting to do."[58] Further, according to O'Donovan, Hauerwas's theological error comes in the unwillingness to see the triumph Christ has won among the nations, a triumph that created the reality whereby those that held power became subject to that very rule. This triumph Hauerwas is not prepared to see, thus relegating Christianity to a return to the catacombs, rendering Hauerwas unable to engage in learning from the shape of Christ's triumph in Christendom lessons for contemporary political theology.[59] O'Donovan's criticism of Hauerwas – that he collapses Christendom into Constantinianism and then rejects them both – applies equally to Yoder, who has, however, acknowledged the *formal* possibility that Christendom could be seen as an example of faithful Christian discipleship. But this limited kind of acknowledgement does not extend to taking Christendom seriously as the locus of faithful Christian political responsibility, but a consistent argument throughout Yoder's work insists that the historical era of Christendom is a prime example of succumbing to the Constantinian temptation.[60] Carter's attempt to defend Yoder's separation of Constantinianism and Christendom, based as it is on these limited, formal concessions by Yoder, must be seen as unsuccessful, since Yoder does not take Christendom seriously as an historical example of the church on mission, as O'Donovan is willing to do.[61]

Despite the conflation, it is nonetheless the case that for Yoder Constantinianism is not identical to Christendom. Rather, Christendom is an historical era in which the church is captive to Constantinianism, which Yoder understands as a particular kind of symbol of unfaithfulness that can exist at any time. Therefore, Constantinianism can exist beyond Christendom, but

---

[57] O'Donovan is quoting Hauerwas, *After Christendom?: How the Church is to Behave if Freedom, Justice, and a Christian Nation are Bad Ideas* (Nashville: Abingdon Press, 1991), 39.
[58] O'Donovan, *The Desire of the Nations,* 216.
[59] O'Donovan, *The Desire of the Nations,* 215-217.
[60] See "Constantinian Sources of Western Ethics" in *Priestly Kingdom,* "Peace Without eschatology," and "Christ, The Hope of the World," both included in Yoder, *The Royal Priesthood: Essays Ecclesiological and Ecumenical.*
[61] Political scientist Thomas Heilke claims that Yoder's work, because it is an analysis and critique of the historical era of Christendom, can be read as political thought in the Western tradition. Heilke therefore uses Yoder's work extensively in his own political writing, and in doing so, perpetuates the tendency to collapse Christendom and Constantinianism. See Heilke, "Yoder's Idea of Constantinianism: An Analytical Framework Toward Conversation," in Ben Ollenburger and Gayle Gerber Koontz, eds. *A Mind Patient and Untamed: Assessing John Howard Yoder's Contribution to Theology, Ethics, and Peacemaking* (Scottdale, Cascadia Publishing House, 2004), 92, 115 for examples of Heilke's conflation of Christendom and Constantinianism.

during the historical era of Christendom, one was collapsed into the other. He traces that same unfaithfulness through a series of changing circumstances that nevertheless exhibit the same basic failures. Classic Constantinianism gives way to *neo-Constantinianism* (1648 -1776), an era wherein the church is a servant, not of humanity at large, but of a particular society. *Neo-neo-Constantinianism* sees a formal separation of church and state, but "the church blesses the society it inhabits (and particularly its own national society) without a formal identification therewith, or without religious rootage in the common people,"[62] as, for example, in the United States and Scandinavia. *Neo-neo-neo-Constantinianism* includes "a preoccupation of the church to be allied with even post-religious secularism, as long as this is effective and popular," in the sense that the church can make common cause with secular government.[63] Finally, *neo-neo-neo-neo-Constantinianism* is " advance approval of an order that does not yet exist, tending to be linked with approval of any means to which people resort that hope to achieve it," as in the case of Latin American churches that give their a priori approval to political revolution.[64] The church assumes that if it provides help to the appropriate secular power structure, it will be possible to achieve for the world the salvation that it is already on the way to achieving; the church is a chaplain for society, providing resources to help people meet specifically spiritual needs. These assumptions underlie each of the forms of Constantinianism - in each of these cases, the church identifies the cause of God with some particular secular power structure.[65]

Yoder's conflation of Christendom into Constantinianism is made possible by a particular understanding of the term 'Constantine,' which serves as a symbol or a code – indeed, even in discussions of the fourth century, Constantine the historical man is not as important as his symbolic function. For example, in the essay "The Kingdom as Social Ethic," Yoder explains the 'function' of Constantine:

> The reference to Constantine in the following exposition has a code function. The first Roman emperor to tolerate, then to favor, and then to participate in the administration of the Christian churches is the symbol of a shift in relationships which had begun before he came on the scene and was not completed until nearly a century after his death. Although his thoughts and his deeds are eminently representative of the nature of the shift, it is not our present task to discharge the task of the historian, to interpret the man by asking questions about his sincerity or his wisdom or his relative causative importance. The symbolic value of Constantine as representative of that change was not an invention of his critics or of Christian radicals either in the twelfth century or more recently. It was rather the adulatory historians of

---

[62] Yoder, *The Royal Priesthood*, 196.
[63] Yoder, *The Royal Priesthood*, 197.
[64] Yoder, *The Royal Priesthood*, 197.
[65] Yoder, *The Royal Priesthood*, 195-203.

The Secular and the Eternal 147

the school of Eusebius of Caesarea who gave to his age and to his person that dramatic centrality. All that the radical historians did was to argue that the change was not all for good, whereas "mainstream" theologians from Eusebius to Bullinger and Bucer saw him as initiator of the millennium.[66]

While Constantine serves as a symbol or code, the historical era of Constantine the man nonetheless functions as an historical hinge, the time of a deep shift in the experience of the church. Such a positioning of Constantine allows Yoder to read Constantinianism both backward and forward from the historical contingencies of the fourth century. For example, Yoder observes that, in a variety of historical settings, "the distinctiveness of the Word's civil reordering has been risked in the common coinage of effective government."[67] Reading the Bible as a source for civil reordering can be, but is not necessarily, a temptation to betrayal which Yoder refers to as the "Solomonic or Constantinian one, when it reduces the *reordering* the prophetic Word demands and enables to the hallowing or reforming of the present order...It becomes betrayal when any power structure is identified as the order God desires."[68] It is precisely the power of Constantine as symbol or code that allows Yoder to read Constantinianism back into the Old Testament, so that rulers such as Solomon and David, or any other attempt to use secular power to do God's work can be seen as prequels, as it were, to Constantine.

Constantinianism serves Yoder most consistently as a way to bring to view the besetting temptations to which the church has too often succumbed, to remind the church of its own unfaithfulness within Christendom, to alert the church to its calling to disavow all forms of Constantinianism. Despite recognizing forms of the temptation in the Old Testament, and bringing to view the 'creeping empire loyalty' of the early church, Yoder still insists that the

---

[66] Yoder, *The Priestly Kingdom,* 201-202 note 3. See also Yoder, "Contrasting Theological Approaches to the Problems of State and Society" (paper presented at Calvin College, Grand Rapids, April 19, 1974), Conrad Grebel College Library, Waterloo, Ontario, 5, where Yoder notes again that "Constantine" is not a reference to the man's biography or personality, "but to the sweeping re-orientation of church-world relationships of which he was only one of the agents but soon became the major symbol. After centuries of persecution and uncertainty, during which time the concept of a Christian responsibility for political structures could never arise directly, the churches were now faced not only with the affirmation in principle of their right to exist but even with their right to power and privilege, under the benevolent intentions of their heirs of that same power which had been sometimes actively persecuting and usually barely tolerating them." In addition, see Yoder, *The Royal Priesthood,* 245, where Yoder, in a discussion of the importance of the disavowal of Constantine for interfaith dialogue, notes "The Roman emperor who began to tolerate, then supported, then administered, then finally joined the church, soon became and has remained until our time the symbol of a sweeping shift in the nature of the empirical church and its relation to the world."
[67] Yoder, "The Bible and Civil Turmoil," in *For the Nations,* 83.
[68] Yoder, "The Bible and Civil Turmoil," in *For the Nations,* 83.

fourth century signals a deep shift that is best understood as a 'fall' of the church. The coming of Christendom under Constantine is not the outworking of the church on mission, not contextual theology done faithfully, not to be celebrated as the triumph of Christ made visible, and not a foretaste of the kingdom of God. Several contemporary stances toward Christendom are possible – the church might continue to defend the classical claims of Christendom in a classic way; or disavow some of the false steps of Christendom while remaining firmly in the history of Christendom; or declare Christendom to be substantially wrong.[69] Yoder obviously prefers the latter option, believing as he does that Christendom is the embodiment of the "Constantinian concubinage,"[70] the beginning of a "great reversal,"[71] the source of a series of unfaithful compromises.

If Christendom and Constantinianism are very nearly conflated, and Constantine as a code/symbol is extended to include a stance both before and after the man Constantine and the historical era of Christendom, then Yoder clearly runs the risk of imposing a template over all of history that would prejudice his historical readings. That is, he has not developed the historical dimensions of his arguments enough to carry the normative weight placed upon it.[72] Yet Yoder is very concerned about the way history is to be read, and often challenges conventional or mainstream readings that in his view are captive to other templates such as cause-effect thinking, readings which assume that meaningfulness is borne by rulers and moved by coercion. Yoder is therefore capable of an heightened alertness to issues of accomodationism, while at the same time criticized for failing to see the positive possibilities and realities within Christendom.

---

[69] Yoder, *The Royal Priesthood*, 249.

[70] Yoder, *The Priestly Kingdom*, 179.

[71] In trying to show that contemporary Christians do not reason as the early Christians did, Yoder argues that the axioms of Western social thought are the product of a *deep shift* in the relation of church and world for which Constantine has become the symbol. Yoder, "The Constantinian Sources of Western Social Ethics," *The Priestly Kingdom*, 135.

[72] As Alex Sider has suggested, "Yoder's argument for increasing acculturation in the pre-Constantinian church and a slow but perceptible drift into a comfortable relationship with the empire begins to look like an attempt to retell the past to furnish it with a suitable denouement." J. Alexander Sider, "Constantinianism Before and After Nicea: Issues in Restitutionist Historiography," in Ollenburger and Gerber Koontz, eds. *A Mind Patient and Untamed*, 132. Sider suggests that Yoder's theses regarding Constantinianism are historical, and yet repeatedly skirt the historical coordinates of the shift. "Yoder's inattention to the effects of Roman law on Christian self-perception and theology, as well as his unnuanced accounts of the political implications of pro-Nicene theology are only two instances in which I take this to be the case." In other words, the historiography on which Yoder based his research in regard to the genetics of Constantinianism was not very good. Sider, 135-136.

O'DONOVAN'S VIEW OF CHRISTENDOM AS CHURCH ON MISSION

O'Donovan rejects the Yoder (and Hauerwas) position regarding Christendom as wrong, because their reading creates within the church a 'catacomb consciousness.'[73] The Yoder position is an unnecessary one in part because it does not take into account the proper meaning of 'secular,' which O'Donovan believes is necessary in order to avoid the temptations that accompany Christendom. That is, two ages are overlapping in an 'eschatological fusion,' one in which "the passing age of the principalities and powers has overlapped with the coming age of God's Kingdom."[74] Thus political authorities are properly secular when that term is understood as belonging to the present age that is passing away. Nonetheless, these conquered powers give indirect testimony to give to the impact of Christ's dawning glory – a witness that is the central core of Christendom.[75] The creation of something like Christendom is not, however, a *project* of the church's mission, but rather a *response* to the church's mission,[76] which means that any historical reading of Christendom should seek to understand the church's attempt to live in the midst of these two overlapping ages.

The contours of O'Donovan's historical narration provide significant clues that indicate his willingness to read Christendom positively without coming to its defence. In its early stages, the success the church experienced gave it the courage to confront rulers, and so throughout the era of Christendom, according to O'Donovan, the church experienced to some significant degree the logical conclusion of its confidence in the mission it was called to by the triumph of Jesus Christ. Instead of seeing the Edict of Milan (313) as a watershed in a negative way, as some kind of lapsarian event to be regretted, O'Donovan construes it as contextual theology. Christendom continues to exert a claim on the church even now, as a witness to the impact of the Christian faith on Western politics, as "the womb in which our late-modernity came to birth."[77] As such, Christendom offers contemporary Christians a reading of the political concepts provided in Scripture, allows Christians to learn about themselves from an era that is not too far removed from their own, and acts as a promise of

---

[73] O'Donovan, interview by Josh Pater, *Chimes Online*, 7 November 2001, available at http://clubs.calvin.edu/chimes/2001.11.09/ess.html.
[74] O'Donovan, *The Desire of the Nations*, 211.
[75] O'Donovan, *The Desire of the Nations*, 211-212. Thus for O'Donovan the terms that corresponds to 'secular' is not 'sacred' but 'eternal.' A secular government then is one that shows the impact of Christ's triumph, and the church rightly involves itself in secular government.
[76] O'Donovan, *The Desire of the Nations*, 195. "The historical Christendom has been neither necessary nor sufficient for the conceptualization of the political." O'Donovan, "Deliberation, History and Reading," 139.
[77] O'Donovan, *The Desire of the Nations*, 194.

the age of Christ's fully unhindered rule.[78] Christendom thus is a response to mission, not the result of it, or, put another way, it is not a seizing of power but an instance of alien power becoming attentive to the mission of the church. The church on mission does not resist the success that comes with pursuing that mission, although it remains constantly preoccupied with the question of the legitimacy of the missionary context in which finds itself. Even in moments that seem on the surface to be capitulations to secular power, O'Donovan insists "there emerge unexpected traits of Christian authenticity."[79]

O'Donovan provides two analytical observations regarding his historical narration of Christendom. First, the Christendom idea has to have mission at its core. This is not to deny the ambiguities that arise especially from the loss of such a focus. The primary "peril of the Christendom idea – precisely the same peril that attends upon the post-Christendom idea of the religiously neutral state – was that of negative collusion: the pretence that there was now no further challenge to be issued to the rulers in the name of the ruling Christ."[80] However, O'Donovan prefers to frame his understanding of Christendom positively, noting that a conversion of empire offered "opportunities for preaching the Gospel, baptizing believers, curbing the violence and cruelty of empire and, perhaps most important of all, forgiving their former persecutors."[81] Second, Christendom describes a mutual service between two authorities predicated in the difference and balance of their roles. The service rendered by the state to the church is to facilitate its mission. This is not to speak of the state's duty to defend the church or reinforce church discipline. Rather, the church helps the state to understand itself as secular, as having "a place on the threshold of the Kingdom, not within it," making it appropriate that the "service the church can render to this authority of the passing world is to help it make that act of self-denying recognition."[82] O'Donovan is insistent at this point that the state *qua* state has a place on the threshold of the kingdom but not within it, suggesting that the church's witness to the state takes a different form than the witness to individuals, families, tribes and nations, which have a place in the church. But the state *qua* state has to be instructed in ways of being appropriately secular.

The Visibility of the Church

The disagreement between Yoder and O'Donovan regarding the possibilities of Christendom, namely the church as Constantinian versus the possibility of Christendom being display of the church on mission, bring to view distinctive

---

[78] O'Donovan, *The Desire of the Nations*, 194-195.
[79] O'Donovan, *The Desire of the Nations*, 197.
[80] O'Donovan, *The Desire of the Nations*, 213.
[81] O'Donovan, *The Desire of the Nations*, 212.
[82] O'Donovan, *The Desire of the Nations*, 217-219.

The Secular and the Eternal 151

understandings of the visibility of the church. That is, the church is seen as an important political entity, but when the move to society is made, the church seems to drop from view for O'Donovan, while Yoder refuses such an understanding.

Yoder believes that the Constantinian era brought about a new ecclesiology in which the true church was rendered invisible. The definitions of the faith after Constantine could no longer take the visible gathering of worshipping Christians as basic. In Yoder's understanding of the necessity of the visibility of the church, any credit for the kind of progress that he acknowledges in the direction of greater humanity and justice is not to be given to Christendom, but to the church, precisely to the degree to which it has provided the embodied biblical and moral paradigm for the world in which it exists. In the Constantinian model, the church's visibility takes on the form of chaplain for society, providing resources to help people meet specifically spiritual needs. The visibility of the church takes form in its relationships with secular power structures. Yoder understands this notion of visibility as deeply unfaithful to God's calling out of a community of faith, a community that seeks an ever-refined understanding of that peoplehood.[83] Further, since Yoder disavows any equation between the faithful church in mission and the triumph of God in history, making it impossible to identify when the church's mission is or has been successful, the church's task is to be the church, which is for Yoder the locus of the meaning of history. That is, if the church begins to identify the structures of secular society as the locus of meaning of history, the visibility of the church as the primary social structure through which the gospel works to change other structures will be compromised.[84] The early church understood that God works in history through the visible, confessing community, and he works invisibly – the risen Christ sits at the right hand of the father, and governs the universe, but how the latter happens is not transparent.

O'Donovan's account of the church acknowledges the church as having the true character of a political society, by which O'Donovan means that it is brought into being and held in being, not by a special function it has to fulfill, but by a government that it obeys in everything. It is ruled and authorized by the ascended Christ alone and supremely; it therefore has its own authority; and it is not answerable to any other authority that may attempt to subsume it.[85] In O'Donovan's view, to lose sight of the church's rooting in the Christ-event is to cease to understand it as a society ruled by another king, which opens the church to the danger of becoming accommodationist and territorial.[86] Secondly, O'Donovan asserts that the political character of the church, its essential nature as a governed society, is hidden, to be discerned by faith. From within, the

---

[83] Yoder, *The Royal Priesthood*, 195-203.
[84] Yoder, *The Politics of Jesus*, 153-154.
[85] O'Donovan, *The Desire of the Nations*, 159.
[86] O'Donovan, *The Desire of the Nations*, 162.

church is a community of freedom and obedience, a society formed by Christ; from the outside, the church presents the appearance of a functional religious organism rather than a political one. This results in the "paradoxical combination of independence and conformity to local law and custom."[87]

There is a tension regarding the visibility of the church in O'Donovan's work. The way O'Donovan moves from Christology to ecclesiology within political theology leaves him vulnerable to the kind of criticism that in his treatment the church has no visible political character.[88] He understands the rule of God to be made visible in the church, and insists that political theology must be grounded in the church, based on Christology, but this visible rule of God in the community founded by Christ too quickly drops from visibility when direct political substance is discussed.[89] In other words, O'Donovan is seemingly unwilling to allow the existence of a churchly community to be the church's political witness to the world. Jonathan Chaplin suggests that fundamental to O'Donovan's theological vision is the conviction that the victory of Christ creates the church and that ecclesiology is prior to political theology. In this respect, O'Donovan is indebted to Hauerwas in asserting that the foundation of the church's witness must be the existence of a faithful witnessing community. Where he departs from Hauerwas is his denial that the mere existence of such a community *just is* the church's political witness to the world.[90]

In a recent interview, O'Donovan clarifies how his own views regarding the relationship of church and society and the visibility of the church within society

---

[87] O'Donovan, *The Desire of the Nations*, 166.

[88] Kroeker, "Why O'Donovan's Christendom is not Constantinian and Yoder's Voluntariety is not Hobbesian," 58. Kroeker notes that it is the public witness of the church that has "no direct political substance, and its identity is not yet clear as its meaning is tied to the ascended Christ," 58.

[89] Daniel Carroll registers a similar complaint, and attributes the problem to the fact that O'Donovan's eschatology offers no sustained exposition of the "not yet" of eschatology, that *The Desire of Nations* suffers from an absence of a "positive" tone in regards to Christian hope, from a lack of expansion of the impact of the eschatological vision—in other words, O'Donovan has neglected important aspects of the "not yet." See M. Daniel Carroll R., "The Power of the Future in the Present: Eschatology and Ethics in O'Donovan and Beyond," in Bartholomew, et al., eds., *A Royal Priesthood?*, 125, 126, 139. Also helpful here is Christopher Rowland's essay in the same book. Rowland argues that the politics of Jesus could be a helpful addition to O'Donovan's political theology. Rowland makes his argument from his discussion of the Apocalypse—i.e., the story of Christ's work casts its shadow over every human transaction, and readers of the Apocalypse are offered the resources to work out what faithfulness to the testimony of Jesus might mean—Rowland believes that Yoder's theology, and indeed the spirit of the early Anabaptists, could fit well into O'Donovan's political theology, whereas O'Donovan takes his work in a direction that is more sympathetic to the spirit of the magisterial Reformers. Christopher Rowland, "The Apocalypse and Political Theology," in Bartholomew, et al., eds., *A Royal Priesthood?*, 241-254.

[90] Jonathan Chaplin, "Political Eschatology and Responsible Government," 269.

The Secular and the Eternal

differ from those held by Yoder and Hauerwas.[91] In response to a question concerning the difference of the communality experienced in society from that within the church, O'Donovan asserts,

> Here is a point where the "doctrine of the two" is invoked. On earth, yes, because the way in which we experience the church as a community is still provisional. We are not yet at rest with the saints of all ages in heaven, in the glory of God united by his worship. We look for that and hope for that, but the full-bodied sociality of the church is not yet wholly present to us. We get tastes of it in our congregations where we worship and foresights of it, but the full city of God to which we are called is not yet part of our experience. But if one says we are called to a city, I think it's important to see that some of the full, concretely structured political, public character that we associate with civil societies is also clinging to the church in the end, that this is the fulfillment not only of the prayer meeting and the quiet little gathering, it's the fulfillment of the public life that we know here on earth.[92]

O'Donovan's response leads to a question that places O'Donovan into a direct confrontation with Yoder and Hauerwas regarding the visibility of the church. The interview pursues this further:

> That last statement almost sounds like something with which Stanley Hauerwas could agree, that there is a political analogue within the church; he sort of envisions the church politically. Yet you move away from Hauerwas's analysis and come to a point that's quite different. What do you make of his argument (following John Howard Yoder) that what he calls Constantinian assumptions are wrong, first because if the church is truly the church it will always be a minority, and second because in turning Christianity into a philosophy suitable to maintain the society, Christians undercut the ability of the church to take a critical stance toward that society?[93]

O'Donovan's reply, in part, brings into sharp relief the fact that he understands the view of the church and society held by Yoder and Hauerwas to

---

[91] Both the interviewer and O'Donovan connect Hauerwas and Yoder very closely in the published conversation referred to here. My interest is in O'Donovan's attempt to differentiate himself from the views that he sees as being represented by Hauerwas and Yoder, and not in the issue of disentangling Yoder and Hauerwas from each other. I have addressed this latter issue in "Share the House: John Howard Yoder and Stanley Hauerwas Among the Nations," in Ben Ollenburger and Gayle Gerber Koontz, eds., *A Mind Patient and Untamed*, 187-204.

[92] O'Donovan, interview by Josh Pater, *Chimes Online*, 7 November 2001, available at http://clubs.calvin.edu/chimes/2001.11.09/ess.html.

[93] O'Donovan, interview by Josh Pater, *Chimes Online*, 7 November 2001, available at http://clubs.calvin.edu/chimes/2001.11.09/ess.html.

be unnecessarily truncated, limited largely as it seems to the confines of the church itself.

> I think his criticisms of the Christendom idea are partly wrong, first because he dismisses the church as always being a minority. I don't know on what theological authority one could make that assertion. The church has very often been a minority. But whether the church is a majority or a minority at any time or place, the church is not given yet to be wholly visible to itself. There is a real temptation in wanting to be a visible minority, a gathered church in which you can say, "We are few, but we know exactly who we are, and we know who is on our side. The line is drawn clearly and unambiguously between us and the world." That kind of visibility and definition is not granted to the church in our age. We know where the church is because we know where the sacraments are and where the word is preached. We see people gathering to the sacraments, we see the church taking form... Even if it's true that the church is going to be a minority, the church is going to be embattled and contested to a certain extent, but it can be so as a majority sometimes. Evil has its ways of challenging the church when it's in an apparently confident position just as much. Even if the church is a minority, it can't be a self-conscious minority which says to itself, "We're perfectly safe because we're a minority." That I have to say I find troubling in the kind of catacomb consciousness I find in Stan and John Howard Yoder. I don't think it was at all typical of the Christians that actually inhabited the catacombs. They didn't huddle down there and say, "How nice. We at least know who we are while we're down here."
>
> The question of the church being unable to criticize society, that seems to me to be wrong, but not wholly wrong. Whenever our mission takes us into a sphere of life, the question is always before us: Can we remain faithful to Christ while engaging in the demands, expectations, and outlook of this sphere of life?... It seems to me extremely clear that the question of the church's assimilation to the ethos of the society in which it lives, particularly western society - which is deep down the thing Stan cares about most, and I honor him for that because I think he is a great prophet against the assimilation of the Church to the world - that question is raised quite irrespective of the church's relation to government. No doctrines of Christendom or against Christendom are going to change the fact that the church in a loud, confident and boisterous society - confident of its position, confident of its own right - is going to have to struggle to keep the authenticity of its gospel. It's going to happen anyway, and relation to government doesn't necessarily make it easier or harder, though in any given situation it might, depending on the government.[94]

O'Donovan's rejection of the so-called 'catacomb consciousness' and the accusation that Hauerwas, following Yoder, "dismisses the church as always

---

[94] O'Donovan, interview by Josh Pater, *Chimes Online,* 7 November 2001, available at http://clubs.calvin.edu/chimes/2001.11.09/ess.html.

being a minority," include a misleading notion. That is, O'Donovan's characterization of Yoder's and Hauerwas's view as somehow dismissive because of a belief in the minority position of the church, or as being satisfied with staying in the catacombs is fundamentally unfair, since it ignores to a large extent the extensive work done by both Yoder and Hauerwas in areas of the church's constructive political engagement with the wider world. Further, to suggest that the concern regarding the church's assimilation to society can be "raised quite irrespective of the church's relation to government" is disingenuous in that O'Donovan himself admits that the church always has to struggle with the authenticity of its gospel, a difficulty which appears directly in the church's relation to the government, whether that relation is located in a minority or majority position. The shape of the struggle against assimilation will in fact be directly related to the church's relation to the government, since presumably the temptations experienced by a minority church will be different than those experienced by a majority or established church, and not just in ways that are dependent on the government itself. That is, to be established or to assume a majority position – these are themselves temptations to assimilation in Yoder's view.

That is, it is not the case that Yoder's church is visible and O'Donovan's invisible, but that the nature and locus of visibility and invisibility is different – for Yoder, visibility happens when the church *is* the church, and the work of God in the world is not fully transparent. For O'Donovan, the church is visible and political, but is invisible when it goes into the world, where the triumph of Christ becomes visible in judicial form. Thus, for O'Donovan, political theology is not simply ecclesial self-description,[95] since the church both is and is not a political society. That is, there can be no concrete representation of the kingdom of God on earth, "except the indirect one afforded by the church."[96] This indirect representation of the kingdom of God suggests to O'Donovan that the visibility of the church is the visibility of faith, and full visibility can only be expected at the last – in the meantime, the church models that eschatological community, but is not identical to it.[97] O'Donovan's struggle to find a way to acknowledge the importance of the church in political theology without equating the two leads him to describe the church both as counter-political and post-political, but never political in the way that Yoder conceives things. On O'Donovan's account, the counter-political moment in the New Testament proclamation of the cross is surely against an a-political theology, "a theology that simply disinterests itself in the order of the social life and the practice of judgment, and presents the Gospel wholly as a realm of the spirit available to solitary individuals."[98] But the temptation that concerns O'Donovan here is the

---

[95] O'Donovan, *The Ways of Judgment*, 239.
[96] O'Donovan, *The Ways of Judgment*, 214-215.
[97] O'Donovan, *The Ways of Judgment*, 261, 264, 318.
[98] O'Donovan, *The Ways of Judgment*, 231.

danger of the totalizing of all of politics within the framework of the counter-political, which centers on the critical dimension of such politics, and thus results in depoliticization, which cannot then undertake the task of judgment.[99] So the church, while counter-political, is, in O'Donovan's view, nonetheless constrained in its counter-politics by the 'not yet' of the eschaton, since the church is not yet identical to the eschatological community of God.[100]

O'Donovan also suggests that the church can be properly understood as a post-political society, one which models life beyond the judgment of the present age, and bears witness to a final judgment. The community of the church is not one of primal innocence that needs no judgment, but is rather "it is a society that has felt the need for judgment, has cried to God for judgment, and has seen it revealed in Christ; and believing what it has seen, it has judged for itself."[101] Such a society can refrain from judgment because it defers to God's judgment, but must still recognize the need for human judgment in society, which takes place in the present age, the age that is the proper arena for consideration of political theology. Thus the church, while it is both counter-political and post-political,[102] nonetheless is not properly the focus of political theology.

Theology of History

These differing positions regarding the era of Christendom, and the disparate understandings of visibility and invisibility can be accounted for in large part by distinctive theologies of history, especially as these are related to eschatology. In other words, it is not simply that Yoder and O'Donovan disagree about historical details of what actually happened in Christendom, or what date should serve as the beginning or end of the era. Rather, a difference can be found between them regarding the question of how history ought to be understood.

YODER'S APOCALYPTIC HISTORIOGRAPHY

Yoder asserts that the level of change that matters the most for the Constantinian shift is that there arises a new understanding of the meaningfulness of history, an issue that is inextricably connected to eschatology. The connection of history and eschatology is a thread that runs throughout Yoder's work, and is one of the key dimensions of his political

---

[99] O'Donovan, *The Ways of Judgment*, 234.

[100] O'Donovan, *The Ways of Judgment*, 261.

[101] O'Donovan, *The Ways of Judgment*, 238.

[102] O'Donovan makes a brief mention of a pre-political society, which is a reference to the "pre-political social harmony of the Garden of Eden." O'Donovan, *Ways of Judgment*, 7.

theology, including as it does his view of the responsibility of the church in the world. When Yoder considers St. John's question in the Apocalypse regarding the opening of the scroll sealed with seven seals, the key issue raised is "precisely the question of the meaningfulness of history."[103] The answer to that exact question changes fundamentally when the church becomes Constantinian, since Christians then begin to assume that the forces which really determine the march of history are in the hands of leaders of armies and markets, with the attendant belief that Christians will want in their turn to become lords of state and market to use their power for their desirable ends. What needs rather to be seen, according to Yoder, is that that the church is the primary social structure through which the gospel works to change other structures.[104]

> We can't immediately say that certain events in secular history or cultural history have been providentially governed so that they must come out this way in the end, but we do (or the early church does) confess that, as a hidden meaning, and as a meaning which the church can know sometimes through the prophets, sometimes through experience and discernment. Thus the risen Lord uses the powers despite themselves, including the economic and political powers, including Caesar, somehow for his hidden purposes... So you know for a fact that there is a church and that God is using the church for certain ministries of proclamation and service, fellowship, etc. You have to take it in faith that God is governing the world.[105]

What is and must remain visible, and what Christian believers are called to contribute to, is the church community. What is invisible, or at least not fully transparent, is God's work in the wider world, which must be taken by faith. Constantinianism reverses visibility and invisibility when compared to the beliefs of the early church, and marks part of the great reversal that is Christendom. The Christian understanding of history changes so that the church becomes convinced that God is governing history through Constantine, whereas previously, "you knew as a fact of experience that there was a church, and you had to take it on faith that God was governing history. Now, you know for a fact that God is governing history (Constantine is one of us), but you have to take it on faith that there is a church. That is the shift in the meaning of salvation history for which Constantine is the symbol. That is the philosophical meaning of the Middle Ages, with the eschatology of the New Testament stood on its head."[106]

Yoder sums up what he considers to be the impact of this change in the view of history:

---

[103] Yoder, *The Politics of Jesus*, 232.
[104] Yoder, *The Politics of Jesus*, 153-154.
[105] Yoder, *Christian Attitudes*, 42-43.
[106] Yoder, *Christian Attitudes*, 44.

> We hardly can imagine how deep a reorientation of the meaning of history was involved when it became obvious, because of the victory of Constantine, that the God of Moses is on the side of the people who come out triumphant in a particular course of events. That means we derive our ethics from the imperative to make history come out right through our actions. God has no way to make history come out right except that we run it, so it's God's responsibility, not ours, when we change our ethics so as to help him win. We are unselfish in the matter. We are just helping God run his world.[107]

Thus for Yoder the deep change inaugurated by Constantine the symbol is not primarily the new view of violence, but the meaning of the *visible* church – Caesar as the bearer of God's providence – the unique bearer of history,[108] which brings about a change in the view of violence, among the many other things noted above (ethics, ecclesiology, and so on).

This deep shift happens in part because of a misunderstanding of the two ages that exist simultaneously in the present age, although they differ in nature or direction. The first age points backwards to human history outside of Christ and is socially manifested in the world; the second points forward to the fullness of the kingdom of God, of which it is a foretaste, and is manifested in the body of Christ. This new age, revealed in Christ, takes primacy over the old and will finally vanquish it. The state did not change with the coming of Christ; what changed was the coming of the new age that proclaimed the doom of the old one. The ultimate meaning of history is to be found in the work of the church. Thus when people look for the meaning of history in the secular powers, a fundamental confusion has taken place, wherein the providential purpose of the state has been confused with the redemptive purpose of the church,[109] or put another way, the kingdom of this world has become the kingdom of God.[110]

The confusion of the two ages, or the collapsing of the two, comes as a result of a reversal in eschatology, which might also be called an immanentization of the future reign of God into the present world, or more specifically, the secular realm. Such an immanentization embodies the temptation to see the kingdom as present before its time. Yoder claims that Augustine, for example, held that the Roman church was the coming of the promised millennium, which led to a "conscious abandon of eschatology,"[111]

---

[107] Yoder, *Christian Attitudes*, 50-51.
[108] Yoder, "Contrasting Theological Approaches to the Problems of State and Society," 6.
[109] Yoder, *The Original Revolution*, 55-61.
[110] Yoder, *Anabaptism and Reformation in Switzerland*, 258.
[111] Yoder, *The Original Revolution*, p. 66. Yoder makes a similar point in "Contrasting Theological Approaches to the Problems of State and Society," 7. In "Ethics and Eschatology," Yoder again says: "Since Constantine, some broad assumptions have been operative which represent a kind of 'fulfilled apocalyptic.' The role of the ruler

since what had been considered as eschatological could now be observed as it was played out in the structures of power. In such a world of realized eschatology, Christian hope was turned inside out,[112] becoming something that was so fully transparent that faith was no longer necessary to see that God's governance in history has become evident in the person of the Christian ruler of the world. As will become clear below, while O'Donovan does not agree with such an assessment of the Constantinian situation, his view cannot be described as Constantinian on these terms, since there is no such thing as a 'nominally Christian mass' in his thinking, but the proper understanding of the differently authorized church and secular power.

Thus we have come to a dimension of Yoder's thought without which it is impossible to understand his political theology - the convergence and mutual interplay of his eschatology and view of history in such a way as to underwrite what he believes to be a biblical philosophy of history, a view that David Toole calls "apocalyptic historiography."[113] One can only recognize the meaningfulness of history as the theater of God's work if a proper eschatology is in place, allowing the Christian to acknowledge that the bearer of history is the church. The church can take history and its role within history seriously precisely because of its eschatology, which understands that the kingdom that broke into this world in Jesus Christ will come in its fullness through the power of God, and not via the manipulation or coercive methods of the church, the state, or some combination of these. So Yoder reads history in an apocalyptic style, which is something of an exercise in skepticism, as it seeks to destroy confidence in traditional historical narratives, especially that of historical necessity. Yoder allows for freedom and resistance by introducing God into a history that is too often understood as a "system-immanent causal nexus,"[114] and by encouraging people to discern God's presence amidst events,[115] albeit in ways that do not depend on the machinations of those who wield state power. The work of God in the Kingdom is a social order and not a hidden one, and consists in "the real accessibility of a new order in which grace and justice are linked, which people have only to accept. It does not assume that time will end tomorrow; it reveals why it is meaningful that history should go on at all."[116] According to Yoder, Christians are called to a believing view of world history, one that sees "the modern world is a subset of the world vision of the gospel,

---

himself is part of the changing history of Christian eschatology. That is, the new era is seen as the new millennium when the great serpent has been chained." Yoder, "Ethics and Eschatology," 121.

[112] Yoder, *The Royal Priesthood*, 57.

[113] Toole, *Waiting for Godot in Sarajevo*, 211.

[114] See Yoder's discussion in Yoder "Armaments and Eschatology," *Studies in Christian Ethics* 1 no 1 (1988): 43-61.

[115] David Toole, *Waiting for Godot in Sarajevo*, 211.

[116] Yoder, *The Politics of Jesus*, 105.

not the other way around. That means we can afford to begin with the gospel notions themselves and then work out from there, as our study has done, rather than beginning with the 'real world' out there (someone else's definition of 'the nature of things') and then trying to place the call of God within it."[117] In other words, an apocalyptic historiography is one that reads history "from below," based as it is on the way of the cross, and participates in history with hope, based as it also is on the kind of power displayed in the cross.[118]

O'DONOVAN'S CONTESTED HISTORY

A reading of history that identifies the church as the bearer of history is too narrow and too suspicious for O'Donovan. His historical reading of Christendom is not confined to the church, is not an attempt to identify a golden age of liberalism, but tries to provide a reading that is provisional, heuristic, and subject to changes of perspective.[119] His work of retrieval[120] of the 'Great Tradition' is given shape by his theology of history that is clearly evident throughout his analysis of Christendom. On the basis of his understanding of history as something public that is the theatre of God's saving purposes and humanity's social undertakings,[121] O'Donovan makes a positive account of Christendom possible, and even makes the Constantinian shift explicable as an instance of Christian faithfulness.[122] O'Donovan's reading of history is theological in that he is seeking to provide an account of the triumph of Christ, and in that he is reading from "a perspective which allows the expectation that the power of the gospel may bring about transformation that goes beyond the sphere of the individual."[123] O'Donovan, in other words, firmly rejects any notion that history is some uninterpretable space that has the timeless character of myth, or is completely open to unfettered acts of human will – an understanding to which he refers as value-totalitarianism. Any concepts that suggest that history is self-contained must be resisted: for example, inevitable progress within history is a view that cannot be sustained in light of a Christian eschatology.[124]

---

[117] Yoder, *Body Politics*, 74.

[118] Yoder, *He Came Preaching Peace*, 44.

[119] O'Donovan, *The Desire of the Nations*, 284.

[120] Stanley Hauerwas and James Fodor point out that O'Donovan variously describes his project as one of recovery, restoration, retrieval, reclamation, re-orientation and renewal, but that this is no "static duplication or prosaic repetition of the past that he is after." Hauerwas and Fodor, "Remaining in Babylon," 34.

[121] O'Donovan, *The Desire of the Nations*, xi.

[122] William Cavanaugh, "Church," 397.

[123] Bernd Wannenwetsch, review of *The Desire of the Nations: Rediscovering the Roots of Political Theology*, 465.

[124] O'Donovan, "History and Politics in the Book of Revelation," 28, 29. O'Donovan also notes that when history is made the categorical matrix for meaning, it cannot be

It might be said that O'Donovan's concerns amount to an attempt to avoid historicism, and thereby steer clear of any understanding of history and political theology that cannot muster anything but suspicion based on a reductionistic account of history. According to Victor Austin,

> O'Donovan looks to history as a means of understanding a modern problem, but he strictly rejects modern historicism. He describes and critiques two sides of a modern debate: those 'liberals' who separate theology and politics (and who are motivated by suspicion), and those 'historicists' who unite them at the fearful costs of totalizing skepticism. Underlying his argumentation is the belief that argumentation is possible: one can have a vision that will render action intelligible.[125]

It is through the elaboration of his theology of history that O'Donovan can pursue the purpose of his political theology – to push back the horizon of commonplace politics and open it up to the activity of God. Earthly events are partial indicators of God's work, but we need God's purposes to see what is happening in political events. Theology needs a full political conceptuality, and the political needs a theological conceptuality - both are concerned with the history that finds its goal in Christ, the desire of the nations.[126] O'Donovan is therefore especially careful to resist modern historicism, a concern pursued vigorously in *Resurrection and Moral Order*. In establishing an evangelical foundation for ethics, a careful distinction between teleology and eschatology is important in that historicism is expressed as historical teleology. That is, any concept of an 'end' in modern historicism is essentially a concept of development in time – nothing can have a point unless it is a historical point, developed within time. Only the moments of time can be the raw material for transformation. But, drawing on the theology of the Reformers, O'Donovan emphasizes the point that is lost in modern historicism – the fulfillment of history cannot be generated from within history alone, but God is at work from beyond history.[127] That is, "God is not merely responding to necessities intrinsic to it, but is doing something new…. The transformation is in keeping with the creation, but in no way dictated by it. That is what is meant by describing the Christian view of history as 'eschatological' and not merely as 'teleological.'…

---

taken seriously as history. O'Donovan, *Resurrection and Moral Order*, 58-60. In a response to Nicolas Wolterstorff, O'Donovan reiterates his view that politics belongs to history, not nature, and therefore, he concludes that "I am afraid that the invocation of history as patient progress towards the ideal leaves me quite skeptical…I see nothing inexorable in the modern state's purification." O'Donovan, "Deliberation, History and Reading" 137-139.

[125] Victor L. Austin, "Method in Oliver O'Donovan's Political Theology," 585. Austin is encapsulating O'Donovan's arguments from *The Desire of the Nations*, 6-11.

[126] O'Donovan, *The Desire of the Nations*, 2.

[127] O'Donovan, *Resurrection and Moral Order*, 58-67.

Only if historical ends are understood in this eschatological way can we understand also the claim that 'Christ alone' brings the world-order to its fulfillment."[128] Historicism thus legitimizes the immanent tendencies of history, and finds too little room to criticize them, whereas the belief that only Christ gives the totality of events their shape and point as history allows for both critical and constructive engagement in and with the events of history.[129]

In his political theology, O'Donovan reiterates his emphasis on history as the theater of God's work while at the same time denying modern historicism. That is, he follows the modern tradition of organizing talk of politics within the category of history, but places that history within the history of God's reign.[130] It is precisely this rejection of historicism while still insisting that history is the theatre of God's action that allows O'Donovan to offer a reading of Christendom, that, while admittedly contested, takes seriously the possibility that Christ's triumph can be visible there. O'Donovan's understanding of history, based as it is on the triumph of Christ, does *not* in fact slide into Constantinianism. O'Donovan's own explanation for his ability to take Christendom seriously is that he does not simplistically substitute theology for history. That is, it is easy to attack Christendom if one allows theology to function in some idealistic manner that truncates the theological task so that it can only be suspicious, a stance which Yoder's work cannot move beyond, according to O'Donovan.

The alliance of Constantine, Eusebius, and monarchical theology was only a momentary configuration, in O'Donovan's view, and indeed, Christendom's ideas can be attributed most directly to monks and bishops, not to secular rulers.[131] For the ancient church, the Edict of Milan was the logical conclusion of its confidence in mission, the confirmation of what it had always predicted,

---

[128] O'Donovan, *Resurrection and Moral Order*, 64. "Classical Christian thought proceeded from a universal order of meaning and value, an order given in creation and fulfilled in the kingdom of God, an order, therefore, which forms a framework for all action and history, to which action is summoned to conform in its making of history. Historicism denies that such a universal order exists." O'Donovan, *Resurrection and Moral Order*, 67.

[129] O'Donovan, *Resurrection and Moral Order*, 73, 157.

[130] O'Donovan suggests that placing political history within the history of God's reign means that three elements are added to historicism: 1) the history of divine rule safeguards and redeems the goods of creation; 2) we are forced to strip away the institutional fashions within which the Western tradition has clothed the idea of authority; 3) history of divine rule is a revealed history which takes place as the history of Israel. In *Resurrection* he established a link between ethics and history; now in *Desire* he extends the connection to politics and history: "As true ethics is grounded in that history because it is a history of the vindication of creation order so it is also grounded in that politics which is the politics of the divine rule. " *The Desire of the Nations*, 19-21.

[131] O'Donovan, "Response to Colin Greene," 342-343.

The Secular and the Eternal 163

and therefore there is no point in regretting one example of contextual theology, or in making it out to constitute the Constantinian 'Fall.'[132] For O'Donovan, theology helps him to read history, not to provide a legitimation of a particular secular power, but rather to "demonstrate how the victory of Christ over 'the rulers of this age' has taken actual historical, institutional effect as political authorities in Christian Europe 'bowed before' the throne of the risen and ascended Christ."[133]

Christian Political Responsibility

Yoder and O'Donovan's respective views of Christendom, which display differing theologies of history, bring to view significantly different understandings of political responsibility. For Yoder, this responsibility is centered in the church, and therefore he does not believe that Christian political responsibility necessarily includes any attempt to assume secular power, while O'Donovan understands political responsibility to be centered in government, which is accountable to the triumph of Christ.

In Yoder's view, Christendom, since Constantinianism is embedded in it, *cannot* serve as the bearer of history, since it has turned hope inside out, and has immanentized eschatology, or put another way, has dragged the future consummation of history into the present, and then described this present as the kingdom of God; this, despite the disavowal of the way of the cross and a willingness to use coercive methods. The belief that God's work is visible in the empire, or that it is possible or necessary to take control of history and move it in whatever direction is thought to be effective or responsible is in Yoder's view a heresy, and not just something that needs to be altered slightly, since heresy must be rooted out. For Yoder, it is precisely a biblical philosophy of history that can root out the heresy of Constantinianism. Such a philosophy, if it understands the church to be the bearer of history, has the resources to take history and the present seriously. To take history seriously means to be able to identify both apostasy and faithfulness, which Yoder believes is possible by adopting "a view which criticizes what has come into being in the course of history, on the grounds of criteria which themselves are also drawn from within the course of history,"[134] grounds that are drawn from Scripture, and most

---

[132] O'Donovan, *The Desire of the Nations*, 194.

[133] Chaplin, "Political Eschatology and Responsible Government," 269. Christendom should not be seen as an age in which the missionary challenge was derailed, but the age was perpetually preoccupied with that question. O'Donovan, *The Desire of the Nations*, 196.

[134] Yoder, *The Priestly Kingdom*, 127. In his doctoral thesis Yoder argues that only those who are capable of questioning history are capable of taking it seriously. That is, the early Anabaptists were not ahistorical by going back to the early church. Rather they were forced to think historically by the fact that they thought the church in its belief regarding the state could not be reformed. Yoder, *Anabaptism and Reformation in*

clearly evident in the suffering servanthood of Jesus. The substantial criteria according to which Jesus defined judgment are concrete deeds of servanthood. Yoder appeals to the apostolic witness, which insisted that any 'larger' claims for Christ as preexistent, as creator or cosmic victor, must not be disengaged from the man Jesus and the cross.

> The criterion of Servanthood is substantial, not merely formal. It throws an especially clear light on one monumental kind of 'discernment of the kingdom in history,' namely, identifying events of statecraft as preeminently worthy of recognition. "God has done it" inaugurated the confusion of Constantine's peace with the reign of God. "God wills it" sent the crusaders off to the Near East. The error was not that no meaning should have been ascribed to events, but that nonservant criteria reversed the relation of church and world.[135]

Therefore, Yoder's view of history tries to discern God's work where it is operative and visible – in the church. "This is where it is already clear that he rules. The kind of ruler he is is a suffering kind of ruler. The church is moving history by her Servanthood. Most of us still think that the way to move history is not by Servanthood but by some other kind of rule, but the church is the instrument through which God is moving history by Servanthood, in the extension of doing that same thing in Jesus."[136] Christian political responsibility, in other words, is centered in the church, a view that O'Donovan sees as truncated because it does not adequately take into account the triumph of Christ. O'Donovan also suggests that Yoder's understanding of Christian political responsibility centered in the church can lead to "high moral pretensions," as in the case of Yoder's suggestion that the early Christian vision of open meetings and evangelical freedom have contributed to the rise of democracy.[137]

Switzerland, 194. Yoder's emphasis on the possibility of the identification of faithfulness and apostasy within the church carries with it an ironic danger. The very reason he embarks on restitutionism at least in part is to be able to engage in what he considers to be a crucial part of the church's work, that is, the "inexhaustible will to dialogue." See Yoder, *Anabaptism and Reformation in Switzerland,*"136. But Yoder's persistent focus on the unfaithfulness of the Christian church, especially in Christendom, actually hinders ecumenical conversation. See Gerald Schlabach, "Deuteronomic or Constantinian: What is the Most Basic Problem for Christian Social Ethics?" in *The Wisdom of the Cross,* 449-471.

[135] Yoder, *For The Nations,* 243.

[136] Yoder, *Preface to Theology,* 248.

[137] O'Donovan, *The Ways of Judgment,* 171. The Yoder reference is from *For the Nations,* 32. O'Donovan characterizes Yoder as the proponent of the religious version of a narrative of democracy that aims to demonstrate irreversible ideological progress, one of a number of twentieth-century apologies for democracy. This seems somewhat misleading, since, according to Yoder, if a Constantinian view of democracy could be

O'Donovan's reading of Christendom as the fruit of Christ's triumph, his insistence on the central importance of the church's focus on its own mission as response to that triumph in navigating the turbulent waters of relationships with secular power, his clear-eyed recognition of the flaws of Christendom, and his cautions regarding the myriad pervasive temptations together constitute a convincing case that fends off accusations that O'Donovan should be labeled as Constantinian. In fact, O'Donovan makes the Constantinian shift explicable, since he rejects the notion that such a shift is from another-worldly church to a worldly church, or from a non-coercive to a coercive church. Rather, as William Cavanaugh points out, "the shift was in the way Christians read what God was doing in salvation history."[138] On this account, the age of Constantine was not the beginning of political theology, but represented a change in Christian thinking and also in practice regarding the manifestation of the kingdom of God in the world. Thus the contemporary ferment of political theology pursued in the way O'Donovan does is an attempt to reimagine what God is doing with the principalities and powers of this present age.[139]

Yoder's theology of history, on the other hand, implies that the responsibility of the church is precisely *not* to seek to take control of history, which is not to say that the church remains uninvolved in society. Rather, if history is borne by the church, then the church is given enormous responsibility, since the church's first duty to society will be the same as her first duty to her Lord.[140] This first duty of servanthood precludes an understanding of responsibility that suggests that the church should seek to grab hold of the handles of history and move it in the right direction.

In a well-known passage in *The Politics of Jesus,* Yoder's view of an understanding of history, responsibility, and eschatology are brought together, embedded, significantly, in a discussion of the Apocalypse of St. John. Yoder observes that much "social ethical concern is moved by a deep desire to make things move in the right direction... part if not all of social concern has to do with looking for the right 'handle' by which one can 'get hold on' the course of history and move it in the right direction." Whatever that 'handle,' such an approach is structured to lift up one focal point which is more important than people, a focal point to which other values are then subordinated. Within such a structure, Yoder identified three assumptions that his own apocalyptic historiography enables him to disavow; namely, that a) cause and effect is visible; b) we are well informed enough about the world to decide for the world; and c) effectiveness in moving toward these goals is itself a moral yardstick. Yoder's biblical philosophy of history prompts him to argue that the

---

rejected, then Christians might well celebrate it as a prophetic ministry of a servant people in a world they do not control. Yoder, *The Priestly Kingdom,* 165-166.
[138] Cavanaugh, "Church," 397.
[139] Cavanaugh, "Church," 397.
[140] Yoder, *The Christian Witness to the State,* 17.

relationship between the obedience of God's people and the triumph of God's cause is not a relationship of cause and effect but one of cross and resurrection. "But this position is nothing more than a logical unfolding of the meaning of the work of Jesus Christ himself, whose choice of suffering Servanthood rather than violent lordship, of love to the point of death rather than righteousness backed by power, was itself the fundamental direction of his life. Jesus was so faithful to the enemy-love of God that it cost him all his effectiveness; he gave up every handle on history."[141] But, as is obvious, to give up any handle on history is to claim a robust eschatology that provides the basis of the work of the church – work that allows for hope (eschatological, that is, open to God's future) and skepticism (historical, that is, open to identifying apostasy as well as faithfulness).[142] The church is not the midwife of history, charged with bringing into reality some immanent vision; if history has a meaning, it is eschatological.[143]

In O'Donovan's non-Constantinian understanding of responsibility, it is not Christendom but an "eschatologically charged notion of 'responsible' government" that is the core of the distinctive political contribution of the gospel.[144] In O'Donovan's words, "the political doctrine that emerged from Christendom is characterised by a notion that government is responsible. Rulers, overcome by Christ's victory, exist provisionally and on sufferance for

---

[141] Yoder, *The Politics of Jesus,* 228-234. The notion that Christians must disavow cause and effect thinking is reiterated in several other places in Yoder's work. See his questioning of the embrace of the system-immanent causal nexus in Yoder, "Armaments and Eschatology," 43-61.

[142] Yoder, *The Priestly Kingdom,* 1-2; "Ethics and Eschatology," 125. Yoder's well-known phrase, 'no handles on history,' is closely connected to another phrase 'with the grain of the universe,' which has been given currency recently by Stanley Hauerwas. People who give up the attempt to grab the handles of history are the ones who are working with the grain of the universe. "The point that apocalyptic makes is not only that people who wear crowns and claim to foster justice by the swords are not as strong as they think – true as that is: we still sing, 'O where are Kings and Empires now of old that went and came?' It is that people who bear crosses are working with the grain of the universe. One does not come to that belief by reducing social process to mechanical and statistical models, nor by winning some of one's battles for the control of one's own corner of the fallen world. One comes to it by sharing the life of those who sing about the Resurrection of the slain Lamb." Yoder, "Armaments and Eschatology," 58. The Hauerwas book is *With the Grain of the Universe.*

[143] Reinhard Hütter, "The Church: Midwife of History or Witness of the Eschaton?," *Journal of Religious Ethics* 18 no 1 (Spring 1990): 27-54. Following Yoder, Hütter claims that the church reveals why there is history … "if history has any meaning at all, it is an *eschatological* one; I.e. it represents nothing else than the result of the very specific kind of 'battle' between the new and the old order." This means participating in the new order in contradiction to and in the middle of the old one and paying the price for it. Hütter, "The Church: Midwife of History or Witness of the Eschaton?," 45.

[144] Chaplin, "Political Eschatology and Responsible Government," 277.

specific purposes."¹⁴⁵ The political authority that results is something that O'Donovan sees as new, since the notion of 'state' is something that is a structure of relations within the community that can coexist with other structures that serve other purposes. The state as subject to Christ's authority does not signify the dissolution of authority, but a "responsible state is therefore minimally coercive and minimally representative," and "legitimated by its judicial function."¹⁴⁶ That judicial function nonetheless encounters the law of the Spirit of Christ, as noted above, wherever that society has made a place for the church in its midst. For O'Donovan, "responsible government, therefore, will be neither the triumphalist service of a Christian empire nor secularist political neutrality."¹⁴⁷ Such a notion of responsibility prevents O'Donovan's work from being understood as underwriting a scenario in which the church is nothing more than a moralistic critic of society that in any event cannot reach society, since the critique is not primarily service of society but moral self-justification of the church.¹⁴⁸

Even if O'Donovan's theology of history allows him to avoid a straightforward defence of Christendom while offering a word of advice to its critics, his reading is in fact contested, a possibility that he has recognized as inevitable. Of the several contested dimensions of his account, perhaps the most compelling, is the question of whether his reading of Christendom has gone too far in moving beyond suspicion. That is, in his zeal to ensure that Christian political theology has more to offer than suspicion of secular power, O'Donovan may have lost an appropriate amount of critical distance. Closely connected with this notion is the related criticism that O'Donovan's political theology is simply too interested in rule – this despite his disclaimers about responsible government, the role of minimal secular coercion and representation. That is, while O'Donovan is not interested in defending any form of monarchical or totalitarian rule, or control of government structures more generally, nonetheless it is the case that he wants to rule morally.¹⁴⁹ This

---

¹⁴⁵ O'Donovan, *The Desire of the Nations*, 231.

¹⁴⁶ O'Donovan, *The Desire of the Nations*, 231-234, 241.

¹⁴⁷ Kroeker, "Why O'Donovan's Christendom is not Constantinian," 57.

¹⁴⁸ Bernd Wannenwetsch, review of *The Desire of the Nations: Rediscovering the Roots of Political Theology,* 466. Wannenwetsch is clear in another context of the dangers of churchly participation in political power. As he puts it, "Ironically – and in contrast to the modern reading of the development – it was exactly Christianity's rise to political power which partially but not completely obscured this nascent theological clarity about the inherent political nature of the church as a worshipping community. We must, of course, avoid the pitfall of presenting the narrative of decline from relatively healthy primitive Christian communities to the compromised church of the Christendom era." Wannenwetsch, "Liturgy," 80. Wannenwetsch might be describing the contours of the disagreement here between O'Donovan and Yoder.

¹⁴⁹ This point is made by Hauerwas and Fodor by way of comparing O'Donovan and John Milbank, who are both seen as interested in rule and in God's rule. "Whereas

interest in (moral) rule makes it more difficult to recognize and avoid the temptations that O'Donovan tries to bring into such sharp relief, and even if it is possible to recognize these dangers, it may be difficult to criticize or extricate the church on mission from such temptations, given O'Donovan's position regarding what he terms as "Christian political discipleship," a notion that O'Donovan identifies as arising from within Christendom. "The political doctrine of Christendom was discovered and elicited from the practical experience of Christian political discipleship, in which Christian rulers were accompanied and assisted by the wider church."[150] O'Donovan's way of putting the matter leaves the door open for the suggestion that Christian political discipleship is a different category than Christian discipleship, and thus reinforces the critique that his political theology is too interested in rule, and concomitantly tends to have a truncated capacity to acknowledge the dangers of such rule. Arne Rasmusson carries forward just such a critique, arguing that the more the church identifies with the ruling elite, the more it tends to see the world through the eyes of that elite. Indeed, if successful regimes are the signs of God's providence, then it becomes difficult to see how the church could challenge one's own nation or system at large, since to do so might well be seen as a questioning of that very providence. The church, through a symbiosis with the power establishment can easily lose the ability to see the world differently, let alone challenge that establishment. If that is the case, Rasmusson argues, then the social creativity of Christianity may well be located in dissenting churches, instead of in those that are part of Christendom.[151] Rasmusson's point is well-taken, but misses the mark in part with O'Donovan, since O'Donovan's understanding of 'success' has to do with an apt view of the possibility of appropriate judgment in the secular realm. Thus there is no reason why the church should not remain critical within a 'successful' regime, if the church remains clear on the distinction between provisional and ultimate judgment. That is, O'Donovan does not commit the church to identification with the elite in order to discharge Christian political responsibility.

It should be noted that one of the reasons that O'Donovan is able to pursue

---

O'Donovan wants to rule morally, Milbank wants to rule intellectually…Being all too cognizant of the sinful proclivities of the human imagination and of the seeming ineradicable human pride which reserves for political life its most virulent manifestations, we find our hope in the prospects of human rule under God to be tempered more by the eschatological 'not yet' than encouraged by the eschatological 'already.' Hauerwas and Fodor, "Remaining in Babylon," 40. Gilbert Meilaender shows a similar hesitation about O'Donovan's emphasis on rule, focusing instead on having less eagerness to "have the force of even a humble state joined too closely to the mission of the church," and emphasizing more eschatological reservation about political rule than he sees displayed in O'Donovan. Meilaender, "Recovering Christendom," 42.

[150] O'Donovan, *The Desire of the Nations*, 219.

[151] Rasmusson, "Not all Justifications of Christendom are Created Equal," 71-73.

his positive reading of Christendom is his decision to treat rule and society separately. That is, he finds the analogy to the church's practices in early modern liberal *society,* not in rule, where judicial activity is the mark of power that is attentive to the triumph of Christ. However, William Cavanaugh warns of the danger of separating notions of the state too sharply from society. The temptation is to see a great advantage in speaking of 'civil society' because it seems to allow the church to avoid privatization without implication in the specter of Constantinian state coercion. Cavanaugh's concern is that unless 'public' is redefined, being public is a game at which Christians will lose, because as soon as a distinction is made between private and public, the church is domesticated by the state, especially if 'society' is seen as a neutral space that can accommodate any number of voices that are nonetheless at the service of the state. The great irony, then, according to Cavanaugh, is that in trying to arrange for the church to influence 'the public,' rather than simply *be* public, the public has reduced the church to its own terms. He concludes that "public Christian presence cannot be the pursuit of influence over the powers, but rather a question of what kind of community disciplines we need in order to produce people of peace capable of speaking truth to power."[152] Cavanaugh's concerns apply to O'Donovan's understanding of the necessity of separating rule and society too sharply, a move that pushes O'Donovan to do just what Cavanaugh warns against – the attempt to pursue influence over the powers as the primary public Christian presence. That is, O'Donovan's view of secular authority depends on separate authorization of the state and the church, proper understanding of secular, and so on, but does not depend on community practices so much as on the way to be political; at the same time, the church does depend on practices when it deals with itself within the pastoral theater.

Yoder challenges any historical reading that is not eschatological enough, and therefore incapable of seeing things as they really are – thus Yoder calls for a doxological reading of history.[153] Or more accurately, Yoder calls for a *rereading* of history, not because each generation needs to write history from scratch, "but that *at certain points* there is specifiable good news about the human condition, the goodness or the newness of which those hitherto have been controlling the storytelling had not yet appropriated."[154] Yoder's 'reading against the grain' in this way challenges a 'necessitarian vision of causation,' and takes actual decisions of people seriously as part of history, a move which allows him to challenge determinism. His readings try to take seriously the

---

[152] William Cavanaugh, *Theopolitical Imagination: Discovering the Liturgy as a Political Act in an Age of Global Consumerism* (New York: T& T Clark, 2002), 88. The argument I summarize here is taken from pages 53-95.

[153] Yoder, "The Burden and Discipline of Evangelical Revisionism," in Louise Hawkley and James Juhnke, eds. *Nonviolent America: History Through the Eyes of Peace* (Kansas: Mennonite Press, Bethel College, 1993), 21-37.

[154] Yoder, "The Burden and Discipline of Evangelical Revisionism," 22.

underdogs of history and challenge the falseness of official ideologies that interpret history to support those very ideologies.[155] Yoder's reading history *against* the grain allows him to live *with* the grain of the universe, and in doing so remain vulnerable to continuing dialogue with other readings in an attempt to see things as they really are.

Yoder's rejection of Christendom, based on his apocalyptic historiography assumes that the church has responsibility, but not primarily to control or shape the judgments of government – or at any rate, it is not those judgments that display the triumph of Christ. Rather the church is responsible and representative – judgment is needed in the church, the practices of the body of Christ are translated into societal norms, so the responsibility of the church to the risen Lord is also responsibility to society. Therefore, Christendom (Constantinianism) has to be rejected as a source for understanding Christian responsibility, and resisted on an ongoing basis in any of its forms, according to Yoder.

It is important to reiterate a point that can easily be lost in this critical comparison of Yoder and O'Donovan's respective visions of Christian political responsibility. That is, Yoder's claims to forego the grasping of 'the handles of history' carry in them an implicit judgment on other visions of political theology, whereby others are seen as doing just that, attempting to grasp power conventionally understood, and thus make things come out right. But to see Yoder as innocent of grasping the handles of history and O'Donovan as guilty of such as charge would be to misunderstand the comparison at this critical juncture. O'Donovan is critically concerned that political responsibility is *not* seen as the imposition of the human will on some blank slate of human history. Thus O'Donovan's constant and consistent warnings against historicism, against seeing history as completely open to unfettered acts of the human will.

The distinctive readings of Christendom and Christian political responsibility found in Yoder and O'Donovan are pursued in both projects into discussions of the legitimacy of the use of violence by secular power, a discussion that brings into sharp relief the divergent social instantiations of these theopolitical visions that both scholars claim are theologically and Biblically based. It is to this issue that the next chapter will turn.

---

[155] These re-readings (and others) are part of Yoder's argument in "The Burden and Discipline of Evangelical Revisionism."

Chapter 4

The Just War Revisited:
The Just War Rejected

Introduction

This critical comparative study of the theopolitical projects of Yoder and O'Donovan will now turn to one dimension of the concrete social instantiation of these two visions – namely, their respective views of the role of the legitimacy of force on the part of secular power. Both projects reject any notion that the church can legitimately use force on its own behalf, or that the state can be justifiably recruited to use force on behalf of the church to resolve some theological dispute or disciplinary issue.

Nonetheless, there is a deep and fundamental disagreement between Yoder and O'Donovan regarding the use of force by secular power in that O'Donovan's political theology leads him to revisit what he considers to be the unjustly neglected Just War tradition in hope of reviving it to an appropriate level of prescriptive use. This initiative of retrieval is consistent with O'Donovan's theologically based politics, his reading of the Bible and the Great Tradition of Christian political thought. It is his reading of these sources that informs his notion of the importance of the political act (not primarily an institution or ideology), an act that seeks to embody law, justice, and political right in the realm of secular power, which is made possible by the rule of Christ. Clarity regarding eschatology is also essential, since, according to O'Donovan, Christ's rule will become fully real and transparent in the eschaton, but it is *not* the role of the Christian, the church, or of secular power to bring about the coming kingdom - that is the work of Christ. Instead, what is required of the secular power is judgment, understood as provisional and penultimate, never under the illusion that the actions that are undertaken in the service of judgment, even if they are violent, can have ultimate status. However, according to O'Donovan, part of the essence of penultimate judgment is power, and the possible use of legitimate force is part of that power. Thus, it is not accurate to understand O'Donovan as a just warrior who goes to theology to underwrite that position. Rather, his revisiting of the Just War tradition comes as a result of his theological project.

Yoder's political theology, on the other hand, leads him to reject killing and war in favor of pacifism, although he engages the Just War tradition seriously as part of an attempt to call that tradition to be honest to its own best impulses, an engagement that Yoder understands as born of his pacifism. Yoder's pacifism, like O'Donovan's support of Just War, should *not* be seen as a position that can be understood apart from his theological project and his reading of the Bible. Yoder's belief that the resurrection vindicates the way of the cross suggests to him that pacifism is the logical and, more importantly, the faithful way to follow Christ in discipleship. His understanding of discipleship includes the view that the community of disciples, the church, cannot underwrite violence by secular power, even if war is fought in the name of justice and order. While allowing for the state to pursue police action that uses minimal force, Yoder nonetheless argues that the pursuit of justice through war is a misunderstanding of eschatology, since such a pursuit relies on a consequentialist calculation that does not take seriously enough the notion that God is in control of history. Yoder's pacifism is not a principle that he is committed to apart from his understanding of discipleship, nor does his pacifism lead him to withdrawal from the world. He does not begin with pacifism and then seek to justify it theologically. Rather, his theological understandings lead him to pacifism. Thus, for Yoder and O'Donovan respectively, pacifism and the Just War tradition are not accounts of violence that can be abstracted from their theological projects, but are embedded in their understandings of Christian political responsibility. I will trace this basic difference through their respective understandings of justice/judgment, eschatology, ecclesiology, and the relationship of peace, war and responsibility. Yoder would criticize O'Donovan for being incapable of escaping Christendom, and therefore Constantinianism, and ultimately grasping for power because there is not enough eschatological tension in his work. O'Donovan would criticize Yoder for being essentially modern – unable to muster anything more than suspicion, focused too narrowly on the opposition between this world and the next, incapable of engaging the responsibilities of power beyond state boundaries, and ultimately stuck in the theater of the pastoral because of a thin theology that ironically finds itself on the same side of issues as supporters of deterrence strategies based on massive arms build-up. In sum, I will argue that while Yoder and O'Donovan share the belief that Christology anchors Christian political thinking, their views on the possibility of the use of force by secular power offer a concrete example that reveals how differently they understand the implications of Christology for political theology.

The Nature of the Disagreement between Yoder's Pacifism and O'Donovan's Just War

While it is true that the Just War tradition and pacifism are not entirely incommensurable, it is nonetheless the case that fundamental differences exist between Yoder and O'Donovan on the question of secular force. However, it is important to frame the nature of these differences accurately, a task that is made difficult by the mutual misunderstandings perpetuated by Yoder and O'Donovan themselves in their respective discussions of the traditions with which they are in disagreement. That is, when Yoder describes Just War theory as an attempt to control history, an attempt based on not taking Jesus seriously enough, his critique misses the mark regarding O'Donovan, whose revisiting of the tradition cannot be reduced to that of a Constantinian just warrior, based as it is on a Christologically centered theology. Conversely, O'Donovan's representation of pacifism as a monolith that can only muster modern suspicion and therefore by its very nature cannot take up Christian responsibility does not take into account Yoder's careful delineation of a messianic pacifism committed to constructive engagement with the world, irreducible to mere suspicion, a position that collapses if taken in isolation from the confession that Jesus is Lord. O'Donovan is reacting to a pacifism other than Yoder's, while Yoder's criticism of the Just War Tradition does not take into account the kind of theological basis O'Donovan employs in his use of that tradition.

Yoder's criticisms of the Just War tradition are often closely connected to his account of Constantinianism, to the extent that he seems to assume that anyone who supports the Just War tradition does so precisely and only because of the prior mistake of acquiescing to a symbiotic relationship of church and secular power in which the source for knowledge is so-called common sense based on empirical data,[1] and not Christ. Yoder sees the Just War tradition as based on the misguided belief that Christians have to guide the emperor and thus have a hand in making history come out right,[2] which results in a calculating consequentialism that seems necessary for the assumption of social responsibility.[3] Yoder also sees support of the Just War tradition as at bottom an issue of unfaithfulness to the call of discipleship, a reversal of the direction

---

[1] Yoder, "The Credibility of Ecclesiastical Teaching on the Morality of War," in Leroy Rouner, ed. *Celebrating Peace* (Notre Dame: University of Notre Dame Press, 1990), 38.
[2] Yoder, *Christian Attitudes to War, Peace, and Revolution,* 46, 49, 51.
[3] Yoder, "War as a Moral Problem in the Early Church: The Historian's Hermeneutical Assumptions," in Harvey Dyck, ed. *The Pacifist Impulse in Historical Perspective* (Toronto: University of Toronto Press, 1996), 96. Yoder offers more nuanced accounts of Just War thinking in his book *When War is Unjust: Being Honest in Just-War Thinking,* 2d ed. (Eugene: Wipf and Stock, 2001), where he engages that tradition on its own terms instead of only subjecting it to his pacifist criticism. When he engages Just War thinkers, he claims to be encouraging them to take their own tradition as seriously as possible. When he writes in other contexts, he subjects that tradition to consistent Constantinian critique of the kind that I am describing here. For example, in writings published both before and after *When War is Unjust,* Yoder retains his Constantinian critique in a fairly consistent manner. Yoder's direct engagement with the Just War tradition will be dealt with further below.

indicated by the incarnation of Christ.[4] Yoder fears that the notion of 'public service' is a euphemism for the exercise of power as benefaction.[5] Since the Bible "raises special doubts concerning the appropriateness of state violence as an instrument of righteousness,"[6] Yoder concludes therefore that the Just War tradition can only take root in a Constantinian situation. However, as I will show, O'Donovan's revisiting of the Just War tradition does not fall easily within the purview of this basic line of critique.

O'Donovan's criticisms of pacifism are most closely related to his belief that it cannot discharge the calling of Christian political discipleship in the theatre of the *saeculum*, that place where can be found "a time to love, to believe, and to hope under a regime of provisional judgment; here, too, it is possible to practice reconciliation, since God's patience waits, and preserves the world against its own self-destruction."[7] According to O'Donovan, pacifism cuts off responsibility to the world outside of the church, because it can only offer suspicion and criticism without engaging in constructive work. Indeed, O'Donovan suggests that pacifism has much in common with the kind of deterrence based on massive arms build-up. That is, both pacifism and deterrence seek to banish force entirely from human history, and as such pacifism is merely a mutant form of deterrence "transformed by a technological and historicist vision of human progress,"[8] whereas, O'Donovan insists, Christians are called to offer to the world a counter-praxis to the violence that is based on the praxis of unmediated conflict. For O'Donovan, pacifism is a Christian strategy that limits counter-praxis to the pastoral theater, and can offer nothing more than endurance and martyrdom in the theater of the world, a criticism which simply fails to do justice to the kind of pacifism endorsed and promoted by Yoder (and others) who argue for much deeper and broader constructive engagement than some kind of endurance. But O'Donovan rejects any notion that there are many and variegated forms of pacifism, claiming instead that "in the face of a praxis of unmediated opposition, it [pacifism]

---

[4] Yoder, *The Priestly Kingdom*, 74, 157.

[5] Yoder, *The Royal Priesthood*, 95, 119.

[6] Yoder, *For the Nations*, 92. While Yoder claims that "the Bible speaks of the people of God as an instrument of God's justice not to be telescoped into the role of civil government," he does not specify the nature of these 'special doubts' any further.

[7] O'Donovan, *The Just War Revisited*, 6.

[8] O'Donovan, *Peace and Certainty: A Theological Essay on Deterrence* (Grand Rapids: Eerdmans, 1989), 28-29. O'Donovan returns to this argument several times throughout his essay on deterrence, arguing that pacifism has unwittingly found itself intertwined with total-war strategy in the search for total peace, and because it is unwilling to engage in a search for the conditions for a sustainable just and stable peace, which might call for *appropriate* use of force. The deterrence O'Donovan refers to in this essay "is the name we have given to the stance of perpetual armed threat with which the two great political blocs of the post-war world confront each other." Ibid., 1.

holds that an evangelical counter-praxis of judgment is not to be looked for."[9] Pacifism contains a serious flaw in that peace is seen only as a gift from God, and therefore nothing can be done in the secular realm (understood as the opposite of the eternal) to create peace. Pacifism thus amounts to a *via negativa*, a praxis whose watchwords seemingly all begin with the prefix 'non,' circumscribing the possibility of action in the world. In sum, pacifism warns people away from war with the attendant effect that it becomes impossible to think practically about the tasks that are necessary for the building of stable peace and justice.[10]

The broad characterizations of opposing positions briefly outlined above amount to caricatures, and perhaps more importantly, seem to ignore the fact that it is misleading to speak of Yoder primarily as a pacifist or of O'Donovan as first and foremost a just warrior. To label them in this fashion suggests that pacifism and just war are starting positions, rather than part of a more comprehensive theological project. However, to suggest that the broad characterizations of these positions are inaccurate is not to suggest that the differences between Yoder and O'Donovan are not real and profound. Rather, the differences cannot be circumscribed by accusations of Constantinianism, lack of social responsibility, or a reluctance to take Jesus seriously.[11] The divergence of views is better located in fundamentally incommensurable understandings of Christian responsibility, which find their orientation in views of justice/judgment, eschatology, and ecclesiology. We turn now to trace the connection of these ideas to the use of secular violence, which will reveal the

---

[9] O'Donovan, *The Just War Revisited*, 7.

[10] O'Donovan, *The Just War Revisited*, 9-15. In a 1985 public debate with Anabaptist thinker Ronald Sider regarding peace and war, O'Donovan presents a number of disagreements with Sider's position as presented, and argues that the real question on the table is whether resort to force is ever justified. O'Donovan suggests that if Sider and other pacifists assume such an *a priori* position, then it becomes impossible to move beyond a discussion of face-to-face confrontation to a consideration of the protection of others, which may entail the use of force, according to O'Donovan, even while remaining faithful to Jesus. See Ronald Sider and Oliver O'Donovan, *Peace and War: A Debate About Pacifism* (Bramcote: Grove Books, 1985), 13-17.

[11] D. Stephen Long has suggested that the disagreement between Paul Ramsey and Yoder also misses the mark in that the description of the other's position is "too easy a characterization." That is, Ramsey accuses Yoder of irresponsibility, and Yoder accuses Ramsey of trying to control history. Long attempts to show that Ramsey and Yoder are not that far apart in their positions, since both proceed not from nationalistic commitments, but from the community of discipleship. While I agree with Long concerning the inadequacy of the mutual characterizations of Ramsey and Yoder, he comes close to papering over fundamental differences that remain on other grounds, some of which are similar to the differences that will be explored between O'Donovan and Yoder. See D. Stephen Long, "Ramseyian Just War and Yoderian Pacifism: Where is the Disagreement?" *Studies in Christian Ethics* 4 no 1 (1990): 58-72.

real nature of the differences between Yoder and O'Donovan's theopolitical projects.[12]

Judgment and Justice

As he makes obvious in *The Desire of the Nations* and *The Ways of Judgment*, O'Donovan understands judgment to be a central dimension of political theology, serving as one of the four political terms that provide a framework for his exegetical work. To recap briefly, O'Donovan reads the Old Testament to reveal the judgments of God both on an individual basis, and with regard to the people as a whole. God's judgments bring the distinction between the just and the unjust to view, and form the basis for the performance of juridical activity.[13] The ministry of Jesus also functioned as a proclamation of the coming judgment of Israel, especially for those on whom the responsibility of misdirecting the nation fell. Further, Jesus' ministry displayed a positive judgment on behalf of the poor. The passion of Jesus also functions as a moment of judgment on this world, as it separates the innocent from the guilty, is recapitulated in the mark of martyrdom in the life of the church, and provides the basis of the corresponding act of worship contained in the Eucharist.[14] The political theme of judgment for O'Donovan is not the basis of some particular institutional form as much as it is the ground of reflection and action that must be undertaken by secular power in order to bring about political right. Put another way, judgment is the gateway to the pursuit of justice.[15] Closely connected to issues of judgment and justice in O'Donovan's thought is the notion of authority. That is, judgment has to do with the dynamic disposal of authority into the place of need.[16] Further, for the principle of authority to be made concrete, it has to be re-ordered to the task of judgment, says O'Donovan.[17] And it is secular authority that has been authorized by the Christ-

---

[12] I have found no explicit discussion of O'Donovan's work in Yoder. O'Donovan mentions Yoder from time to time, but does not in fact treat Yoder's writings on pacifism seriously. Indeed, aside from the published debate between Sider and O'Donovan, there is a minimal amount of direct engagement with pacifist interlocutors in O'Donovan's work.

[13] O'Donovan, *The Desire of the Nations*, 37-40; *The Ways of Judgment*, 6.

[14] O'Donovan, *The Desire of the Nations*, 138-141; 178-181.

[15] As O'Donovan puts it, "'Judgment,' then, is more sharply focused than the abstract noun 'justice,'" in that the latter term has been used in Western moral discourse in three ways, which have converged in Western Christian thought – justice-as-right, justice-as-virtue, and justice-as-judgment. O'Donovan's working definition of judgment as "an act of moral discrimination that pronounces upon a preceding act or existing state of affairs to establish a new public context" seeks to provide this more sharply focused political concept. O'Donovan, *The Ways of Judgment*, 6, 7.

[16] O'Donovan, *The Desire of the Nations*, 106.

[17] O'Donovan, *The Desire of the Nations*, 286.

event to ensure the social space needed for the mission of the church. The secular authority, to be sure, is called to serve God's purpose, which, according to O'Donovan, is judgment, so that "the whole rationale of government is seen to rest on its capacity to effect the judicial task."[18] Thus secular power is authorized to carry forward the task of judgment to bring about justice for others, not for purposes of self-defense.[19] The task of judgment is to be understood in the central political sense of responding to wrong done in the public realm.[20] That is, "political judgment ... is a response to wrong as injury to the public good."[21]

Judgment within the church is one kind of counter-praxis, which can only be understood as taking place within the community of belief and worship, and thus takes the shape of "mutual forgiveness, by which enemies who believe the Gospel are made enemies no longer."[22] This is not to say that Christians are not subject to the judgment of secular authority. However, within the community itself, O'Donovan maintains that the church "functions on an almost totally opposite principle to the judicial principle that serves the general needs of the world."[23] That is, Christians within their own church community do not seek retaliation for evil, nor vengeance or vindication, but rather entrust such judgment to the decisive act of God. The church community's disavowal of such judgment contrasts sharply with the pursuit of judgment in the secular realm, which deals with penultimate and provisional judgments. "By embracing the final judgment of God Christians have accepted that they have no need for penultimate judgments to defend their rights. The continued presence of such judgments in the world, however, is an important witness to those to whom the word of final judgment has yet to come."[24] Indeed, O'Donovan claims that the decisive test of a political theology is whether it can articulate what he refers to as the counter-political movement of the cross along with the moral implication that those who live by the cross may not judge. Political theology has to be careful not to be trapped by the totalizing of the political within the counter-political, an arena in which everything is political, but with severely limited meaning that cannot get past a self-assertive and anti-authoritarian spirit. Such a totalizing of the political within the counter-political creates something that cannot be actualized, and tends toward depoliticization. Rather, O'Donovan

---

[18] O'Donovan, *The Desire of the Nations*, 148.
[19] Sider and O'Donovan, *Peace and War*, 15.
[20] O'Donovan, *The Ways of Judgment*, 32. O'Donovan's point here is embedded in a larger discussion of justice and equality, in which he argues that judgment is not to be understood within a framework of reciprocity, which, if taken as the sole matrix of justice, can easily lead to the "totalizing of market-theory which was such a feature of late twentieth-century political and social thought." Ibid., 36.
[21] O'Donovan, *The Ways of Judgment*, 59.
[22] O'Donovan, *The Just War Revisited*, 6.
[23] O'Donovan, *The Desire of the Nations*, 149.
[24] O'Donovan, *The Desire of the Nations*, 151.

suggests that when Jesus calls for judgment, what is required is to judge the good that God by his judgment has set before his people to do, and is now open to be done. The society that has felt the need for judgment has cried to God for judgment, has seen such judgment revealed in Christ, and believed what it has seen, then begins to judge for itself, because it can recognize the 'moment,' the interim which is a definite something. While the church as a community judges not, it bears witness to a final judgment. Yet that witness is not the whole story for O'Donovan, since to stop there would be to become mired in ecclesial self-description, or ecclesiology. But political theology carries on as "an intellectual enquiry located on the horizon of the theology of the church... a description of the world as it appears on this horizon..."[25]

In the theatre of the *saeculum*, which is the world of unbelief and disobedience, judgment is found as "the interim provision of God's common grace, promising the dawning of God's final peace ... a time to live, to believe and to hope under a regime of provisional judgment; here, too, it is possible to practise reconciliation, since God's patience waits, and preserves the world against its own self-destruction."[26] It is in this context that war becomes not only possible, but also potentially a calling, since war can be authority practicing judgment, whereby it becomes possible to speak of the judicial model of war.[27] On this account, Just War tradition is not an attempt to assume control, or to recruit the state to do the work of the church, or to ask the state to use coercion in church disciplinary matters, *contra* Yoder's generalized complaints regarding Just War tradition. Rather, O'Donovan expects that secular power must do what it is called to do by the reality of the triumph of Christ – that is, to dispose authority into the place where justice is needed, where the powerless are mistreated, where what is needed is not being done and so on. Judgment thus disposed can be understood as both reactive, since it is a response to wrong as injury to the public good, and proactive, since it seeks to anticipate harm from private neglect or ignorance, and thus avert the threat of harm.[28]

So O'Donovan speaks of judgment as the gateway to justice, wherein

---

[25] O'Donovan, *The Ways of Judgment*, 239. The larger argument extends from 233-241.

[26] O'Donovan, *The Just War Revisited*, 6.

[27] O'Donovan assumes that a similar argument can be used in the case of capital punishment. That is, capital punishment by the state is not an attempt to defend itself, but comes from the office of judgment that is legitimately part of the calling of secular power. That is, O'Donovan insists that it is important to see any connection secular power has to coercion that might include death has to be related to judgment. See O'Donovan, "The Death Penalty in *Evangelium Vitae*," in Reinhard Hütter and Theodor Dieter, eds. *Ecumenical Ventures in Ethics: Protestants Engage Pope John Paul II's Moral Encyclicals* (Grand Rapids: Eerdmans, 1998), 216-236. O'Donovan also includes a discussion of punishment as an instance of judgment in *The Ways of Judgment*, 101-124.

[28] O'Donovan, *The Ways of Judgment*, 62.

judgment happens both in the theatre of the church and the theatre of the secular, but differently, since violence can never be dispatched in the church *by* the church or by the state *for* the church, whereas in the theatre of the secular, Christians must submit to and participate in judgment, the bearings for which are found in love, which can, paradoxically, on this account, smite and even slay.[29] To resist or ignore the task of judgment in the theatre of the secular, as O'Donovan accuses pacifists of doing, is to remain committed to a 'bi-polar' rather than the required 'tri-polar' configuration to which Christians are called. That is, pacifists may well be willing to forego self-protection in face-to-face encounters, but are remiss when they do not adequately take into account responsibility for the protection of other people.[30] O'Donovan's critique is intensified when the discussion moves beyond the confines of a single given state, since he claims that pacifism will not even contemplate the improvisation of judgment where it is not provided for in the state structure. Therefore, pacifism, despite claims to the contrary, is monolithic in that "it holds that an evangelical counter-praxis of judgment is not to be looked for."[31] Just War tradition, on the other hand, asserts the practical claim "that God's mercy and peace may and must be witnessed to in this interim of salvation history through a praxis of judgment, even beyond the normal reach of states."[32]

While O'Donovan insists that secular power must execute judgment and be willing to use war as part of the practice of judgment, Yoder is unwilling to make such a move. The topic of judgment plays a relatively minor role in Yoder's political theology, and in any case, could not play the role of

---

[29] O'Donovan, *The Just War Revisited*, 9.

[30] Sider and O'Donovan, *Peace and War*, 15. O'Donovan reiterates the point in *The Ways of Judgment*, 209, where he argues that this tri-polar structure is fundamental to the public ownership of an act of force, and therefore the community is not represented in a bi-polar confrontation.

[31] O'Donovan, *The Just War Revisited*, 7.

[32] O'Donovan, *The Just War Revisited*, 9. Here O'Donovan sounds remarkably similar to his mentor, Paul Ramsey, whose notion of the political act as an "exercise of power and an exercise of purpose," is taken up by O'Donovan in the early part of *The Desire of the Nations* and carried forward into discussions of Just War in *Just War Revisited*. Ramsey's book, *The Just War: Force and Political Responsibility* collects many of Ramsey's essays in which he sets forth his understanding of how a truer doctrine of Just War can be restored. Such a doctrine would show that it is the work of love and mercy to deliver God's children from tyranny and protect them from oppression, which can be done through the just exercise of force. Indeed, according to Ramsey, if the Just War doctrine did not exist, Christians would have to invent it in order to find a way to be faithful to God in terms of political responsibility. See Ramsey, *The Just War: Force and Political Responsibility* (New York: Charles Scribner's Sons, 1968), 8, 54, 143, 146; O'Donovan, *The Desire of the Nations*, 20. While I will not develop the relationship of Ramsey's thought to O'Donovan's work in a systematic manner, there will be occasions to show the connections between them.

underwriting a judicial account of war. Rather, any suggestion that the judicial model of war is legitimized by the triumph of Christ and finds its bearings in the expression of Christian love[33] would be strongly resisted by Yoder on the basis that such a view assumes a calculating link between that which is in God's hands (judgment) and the actions of secular power. Any such calculating link has been broken, according to Yoder, whose point is not to avoid the pursuit of the right, but rather that

> the triumph of the right is assured not by the might that comes to the aid of the right, which is of course justification of the use of violence and other kinds of power in every human conflict. The triumph of the right, although it is assured, is sure because of the power of the resurrection and not because of any calculation of cause and effects, nor because of the inherently greater strength of the good guys. The relationship between the obedience of God's people and the triumph of God's cause is not a relationship of cause and effect but one of cross and resurrection.[34]

Yoder disavows a kind of calculus or justification that is not rooted in the logic of cross and resurrection, which he believes can never justify violence. Any argument that in the end permits the taking of life is based on calculations of right and merit, and thus displays a lack of faith in Jesus Christ, according to Yoder.[35]

In addition, Yoder sees as dubious a position that uses justice as a means of arguing for the legitimacy of war. He suspects that in such a view, justice simply acts as a caricature that commits people to be guided by some other standards than the incarnation of Jesus Christ.[36] This is not to suggest that secular power has no legitimate function. To the contrary, the state has a role that is determined by the Lordship of Christ. However, Yoder's understanding of the role of the state is significantly different here than O'Donovan's. While the secular state is not separately authorized, according to Yoder, it nonetheless serves a function within God's plan by encouraging good and restraining evil. The Christian who is a pacifist is not relegated to irrelevance, since the Christian nonetheless speaks to the state of how it can best fulfill its responsibilities.[37] But the role of secular power in Yoder's view is not judgment; he argues that while God's judgment is sure, that judgment is to be realized in the future.

However, it is important to understand just what Yoder means by this

---

[33] O'Donovan, *The Just War Revisited*, 9. O'Donovan argues here that in the Just War tradition, we find the paradoxical form of the thought that love can smite and even slay, which is clearly a parting of the ways with pacifism.

[34] Yoder, *The Politics of Jesus,* 232.

[35] Yoder, *The Original Revolution,* 48.

[36] Yoder, *The Royal Priesthood,* 119.

[37] Yoder, *The Christian Witness to the State,* 5, 13, 32.

The Just War

pushing of God's judgment into the future. His point is that, according to his reading of the New Testament, there can be no instrumental linkage between a trust in God's future victory and present progress in the pursuit of justice through the political act of judgment.[38]

> The language of the Bible, we saw, is, 'He will come to judge.' That divine intervention is sure. It is this-worldly. It is not set apart from this world by an antipolitical or apolitical dualism or 'division of planes.' It vindicates our faithfulness, but without mandating us to be manipulative or coercive. It condemns the oppressor, yet without vengefully doing to him what he has done. The Lord's coming 'to judge,' i.e., to set things right, will be soon, but not right now. It does not bypass our ongoing struggle; yet the criterion guiding us in the struggle is not whether we win, not whether we can implement lesser-evil calculations to get there, but whether we keep the faith.[39]

The key distinction between Yoder and O'Donovan regarding the role of judgment, especially as it relates to the use of coercion by the state, is made clear in this statement. That is, Yoder simply refuses to talk about judgment apart from the church. For example, in making the 'Christian Case for Democracy,' Yoder argues that it is in the Christian community where people should be allowed to speak freely and listen critically, skills that it should be possible to transfer to debates about human justice. The point is not that the Bible speaks to every issue of justice, but that the people of God should know how to process such issues once they have learned to do so within the Christian community,[40] and presumably what has been learned there does not include the use of violence. So there may be a foundation for optimism regarding the pursuit of justice outside the church, but that optimism must be founded "on the logic of servanthood rather than mixing coercive beneficence with claimed theological modesty."[41] Yoder goes as far as to say that the church accepts living under an unjust social order. He is quick to point out, however, in the face of anticipated criticisms of such a statement, that this is not to acquiesce to orders of power that keep people poor and downtrodden as though such orders were just. Instead, the Christian church remains concerned about the relative improvement of the society in which it lives, with the proviso that "these efforts must not be carried on with a rationale which gives people the hope that

---

[38] Yoder, *For the Nations*, 133.

[39] Yoder, *For the Nations*, 137. The context of Yoder's paragraph is a discussion of the politics of Martin Luther King, Jr. Yoder's analysis of King's work to combat racism in American society centers on bearing the cross as an ethical and strategic category.

[40] This is not part of a religious demonstration of "irreversible ideological progress" that O'Donovan suggests it might be in *The Ways of Judgment*, 171.

[41] Yoder, *The Priestly Kingdom*, 166, 167. The essay in which Yoder makes the argument is entitled "The Christian Case for Democracy."

somehow just around the very next corner "Freedom Land" will come into view."[42]

O'Donovan would see Yoder's refusal to speak of justice apart from the church as irresponsible in that it ignores the theatre of the secular in which the pursuit of justice is important and made possible precisely by the triumph of Christ.[43] O'Donovan suspects that Yoder's theology leads him to the point where it is impossible not only to exercise judgment as political act, but to allow persuasions of any kind to shape society. In other words, O'Donovan suspects Yoder of being fully modern in his belief that any and all social agreements are unjustifiably coercive. O'Donovan's explicit complaint about Yoder in this regard comes within the context of an argument O'Donovan makes regarding the possibility of holding social agreements that are not considered to be coercive simply by their very existence within a society. That is, while early modern liberals thought that there was nothing to fear from shared convictions rationally reached and rationally held, it is now the case that it has come to seem perilous to allow persuasions of any kind to shape society. If social agreements of any kind are potentially coercive, then surely the agreements that constitute the church are also unjustifiably coercive, according to this way of seeing things. O'Donovan believes that narrative theology is guilty of exactly this move; that is, while the narrativists profess that agreement on a common story is an essential element in social identity, their customary repudiation of Christendom on the basis of its having embraced the wrong story is the point at which they succumb to the liberal thesis that any society defined by its belief is to be banned. Says O'Donovan, "in resolving to deconstruct the self-storying of Christendom the narrativists have simply followed the principle proposed by their adversaries: social doctrine of whatever kind is coercive; those who claim a social identity in terms of unnecessary belief do violence to those who do not share it."[44]

It is in the context of this discussion of narrative theology's collapse into neo-liberal patterns that O'Donovan charges Yoder of being guilty of espousing a view that cannot account for any kind of shared convictions that might form social identity without being unjustifiably coercive. Yoder, says O'Donovan, can only muster the weak notion of voluntariety as a basis for church community precisely because he has not escaped the modern liberal view.

---

[42] Yoder, *For the Nations*, 118.

[43] Here Chris Huebner is incorrect in suggesting that O'Donovan (and Paul Ramsey) have an account of justice that is somehow prior to Christology. See Stanley Hauerwas and Chris Huebner, "History, Theology, and Anabaptism: A Conversation on Theology after John Howard Yoder," in *The Wisdom of the Cross*, 402. O'Donovan's account of justice is predicated on his Christology, both in the shape of the justice and in an understanding of how it is to be pursued, and in any case, judgment precedes justice, as previously noted.

[44] O'Donovan, *The Desire of the Nations*, 222-223.

According to O'Donovan, Yoder's view of the church's social identity can be distilled without loss to the single issue of the exercise of individual liberty.

> A voluntary society is one that I could leave without incurring grave or irremediable loss, which might seem strange for a Christian to think about the church. Finally, does the concept of the church as a voluntary society not commend itself chiefly because it fits late-modern expectations of how civil society will be organized? Is Yoder, in the name of non-conformity, not championing a great conformism, lining the church up with the sports clubs, friendly societies, colleges, symphony subscription-guilds, political parties and so on, just to prove that the church offers late-modern order no serious threat?[45]

O'Donovan's rhetorical flourish disguises a flattened description of Yoder's work, drained of the theological distinctiveness of notions such as freedom, voluntariety, ecclesiological identity and discipline, and social doctrine. The charge that Yoder is guilty of espousing the notion that any implementation of social doctrine is coercive is inadequate on several counts. First, but perhaps least important here, is the casual lumping of Yoder amongst the narrative theologians.[46] But appropriate categorization is not really at issue; rather, the important issue here is Yoder's construal of voluntariety, which simply cannot be reduced to the liberal notion of unfettered, ultimately inconsequential individual choice.[47] For Yoder, the notion of voluntariety is just as important

---

[45] O'Donovan, *The Desire of the Nations*, 223, 224.

[46] See Chris Huebner, "Mennonites and Narrative Theology: The Case of John Howard Yoder," 15-38. Huebner argues that while there are some affinities such as an emphasis on theological and ecclesiological particularity between narrative theology and Yoder's thought, Yoder "resists appealing to the general category of narrative and according it primacy in a way characteristic of the general movement of narrative theology," due in large part to the fact that narrative theology "is insufficiently particular, standing above, or perhaps beside, but in any case not adequately rooted in the church." Huebner, "Mennonites and Narrative Theology," 22, 29.

[47] Yoder cannot, however, escape criticism of his voluntarism entirely, in my view. See for example, Stanley Hauerwas's comment made during a public debate with John Milbank. The connection between the issue of voluntariety and violence is nicely highlighted by Hauerwas here. "I have criticized John Yoder because sometimes I think John's language of the voluntary is overdetermined in modernity exactly because it puts too much stress on process separate from the material convictions that you want the process to serve... But what I think is worrisome, John [Milbank], about starting with an issue that begins by saying "if you don't wear your jacket, you don't get to go outside, because it is twenty degrees" is that before long you are saying, "We have to defend the Western world." Among people who want to use the kind of phenomenology of violence that you are insisting upon there has been that kind of slide. The reason why you need a community that will allow you to make the kinds of discriminations for which I am calling is so that purposiveness is never lost. Of course, there are certain kinds of force

for those outside the church as those who make up the church; that is, it is essential that decisions of unbelievers are taken as seriously as those of believers.[48]

Further, Yoder's view of church membership goes far beyond the issue of 'individual freedom.' To become part of the church entails a dimension of voluntary commitment, but such a commitment brings in its wake the immersion (baptism) into a disciplined community, with practices such as binding and loosing, submission to church discipline and so on. The community of God has been a voluntary community from the time of Abraham.[49]

The basic issue here is that O'Donovan sees Yoder's refusal to legitimate secular coercion as evidence that Yoder will not stand for the implementation of any social doctrine at all because any such doctrine is coercive by its very nature. O'Donovan's suggestion that Yoder then turns to a liberal notion of voluntariety is a misunderstanding of Yoder, who calls for involvement in the secular, but in the form of church practice and witness that comes from within the disciplined church community. His voluntariety is not the sort of which O'Donovan accuses him.

The bottom line for Yoder is that secular power is not the appropriate bearer of justice.[50] Rather, the church as God's people functions as the instrument of God's justice. In an extended discussion entitled "The Bible and Civil Turmoil," Yoder argues that Catholic and Puritan visions for society seek to impose normative visions on society as a whole, in God's name. Whereas they claim differing warrants for such an understanding, Yoder argues that nonetheless

> both make the state, in its national form, the primary instrument of governing the implementation of divinely mandated righteousness. Both envisage the problem of constructing a social ethic as if it were to be applied from scratch, or from above; that is why their call for a generalized systemic blueprint comes at the outset. Both justify war if necessary. Both are very selective in their use of biblical perspectives. For both, 'the church' relates to the realm

---

and power being used, but power is not violent in and of itself." Hauerwas and Milbank, "Christian Peace: A Conversation between Stanley Hauerwas and John Milbank," in Kenneth Chase and Alan Jacobs, eds. *Must Christianity be Violent?: Reflections on History, Practice, and Theology* (Grand Rapids: Brazos Press, 2003), 215. I will take up below O'Donovan's suggestion that pacifism is modern at heart.

[48] Yoder, "The Burden and Discipline of Evangelical Revisionism," 22-29.

[49] Yoder, *For the Nations,* 174, 175.

[50] It is in this context that Travis Kroeker suggests that O'Donovan is disingenuous to say that Yoder is guilty of succumbing to the liberal notion that all social doctrine is coercive. Rather, "for Yoder, the social body politic of the church is precisely not so, and precisely because it is not in the business of enacting and enforcing judicial authority – it proceeds on a different paradigm of divine rule and justice." Kroeker, "Why O'Donovan's Christendom is not Constantinian," 55-56.

of justice through the privileged instrument of the clergy structure speaking to rulers.[51]

However, Yoder is suspicious of this understanding, since "the Bible speaks of the people of God as an instrument of God's justice not to be telescoped into the role of civil government."[52] This community of God's people would have to disavow any Solomonic or Constantinian vision that does not allow the civil community any choice. Rather the community of God that is an instrument of justice would "need to be a community committed to the ministry of 'firstfruits,' prefiguring in its own life the kingdom reality to which the whole world is called."[53] Yoder is obviously optimistic about the "community's capacity to carry the biblical paradigms creatively from one culture to another,"[54] from the church to the secular arena, but no doubt he would consider such optimism more 'realistic' than the notion that the triumph of Christ can be displayed in the judicial activity of government, especially as that includes the judicial model of war.

Eschatology

Yoder's and O'Donovan's understandings of eschatology formulate part of the rationale for their respective views regarding judgment insofar as eschatology is connected to the possibilities of the secular pursuit of war on the judicial model. But as is the case for a number of issues (church, judgment, responsibility), agreement regarding the importance of eschatology does not lead to a similar conclusion about its importance for the issues of peace and war. Yoder, on the one hand, insists that the pursuit of peace without eschatology is misguided, and that it is an apocalyptic vision that provides the way to undercut a pragmatic case for casuistic compromise resulting in the use of violence.[55] That is, a robust eschatology resists both an inappropriate liberal pacifism, and a decidedly unrealistic view that war will bring about peace and justice. O'Donovan, on the other hand, following Paul Ramsey, believes that without the "essential structure of government to harness representative status and power to the service of judgment and law,"[56] a structure which is a provision of common grace, any efforts at peace will be doomed. Real peace, which is an eschatological reality, and therefore of an ultimate nature, can only come from God. An appropriate understanding of such a future ultimate reality

---

[51] Yoder, *For the Nations*, 91.
[52] Yoder, *For the Nations*, 92.
[53] Yoder, *For the Nations*, 92.
[54] Yoder, *For the Nations*, 92.
[55] Yoder, *For the Nations*, 134.
[56] O'Donovan, *The Just War Revisited*, 32.

frees secular authority to exercise judgment in the in-between time[57] with the understanding that any such judgment and its attendant means are of a penultimate nature. Such a view is not an attempt to control history, or to bring it to an end imposed by exercise of the human will.

Perhaps the most important dimension of Yoder's eschatology as it relates to pacifism is the breaking of any calculating link between human action and God's purposes. Yoder's retrieval of the idiom of evangelical apocalyptic, or an apocalyptic stance, includes a resistance to being captured by the determinism of a system-immanent causal nexus[58] by allowing the possibility to imagine and to speak of "a frame of reference in which we acknowledge being the graced objects of a meaning from beyond ourselves."[59] Reasoning in a mode of systemic determinism assumes that it is possible to know the global social process with enough certitude to make consequentialist judgments that justify casuistically taking into our own hands coercive and violent measures toward adversaries.[60] In order to break out of this kind of thinking, which is surely not evangelical in that it does not take into account the fact that God is the ultimate mover of history, an eschatological stance ought to give pause to those who think that it is their task and calling to take hold of the handles of history and move it in the direction they think can be discerned through some immanent process. Such a stance allows Christians to resist system-immanent thinking, but also to recognize the freedom to live meaningfully in a world with an open future, a world in which the rule of Christ has come, but not yet in its fullness. Christian hope is thus not immanentized, but actually believes with the good news of the gospel that God has reached out and spoken into the world from elsewhere, and displayed the way the world really works in the incarnation of Jesus Christ.[61]

All of this suggests that the current age is one that is properly filled with eschatological tension – "tension that will be resolved by the triumph of the new in the fullness of the kingdom of God."[62] Not to recognize this tension is either to have pushed God's work completely into the future or to have brought the future into the present and called that God's will and work. To live in evangelical eschatological tension is to be involved in doxology, "a way of seeing; a grasp of which end is up, which way is forward,"[63] and not engineering. Yoder points out that the believer agrees with the liberal that

---

[57] O'Donovan, *The Desire of the Nations,* 146.

[58] This phrase, and others like it (eg. 'necessitarian vision of causation') are used by Yoder in many of his discussions of eschatology.

[59] Yoder, "The Burden and Discipline of Evangelical Revisionism," 34.

[60] Yoder, "Armaments and Eschatology," 55, 56. The idea of 'handles of history' appears at various points throughout Yoder's writings, most prominently in *The Politics of Jesus,* 232ff.

[61] Yoder, "Armaments and Eschatology," 49; "Ethics and Eschatology," 126.

[62] Yoder, *The Royal Priesthood,* 153.

[63] Yoder, *The Royal Priesthood,* 129.

persistent pressure on the system is important, and with the utopian that just because we cannot see a clear line from here to there does not mean we have to be quiet. Thus faith frees us from the bondage of an engineering model of the social order and from the hubris of identifying and grabbing the handles on the system.[64]

This construal of the relationship between eschatology and pacifism is the burden of Yoder's essay entitled "Peace Without Eschatology?"[65] As the title suggests, Yoder argues that certain kinds of peace initiatives are misguided, particularly those that take no account of eschatology.

> "Peace" is not an accurate description of what has generally happened to nonresistant Christians throughout history, nor of the way the conscientious objector is treated in most countries today. Nor does Christian pacifism guarantee a warless world. "Peace" describes the pacifist's hope, the goal in the light of which Christians act, the character of Christian actions, the ultimate divine certainty that lets the Christian position make sense; it does not describe the external appearance or by the observable results of Christian behavior. That is what we mean by eschatology: a hope that, defying present frustration, defines a present position in terms of the yet unseen goal that gives it meaning.[66]

Yoder connects this sense of hope with a reading of Christ's love that marks the new age brought on by the incarnation, life, death, and resurrection of Jesus, wherein "effectiveness and success had been sacrificed for the sake of love, but this sacrifice was turned by God into a victory that vindicated to the utmost the apparent impotence of love."[67] Thus the pacifism adopted by Christians is a matter of discipleship, not legalism, and is right not because it works, but because it anticipates the final triumph of the slain Lamb.[68]

It is this robust eschatology that enables Yoder (along with other thinkers such as Reinhold Niebuhr and Paul Ramsey, and not least, O'Donovan) to reject the "multi-faceted optimism of liberal Protestant pacifism."[69] Yoder's critique of the peace vision of Enlightenment humanism is that it is a false

---

[64] Yoder, *For the Nations,* 150.

[65] This essay was first written for a conference in the Netherlands in May 1954, published as a pamphlet in the *Concern* series in 1961, published as an essay entitled "If Christ is Truly Lord" in *The Original Revolution,* and then reprinted with minor revisions as "Peace Without Eschatology?" in *The Royal Priesthood.* References here are to the latter publication. Michael Cartwright suggests that this is one of Yoder's "most carefully wrought responses to 'responsibility ethics' argumentation" prior to *The Politics of Jesus* and *Nevertheless.* See *The Royal Priesthood,* 143-144 for Cartwright's introduction to the essay.

[66] Yoder, *The Royal Priesthood,* 145.

[67] Yoder, *The Royal Priesthood,* 148.

[68] Yoder, *The Royal Priesthood,* 148, 151.

[69] Yoder, *Christian Attitudes To War, Peace, and Revolution,* 322.

gospel that puts hope in the wrong place, based as it is on minimal, natural, universal moral insight.[70] The rise of liberal Protestant pacifism in the twentieth century entails an optimistic vision that reasonable humane moral insight can and will lead to solving problems of truth, education, and so on. Yoder rejects pacifism as it appears on these terms, and is explicit about the differences between messianic pacifism of the type he espouses and liberal Protestant pacifism, as it is exemplified by social gospel pacifism of early twentieth century America:

> Obviously war is a social evil. If it is an evil, you stop it. You stop it by teaching people that it is evil. You stop it by educating. You stop it by forbidding it and putting sanctions behind the prohibition. You stop it by creating alternative structures. This will obviously have to be a specific kind of pacifism, a social gospel kind of pacifism, that does not need to struggle deeply with failure, or with the continuing power of tyranny, or the challenge of the cross. That's all part of what we are winning out against. You don't have to debate about revelation versus other claims, e.g. whether to follow Jesus or effectiveness or rationality or the data of experience. All the moral authorities are on the same side. You have no deep choice between obedience or effectiveness, or between social pragmatism and divine command, because they are all on the same side. This position will obviously be the position of the church. Obviously it is what Jesus taught, but it would be just as true without Jesus or the church. It doesn't need Jesus as an authority, because it is true anyway. It doesn't need the church, either as a teacher or as embodiment. You don't need the church as teacher, because everybody knows already that war is a destructive stupid thing to do and ought to be stopped. The church accredits herself by reinforcing what people already know. We don't need a church as embodiment of obedience because this is a vision everybody can embody, especially statesmen and the bureaucrats of the League of Nations. You don't need any deep critical social analysis of the economic structures that make for war, or of the ethnic and racial egoisms that make for abiding polarizations, hatred and insoluble problems because we are moving past all that. Obviously there are no racial or ethnic problems that can't be solved by an expansion of the beautiful experience of the American melting pot.[71]

As is evident here, Yoder's rejection of liberal pacifism is rooted in his prior rejection of liberal optimism that he finds to be unsustainable and even unrealistic, primarily because it does not need Jesus or the church. If the substance of pacifism is not based on the logic of the cross and resurrection of

---

[70] Yoder, *Christian Attitudes To War, Peace, and Revolution*, 244-247.

[71] Yoder, *Christian Attitudes To War, Peace, and Revolution*, 333-334. The obviously informal nature of this passage reflects the fact that the book being quoted consists of transcribed course lectures. Yoder's own views are clear in the manner in which he describes this stream of social gospel pacifism.

Jesus, nor embodied in the suffering servanthood of the church, Yoder believes that such a pacifism cannot take into account the reality of the world in which it seeks to operate. To convince people to embrace pacifism on the basis that war is a social evil, or by constructing educational systems or other alternative structures is seen as hopelessly naïve by Yoder, since such beliefs refuse to take into account the real distinctions that exist between the different understandings of the world works; distinctions that Yoder believes cannot be arbitrated by education or some such initiative which is finally based on universal human reason. To assume that the church works in the same way as the world suggests that church and world can simply cooperate fully without loss in either case, an assumption that Yoder rejects largely because of his eschatology, without which there can be no real peace.

It is on the basis of eschatology that Yoder is able to resist the false optimism of liberal pacifism and yet retain his Christian messianic pacifism. The distinction between these two types of pacifism is profound, and challenges O'Donovan's characterization of pacifism as a monolith that rejects killing first and foremost. Peace *with* eschatology allows Yoder to suggest that it is possible to pursue peace without resorting to violence, that the church is called to practice peace and exemplify it, and as noted above, even live with injustice.[72]

According to O'Donovan, the right of the state to impose coercive measures against wrong-doers arises not from its need to defend itself, but from its office of judgment[73] that takes place in the 'in-between time.' This 'in-between time' is described by O'Donovan as a 'definite something,' which finds its existence between the pre-political society of God's creation and a post-political society which refrains from judgment because it has the judgment of God to defer to.[74] Put another way, political leaders, along with their authority are constituted "as a secondary theatre of witness to the appearing grace of God, attesting by their judicial service the coming reality of God's own act of judgment."[75] This witness of the church is one that bears witness to a final judgment of God. O'Donovan refers to this responsibility as an eschatological summons to social communication, which is both an announcement and a lived display of a community within the moment of God's patience, and that bears witness to the

---

[72] With specific reference to the racial revolution in the United States, Yoder claims that "our continuing attention to the racial revolution shall therefore first of all be illuminated by the awareness that *the vision* of creating, through a merging or fusion of the structures of church and society, *a truly human* and thereby truly Christian *total society needs to be abandoned.* This is by no means a position of resignation or of conservatism; it simply places in a more biblical, more realistic, and more eschatological framework the abiding Christian claims, demands, and hopes for the social order." Yoder, *For The Nations,* 107, emphasis in original.
[73] O'Donovan, "The Death Penalty in *Evangelium Vitae,"* 232.
[74] O'Donovan, *The Ways of Judgment,* 238.
[75] O'Donovan, *The Ways of Judgment,* 5.

final judgment.⁷⁶ To speak of the 'in-between time,' that 'definite something,' is itself an eschatological statement. According to O'Donovan, the primary eschatological assertion about political and demonic authorities that govern the world is that they have been made subject to God's sovereignty because of the triumph of Christ. Along with the secondary assertion, that this reality awaits its full revelation in the final universal presence of Christ, a framework is created in which "there opens up an account of secular authority which presumes neither that the Christ-event never occurred nor that the sovereignty of Christ is now transparent and uncontested."⁷⁷ Here a significant difference between Yoder and O'Donovan is brought to view, in that O'Donovan is wary of assuming that the sovereignty of Christ is apparent and uncontested even in the church, and especially that the church itself does not constitute the sole public sign of God's work.⁷⁸ To make such an assumption is only possible when secularity is misunderstood and misused. That is, it is essential, according to O'Donovan, to rightly understand secularity, which requires an eschatological faith to be sustained, a belief in the 'not yet.'⁷⁹ When the Christian has a robust view of the 'not yet,' it then becomes possible to distinguish between the time that is to come and the interim age in which provisional judgments are necessary. O'Donovan expresses concern that the inability to make this distinction can lead to idolatry, "locking the transcendence of God into the structures of its own particularity."⁸⁰ Such is the danger when Christians cannot see beyond the realm of the church when considering tasks of judgment that are necessary prior to the full revelation of Christ's triumph. Therefore O'Donovan counsels expectant patience, since "if we allow the 'not yet' to slide toward 'never,' we say something entirely different and wholly incompatible, for the virtue that undergirds all secular politics is an expectant patience."⁸¹ This stance of expectant patience suggests that what is to be waited for is God's peace, which cannot be produced by human action. That is, war pursued in this interim age is not intended as way of bringing about the end that is only God's. O'Donovan is clear that "we must deny the supposed cultural value of war, its heroic glorification as an advancement of civilisation. For war serves the ends of history only as evil serves good, and the power to bring good out of evil belongs to God alone."⁸² If war is seen as an attempt to bring about God's triumph, a mistake has been made which does not take into account an appropriate view of eschatology,

---

[76] O'Donovan, *The Ways of Judgment,* 240. O'Donovan is clear that while the church models the eschatological community, it is not identical to it. Ibid., 261.
[77] O'Donovan, *The Desire of the Nations,* 146.
[78] O'Donovan, *The Desire of the Nations,* 25.
[79] O'Donovan, *Common Objects of Love,* 42.
[80] O'Donovan, *Common Objects of Love,* 41.
[81] O'Donovan, *Common Objects of Love,* 42.
[82] O'Donovan, *The Just War Revisited,* 2.

which carries in its train a misunderstanding of secularity.[83] However, it is important to recognize that the expectant patience counseled by O'Donovan in light of his eschatology is not the same as the kind of patience Yoder has in mind when he also advocates patience in the face of eschatological expectations. Yoder's patience includes the belief that true peace cannot be had without eschatology, but nevertheless, the Christian is called in the interim to resist the temptation to justify the use of secular violence and war, whereas O'Donovan's patience leaves room for just such actions, if it is understood that secular violence war and violence are acts of judgment required in the interim time.

O'Donovan argues that the purpose of secular government is judgment, that "the whole rationale of government is seen to rest on its capacity to effect the judicial task."[84] O'Donovan's view that the notion of secular judgment presumes an account of the secular that is itself eschatologically constituted is similar to that of Paul Ramsey, who argues that because the Bible contains the book of Revelation, it ought to be impossible for Christians to suppose that the political life of mankind is anything other than the realm of patient endurance.[85] Rather, the eschatological horizon, the belief that the future is in God's hands and can only be brought about by God, puts politics in its place and frees the Christian for participation in the making of peace.[86] Further, Ramsey notes that there is not just a 'slash' between the 'already' and the 'not yet' that is often used when speaking eschatologically. Rather, Ramsey sees an "aeonic slash" between the 'already' and the 'not yet,'[87] suggesting that the border between them is not porous, or permeable; the 'not yet' cannot impinge on the 'already,' except in the sense that it determines the nature of the already as provisional and penultimate.

It is just such a decisive eschatological move of making a sharp distinction between ultimate and penultimate judgment that frees O'Donovan to consider force as not only legitimate but necessary part of Christian political responsibility, thus giving him an "eschatologically charged notion of

---

[83] In a related discussion regarding the dangers of universalizing ambitions within modern communication, O'Donovan warns: "In this universalizing thrust we may observe how Western society has forgotten how to be secular. Secularity is a stance of patience in the face of plurality, made sense of by eschatological hope; forgetfulness of it is part and parcel with the forgetfulness of Christian suppositions about history." O'Donovan, *Common Objects of Love*, 69.

[84] O'Donovan, *The Desire of the Nations*, 148.

[85] As previously argued, pacifism as espoused in Yoder's work does not argue for such an understanding.

[86] Ramsey, *The Just War*, 179-181.

[87] Ramsey, *Speak Up For Just War or Pacifism: A Critique of the United Methodist Bishops' Pastoral Letter "In Defense of Creation,"* (University Park and London: The Pennsylvania State University Press, 1988), 37.

'responsible' government"[88] that includes the possibility of war as a judicial means for pursuing justice.

Ecclesiology

The church as a political entity plays an important role in the political theology of Yoder and O'Donovan. O'Donovan asserts that describing the true character of the church as a political society "means to say that it is brought into being and held in being, not by a special function it has to fulfill, but by a government that it obeys in everything. It is ruled and authorized by the ascended Christ alone and supremely; it therefore has its own authority; and it is not answerable to any other authority that may attempt to subsume it."[89] But it is important to recognize that O'Donovan goes on to argue that the political character of the church "is hidden, to be discerned by faith as the ascended Christ who governs it is to be discerned by faith."[90] O'Donovan is careful in this discussion of the hidden character of the political nature of the church not to give the impression that human judgment must be suspended. It might be possible, O'Donovan says, to read accounts such as that of the woman take in adultery (John 7:53-8:11) as pointing the church toward complete abstention from judicial activity, and from governmental activity that is judicial in nature. Against this possibility, O'Donovan argues that such a reading

> would be to proclaim the cross without the resurrection. In the light of the resurrection the cross is seen to be a judgment which is, at the same time and completely, an act of reconciliation: an act of judgment, because it effected a separation between right and wrong and made their opposition clear; an act of reconciliation, because by this judgment the way was opened for the condemned to be included in the vindication of the innocent. What appears, then, to deprive us of all confidence in judgment actually restores our confidence. Where this merciful judgment has been shown us, we are bound to show it. We too, to the limited extent that we are able, must point to the redemptive unity of judgment and reconciliation.[91]

O'Donovan displays a hesitancy here to speak in terms of embodiment – the church acting as a display to the secular world of the forgiveness it offers to others in the church is not part of O'Donovan's understanding of the relationship between the church and society. Instead, "the secular function in society was to witness to divine judgment by, as it were, holding the stage for it; the church, on the other hand, must witness to divine judgment by no

---

[88] Jonathan Chaplin, "Political Eschatology and Responsible Government," 277.
[89] O'Donovan, *The Desire of the Nations*, 159.
[90] O'Donovan, *The Desire of the Nations*, 166.
[91] O'Donovan, *The Desire of the Nations*, 256-257.

judgment, avoiding litigation and swallowing conflict in forgiveness."[92] The church can cross into the sphere of judgment without leaving the Christian faith behind, claims O'Donovan, but cannot assume to achieve politically the forgiveness God has achieved on the cross in Jesus Christ. While it may be possible to offer mercy as an exception within secular judgment, the forgiveness practiced within the church cannot be taken from that sphere to the sphere of secular judgment.[93] That is, O'Donovan cannot see the church's embodiment of its practices as the fulfillment of Christian responsibility, even if the church offers those practices as paradigms to the secular world. Such an understanding simply does not extend far enough into the world, and, in addition, does not understand the effect of the triumph of Christ in the world outside of the church. Since O'Donovan cannot see the church as itself being the primary locus of Christian witness,[94] he suggests that it is judicial activity properly understood that is constitutive of Christian political responsibility.

For O'Donovan, then, moral reflection, which establishes an evangelical counter-praxis to the world's antagonistic praxis, is not the counter-praxis of the church only, but the acknowledgement of participation in another theatre. In other words, to restrict discussion of the political act of judgment to the theatre of the church is to truncate the Christian notion of political responsibility in an unfaithful manner. For Yoder, to extend consideration of Christian responsibility to a place outside of the church, or, to use O'Donovan's terms, to the second theatre of secular government, would be a sign of unfaithfulness. Moral reflection and the taking up of responsibility begin in the community created by Jesus Christ and continue as the church, which Yoder considers to be the locus of true internationalism, witnesses to the state and seeks to act as a specimen of peace to the wider world, as a display of the new world on the way.

The question of the use of violence by secular authority brings to view this fundamental difference between O'Donovan and Yoder on their understandings of the church. It is significant that in O'Donovan's explicit use of Just War tradition, the church essentially disappears from view. When the church is mentioned, the point is basically one of defending this very lacuna. That is, the discussion of Just War is one that is different from the theatre of the pastoral. While the basis of O'Donovan's move is theological, he is also at pains to argue that historically the church has not been pacifist for the reasons cited by modern Christian pacifists. If the early church seemed to be pacifist it was not

---

[92] O'Donovan, *The Desire of the Nations,* 259.
[93] O'Donovan, *The Ways of Judgment,* 92-99. The mercy extended within the secular theatre "arises from a discontinuity in the judicial regime, a reflective self-transcendence evoked by the recognition that judgment is imperfect." Ibid., 95. It is of course also the case that control of the exception can be an instance of absolute power.
[94] Jonathan Chaplin, "Political Eschatology and Responsible Government," 269.

because participation on the judicial model of warfare was considered wrong.[95] O'Donovan finds the notion that the early church's putative pacifism remains normative in perpetuity to be a fundamental misreading of that era. While O'Donovan is able to acknowledge that the Constantinian era brought about a discontinuity with the early church view of war, he nonetheless understands the earlier situation as a complex one, which upon close examination does not yield a singular attitude toward military matters. That is, O'Donovan sees an ambiguity that cannot be reduced to a single pacifist stance. He refuses to accept that evidence for the presence of Christians in the military can be explained in terms of where these Christians found themselves at the time of conversion; the church seems to change its attitude toward military service without much anxiety. The real difficulty in military service was the military oath and the shedding of blood, which made civil magistracy and military service problematic, although O'Donovan finds it rare for Christians to say that judicial bloodshed is intrinsically wrong.[96] But the heart of the ambiguity, for O'Donovan, is the early practice of deferred baptism, which protected contradictory attitudes, whereby the church could retain large numbers of unbaptized Christians while insisting on rigorous principles for baptized Christians, principles later transferred to the clergy. Therefore, "the legal

---

[95] Indeed, O'Donovan even notices a move toward an elementary Just War code in the Deuteronomic law in *The Desire of the Nations*, 53-55. That is, the sacral concept of war, in which God's initiative is central while downplaying human military action, nonetheless makes provisions such as protection of fruit trees and protection of women and children. O'Donovan notices a rudimentary Just War code, whereas Yoder reads the accounts in the Hebrew Scripture as evidence that holy war shows believers God will fight for them, and therefore they do not have to. Where O'Donovan sees the seeds of Just War, Yoder sees the nudge toward pacifism, reading both back and forward from Christ. There is a parallel disagreement between O'Donovan and Yoder regarding Karl Barth's stance toward violence by the secular state. O'Donovan reads Barth as one who pulls back at the last moment from the conclusion to which his work is logically progressing – that conclusion, according to O'Donovan, is the legitimate use of violence by the state, not the treatment of violence or coercion as an abnormal exception. See O'Donovan, "Karl Barth and Paul Ramsey's 'Uses of Power,'" in Oliver O'Donovan and Joan Lockwood O'Donovan, *Bonds of Imperfection: Christian Politics, Past and Present* (Grand Rapids: Eerdmans Publishing, 2004). Yoder, on the other hand, argues that the direction of Barth's work leads inexorably toward full embrace of pacifism within a free church context. Barth's use of the concept of the 'borderline situation' provides him with a way to insert the possibility of violence and coercion into his thought, a move that Yoder believes to be out of step with Barth's own best insights. See the extended argument in Yoder, "Karl Barth and the Problem of War," in Yoder, *Karl Barth and the Problem of War and Other Essays on Barth*, ed. Mark Thiessen Nation (Eugene: Cascade Books, 2003), 1-104.

[96] Oliver O'Donovan and Joan Lockwood O'Donovan, eds. *From Irenaeus to Grotius: A Sourcebook in Christian Political Thought, 100-1625* (Grand Rapids: Eerdmans Publishing, 1999), 2-3.

exemption and exclusion of the priesthood from military service developed in the fourth century just when the presence of lay soldiers in the church was becoming unremarkable."[97] Even in the writings of Tertullian, which O'Donovan describes as "the pre-Nicene church's fullest and strongest statement of opposition to Christians accepting military office," what stands out to him are the "ambiguities which surround that opposition."[98] This focus on the ambiguities which he finds in early church writings and practice lead O'Donovan to conclude that "the association of civil society and its institutions with idolatry was so much the fundamental reality for the pre-Nicene church, that it swallowed up all other reasons."[99] In sum, O'Donovan sees no historical evidence that pacifism has ever been the unambiguously normative stance of the church, and therefore it would be inaccurate to lay the blame for the embracing of Just War tradition at the feet of Christendom, to which, in any case, violence is not endemic.[100]

Therefore, while O'Donovan remains unconvinced about the church's pacifism, this is not because he drops his political theological underpinnings when he considers issues of war. Indeed, it is his political theology that underwrites his vigorous revisiting of the Just War tradition.[101] For O'Donovan, Just War is not an attempt to control history, but an illustration of the fact that political choices are already spiritual choices.[102] By the 'spirituality' of Just War, O'Donovan means "its capacity to make the reflecting subject conscious of his or her own responsible position before God in relation to other members of society who have their own differently responsible positions." Thus Just War is meant to be "the exercise of Gospel faith within the theatre of unbelief and disobedience."[103]

For Yoder, the church plays the political role it is called to when it acts as a faithful church. This unrelenting focus on the visibility of the church does not

---

[97] O'Donovan and Lockwood O'Donovan, eds. *From Irenaeus to Grotius*, 3.

[98] O'Donovan and Lockwood O'Donovan, eds. *From Irenaeus to Grotius*, 24.

[99] O'Donovan and Lockwood O'Donovan, eds. *From Irenaeus to Grotius*, 24.

[100] O'Donovan, "Response to Colin Greene," 343.

[101] In his revisiting of the Just War tradition, O'Donovan's language becomes less overtly theological and exegetical in nature than the discourse of *The Desire of the Nations*. It seems to me that this change in language is deliberate because O'Donovan sees himself as engaging a different audience, but without losing the ground gained in his political theology. "Political ethics has to carry forward into detailed deliberation the principle established by political theology: authority is reordered towards the task of judgment." See *The Desire of the Nations*, 286. The publication of *Ways of Judgment* might be said to embody this carrying forward into detailed deliberation what has been established in *The Desire of the Nations*, but without making unnecessarily strict distinctions between the tasks of political theology and political ethics.

[102] O'Donovan, *Common Objects of Love*, 23.

[103] O'Donovan, *The Just War Revisited*, ix, 6.

drop from view when Yoder takes up discussions of pacifism and Just War.[104] In a telling move, Yoder begins his series of essays on Christian pacifism in *The Original Revolution* with his belief that God has called into being a new community.[105] In direct opposition to the kind of historical reading of early church pacifism put forward by O'Donovan, Yoder refuses to accept that the early church practice regarding the military is anything but normative, since that practice cannot be reduced to its links with a purely religious notion of idolatry. Yoder sees far less ambiguity in the early church's stance toward violence than does O'Donovan, but without denying the importance and relatedness of attitudes toward idolatry and other cultural dimensions of life in the Roman Empire. Yoder sees a fundamental polarity between Caesar and God, reflected in the polar relationship of the early Christians to the whole authority structure for a cluster of reasons that included idolatry, military service and so on. However, the rejection of military service cannot be reduced to the issue of emperor worship. The early church's clash with the military was not restricted to disagreements about killing *or* idols, but rather "was rooted in a fundamentally anti-tyrannical and anti-provincial vision of who God is and of God's saving purposes in the world."[106] This dualism Yoder understands as total, but practical in its nature rather than systematic. The total dualism of the early church was not based on opposition to the 'state as such,' but to the kind of state the early Christians faced, one in which idolatry, violence, public abuse of minorities, war, and empire were part of *that* state. Yoder believes that the early church, within the sharp dualism that can be observed, was pacifist for the sake of being pacifist, that the early Christians rejected military service because it was wrong in principle.[107] He acknowledges the changes in early church practice and policy, but identifies these as 'creeping empire loyalty.' Yoder is adamant that early church pacifism was not just contextual, but that the Constantinian shift, that fundamental reorientation of the relationship of church and world, opened the way for Just War thinking.[108]

What Yoder understands to be important is the communal quality of moral engagement, an "ethical style" in which "the lordship of Christ is the center which must guide critical value choices, so that we may be called to subordinate or even to reject those values which contradict Jesus."[109] However, such a subordination of values does not exclude or deny the issues of the wider society, claims Yoder. Rather, "the obedient Christian community becomes at the same time an instrument for serving and saving the larger culture."[110]

---

[104] Yoder, et al., *On Earth Peace*, 138.

[105] Yoder, *The Original Revolution*, 27.

[106] Yoder, "War as a Moral Problem," 102.

[107] Yoder, *Christian Attitudes to War, Peace, and Revolution*, 26-27.

[108] Yoder, *Christian Attitudes to War, Peace, and Revolution*, 49.

[109] Yoder, *The Priestly Kingdom*, 11.

[110] Yoder, *The Priestly Kingdom*, 11.

Indeed, Yoder claims that the visible, voluntary community of the church is by its nature a truer, more properly ordered community than is the state. The church also has the capacity to extend beyond the modern state, according to Yoder, since it is Christian unity that is the true internationalism, and Christian internationalism is the truest unity.[111] Thus Yoder contends basically that Christian political theology is not statecraft as conventionally understood,[112] but is the church as the beginning of what is to come, authentic exemplarity that communicates

> to the world what God plans to do, because it shows that God is beginning to do it... The church is also pilot project, and podium, pedagogical base and sometime power base. In none of these ways does it really depend on the church's presence or its day-to-day faithfulness whether, or when, the new world, to which the church witnesses and from which its being is derived, shall actually come upon us in power. Part of the grace from which the church lives is the grace of not needing to be responsible for that. But the church is responsible for the congruence between its ministry and that new world that is the church's way, because it is on the way.[113]

Nonetheless, as part of his pacifist stance, which extends to the dialogical engagement with other traditions and positions, Yoder attempts to take the Just War tradition seriously on its own terms through respectful dialogue.[114] This

---

[111] Yoder, *The Royal Priesthood*, 180. Although Yoder's notion of internationalism has a certain vagueness to it, his ecumenical work serves as a display of what he is putting forward. See Mark Thiessen Nation, *John Howard Yoder: Mennonite Patience, Evangelical Witness, Catholic Convictions* (Grand Rapids: Eerdmans Publishing, 2006) for a book-length study of Yoder's ecumenism. It must be said that Yoder's notion of church internationalism is no more vague than O'Donovan's notion of an international community of plurality, or a 'Western Christian public,' both of which seem like formal categories rather than an identifiable entity. O'Donovan, *The Just War Revisited*, 96, viii.

[112] Drawing largely on Yoder's work, Stanley Hauerwas makes this same point in a lengthy epilogue to a book written by Paul Ramsey, in which Hauerwas argues that it is often expected that pacifism will be presented as an alternative to Just War, "a principled position that is meant to determine the policy of states." Hauerwas believes that Ramsey's use of Just War is exactly that – a theory of statecraft. However, argues Hauerwas, while it is the case that Christians are called to serve the neighbor, it is not necessarily the state which is authorized by God to provide that service. Hauerwas, "Epilogue: A Pacifist Response to the Bishops," in *Speak Up for Just War or Pacifism*, 164, 167, 175.

[113] Yoder, *The Royal Priesthood*, 126.

[114] This is Yoder's own description of his initiative in a book-length engagement with the Just War tradition. Yoder, *When War is Unjust*, ix.

dialogue is an attempt to hold Just War accountable on its own terms.[115] The extent of the engagement is quite remarkable, ranging from Yoder's involvement on the campus of the University of Notre Dame with Catholic interlocuters amidst the military officer training program there to an extensive number of essays that directly engage Just War thinking.[116] Yoder makes the claim that in none of this respectful dialogue is he being disingenuous, but is simply calling the Just War tradition to its own best principles.[117] He couches his exposition and critique of the tradition in terms of seeking an ecumenical way of giving "the benefit of the doubt to the mainstream theological tradition," and in doing so "is not advocating backhandedly my own pacifist ideals," an

---

[115] This engagement has garnered some serious responses from those within the Just War tradition, including Paul Ramsey, *Speak Up For Just War or Pacifism,* 96-122, 159-162; Charles Lutz in the foreword to *When War is Unjust,* xi-xx; Reinhard Hutter, "Be Honest in Just War Thinking! Lutherans, the Just War Tradition, and Selective Conscientious Objection," in *The Wisdom of the Cross,* 69-83; Tobias Winwright, "From Police Officers to Peace Officers," in *The Wisdom of the Cross,* 84-114.

[116] Yoder, "Bluff or Revenge: The Watershed in Democratic Awareness" in Todd Whitmore, ed. *Ethics in the Nuclear Age* (Dallas: SMU Press, 1989), 79-94; "The Challenge of Peace: A Historic Peace Church Perspective" in Charles J. Reid, Jr., ed. *Peace in a Nuclear Age: The Bishops' Pastoral Letter in Perspective,* (Washington, Catholic University of America Press, 1986), 273-290; "The Credibility of Ecclesiastical Teaching on the Morality of War" in Leroy S. Rouner, ed. *Celebrating Peace,* 33-51; "How Many Ways are There to Think Morally About War?" *The Journal of Law and Religion* 11 no 1 (1994): 83-107; "Just War Tradition: Is it Credible?" *Christian Century* 108 no 9 (March 13 1991): 295-98; "Military Realities and Teaching the Laws of War" in Theodore Runyon, ed. *Theology, Politics, and Peace* (Maryknoll: Orbis Press, 1989), 176-180; "The Reception of the Just War Tradition by the Magisterial Reformation" *History of European Ideas* 9 (1988): 1-23; "Surrender: A Moral Imperative?" *The Review of Politics,* 48 no 4 (Fall 1986): 576-595.

[117] Yoder complains that while his own articulation of pacifism has been dialogical, he in turn has been treated like a foil in the minds and writings of Just War thinkers. See *The Priestly Kingdom,* 1. He sees an exception in the case of Lisa Sowle Cahill, *Love Your Enemies: Discipleship, Pacifism, and Just War Theory* (Minneapolis: Fortress Press, 1994). See Yoder, "Review Symposium," *Horizons* 22 no 2 (Fall 1995): 277-281. Yoder notes "the great improvement which this account represents over earlier histories is the effort to be fair to each position in its own terms." Further, Cahill acknowledges that pacifism has its own logic. Yoder approvingly states that "her intention to describe a position other than her own in its own terms, rather than in those of its critics, is fundamentally to be welcomed, and relatively new in the field." "Review Symposium," 277. The kinds of 'best principles' that Yoder wants the Just War tradition to uphold include being willing to apply the doctrine negatively so that some intrinsically just cause might for example go undefended because there would be no legitimate authority to defend it; that war would truly function as a last resort and not an only resort; that strategies of nonviolence would be put forward as part of Just War thinking; and so on. Yoder, *When War is Unjust,* 71-80.

exercise that "would call for a biblical and a pastoral argument."[118]

Despite such disclaimers, a reading of Yoder's dialogue with the Just War tradition reveals a distinct reservation of positive judgments for those occasions when the tradition acts like pacifism. Put another way, Yoder is willing to approve of the Just War tradition when that tradition leads, on its own terms, to conclusions that coincide with pacifism. At most, his respectful dialogue is an attempt to acknowledge the tradition as credible, but that attempt will never extend to a concession that it is right or faithful.

Yoder's treatment of the Just War tradition includes several dimensions. First, he argues that pacifism and the Just War tradition are part of the same universe of discourse, that they interlock in several ways: "a moral presumption against violence (although they differ on whether it may be over-ridden); a stake in the rejection of total war, which issues in politically making common cause against unacceptable national policies; support for maximizing the potential of nonmilitary means of pursuing just social objectives, including national defense."[119] Given these areas of overlap, Yoder believes that pacifism and the Just War tradition can work together in resisting less restrained views.[120] Nonetheless, whatever the commonalities that can be embraced within a common universe of discourse, Yoder is clear in all of his forays into the Just War tradition that even if such thinking is honest, "Just War discourse deceives sincere people, by the very nature of its claim to base moral discernment upon the facts of the case and on universally accessible rational principles. It lets them think that their morality is somehow less provincial and more accessible to others than if it referred specifically to the data of Christian faith, including the words and the work of Jesus."[121] Herein the shape of Yoder's dialogue with Just War tradition becomes clear - he finds specific flaws which ultimately bring to view the fact that the tradition needs to become more credible by being true to its own best principles. However, it seems equally clear that in the event that the Just War tradition were to be credible, by which is meant that the tradition would be able to say that some wars are not justifiable, Yoder would still declare it to be unfaithful to Jesus Christ. For example, Yoder is quite specific about some of the flaws in the tradition, especially in his book *When War is Unjust*, but not only there. Many of the shorter pieces cited above show Yoder assessing the credibility of the tradition in historically specific cases, and

---

[118] Yoder, "The Credibility of Ecclesiastical Teaching on the Morality of War," 37.

[119] Yoder, "'Just War and 'Non-violence': Disjunction or Dialogue?" 172.

[120] For example, both traditions resist notions that reduce moral accountability on the basis that war consists in a breakdown of civility. Further, the traditions agree that war cannot be justified by a transcendent cause declared by a prophetic person (the 'Crusade' option). They also resist the idea that war removes restraints by offering a setting that acts as an opportunity to prove the virility or dominance of a state. Yoder, "The 'Just War' Tradition: Is it Credible?" 298.

[121] Yoder, "The 'Just War' Tradition: Is it Credible?" 298.

in each case finding it wanting in some way. Some of his complaints include his fear that the restraints of the tradition are continually being weakened as exceptions are ruled out, as war becomes total, through technological escalation, and through a sliding scale that continues to be less and less rigorous in terms of what is considered acceptable.[122] Paul Ramsey, in *Speak Up For Just War or Pacifism*, takes on some of the specific details of Yoder's arguments. While the details of these arguments are important, it is essential to see that the difference between Ramsey and Yoder, and by extension, Yoder and O'Donovan, is a disagreement regarding what it means for disciples of Jesus to be responsible. Yoder and Ramsey agree, for example, that the difference between them lies not so much in the details, but in prior issues. Yoder, in response to Ramsey, claims that the issue between them is not one of principles versus consequences, as it is those categories that are themselves problematic.[123]

Peace, War, and Responsibility

The disagreement between Yoder and O'Donovan circles around an understanding of the role of legitimate force as part of what it means for Christians to assume responsibility within the world. The disagreement is *not* about whether or not it is necessary or desirable to take hold of the handles of history, or striking a bargain with the state in order to enforce standards or beliefs on the part of the church. However, Yoder understands thinkers such as O'Donovan to have made a fundamental error in framing the debate in terms that seem to force a decision between responsibility and faithfulness to what it means to be a disciple of Jesus Christ. Even here, however, it is important not to miss the nuances. That is, O'Donovan never advocates the embracing of Just War in such a way as to forego moral standards within the theatre of war, as though once the decision to go to war has been taken, licence has somehow been granted to act in ways that are dictated by war itself. Rather, it is precisely this kind of idea that O'Donovan argues against when he revisits the Just War tradition – his interest is to extend just war thinking beyond *ius ad bellum* into *ius in bello*.

Yoder also is careful to acknowledge that if forced, he would choose

---

[122] See especially chapter 5 of *When War is Unjust*.

[123] Yoder commends Ramsey for the extent to which he "respected and listened to pacifists, while rejecting their views." Yoder, "The Burden and Discipline of Evangelical Revisionism," 31. Ramsey's specific interaction with Yoder on issues of pacifism and Just War shows that while the respect is mutual, Ramsey is tired of hearing that it is only pacifists who take Jesus seriously, and argues instead that Christology is the heart of the matter for both pacifists and the Just War tradition, and that the real differences come after this crucial starting point. Ramsey, *Speak Up For Just War or Pacifism*, 96-123.

faithfulness, all the time denying that this way of putting the issue is adequate. Yoder blames what he calls 'hard Niebuhrians' for forcing the choice of responsibility versus faithfulness on issues of war and ethics more generally, claiming that this choice dominates the debate. This is not simply a matter of ethical methodologism for Yoder, but of the substance of the Christian faith:

> To assume that fidelity to principle and useful impact on the course of events must *a priori* be alternatives is to deny the substance of the faith; that one God is Creator of heaven and earth, that Jesus was authentically (politically) human, that he was raised from the dead and is at the father's right hand, and that they sent the Holy Spirit. Each of these components of the Good News contributes to our evaluation of the tension between faithfulness and integrity. *If* I had to choose between *apparent* effectiveness and *apparent* fidelity, I would choose the latter, but *not* because I would grant the adequacy of that way of putting the issue. My reason for preferring *apparent* faithfulness to *apparent* effectiveness would not be moral purism but rather the very realistic awareness that the kinds of consideration pertinent to the definition of "fidelity" are knowable, trustable, and binding, on grounds qualitatively different from those pertinent to claims of "effectiveness" or "responsibility."[124]

Part of the issue for Yoder is that he cannot concede that the assumption of responsibility is constitutive of faithfulness, since, construed in certain ways, responsibility is not necessarily Christian in nature. For example, Yoder argues that it is relatively easy to make several "natural misinterpretations of historical responsibility," especially if the "irreducible historicity of Jesus' servanthood" is downplayed, replaced, or entirely ignored.[125] These several misinterpretations include a move from that which is considered to be right (substance), to that which is rightly intended (form). In this view, "'love' is a positive subjective intention, which may be called on to justify any action done in its name."[126] The second misinterpretation, a move from deeds to goals, understands intention in an objective sense as the goal sought, "justifying any means claiming to reach it."[127] Yoder rejects any notion of the 'benefaction' that can ostensibly come from good intentions, since the call to the Christian is not "to will the good or to achieve it, nor to be justified, so much as to be present as servant."[128]

But Yoder's central concern focuses on the connection of Constantinianism to notions of responsibility. He assumes that any attempt to find approval of war in Scripture is doomed to failure. Of more concern is the notion that in society people have the responsibility for the protection of the good neighbor

---

[124] Yoder, "Burden and Responsibility," 32-33. Emphasis in original.
[125] Yoder, *For the Nations*, 243.
[126] Yoder, *For the Nations*, 243.
[127] Yoder, *For the Nations*, 244.
[128] Yoder, *For the Nations*, 244.

against the bad one, a responsibility that Yoder understands to be the police function of the state. However, others believe that it is the Christian's duty through the functions of the state to contribute to the maintenance of order and justice. According to Yoder, the problem is that this view is based on a 'realistic' analysis of the old aeon and knows nothing of the new, and therefore "is not specifically Christian and would fit into any honest system of social morality. If Christ had never become incarnate, died, risen, ascended to heaven, and sent his Spirit, this view would be just as possible, though its particularly clear and objective expression may result partly from certain Christian insights."[129] To reject a view of responsibility that embraces the possibility of war as a way of defending the good neighbor from the bad is not to reject responsibility, but is to disagree regarding the nature of responsibility. For Yoder, the Christian responsibility to the social order has to distinguish between the objects of its witness, and when proper distinctions are not made between the aeons, the Constantinian point of departure is brought to view. This misguided point of departure reasons by way of notions such as universal morality and 'lesser evil' arguments, which are anathema to Yoder's way of construing responsibility. Once the Constantinian point of departure is in place, once the Christian believes that responsibility can be defined from within the given order rather than from the gospel, "once the nation is authorized exceptionally to be the agent of God's wrath, the heritage of paganism makes quick work of generalizing that authorization into a divine rubber stamp."[130] As noted above, to pursue war as a tool of social responsibility is to succumb unnecessarily to consequentialist thinking,[131] which is evidence that the appropriate eschatological tension is missing.

Throughout Yoder's writings runs a basically consistent thread that takes exception to the inclination to think of political involvement as somehow attempting to work within given governmental structures, by trying to control who is elected, by attempting to get things done through political power as conventionally understood. Instead, Yoder argues that the ultimate justification for the mandate of the state is to be found within the mandate of the church. Rather than seeing the church as a support system for the state, Yoder insists that "the Christian faith inverted this relationship and viewed the world-embracing empire as merely a support system, subservient to the real work God is accomplishing in the world."[132] Put another way, the state is there for the sake of the church.[133] Instead of suggesting that in order to have any effect in this world, standards foreign to the Christian way may have to be appropriated,

---

[129] Yoder, *The Royal Priesthood*, 162.
[130] Yoder, *The Royal Priesthood*, 167. Yoder's treatment of 'Constantine and Responsibility' is found in *The Royal Priesthood*, 161-167.
[131] Yoder, "War as a Moral Problem," 96.
[132] Yoder, *Discipleship as Political Responsibility*, 23.
[133] Yoder, *Discipleship as Political Responsibility*, 62.

Yoder points to the priority of the church. Such a priority does not, however, lead to withdrawal from society, or from political responsibility. Despite the state's violence, Christians are called to be involved, by calling the state to humane actions and policies, to reduce violence in keeping order and so on. It is also the case that such involvement could take the form of refusal to participate in activities where the state oversteps its own boundaries.[134]

Whereas Yoder considers the 'responsible' taking up of war to be a sign of unfaithfulness, and as lacking eschatological tension, O'Donovan is equally adamant that the embracing of pacifism cannot discharge Christian responsibility – indeed, to be pacifist is to cut oneself off from the very possibility of being responsible. It is essential that there be a 'deliberating public' that can discern the necessity of political acts which serve as part of the shaping of faithful judgments, that does not somehow surround itself with a sacred boundary by which responsibility is cut off.[135] Yoder's refusal to move out of the church in his discussions of responsibility therefore simply cuts the nerve, as it were, of the possibility for responsible, faithful action. Even Yoder's notion of the church's role as a witness to the state would no doubt fall short in O'Donovan's understanding, since this is still too far removed from life in the *saeculum*. O'Donovan argues that any Christian position that cannot make the important distinction between Christian witness and Christian reflection is doomed to remain forever stuck in the pastoral arena of the church. O'Donovan expresses his concern about an appropriate understanding of duality by suggesting that "proclaiming the unity of God's rule in Christ is the task of Christian witness; understanding the duality is the chief assistance rendered by Christian reflection."[136] The duality O'Donovan addresses here is that of the political and the spiritual, the dual authority that O'Donovan struggles to treat appropriately in light of the proclamation of the Kingdom of God, which spans the two.[137] To suggest as Yoder does that it is appropriate to understand this duality as one of response (obedience to or confession of Christ as Lord; disobedience to or rejection of Christ as Lord) does not go far enough in O'Donovan's view, leaving as it does the Christian mired in the confines of the church without making the move to politics properly understood as "the theatre of divine self-disclosure."[138] As O'Donovan points out, in a move that Yoder steadfastly refused to make, Christian political discipleship is different than Christian discipleship.[139] It is important to observe that O'Donovan's distinction between Christian political discipleship and Christian discipleship does not carry in its wake a Constantinian notion of looking somewhere other

---

[134] Yoder, *Discipleship as Political Responsibility*, 41-44.
[135] O'Donovan, *The Just War Revisited*, 15.
[136] O'Donovan, *The Desire of the Nations*, 82.
[137] O'Donovan, *The Desire of the Nations*, 82.
[138] O'Donovan, *The Desire of the Nations*, 82.
[139] O'Donovan, *The Desire of the Nations*, 219.

than to the Lordship of Christ for guidance. Rather, it is precisely the Lordship of Christ that calls for these appropriate distinctions to be made.

Since O'Donovan does not see the church itself as the locus of the pursuit of judgment through political responsibility, and since the secular government is authorized by the triumph of Christ to shape and pursue judgment, the notion of the possibility of war as the continued judicial activity of a responsible government becomes centrally important. War is not an exceptional activity, but rather should be understood as the extraordinary extension of *ordinary* acts of judgment.[140]

It is Yoder's reluctance to speak of responsibility outside of the church in his embrace of pacifism that is at the heart of O'Donovan's suspicion that Yoder has succumbed to the temptations of modernity. According to O'Donovan, Yoder specifically and pacifism generally cannot move beyond suspicion, not because of a commitment to discipleship, but because of an inability to recognize and therefore cast off a lingering and pervasive modern notion of the state.

O'Donovan's suspicion of pacifism in this regard can be seen early in his career in his published debate with Ronald Sider, whom O'Donovan suspects of being "an unremittingly modern man,"[141] especially with regard to the use of modern technology. That is, Sider's suggestions of pacifist non-lethal methods seem to O'Donovan to be dependent on modern international communications and advanced technology. Arguing that for centuries the kinds of technology that Sider seems to assume were out of reach, O'Donovan is prompted to ask "what is a society without advanced communications and advanced technology supposed to do about fighting war non-lethally?"[142] The essential critique of Sider amounts to the suspicion that too much of his moral programme depends on modern technology, a move that in O'Donovan's view allows Sider to unfairly accuse a thousand years of Christianity of being unfaithful to Jesus Christ.[143]

O'Donovan extends his critique of pacifism as modern on technological grounds in his work on deterrence, where he makes the argument that "deterrence is, in fact, a tough-minded mutation of pacifism, a pacifism

---

[140] O'Donovan, *The Just War Revisited,* 14. O'Donovan is elsewhere concerned that if Just War is only an emergency measure, then the inclination will be to create emergencies. O'Donovan, "The Death Penalty in *Evangelium Vitae,*" 232-233.
[141] Sider and O'Donovan, *Peace and War,* 23.
[142] Sider and O'Donovan, *Peace and War,* 16.
[143] Sider and O'Donovan, *Peace and War,* 23. The specific kinds of technology O'Donovan has in mind (non-lethal gases, advanced international communications) he deems to be necessary for a non-lethal international police force to operate successfully. In O'Donovan's view, if a moral theory is dependent on such technology to be functional (as he suspects Sider's to be), then it is inadequate because it has nothing to say to societies where such technology is out of reach. Sider and O'Donovan, *Peace and War,* 16.

transformed by a technological and historicist vision of human progress. Many of the traditional arguments made against pacifism are also *mutatis mutandis* arguments against deterrence."[144] Here O'Donovan's concern regarding pacifism has changed slightly. At issue more than technological development itself, according to O'Donovan, is the misguided notion that total peace is possible – a notion shared by deterrence and pacifism.

O'Donovan's criticism of pacifism as modern takes on a different dimension in his more recent work, centering on pacifism's inability to move beyond suspicion. O'Donovan's suspicion of modern suspicion could perhaps be said to serve as the generative impulse for his own theopolitical project. That is, his is an attempt to move beyond the suspicion that marks the age of late modernity, the suspicion that politicians corrupt morality, and that politics is corrupted by theology.[145] If theology purports to be offering an alternative vision for politics, but serves only a reactive critical function, and never rises above the rhetoric of skepticism, then that theology itself can be described as modern. After all, "a politics that does not encompass the direction of society ceases to be a politics at all. But there is no room for direction is a society ruled by the imperative of universal suspicion."[146] Such criticism may well be useful as an interpretive tool, but, "once totalized, criticism merely evacuates itself of content and turns into a series of empty gestures."[147] While O'Donovan's explication of and warning against totalizing suspicion is fairly broad in *The Desire of Nations,*[148] it is in his explicit discussion of Just War that it becomes clear that pacifism is a prime example of a theology that is a modern development. The accusation that pacifism cannot think in terms other that those of opposition is reiterated in the context of pacifism's putative preoccupation with the distinction between this world and the next.[149] Further, pacifism, which O'Donovan refuses to treat in its plurality, cannot move beyond 'statism.' The "pacifist position, will not contemplate the *improvisation* of judgment where it is not provided for within a state structure, and to that extent cannot treat international politics wholly seriously *as* politics, a God-given sphere of peaceful interaction. Here we begin to see why pacifism is a modern development."[150] O'Donovan's complaint here goes deeper than his

---

[144] O'Donovan, *Peace and Certainty,* 28-29. O'Donovan is following Paul Ramsey's argument that both deterrence and pacifism think it is possible to eliminate the use of force from history. See Ramsey, *The Just War,* 141.

[145] O'Donovan, *The Desire of the Nations,* 6-8.

[146] O'Donovan, *The Desire of the Nations,* 10.

[147] O'Donovan, *The Desire of the Nations,* 11.

[148] O'Donovan offers the contemporary example of liberation theology (the Southern school, in his terms), as an initiative that can be describes as "an unsustainable combination of political affirmation and universal suspicion." O'Donovan, *The Desire of the Nations,* 11.

[149] O'Donovan, *The Just War Revisited,* 10.

[150] O'Donovan, *The Just War Revisited,* 8. Italics in original.

previous contention that pacifism is based on technological development. Rather, he believes that a position that purports to be Christian but relies on a modern notion of the limits of state boundaries, and then calls such a view more Christian than others hides the fact that pacifism simply cannot move beyond a hidebound presumption against the use of force.

In *Nevertheless,* an account of the varieties of religious pacifism, Yoder makes the overdrawn claim that the pacifism he puts forward, that of the messianic community, is the only one in his typology for which the person of Christ is indispensable.[151] This is overdrawn, because while it is the case that his position falls apart if the dependence on the confession that Jesus is Christ and Lord is withdrawn, other positions, such as the one put forward by O'Donovan, also collapse under similar circumstances.[152] Nonetheless, Yoder's point is important as a self-description. Prior to asking questions regarding violence or nonviolence, responsibility or faithfulness, Yoder seeks to answer the question of discipleship. An ethic of discipleship, he suggests, is guided not by goals, but by the Lord it seeks to reflect.[153] Put another way, pacifism has its theological basis in the character of God and in the work of Jesus Christ.[154]

> To say that this is the pacifism of the *messianic* community is to affirm its dependence upon the confession that Jesus is the Christ and that Jesus Christ is Lord. To say that Jesus is the Messiah is to say that in him are fulfilled the expectations of God's people regarding the coming one in whom God's will would perfectly be done. Therefore, in the person and work of Jesus, in his teachings and his passion, this kind of pacifism finds its rootage, and in his resurrection it finds its enablement.[155]

This rootage in Christology provides the basis of the creation of a human community dedicated to a deviant value system, one which finds Christian

---

[151] Yoder, *Nevertheless,* 134.

[152] Paul Ramsey is adamant that claims such as the ones Yoder makes here stop the very thing Yoder claims to want – honest dialogue. Ramsey insists that Christologies other than that held by Yoder and Hauerwas take the life, teachings, and death of Jesus with equal seriousness. As Ramsey puts, "there is nothing to be gained from adherents of one or another of these actual or possible accounts of the person and work of Christ saying of the others, 'We all participate in Jesus; you in your way, I in *his.*'" Ramsey, *Speak Up for Just War or Pacifism,* 114, italics in original. Similarly, O'Donovan suggests that his disagreement with the Anabaptist theologian Sider is not about what Jesus says, but about its implications. Sider and O'Donovan, *Peace and War,* 15.

[153] Yoder, *The Original Revolution,* 39.

[154] Yoder, *The Politics of Jesus,* 239. Hauerwas equates discipleship with pacifism, and argues that for Yoder pacifism is not about nonviolence as much as it is about Christ. Hauerwas, "Notes For a Conversation With John Milbank," in *Must Christianity be Violent?,* 173-176. See also Hauerwas, "Messianic Pacifism: Non-resistance as a Defense of a Good and Just Social Order," *Worldview* 16 no 6 (June 1973): 29-33.

[155] Yoder, *Nevertheless,* 133-134.

hope, but not of the sort found in Just War thought, which finds at least some probability of success based on its calculations of possible violent action. That is, Yoder claims that it is only the pacifism of messianic community that collapses completely if Jesus is not Lord. This kind of pacifism does not promise to 'work,' says Yoder, but offers hope in the form of faith, which "is not the preponderant probability of early success which is desired by the just-war theory or by a prudential ethic."[156]

Here it is clear that Yoder believes that any position which claims to confess Jesus as Lord, that is centered in Christology, is inadequately Christological if it can find within such a position room for Just War. But he cannot seem to see that the difference is in an understanding of responsibility, and in disagreement about eschatology – not in degrees of seriousness regarding Jesus. That is, while Yoder and O'Donovan diverge significantly in their understanding of Christology, it is inaccurate to suggest that O'Donovan takes Jesus less seriously than does Yoder. Christian political theology and ethics is made possible by the triumph of Christ, and the rule of Christ is made visible in both the theatre of the church and the secular, although not in a fully transparent way. Clarity regarding the eschaton, the coming age in which that rule will become fully real and transparent, provides a way to understand that the control of history is in God's hands, but the present age calls for political acts in the form of judgment, understood as penultimate and provisional. Thus being faithful to Jesus Christ entails the possibility of the use of force, which is an essential part of what it means to engage in faithful witness, in faithful political discipleship. Violence is not necessarily endemic to either a Christian state or appropriate political acts in the form of judgment, but to deny the possibility of coercion is to deny the possibility of faithfulness in all arenas that extend beyond the church, according to O'Donovan. To accept this possibility is to open the door to involvement not only in abstract discussions of whether some war is just or unjust, but also the pursuit of justice within wars that can be considered just and therefore part of Christian political discipleship. Accordingly, O'Donovan's treatment of pacifism as monolithic is made intelligible. That is, if pacifism cannot move beyond the pastoral realm, then whatever nuances might be introduced by typologies that seek to recognize distinctions within pacifism are irrelevant to O'Donovan, since none of those distinctions are adequate to move pacifism toward the appropriate assumption of political responsibility.

---

[156] Yoder, *Nevertheless*, 136-137.

Concluding Reflections on Post-Christendom Christian Political Theology

Recent political discussions have witnessed significant interest in Christian political theology, whereby theologians have become significant interlocuters in political philosophy.[1] My project has sought to contribute to this lively conversation through a careful critical comparative study of two theopolitical visions, which claim to find authority and warrant in the Bible for these visions.

Both Yoder and O'Donovan refuse to relegate religion to the realm of the personal, and also refuse the kind of conventional separation of church and state that is expressed in a parallel separation of public and private spheres. Yet both thinkers believe that explicitly Christian theopolitical visions have much to offer as part of public political discourse, precisely because they both believe that that secular realm is not to be ignored, but is a theater in which the triumph of Christ takes effect. While the embrace of the secular takes shape in distinctive ways according to Yoder and O'Donovan, they both agree that theology is not a conversation-stopper in discussions of politics.[2]

Yoder's attempt to engage the secular realm consists in a posture that he claims is 'for the nations.'[3] He insists that the "very shape of the people of God

---

[1] To provide just a few examples of these kinds of discussions, see Creston Davis, John Milbank, and Slavoj Žižek, eds., *Theology and the Political : The New Debate* (Durham and London: Duke University Press, 2005), Slavoj Žižek, *The Fragile Absolute – or, why is the Christian legacy worth fighting for?* (London: Verso, 2000); Slavoj Žižek, *The Puppet and the Dwarf: The Perverse Core of Christianity* (Cambridge, Massachusets: The MIT Press, 2003); Alain Badiou, translated by Ray Brassier, *Saint Paul: The Foundation of Universalism* (Stanford: Stanford University Press, 2003); Giorgio Agamben, trans. Patricia Dailey, *The Time That Remains: A Commentary on the Letter to the Romans* (Stanford: Stanford University Press, 2005); Jacob Taubes, trans. Dana Hollander, *The Political Theology of Paul* (Stanford: Stanford University Press, 2004); Romand Coles, *Beyond Gated Politics: Reflections for the Possibilities of Democracy* (Minneapolis: University of Minnesota Press, 2005); Jeffrey Stout, *Democracy and Tradition* (Princeton: Princeton University Press, 2004). See also the journal entitled *Political Theology*, which has been in publication since 1999.

[2] Jeffrey Stout resists Richard Rorty's notion that religion is a conversation-stopper, since Stout believes that there is room for religious voices in democratic culture. Stout, *Democracy and Tradition*, 85-91.

[3] Yoder has often been categorized as being sectarian, a description to which he explicitly takes exception. Despite Ernest Troeltsch's attempt to categorize religious expression in purely descriptive terms, Yoder claims that the term 'sectarian' has become irredeemably pejorative, in part because of the work of H. Richard Niebuhr and

in the world is a public witness, or is 'good news,' for the world, rather than first of all rejection or withdrawal."[4] Put another way, Yoder gives relatively little attention to drawing exact lines between the church and the secular realm, arguing instead for the duality of response (faithful versus unfaithful) to the Lordship of Christ. For example, in an essay entitles "The Paradigmatic Role of God's People," Yoder takes four pages to show the ambiguity of terms such as 'public,' 'private,' concluding that the goods to which he attends in his writing – egalitarianism, open speech, forgiveness, and so on – are sufficiently public for him to address them by talking about gospel values in public.[5] Drawing on the early work of H. Richard Niebuhr and Karl Barth, Yoder claims that "believers together are not called out of but sent into the real (public) world where sacrifice and sovereignty happen."[6] This appearance in the 'real world' is made possible precisely because of the Lordship of Christ. According to Yoder, "because the risen Messiah is at once head of the church and *kyrios* of the *kosmos,* sovereign of the universe, what is given to the church through him is in substance no different from what is offered to the world. The believing

---

James Gustafson. Yoder, *For the Nations,* 3-4. For a helpful discussion of the genealogy of the charge of sectarianism, see Arne Rasmusson, *The Church as Polis,* 231-247. It is interesting to note that Jeffrey Stout, in his recent discussion of democratic traditions, takes exception to the 'new traditionalism' of theologians such Stanley Hauerwas and John Milbank and the philosopher Alasdair MacIntyre, which, according to Stout, leads to making of the church an enclave that can only muster anti-liberalism. Stout traces Yoder's impact on Hauerwas's thought specifically in the area of ecclesiology, but blames MacIntyre's influence for Hauerwas's withdrawal into an ecclesial enclave. For Stout, then, Yoder (and Barth) is, at the very least, less of a danger to American democracy than is Hauerwas. Stout, *Democracy and Tradition,* 92-179. Craig Hovey has argued that the difference between Hauerwas and Yoder is Hauerwas's embrace of MacIntyre's anti-liberalism, a dimension not found in Yoder. See Hovey, "The Public Ethics of John Howard Yoder and Stanley Hauerwas: Difference or Disagreement?" in *A Mind Patient and Untamed,* 205-220.

[4] Yoder, *For the Nations,* 6. The notion of the church as public witness, or as 'public' in its own right is taken up and developed by other thinkers such as William Cavanaugh, *Theopolitical Imagination*; Reinhard Hütter, especially "The Church as Public: Dogma, Practice, and the Holy Spirit," in *Pro Ecclesia* 3 no 3 (Summer 1994): 334-360, and "The Church: Midwife of History or Witness of the Eschaton?" in *Journal of Religious Ethics* 18 no 1 (Spring 1990): 27-54; see also Hütter, *Suffering Divine Things: Theology as Church Practice,* trans. Doug Stott (Grand Rapids: Eerdmans Publishing Company, 2000). Hauerwas also suggests that Dietrich Bonhoeffer's ecclesiology also bears striking similarity to Yoder's. See Hauerwas's two essays, "Dietrich Bonhoeffer's Political Theology," and "Dietrich Bonhoeffer on Truth and Politics," in *Performing the Faith: Bonhoeffer and the Practice of Nonviolence* (Grand Rapids: Brazos Press, 2004), 33-72.

[5] Yoder, *For the Nations,* 15-21.

[6] Yoder, *For the Nations,* 36.

community is the new world on the way."[7]

O'Donovan's theopolitical vision leads him to a deep concern and embracing of the secular realm, if 'secular' is theologically conceptualized. His understanding of the secular as opposite to the eternal, rather than opposition to the sacred, along with his belief that the triumph of Christ has given separate authorization to the state allows O'Donovan to treat the secular realm as something substantive. O'Donovan therefore is able to avoid the mistake of equating all that happens in the secular realm with secularism.[8] The positing of the secular as a separately authorized space creates a way for O'Donovan to shape a political theology wherein the political act of judgment functions in a provisional, penultimate manner. O'Donovan is therefore never in danger of being understood as a sectarian (as Yoder has often been).

The political theology put forward by Yoder and O'Donovan, even when their significant differences are taken into account, consists largely in the recovery of Christian tradition and practice – and that not as yet another form of accommodation to various secular political philosophies. O'Donovan's self-conscious recovery of what he calls the Great Tradition, and Yoder's self-conscious attempts at perpetual restitution hold in common a commitment to proceed along exegetical, theological, and ecclesiological lines – these are the sources which play the primary generative roles for both Yoder and O'Donovan, suggesting and displaying the belief that political theology ought to seek to remain fully Christian even when as it engages in constructive political work. The point is not to shy away from sources and interlocuters which are not Christian, but precisely to approach engagements as Christians, and not abandoning the stance or content of Christian tradition at the moment of engagement.

This recovery of Christian tradition and practice also pushes Christian political theology to avoid any false dualisms between theology and ethics, faith and practice. Yoder has been more explicit about resisting any such dualisms than has O'Donovan, arguing throughout his career that false dualisms have the effect of being able to put aside political engagement at the very moment when that engagement can be expressed in fully Christian ways.[9]

---

[7] Yoder, *For the Nations*, 50. The distinction between Christian believers and secular world is not to be found in terms of withdrawal or engagement with that world, according to Yoder. "The distinctness is not a cultic or ritual separation, but rather a nonconformed quality of ("secular") involvement in the life of the world. It thereby constitutes an unavoidable challenge to the powers that be and the beginning of a new set of social alternatives." Yoder, *The Politics of Jesus*, 39.

[8] Jeffrey Stout believes that John Milbank makes this mistake. See Stout, *Democracy and Tradition*, 93.

[9] Yoder's clearest discussion of false dualisms which allow Christians to avoid political responsibility is part of *The Politics of Jesus*. For example, he complains about false choices between the Jesus of history and the Christ of faith; the prophet and the institution; the catastrophic kingdom and the inner kingdom; the political and the

O'Donovan's work on the other hand displays some ambivalence here, but he also testifies to the importance of resisting distinctions between theology and ethics, especially in his more recent work. Whereas his original intention was to write a two-part project, dealing first with political theology, and then writing a sequel which he anticipated as a "Christian political ethics," which would deal with an agenda set by political rather than theological questions. But that intention, that way of structuring these matters has undergone a change by O'Donovan's own description of things. He describes himself as having become much more cautious about "pseudo-disciplinary distinctions" between theology and ethics, theology and politics.[10] Surely separate discussions of certain matters can serve positive heuristic functions, but Christian theopolitical visions, if they follow Yoder and O'Donovan, will continue to resist any false dualisms as they seek to draw on the Christian tradition as a way of being political. That is, political theology is primarily an exegetical, theological, and ecclesiological task.

Nevertheless, it bears repeating that to envision the political task is such terms is not a way of avoiding constructive engagement, but as the way for Christians to engage the world. Yoder's theopolitical project claims to be 'for the nations,' while O'Donovan's project claims to give an account of the way in which Christ fulfills the 'desire of the nations' for those things that make up the common good. While both Yoder and O'Donovan claim that their biblically-based Christian theopolitical visions have the good of humanity in view, neither theologian places fundamental confidence in any one institutional form of government as the embodiment of the will of God, or the providential bearer of the common good. They share a deep wariness of imperialism and totalitarianism; they cannot be understood as promoting theocracy as the goal of political theology; they are opposed to the notion of seeing the world as a place where the will of the human can simply be imposed without regard for the transcendent.[11] Despite this shared reticence in designating any institutional form of government as the embodiment of providence or as the *telos* of history, both Yoder and O'Donovan underwrite support of democracy, albeit in a

---

sectarian; and the individual and the social. Yoder claims that if Jesus is Lord, then these disjunctions must be denied. Yoder, *The Politics of Jesus*, 103-109.

[10] O'Donovan, *The Ways of Judgment*, ix.

[11] Rowan Williams suggests that there is a significant discourse within political theology that shares "a conviction that the fundamental requirement of a politics worth the name is that we have an account of human action that decisively marks its distance from assumptions about action as the successful assertion of will. If there is no hinterland to human acting except the contest of private and momentary desire, meaningful action is successful action, an event in which a particular will has imprinted its agenda of the 'external' world. Or, in plainer terms, meaning is power..." Williams, "Introducing the Debate: Theology and the Political," in Davis, et al., eds., *Theology and the Political*, 1. Clearly both Yoder and O'Donovan would concur with Williams' statement.

somewhat chastened manner.[12]

The extent of the support for democracy is not identical in Yoder and O'Donovan, but both argue that democratic participation cannot be reduced to casting one's vote in elections at any and all levels of government. Rather, participation in democratic discourse must include the opportunity for deliberation, which is the kind of participation that is welcomed, for example, by Jeffrey Stout.[13] But it is important to observe that Stout is trying to prop up democracy, in which neither Yoder nor O'Donovan have a primary stake, but only insofar as democracy may provide a place where the Lordship of Christ can be expressed, but not only there.

Thus Yoder and O'Donovan provide a way forward for theopolitical work that seeks to be fully post-Christendom, that does not depend on Christendom, has not been seduced by Constantinianism, and is neither contingent on some particular form of institutional government to pursue constructive political engagement, nor interested in making a case for hegemony of the church or some version of theocracy. Political theology along these lines does not require formal establishment status, and indeed may seek to avoid any such structural role precisely in order to leave open the possibility of faithful political engagement. Here Yoder's work is especially compelling as he is evidently less interested in 'rule' of any kind than is O'Donovan, who is interested at least in 'moral rule.' Put another way, Yoder's stance in the world, his engagement with the world, seeks to embody a vulnerability that is less obvious in O'Donovan. This stance in the world opens possibilities for vigorous engagement that is beginning to be taken up and applied in a variety of settings and on-going conversations and initiatives. Perhaps most prevalent among

---

[12] Yoder, assuming a minority position for the Christian church, argues that "if we claim for democracy the status of a social institution *sui generis,* we shall inflate ourselves and destroy our neighbors through the demonic claims we make for our system and we shall pollute our Christian faith by making of it a civil religion. If on the other hand we protect ourselves from the Constantinianism of that view of democracy, we may find the realistic liberty to foster and celebrate relative democratization as one of the prophetic ministries of a servant people in a world that we do not control." Yoder, "The Christian Case for Democracy," in *The Priestly Kingdom,* 165-166. O'Donovan argues that history does not allow the strong thesis that democracy is a necessary or sufficient condition for the cultivation of liberal values. Electoral forms fail to guarantee just liberal governments and are not the guarantee of material representation. However, O'Donovan suggests that democracy is specifically appropriate for Western society at this moment, although it still needs reflective deliberation. O'Donovan, *The Ways of Judgment,* 169-185.

[13] Stout argues that antidemocratic tendencies displayed by the 'new traditionalists' such as Hauerwas do not stem from Christian theological orthodoxy. Therefore, Stout welcomes what he calls "a commendable commitment to democracy" on the part of "orthodox Trinitarians," theologians "who have connected theological orthodoxy with democratic practice…" Stout, *Democracy and Tradition,* 298.

these initiatives is the recent interaction between the radical democracy on the one hand, of the sort practiced and given theoretical underpinnings by Romand Coles, and radical ecclesiology, represented in part by the recent work of Stanley Hauerwas, on the other. In a recent collection of essays, letters, lectures and conversations, Hauerwas and Coles seek to exhibit a politics that refuses to let death dominate our lives; a politics that resists fear and seeks to uncover the violence that is at the heart of liberal political doctrine. And not only does this book try to write about such matters, it tries to display some of the practices it is bringing to view. That is, the practices that are central to this ongoing conversation include attention, engagement, vulnerability, receptive patience, tending, microdispositions, micropractices, waiting, and gentleness. Such practices, patiently pursued, might make up a life that is political, claim Hauerwas and Coles, yet not beholden to conventional politics.

Coles and Hauerwas engage not only each other but also a vast array of interlocuters in their attempts cultivate a politics of 'wild patience' – Sheldon Wolin, Cornell West, Ella Baker, Will Campbell, Rowan Williams, Jean Vanier, Samuel Wells, Gregory of Nanzianzus, and importantly for my point, the thought of John Howard Yoder. Nonetheless, Hauerwas and Coles, in the midst of their respectful and deep mutual engagement, exhibit a certain wariness at times in relation to each other. Hauerwas worries that radical democracy will be an end in itself to which God becomes an afterthought, a superfluous place-holder, domesticated and tamed in service of some other agenda. In fairness, Hauerwas is also worried that Christians do something very similar when they mistake the Christian faith for some garden variety of humanism. Coles, on the other hand, is concerned that the Christian jealousy regarding Jesus may prevent proper vulnerability and underwrite a kind of territoriality. Further, Coles believes that no matter how sincere the upside-down practices of the church may be, it is the case that these kinds of practices have a way of turning themselves right side up, and that without an appropriate discernment on the part of the church. Sometimes it feels as though Coles comes close to equating the insurgent grassroots political practices of radical democracy with the politics of Jesus. It also seems that Coles is tempted to turn the church and its practices into an instance of radical democracy. Perhaps this is one of the reasons why he claims to be so 'haunted' by Yoder, who, as I have pointed out, is open to the criticism that he thinks the practices of the church can be translated into the world without loss. Further, the extended conversation in this book, while richly informed by a wide variety of interlocuters, ranging from political theorists, activists of many kinds, theologians, a number of Mennonite thinkers and so on, is in the end strangely thin on the Christian exegetical tradition. That is, we see close, nuanced readings of Wolin, West, Campbell, et al, but search in vain for the same kind of close attention being paid to sustained readings of the Biblical text. This is of course not to say that the conversation between Coles the radical democrat and Hauerwas the Christian is not informed by biblical ideas. However, I wonder if

Coles' stated concern for Christian jealousy of Jesus might also extend to the Christian privileging of the Scriptural text, and if so, what implications this might have for a long term continuing conversation.

Jeffrey Stout of Princeton, who in his own attempt to revitalize the American democratic tradition often converses with Christian theologians such as Hauerwas, claims that this book gives him hope, since it takes the conversation between Christianity and democracy in a most welcome direction.[14] The impetus for this kind of hopeful conversation and its attendant engagements is found in part by Yoder's theopolitical work, as both Coles and Hauerwas draw extensively on his writing.

Yoder's vulnerability, his will to dialogue also opens up interesting possibilities concerning the pursuit of peace on a scale that goes beyond the local level. Yoder's openness to conversation holds considerable promise for ecumenism, which itself is an important dimension of constructive political engagement.[15] Yoder's approach or stance in ecumenical conversations can be seen as part of the stance that I have brought to view in theopolitical terms – an openness to engage on Christian terms, seeking to bear witness in faithful discipleship. Thus ecumenism and political engagement are part of the same stance in the world. As I have shown previously, Yoder's engagements are not without their difficulties, but it is important to notice that a significant dimension of Yoder's ecumenical work is directly connected to his peace witness. That is, the role of Yoder's thought in ecumenical initiatives such as the World Council of Churches (WCC) has been to promote and focus on the reduction of violence in the world, and consideration of how churches across the world might seek to transcend nationalistic issues in order to overcome violence. One such initiative, which is currently underway, is the *Decade to Overcome Violence,* which seeks to engage in grass-roots reflection and action that pursue peace.[16] This initiative, which runs from 2001-2010 calls on all

---

[14] Stanley Hauerwas and Romand Coles, *Christianity, Democracy, and the Radical Ordinary: Conversations between a Radical Democratic and a Christian* (Eugene, Oregon: Cascade Books, 2008).

[15] Yoder's ecumenical work has not been an explicit dimension of this study, and I bring to view at this late stage in order to suggest some of the constructive directions that Yoder's work has and could be taken. See Mark Thiessen Nation, *John Howard Yoder: Mennonite Patience, Evangelical Witness, Catholic Convictions* (Grand Rapids: Eerdmans Press, 2006) for a book-length explication of Yoder's ecumenism. See also Fernando Enns, *The Peace Church and the Ecumenical Community: Ecclesiology and the Ethics of Nonviolence,* trans. Helmut Harder (Kitchener: Pandora Press and World Council of Churches Publications, 2007).

[16] See for example Donald Miller, Scott Holland, Lon Fendall, and Dean Johnson, eds., *Seeking Peace in Africa: Stories From African Peacemakers* (Telford: Cascadia Publishing House, 2007); Alan Kreider, Eleanor Kreider, and Paulus Widjaja, *A Culture of Peace: God's Vision for the Church* (Intercourse: Good Books, 2005); Fernando

churches to address the universal problem of violence, and is intended to run parallel to the United Nations *Decade for a Culture of Peace and Nonviolence for the Children of the World*.[17] The motion to initiate the *Decade to Overcome Violence* was put forward tot eh WCC by Fernando Enns, a German Mennonite theologian

Finally, the contours of Yoder and O'Donovan's respective theopolitical visions also have different 'sizes,' as it were. As previously discussed, Yoder does not intentionally set out to produce a full-blown political theology, since to do so would be a Constantinian endeavor at its heart, as he perceives it. This is not to say that he does not produce something like a political theology, since it is obviously possible to discern just such a project through a reading of his essays. After all, someone as interested in the politics of Jesus, the politics of pacifism, the Christian witness to the state and so on, is obviously involved in working out theopolitical questions. However, Yoder's *ad hoc* ecclesial approach to politics suggests that he would not have seen the necessity of supplying anything but discussions of *ad hoc* engagements, and further, that these deliberations be conducted primarily in a church context. So, Mark Thiessen Nations's suggestion that Yoder could have improved his work by reading more political philosophy may well have struck Yoder as a misplaced criticism.[18] Indeed, in response to the kind of challenge O'Donovan issued to Anabaptist scholar A. James Reimer, that Mennonites need a social theory, Yoder would not have done what Reimer has done – i.e., set out to provide exactly what O'Donovan called for.[19] Instead, Yoder's response, as seen in his

---

Enns, Scott Holland, and Ann Riggs, eds., *Seeking Cultures of Peace: A Peace Church Conversation,* (Telford: Cascadia Publishing House, 2004).

[17] Samuel Kobia, "Foreword," in Donald Miller, Scott Holland, Lon Fendall, and Dean Johnson, eds., *Seeking Peace in Africa: Stories From African Peacemakers*, 13, 14.

[18] Nation's rather gentle criticism on this point consists of suggesting that Yoder's views "could have been enriched by deep reading in certain recent writings by political philosophers. His own perspective might have been updated in light of this reading." Nation, *John Howard Yoder: Mennonite Patience, Evangelical Witness, Catholic Convictions* (Grand Rapids: Eerdmans Press, 2006), 198-199. Nation is not specific about which political philosophers Yoder might have benefited from reading, and in what ways his views might have been updated, and therefore the criticism lacks substance. My point here is not to suggest that political philosophers ought not to be read by theologians, but more modestly, that Yoder's response to such a comment might well have been that he was more interested in deepening his understanding of the Lordship of Christ, rather than expanding his specific knowledge of political philosophy. This also does not mean that Yoder would disavow such an enterprise out of hand, but that gaining command of some field of knowledge would not be a *necessary* prerequisite to understanding questions of Christian political responsibility.

[19] Reimer describes the challenge and his response: "A number of years ago I was challenged by Oliver O'Donovan, moral philosopher and canon of Christ Church, Oxford, who claimed that he could not find any coherent and systematic treatment of pacifist social theory by Anabaptist or Mennonite writers. I denied this at the time but

extensive body of work, might be to suggest that political theology is whatever emerges as Christians seek to understand what it means to be a faithful disciple of Jesus Christ. Put another way, political theology might be understood as an epiphenomenon of Christian discipleship.

O'Donovan's project seeks to be comprehensive, one that is fully conceptualized in both theological and political dimensions. Thus O'Donovan's continued work in the field comes not so much as *ad hoc* engagements with specific issues, although it surely does that, as in the extension and expansion of the project begun in earnest with the publication of *The Desire of the Nations*. Thus when O'Donovan's attention turns to political ethics or the Just War Tradition, his language may take a more overtly political turn (*The Ways of Judgment*), or a more humanistic vocabulary (*The Just War Revisited*), but all of this work is premised on the theological and exegetical work previously done. Nevertheless, the use of less overtly theological language also seems to be a way of addressing audiences that may not share O'Donovan's theological views. In other words, it may be that someone who reads *The Just War Revisited* without having read *The Desire of the Nations* can nonetheless engage questions of war in discussion with a theologian who is interested in having an impact on secular government, and in calling for constraints within modern warfare.

In sum, this project, through a comparative analysis of John Howard Yoder and Oliver O'Donovan, has shown that, in a post-Christendom, secular, liberal Western society, Protestant political theology has tried in two different ways to relate discourse about God to political thought and social structure.

---

have since pondered his comments at length and come to suspect that he may at least be partly right. It's not that we don't have biblical, historical and ethical apologetics for our peace position but we lack a systematic political theory in which the positive role of civil institutions outside of the church is elaborated from the perspective of the Historic Peace Church Tradition. We have worked out systematically our own view of Christian social ethics from within the womb of the church but not thought a great deal about the positive function of the whole range of human institutions outside church and parachurch agencies. It is this task to which I turn my attention in a larger project of which this essay is but a small part." Reimer, "'I came not to abolish the law but to fulfill it': A Positive Theology of Law and Civil Institutions," in *A Mind Patient and Untamed*, 246. Reimer is still engaged in the larger project, but has not yet completed it to date.

Appendix

Old Testament	Jesus' Ministry	4 Moments of the Christ-Event	Recapitulation of 'moments' in 4 marks of the church's identity	4 Corresponding Practices of Worship	Liberal Society	Liberal Parody – Anti-Christ
Salvation	Works of power, Salvation from the powers	Advent: Christ's action in time – dated coming of the kingdom	Gathering Community – unity in diversity	Baptism	Freedom as social reality	Indifferent, indeterminate free choice
Judgment	Proclamation of the coming judgment of Israel	Passion – Christ's death as judgment, separation of guilt and innocence	Suffering community – martyrdom	Eucharist	Mercy in judgment	Unintelligible suffering
Possession – land and law	Jesus' ultimate exposition of the law, communal identity	Resurrection – restoration of life, of creation; continuity of inheritance	Glad Community – worship, confession, forgiveness	Keeping the Lord's Day	Respect for natural right: equality, affinity (community),reciprocity (universality), creaturely (human and non-human) cohabitation	Individual self-interest
Praise	Faith with which Jesus is received – political recognition of Jesus as King	Exaltation – Praise from God's obedient people	Proclaiming Community – God's words in prophecy and prayer	Laying on of Hands – confirmation, ordination, anointing of the sick	Freedom/openness: public deliberation	Totalizing speech – mass communication and competing interests

Source: I have drawn on Austin, "Method in Oliver O'Donovan's Political Theology," and Kroeker, "Why O'Donovan's Christendom is not Constantinian and Yoder's Voluntariety is not Hobbesian," for the material in this chart.

Bibliography

Oliver O'Donovan

_____. *The Problem of Self-Love in St. Augustine.* New Haven: Yale University Press, 1980.
_____. "Usus and fruitio in Augustine, De doctrina Christiana I." *Journal of Theological Studies* 33 (October 1982): 361-397.
_____. *Begotten or Made?* Oxford: Clarendon Press, 1984.
_____. "A Survey of Recent Christian Ethics." *Religious Studies* 20 (December 1984): 694-695.
_____. and Ronald Sider. *Peace and War: A Debate About Pacifism.* Bramcote: Grove Books, 1985.
_____. *On the 39 Articles: A Conversation with Tudor Christianity.* Carlisle: The Paternoster Press, 1986.
_____. "Augustine's City of God." *Dionysus* 11 (1987): 89-110.
_____. "Christian Morality: The Word Becomes Flesh." *Journal of Theological Studies* 40 (April 1989): 331-337.
_____. *Peace and Certainty: A Theological Essay on Deterrence.* Grand Rapids: Eerdmans Publishing, 1989.
_____. "Speak Up for Just War or Pacifism: A Critique of the United Methodist Bishops' Pastoral Letter 'In Defense of Creation.'" *Journal of Theological Studies* 41 (April 1990): 328-330.
_____. "Limits and Renewals, V. 1: Civil Peace and Sacred Order." *Journal of Theological Studies* 42 (April 1991): 441-444.
_____. *Resurrection and Moral Order: An Outline for Evangelical Ethics.* 2d ed. Grand Rapids: Eerdmans Publishing, 1994.
_____. *The Desire of Nations: Rediscovering the Roots of Political Theology.* Cambridge: Cambridge University Press, 1996.
_____. "Response to Respondents: Behold the Lamb!" *Studies in Christian Ethics*, 11 no 2 (1998): 91-110.
_____. "The Death Penalty in *Evangelium Vitae.*" In *Ecumenical Ventures in Ethics: Protestants Engage Pope John Paul II's Moral Encyclicals*, ed. Reinhard Hütter and Theodor Dieter, 216-236. Grand Rapids: Eerdmans, 1998.
_____. "Political Theology, Tradition, and Modernity." In *The Cambridge Companion to Liberation Theology*, ed. Christopher Rowland, 235-247. Cambridge: Cambridge University Press, 1999.
_____. "Government as Judgment." *First Things* 92 (April 1999): 36-44.
_____ and Joan Lockwood O'Donovan, eds. *From Irenaeus to Grotius: A Sourcebook in Christian Political Thought.* Grand Rapids: Eerdmans Publishing, 1999.
_____. "Deliberation, History and Reading: A Response to Schweiker and Wolterstorff." *Scottish Journal of Theology* 54:1 (2001): 127-144.
_____. Interview by Josh Pater, *Chimes Online,* 7 November 2001, available at http://clubs.calvin.edu/chimes/2001.11.09/ess.html.
_____. *Common Objects of Love: Moral Reflection and the Shaping of Community.* Grand Rapids: Eerdmans Publishing, 2002.

_____. *The Just War Revisited.* Cambridge: Cambridge University Press, 2003.
_____ and Joan Lockwood O'Donovan. *Bonds of Imperfection: Christian Politics, Past and Present.* Grand Rapids: Eerdmans Publishing, 2004.
_____. *The Ways of Judgment.* Grand Rapids: Eerdmans Publishing, 2005.

John Howard Yoder

_____. *The Christian Witness to the State.* Newton: Faith and Life Press, 1964.
_____. *The Original Revolution: Essays on Christian Pacifism.* Scottdale: Herald Press, 1971.
_____. *The Legacy of Michael Sattler.* Scottdale: Herald Press, 1973.
_____. "Contrasting Theological Approaches to the Problems of State and Society." Paper presented at Calvin College, Grand Rapids, April 19, 1974. Conrad Grebel College Library, Waterloo, Ontario.
_____. "The Spirit of God and the Politics of Men." *Journal of Theology for South Africa* 29 (December 1979), 62-71.
_____. Introduction to *Yahweh is a Warrior: The Theology of Warfare in Ancient Israel*, by Millard Lind. Scottdale: Herald Press, 1980.
_____. *Christian Attitudes to War, Peace, and Revolution: A Companion to Bainton.* Elkhart: Co-op Bookstore, 1983.
_____. *To Hear the Word.* Wipf and Stock: Eugene, Oregon, 2001.
_____. *The Priestly Kingdom: Social Ethics as Gospel.* Notre Dame: University of Notre Dame Press, 1984.
_____. *He Came Preaching Peace.* Scottdale: Herald Press, 1985.
_____. "Biblical Roots of Liberation Theology." *Grail* 1 no1 (September 1985): 55-74.
_____. "The Challenge of Peace: A Historic Peace Church Perspective." In *Peace in a Nuclear Age: The Bishops' Pastoral Letter in Perspective,* ed. Charles J. Reid, Jr., 273-290. Washington, Catholic University of America Press, 1986.
_____. "Surrender: A Moral Imperative?" *The Review of Politics*, 48 no 4 (Fall 1986): 576-595.
_____. *The Fullness of Christ: Paul's Revolutionary Vision of Universal Ministry.* Elgin: Brethren Press, 1987.
_____. "Armaments and Eschatology." *Studies in Christian Ethics* 1 no1 (1988): 43-61.
_____. "The Reception of the Just War Tradition by the Magisterial Reformation," *History of European Ideas* 9 (1988): 1-23.
_____. "Bluff or Revenge: The Watershed in Democratic Awareness." In *Ethics in the Nuclear Age,* ed. Todd Whitmore, 79-94. Dallas: SMU Press, 1989.
_____. "Military Realities and Teaching the Laws of War." In *Theology, Politics, and Peace,* ed. Theodore Runyon, 176-180. Maryknoll: Orbis Press, 1989.
_____. "The Credibility of Ecclesiastical Teaching on the Morality of War." In *Celebrating Peace,* ed. Leroy Rouner, 33-51. Notre Dame: University of Notre Dame Press, 1990.
_____. "Thinking Theologically From a Free-Church Perspective." In *Doing Theology in Today's World: Essays in Honor of Kenneth S. Kantzer,* eds. John Woodbridge and Thomas McComiskey, 251-265. Grand Rapids: Zondervan Publishing House, 1991.
_____, Douglas Gwyn, George Hunsinger, and Eugene Roop. *A Declaration on Peace: In God's People the World's Renewal Has Begun.* Scottdale: Herald Press, 1991.
_____. "Just War Tradition: Is it Credible?" *Christian Century* 108 no 9 (March 13

1991): 295-98.

____. *Body Politics: Five Practices of the Christian Community Before the Watching World*. Nashville: Discipleship Resources. 1992.

____. "Texts That Serve or Texts That Summon?: A Response to Michael Walzer." *Journal of Religious Ethics* 20 no 2 (1992): 229-234.

____. "On Not Being Ashamed of the Gospel: Particularity, Pluralism, and Validation," *Faith and Philosophy* 9 no 3 (July, 1992): 285-300.

____. "Cult and Culture In and After Eden: On Generating Alternative Paradigms." In *Human Values and the Environment: Conference Proceedings, Report 140* by the University of Wisconsin Academy of Sciences, Arts, and Letters, University of Wisconsin, 1992.

____. "The Burden and Discipline of Evangelical Revisionism." In *Nonviolent America: History Through the Eyes of Peace*, eds. Louise Hawkley and James Juhnke, 21-37. Kansas: Mennonite Press, Bethel College, 1993.

____ and Michael Cartwright, eds. *The Royal Priesthood: Essays Ecclesiological and Ecumenical*. Grand Rapids: W.B. Eerdmans, 1994.

____. "How Many Ways are There to Think Morally About War?" *The Journal of Law and Religion* 11 no 1 (1994): 83-107.

____. *The Politics of Jesus: Vicit Agnus Noster*. 2d ed. Grand Rapids: Eerdmans Publishing, 1994.

____. "Review Symposium." *Horizons* 22 no 2 (Fall 1995): 277-281.

____. "Meaning After Babble: With Jeffrey Stout Beyond Relativism." *Journal of Religious Ethics* 24:1 (Spring, 1996): 125-139.

____, D.M. Yeager, and Glen Stassen. *Authentic Transformation: A New Vision of Christ and Culture*. Nashville: Abingdon Press, 1996.

____. "War as a Moral Problem in the Early Church: The Historian's Hermeneutical Assumptions." In *The Pacifist Impulse in Historical Perspective*, ed. Harvey Dyck, 90-110. Toronto: University of Toronto Press, 1996.

____. "Confessing Jesus in Mission." *Wereld en Zending*, 24 (1996). Translation available from http://www.nd.edu/~theo/jhy/writings/christology/confessing.htm.

____. *For the Nations: Essays Public and Evangelical*. Grand Rapids: W.B. Eerdmans, 1997.

____. *Preface to Theology: Christology and Theological Method*. eds. Stanley Hauerwas and Alex Sider. Grand Rapids: Brazos Press, 2002.

____. *The Jewish-Christian Schism Revisited*. eds. Michael Cartwright, Peter Ochs. Grand Rapids: Eerdmans Publishing, 2003.

____. *Karl Barth and the Problem of War and Other Essays on Barth*. ed. Mark Thiessen Nation. Eugene: Cascade Books, 2003.

____. *Discipleship as Political Responsibility*. Translated by Timothy Geddert. Scottdale: Herald Press, 2003.

____. *Anabaptism and Reformation in Switzerland: An Historical and Theological Analysis of the Dialogues Between Anabaptist and Reformers*, Edited by C. Arnold Snyder, translated by David Carl Stassen and C. Arnold Synder. Kitchener: Pandora Press, 2004.

Other Sources

Agamben, Giorgio. *The Time That Remains: A Commentary on the Letter to the*

Romans. Translated by Patricia Dailey. Stanford: Stanford University Press, 2005.

Aquinas, Thomas. *St. Thomas Aquinas on Politics and Ethics.* Edited and translated by Paul Sigmund. New York: W.W. Norton, 1988.

Augustine. "On the Morals of the Catholic Church." In *Basic Writings of Saint Augustine, Vol. 1.* Translated by Whitney Oates. New York: Random House, 1948.

_____. *City of God.* Translated by Henry Bettenson. London: Penguin Books, 1972.

Austin, Victor L. "Method in Oliver O'Donovan's Political Theology." *Anglican Theological Review* 79 (Fall 1997): 583-594.

Bader-Saye, Scott. *Church and Israel After Christendom.* Boulder: Westview Press, 1999.

Badiou, Alain . *Saint Paul: The Foundation of Universalism.* Translated by Ray Brassier. Stanford: Stanford University Press, 2003.

Barth, Karl. *Ethics.* New York: Seabury Press, 1981.

_____. "The Christian Community and the Civil Community." In *Karl Barth: Theologian of Freedom,* ed. Clifford Green, 265-296. Minneapolis, Fortress Press, 1991.

Bartholemew, Craig; Jonathan Chaplin, Robert Song, and Al Wolters, eds. *A Royal Priesthood? The Use of the Bible Ethically and Politically – A Dialogue with Oliver O'Donovan.* Grand Rapids: Zondervan Press, 2002.

Beiner, Ronald. "Machiavelli, Hobbes, and Rousseau on Civil Religion." *The Review of Politics.* 55 (Fall 1993): 617-38.

Bell, Jr. Daniel. "State and Civil Society." In *Blackwell Companion to Political Theology,* ed. William Cavanaugh and Peter Scott, 423-438. Oxford: Blackwell Publishers, 2004.

Berkhof, Hendrikus. *Christ and the Powers.* Translated by John Howard Yoder. Scottdale: Herald Press, 1962.

Blough, Neal. "The Historical Roots of John Howard Yoder's Theology." In *Anabaptism and Reformation in Switzerland: An Historical and Theological Analysis of the Dialogues Between Anabaptist and Reformers.* Edited by C. Arnold Snyder, translated by David Carl Stassen and C. Arnold Synder, xli-lx. Kitchener: Pandora Press, 2004.

Cahill, Lisa Sowle. *Love Your Enemies: Discipleship, Pacifism, and Just War Theory.* Minneapolis: Fortress Press, 1994.

Calvin, John. "On Civil Government." In *Luther and Calvin on Secular Authority.* Edited and translated by Harro Hopfel. Cambridge: Cambridge University Press, 1991.

Carroll, M. Daniel. "The Power of the Future in the Present: Eschatology and Ethics in O'Donovan and Beyond." In *A Royal Priesthood? The Use of the Bible Ethically and Politically – A Dialogue with Oliver O'Donovan,* eds. Craig Bartholomew, Jonathan Chaplin, Robert Song, and Al Wolters, 116-143. Grand Rapids: Zondervan Press, 2002.

Carter, Craig. *The Politics of the Cross: The Theology and Social Ethics of John Howard Yoder.* Grand Rapids: Brazos Press, 2001.

Cartwright, Michael. Introduction in *The Jewish-Christian Schism Revisited.* eds. Michael Cartwright, Peter Ochs. Grand Rapids: Eerdmans Publishing, 2003.

Cavanaugh, William, and Peter Scott, eds. *Blackwell Companion to Political Theology.* Oxford: Blackwell Publishers, 2004.

Cavanaugh, William. "Church." In *Blackwell Companion to Political Theology,* ed.

William Cavanaugh and Peter Scott, 393-406. Oxford: Blackwell Publishers, 2004.
_____. *Theopolitical Imagination: Discovering the Liturgy as a Political Act in an Age of Global Consumerism*. London: T & T Clark, Continuum, 2002.
Chaplin, Jonathan. "Political Eschatology and Responsible Government." In *A Royal Priesthood? The Use of the Bible Ethically and Politically – A Dialogue with Oliver O'Donovan*, eds. Craig Bartholomew, Jonathan Chaplin, Robert Song, and Al Wolters, 265-308. Grand Rapids: Zondervan Press, 2002.
Coles, Romand. "The Wild Patience of John Howard Yoder: 'Outsiders' and the 'Otherness of the Church.'" *Modern Theology* 18:3 (July 2002): 305-331.
_____. *Beyond Gated Politics: Reflections for the Possibilities of Democracy*. Minneapolis: University of Minnesota Press, 2005.
Davis, Creston, John Milbank, and Slavoj Zizek, eds., *Theology and the Political: The New Debate*. Durham and London: Duke University Press, 2005.
Davis, Grady Scott. "Tradition and Truth in Christian Ethics: John Yoder and the Bases of Biblical Realism." In *The Wisdom of the Cross: Essays in Honor of John Howard Yoder*, eds. Stanley Hauerwas, Chris Huebner, Harry Huebner, and Mark Thiessen Nation, 278-305. Grand Rapids: Eerdmans, 1999.
Doerksen, Paul. "Share the House: Yoder and Hauerwas Among the Nations." In *A Mind Patient and Untamed*: *Assessing John Howard Yoder's Contribution to Theology, Ethics, and Peacemaking*, eds. Ben Ollenburger and Gayle Gerber Koontz, 187-204. Scottdale, Cascadia Publishing House, 2004.
_____. "Christology in the Political Theology of Oliver O'Donovan." *Mennonite Quarterly Review* 78 no 3 (July 2004): 433-447.
Durnbaugh, Donald, ed., *On Earth Peace*. Elgin: The Brethren Press, 1978.
Enns, Fernando, Scott Holland, and Ann Riggs, eds. *Seeking Cultures of Peace: A Peace Church Conversation*. Telford: Cascadia Publishing House, 2004.
Enns, Fernando. *The Peace Church and the Ecumenical Community: Ecclesiology and the Ethics of Nonviolence*. Translated by Helmut Harder. Kitchener: Pandora Press and World Council of Churches Publications, 2007.
Forrester, Duncan B. "The Desire of the Nations: Rediscovering the Roots of Political Theology." *Journal of Theological Studies* 48 (October 1997): 756-758.
_____. *Theology and Politics*. Oxford: Blackwell Publishers, 1988.
Furnish, Victor Paul. "How Firm a Foundation? Some Questions About Scripture in *The Desire of the Nations*." *Studies in Christian Ethics* 11 no 2 (1998): 18-23.
Greene, Colin J.D. "Revisiting Christendom: A Crisis of Legitimation." In *A Royal Priesthood? The Use of the Bible Ethically and Politically – A Dialogue with Oliver O'Donovan*, eds. Craig Bartholomew, Jonathan Chaplin, Robert Song, and Al Wolters, 314-340. Grand Rapids: Zondervan Press, 2002.
Gustafson, James. "The Sectarian Temptation." *The Annual of the Catholic Theological Society* 40 (1985): 83-94.
Hamburger, Philip. *Separation of Church and State*. Cambridge: Harvard University Press, 2002.
Harink, Doug. *Paul Among the Postliberals: Pauline Theology Beyond Christendom and Modernity*. Grand Rapids: Brazos Press, 2003.
Hauerwas, Stanley. "Messianic Pacifism: Non-resistance as a Defense of a Good and Just Social Order." *Worldview* 16, no. 6 (June 1973): 29-33.
_____. "Pacifism: Some Philosophical Considerations." *Faith and Philosophy* 2 (1985): 99-104.

_____. *Against the Nations: War and Survival in a Liberal Society.* Minneapolis: Winston Press, 1985.

_____. "Will the Real Sectarian Please Stand Up?" *Theology Today* 44 (1987): 87-94.

_____. "Epilogue: A Pacifist Response to the Bishops." In *Speak Up For Just War or Pacifism: A Critique of the United Methodist Bishops' Pastoral Letter "In Defense of Creation,"* Paul Ramsey, 149-182. University Park, Pa.: Pennsylvania State University Press, 1988.

_____. *After Christendom?: How the Church is to Behave if Freedom, Justice, and a Christian Nation are Bad Ideas.* Nashville: Abingdon Press, 1991.

_____. *Dispatches From the Front: Theological Engagements With the Secular.* Durham: Duke University Press, 1994.

_____. *Wilderness Wanderings: Probing Twentieth-Century Theology and Philosophy.* Boulder, Colorado: Westview Press, 1997.

_____, Chris Huebner, Harry Huebner, and Mark Thiessen Nation, eds. *The Wisdom of the Cross: Essays in Honor of John Howard Yoder.* Grand Rapids: Eerdmans, 1999.

_____ and Chris Huebner, "History, Theology, and Anabaptism: A Conversation on Theology after John Howard Yoder." In *The Wisdom of the Cross: Essays in Honor of John Howard Yoder*, ed. Stanley Hauerwas, Chris Huebner, Harry Huebner, and Mark Thiessen Nation, 391-408. Grand Rapids: Eerdmans, 1999.

_____. *With the Grain of the Universe.* Grand Rapids: Brazos Press, 2001.

_____ and John Milbank. "Christian Peace: A Conversation between Stanley Hauerwas and John Milbank." In *Must Christianity be Violent?: Reflections on History, Practice, and Theology,* ed. Kenneth Chase and Alan Jacobs, 207-223. Grand Rapids: Brazos Press, 2003.

_____. "Notes For a Conversation With John Milbank." In *Must Christianity be Violent?: Reflections on History, Practice, and Theology.* ed. Kenneth Chase and Alan Jacobs, 172-182. Grand Rapids: Brazos Press, 2003.

_____. *Performing the Faith: Bonhoeffer and the Practice of Non-violence.* Grand Rapids: Brazos Press, 2004.

Hays, Richard. *The Moral Vision of The New Testament: A Contemporary Introduction to New Testament Ethics.* San Francisco: Harper Collins, 1996.

Heilke, Thomas. "On Being Ethical Without Moral Sadism: Two Readings of Augustine and the Beginnings of the Anabaptist Revolution." *Political Theory* 24:3 (Summer 1996): 493-517.

_____. "Yoder's Idea of Constantinianism: An Analytical Framework Toward Conversation." In *A Mind Patient and Untamed*: *Assessing John Howard Yoder's Contribution to Theology, Ethics, and Peacemaking*, eds. Ben Ollenburger and Gayle Gerber Koontz, 89-125. Scottdale, Cascadia Publishing House, 2004.

Herbert, David. "Getting by in Babylon: MacIntyre, Milbank and a Christian Response to Religious Diversity in the Public Arena." *Studies in Christian Ethics* 10, no. 1 (1997): 61-81.

Hobbes, Thomas. *Leviathan, with selected variants from the Latin edition of 1668.* Edited by Edwin Curley. Indianapolis/Cambridge: Hackett Publishing Company, 1994.

Hollerich, Michael. "Carl Schmitt." In *Blackwell Companion to Political Theology,* ed. William Cavanaugh and Peter Scott, 107-122. Oxford: Blackwell Publishers, 2004.

Hovey, Craig. "The Public Ethics of John Howard Yoder and Stanley Hauerwas: Difference or Disagreement?" In *A Mind Patient and Untamed*: *Assessing John*

Howard Yoder's Contribution to Theology, Ethics, and Peacemaking, eds. Ben Ollenburger and Gayle Gerber Koontz, 205-220. Scottdale, Cascadia Publishing House, 2004.

Huebner, Chris. "Globalization, Theory, and Dialogical Vulnerability: John Howard Yoder and the Possibility of a Pacifist Epistemology." *Mennonite Quarterly Review* 76:1 (January 2002): 49-62.

_____. "Mennonites and Narrative Theology." *The Conrad Grebel Review* 16 no 2 (1998): 15-38.

Hütter, Reinhard. "The Church: Midwife of History or Witness of the Eschaton?" *Journal of Religious Ethics* 18 no 1 (Spring 1990): 27-54.

_____. "The Church as Public: Dogma, Practice, and the Holy Spirit." *Pro Ecclesia* 3 no 3 (Summer 1994): 334-360.

_____. "Be Honest in Just War Thinking! Lutherans, the Just War Tradition, and Selective Conscientious Objection." In *The Wisdom of the Cross: Essays in Honor of John Howard Yoder*, ed. Stanley Hauerwas, Chris Huebner, Harry Huebner, and Mark Thiessen Nation, 69-83. Grand Rapids: Eerdmans, 1999.

_____. *Suffering Divine Things: Theology as Church Practice*. Translated by Doug Stott. Grand Rapids: Eerdmans Publishing Company, 2000.

Jenson, Robert. "Eschatology." In *Blackwell Companion to Political Theology*, ed. William Cavanaugh and Peter Scott, 407-420. Oxford: Blackwell Publishers, 2004.

Jones, L. Gregory. "Resurrection and Moral Order." *Books and Religion* 15:5 (Fall 1987): 28-29.

Kee, Alistair, ed. *A Reader in Political Theology*. London: SCM Press, 1974.

Kreider, Alan, Eleanor Kreider, and Paulus Widjaja. *A Culture of Peace: God's Vision for the Church*. Intercourse: Good Books, 2005.

Kroeker, P. Travis. "Why O'Donovan's Christendom is not Constantinian and Yoder's Voluntariety is not Hobbesian: A Debate in Theological Politics Re-defined." in *The Annual of the Society of Christian Ethics*, 20 (2000): 41-64.

_____. "The War of the Lamb: Postmodernity and John Howard Yoder's Eschatological Genealogy of Morals." *Mennonite Quarterly Review* 74 (April 2000): 295-310.

_____. Review of *The Politics of the Cross*, by Craig Carter. *Journal of Mennonite Studies* 20 (2002): 268-270.

Lind, Millard. "The Concept of Political Power in Ancient Israel." *Annual of the Swedish Theological Institute* 7 (1970): 4-24.

Locke, John. "An Essay Concerning Toleration." In *Treatise of Civil Government and A Letter Concerning Toleration*. Edited by Charles Sherman. New York: D. Appleton-Century Company, 1937.

Long, D. Stephen. "Ramseyian Just War and Yoderian Pacifism: Where is the Disagreement?" *Studies in Christian Ethics* 4 no 1 (1990): 58-72.

Luther, Martin. "On Secular Authority," In *Luther and Calvin on Secular Authority*. Translated and edited by Harro Hopfel. Cambridge: Cambridge University Press, 1991.

MacIntyre, Alasdair. *After Virtue: A Study in Moral Theory*, 2d. ed. Notre Dame: University of Notre Dame Press, 1983.

Manenschijn, Gerrit. "'Jesus Is the Christ,' The Political Theology of Leviathan." *Journal of Religious Ethics* 25 (Spring 1997): 35-64

Martinich, A. P. *The Two Gods of Leviathan: Thomas Hobbes on Religion and Politics*. Cambridge: Cambridge University Press, 1992.

McClendon, James. *Systematic Theology: Ethics*. Nashville: Abingdon Press, 1986.
McConnville, J. Gordon. "Law and Monarchy in the Hebrew Scriptures." In *A Royal Priesthood? The Use of the Bible Ethically and Politically – A Dialogue with Oliver O'Donovan*, eds. Craig Bartholomew, Jonathan Chaplin, Robert Song, and Al Wolters, 69-77. Grand Rapids: Zondervan Press, 2002.
Meilaender, Gilbert. "Recovering Christendom." *First Things* 77 (November 1997): 36-42.
_____. "Resurrection and Moral Order." *Dialog* 26 (Spring 1987): 156-158.
Milbank, John. *Theology and Social Theory: Beyond Secular Reason*. Oxford: Blackwell Publishers, 1990.
Miller, Donald, Scott Holland, Lon Fendall, and Dean Johnson, eds. *Seeking Peace in Africa: Stories From African Peacemakers*. Telford: Cascadia Publishing House, 2007.
Mitchell, Joshua. "Luther and Hobbes on the Question: Who was Moses? Who was Christ?" *The Journal of Politics* 53 (Aug. 1991): 676-700.
Moberly, R.W.L. "The Use of Scripture in *The Desire of the Nations*." In *A Royal Priesthood? The Use of the Bible Ethically and Politically – A Dialogue with Oliver O'Donovan*, eds. Craig Bartholomew, Jonathan Chaplin, Robert Song, and Al Wolters, 46-64. Grand Rapids: Zondervan Press, 2002.
Moltmann, Jürgen. "Covenant or Leviathan? Political Theology for Modern Times." *Scottish Journal of Theology* 47:1 (1994): 19-41.
Murphy, Nancey. "John Howard Yoder's Systematic Defense of Christian Pacifism." In *The Wisdom of the Cross: Essays in Honor of John Howard Yoder*, eds. Stanley Hauerwas, Chris Huebner, Harry Huebner, and Mark Thiessen Nation, 45-68. Grand Rapids: Eerdmans, 1999.
Nation, Mark Thiessen. "Theology as Witness: Reflections on Yoder, Fish, and Interpretive Communities." *Faith and Freedom* 5:1,2 (June 1996): 42-47.
_____. "A Comprehensive Bibliography of the Writings of John Howard Yoder." *Mennonite Quarterly Review* 71:1 (January 1997): 93-145.
Nation, Mark Thiessen. *John Howard Yoder: Mennonite Patience, Evangelical Witness, Catholic Convictions*. Grand Rapids: Eerdmans, 2006.
Nicholls, David. *Deity and Domination: Images of God and the State in the Nineteenth and Twentieth Centuries*. London and New York: Routledge, 1989.
Okholm, Dennis. "Defending the Cause of the Christian Church: Karl Barth's Justification of War." *Christian Scholar's Review* 16:2 (1987): 144-162.
Ollenburger, Ben, and Koontz, Gayle Gerber. *A Mind Patient and Untamed: Assessing John Howard Yoder's Contribution to Theology, Ethics, and Peacemaking*. Scottdale: Cascadia Publishing House, 2004.
Pabel, Hilmar. "Give to Caesar That Which Is Caesars: Hobbes's Strategy in the Second Half of Leviathan." *Journal of Church and State* 35 (Spring, 1993): 335-349.
Penner, Carol. "Mennonite Silences and Feminist Voices: Peace Theology and Violence Against Women." Ph.D. diss., University of St. Michael's College, 1999.
Ramsey, Paul. *Basic Christian Ethics*. New York: Charles Scribner's Sons, 1950.
_____. *The Just War: Force and Political Responsibility*. New York: Charles Scribner's Sons, 1968.
_____. *Speak Up For Just War or Pacifism: A Critique of the United Methodist Bishops' Pastoral Letter "In Defense of Creation,"* University Park, Pa.: Pennsylvania State University Press, 1988.

Rasmusson, Arne. "Not All Justifications of Christendom Are Created Equal: A Response to Oliver O'Donovan." *Studies in Christian Ethics*, 11 no 2 (1998): 69-76.

_____. "Ecclesiology and Ethics: The Difficulties of Ecclesial Moral Reflection." *Ecumenical Review* 52:2 (April 2000): 180-194.

_____. *The Church as Polis: From Political Theology to Theological Politics as Exemplified by Jurgen Moltman and Stanley Hauerwas*. Notre Dame: University of Notre Dame Press, 1995.

Reimer, A. James. "Mennonites, Christ, and Culture: The Yoder Legacy." *Conrad Grebel Review* 16, no. 2 (Spring 1998): 5-14.

_____. "Theological Orthodoxy and Jewish Unity: A Personal Tribute to John Howard Yoder." In *The Wisdom of the Cross: Essays in Honor of John Howard Yoder*, eds. Stanley Hauerwas, Chris Huebner, Harry Huebner, and Mark Thiessen Nation, 430-448. Grand Rapids: Eerdmans, 1999.

_____. *Mennonites and Classical Theology: Dogmatic Foundations for Christian Ethics*. Kitchener, ON: Pandora Press, 2001.

Richardson, Cyril. trans. and ed. *Early Christian Fathers*. New York: Collier Books, 1970.

Rousseau, Jean Jacques. *On the Social Contract*. Translated by Donald Cress. Indianapolis: Hackett Publishing Company, 1987.

Rowland, Christopher. "The Apocalypse and Political Theology." In *A Royal Priesthood? The Use of the Bible Ethically and Politically – A Dialogue with Oliver O'Donovan*, eds. Craig Bartholomew, Jonathan Chaplin, Robert Song, and Al Wolters, 241-254. Grand Rapids: Zondervan Press, 2002.

Schlabach, Gerald. "Anthology in Lieu of System: John H. Yoder's Ecumenical Conversations as Systematic Theology." *Mennonite Quarterly Review* 71 (April 1997): 305-309.

_____. "Deuteronomic or Constantinian: What is the Most Basic Problem for Christian Social Ethics?" In *The Wisdom of the Cross: Essays in Honor of John Howard Yoder*, eds. Stanley Hauerwas, Chris Huebner, Harry Huebner, and Mark Thiessen Nation, 449-471. Grand Rapids: Eerdmans, 1999.

Schmitt, Schmitt. *Political Theology*. Translated by George Schwab. Cambridge: MIT Press, 1985.

Schweiker, William. "Freedom and Authority in Political Theology: A Response to Oliver O'Donovan's 'The Desire of the Nations,'" *Scottish Journal of Theology* 54:1 (2001): 110-126.

Shaffer, Thomas. *Moral Memoranda From John Howard Yoder: Conversations on Law, Ethics and the Church Between a Mennonite Theologian and a Hoosier Lawyer*. Eugene: Wipf and Stock, 2002.

Siebert, Rudy. "From Conservative to Critical Political Theology." In *The Influence of the Frankfurt School on Contemporary Theology: Critical Theory and the Future of Religion: Dubrovnik Papers in Honour of Rudolf J. Siebert*, ed. A. James Reimer, 147-219. Lewiston: Edwin Mellen Press, 1992.

Sider, J. Alexander. "Constantinianism Before and After Nicea: Issues in Restitutionist Historiography." In *A Mind Patient and Untamed: Assessing John Howard Yoder's Contribution to Theology, Ethics, and Peacemaking*, eds. Ben Ollenburger and Gayle Gerber Koontz, 126-144. Scottdale, Cascadia Publishing House, 2004.

Southern, R.W. *Western Society and Church in the Middle Ages*. Middlesex: Penguin Books, 1970.

Stout, Jeffrey. *Ethics After Babel: The Languages of Morals and Their Discontents.* Boston: Beacon Press, 1988.

_____. *Democracy and Tradition.* Princeton: Princeton University Press, 2004.

Strauss, Leo. *Natural Right and History.* Chicago: University of Chicago Press, 1953.

Tanner, Katherine. "Trinity." In *Blackwell Companion to Political Theology,* ed. William Cavanaugh and Peter Scott, 319-332. Oxford: Blackwell Publishers, 2004.

Taubes, Jacob. *The Political Theology of Paul.* Translated by Dana Hollander. Stanford: Stanford University Press, 2004.

Tilley, W Clyde. "World-affirmation and the Resurrection of Jesus Christ." *Perspectives in Religious Studies* 15 (Summer 1988): 165-176.

Toole, David. *Waiting for Godot in Sarajevo: Theological Reflections on Nihilism, Tragedy, and Apocalypse.* Colorado: Westview Press, 1998.

Voegelin, Eric. *The New Science of Politics: An Introduction.* Chicago: University of Chicago Press, 1952.

Wainwright, Tobias. "From Police Officers to Peace Officers." In *The Wisdom of the Cross: Essays in Honor of John Howard Yoder,* ed. Stanley Hauerwas, Chris Huebner, Harry Huebner, and Mark Thiessen Nation, 84-114. Grand Rapids: Eerdmans, 1999.

Wannenwetsch, Bernd. Review of *The Desire of the Nations: Rediscovering the Roots of Political Theology,* by Oliver O'Donovan. *Modern Theology* 14 (July 1998): 463-467.

_____. "Liturgy." In *Blackwell Companion to Political Theology,* ed. William Cavanaugh and Peter Scott, 76-90. Oxford: Blackwell Publishers, 2004.

_____. *Political Worship: Ethics for Christian Citizens.* Translated by Margaret Kohl. Oxford: Oxford University Press, 2004.

Weaver, Alain Epp. "The Politics of Jesus, 20 Years Later." *Mennonite Life* 50 (September 1995): 14-17.

_____. "After Politics: John Howard Yoder, Body Politics, and the Witnessing Church." *Review of Politics* 61:4 (Fall 1999): 637-674.

_____. "Missionary Christology: John Howard Yoder and the Creeds." *Mennonite Quarterly Review* 74:3 (July 2000): 423-439.

_____. "On Exile: Yoder, Said, and a Theology of Land and Return," *Cross Currents* 52 no 4 (2003): 439-461.

Williams, Rowan. "Introducing the Debate: Theology and the Political." In *Theology and the Political: The New Debate,* ed. Creston Davis, John Milbank, and Slavoj Zizek, 1-3. Durham and London: Duke University Press, 2005.

Wogaman, J. Philip. *Christian Perspectives on Politics.* 2d. ed. Louisville: Westminster John Knox Press, 2000.

Wolterstorff, Nicholas. "A Discussion of Oliver O'Donovan's *The Desire of the Nations.*" *Scottish Journal of Theology* 54:1 (2001): 87-109.

Žižek, Slavoj. *The Fragile Absolute – or, why is the Christian legacy worth fighting for?* London: Verso, 2000.

_____. *The Puppet and the Dwarf: The Perverse Core of Christianity.* Cambridge, Massachusetts: The MIT Press, 2003.

General Index

Anabaptism 2, 4, 18-19, 47
antiroyal reading of Hebrew Scripture 4, 15, 36, 40-42, 50, 66
Austin, Victor 30, 32, 161

Barth, Karl 20, 25, 78-79, 90, 194
Bartholomew, Craig 30
Bell, Daniel 2, 13, 69
Berkhof, Hendrik 99-100
Blough, Neal 25

Cahill, Lisa Sowle 198
capital punishment 178
Carroll R., M. Daniel 107, 152
Carter, Craig 1, 3, 24-25, 75-76, 90, 98, 104, 127, 144
Cartwright, Michael 26, 41, 49, 187
Cavanaugh, William 107, 140, 160, 165, 169
Cavanaugh, William and Scott, Peter 1, 14
Chaplin, Jonathan 133, 152, 163, 193
Christendom 1, 2, 6, 128ff.
Coles, Romand 18
common good 124
Constantinianism 27-28, 128ff.

Davidic monarchy 40, 41
Davis, Grady Scott 20, 24
diaspora 4, 42-43, 46
discipleship 11-116, 144, 203
Durnbaugh, Donald 27, 86

exile 42-50

Furnish, Victor Paul 62, 84, 107

God as Warrior 16, 39
grain of the universe 77-78

Harink, Doug 74, 101, 110
Hauerwas, Stanley 2, 12-13, 29, 77, 79, 197, 209

Hauerwas, Stanley and Coles, Romand 213-214
Hauerwas, Stanley and Fodor, James 35, 61-62, 106, 132, 160
Hauerwas, Stanley and Sider, Alex 17, 93
holy war 22, 39-41, 66
Huebner, Chris 20, 183
Hütter, Reinhard 166, 198, 209

incarnation 83, 86

Jeremian shift 16, 42-50, 57-59, 66, 95
'Jesuology' 69-70, 72, 83-84, 91-93, 126-127

Kee, Alistair 7, 11
kenosis 74, 77
Kroeker, P. Travis 7, 24, 27, 107-108, 152, 167, 184

Latin American theology 10, 11, 31
Lind, Millard 21, 37

McConnville, J. Gordon 62-63
Meilander, Gilbert 132, 168
Milbank, John 13, 183, 210

narrative theology 20, 23-24
Nation, Mark Thiessen 25, 197, 214-215

peoplehood 17, 39, 65, 109ff.

Ramsey, Paul 175, 179, 185, 191, 197, 200, 206
Rasmusson, Arne 11, 13-14, 135, 168,
royal reading of Hebrew Scripture 14-15, 31-33, 53ff.
Reimer, A. James 46-47, 89-92, 107, 131, 143, 215-216
Rowland, Christopher 4, 106, 152

Schlabach, Gerald 26, 49, 164

Schmitt, Carl 7-11
Schweiker, William 33-34
Sider, Ron 175, 177, 179, 204, 206
Snyder, C. Arnold 25, 139
Stout, Jeffrey 44, 208, 210, 212

temptations of Jesus 87-88

Toole, David 77, 159
Tower of Babel 43-45

Wannenwetsch, Bernd 35, 47, 160, 167
Weaver, Alain Epp 43, 48-49, 92, 131
Williams, Rowan 3, 83, 211

Evangelical Quarterly

An International Review of Bible and Theology

Editors: I Howard Marshall, John-Paul Lotz

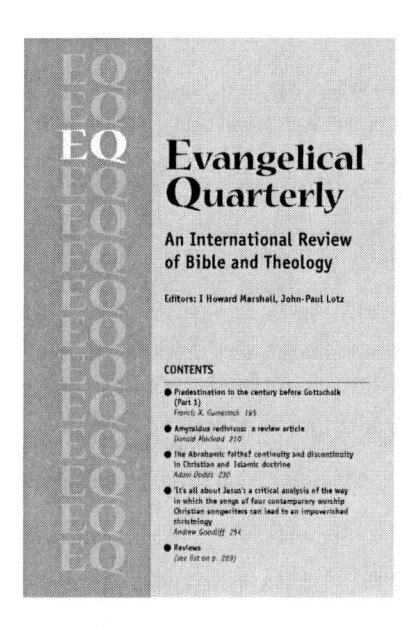

CONTENTS
- Predestination in the century before Gottschalk (Part 1)
  Francis X. Gumerlock 195
- Amyraldus redivivus: a review article
  Donald Macleod 210
- The Abrahamic faiths? continuity and discontinuity in Christian and Islamic doctrine
  Adam Dodds 230
- 'It's all about Jesus': a critical analysis of the way in which the songs of four contemporary worship Christian songwriters can lead to an impoverished christology
  Andrew Goodliff 254
- Reviews
  (see list on p. 289)

Edited by I. Howard Marshall and John-Paul Lotz
EVANGELICAL QUARTERLY
96pp., 210x145mm,
ISSN 0014-3367
This well-established academic journal includes articles on a wide variety of biblical and theological topics. Books of current interest are reviewed in depth by well-known scholars.
Edited in association with the London School of Theology.

Edited by Denis Alexander and Rodney Holder
SCIENCE AND CHRISTIAN BELIEF
96pp., 243x170mm (April and October),
ISSN 0954-4194
Science and Christian Belief, sponsored by Christians in Science and the Victoria Institute, offers an important resource to all whose interests extend across the boundary between science and religion. Each issue contains two or three major features in addition to shorter articles, abstracts and book reviews.
Science and Christian Belief is also available in electronic form.

All USA and Canada subscriptions to:
EBSCO Subscription Services, P.O. Box 1943, Birmingham, AL 35201-1943, USA

All UK and other international subscriptions to:
Paternoster Periodicals, c/o AlphaGraphics, 6 Angel Row, Nottingham NG1 6HL, UK
Tel UK: 0800 597 5980 • Fax 0115 852 3601
Tel: Overseas +44 (0)115 852 3614 • Fax: +44 (0)115 852 3601
email: periodicals@alphagraphics.co.uk

Subscriptions can be ordered online at:
www.paternosterperiodicals.co.uk (non USA and Canada subscriptions only)
All orders placed via our website will receive a 5% discount off the total price.
Rates displayed on the website will reflect this discount.

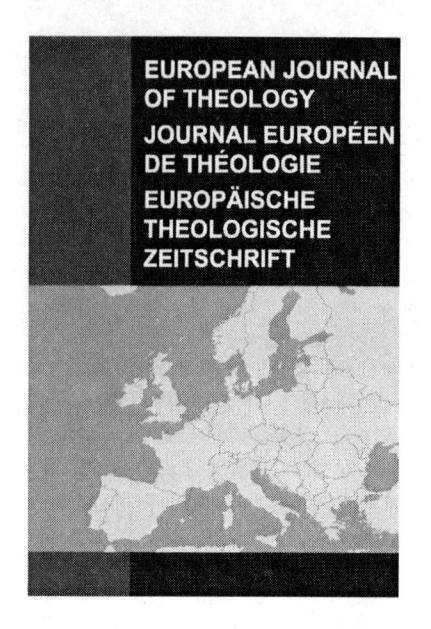

Edited by Pieter Lalleman
THE EUROPEAN JOURNAL OF THEOLOGY
96pp., 245x185mm (April and October),
ISSN 0960-2720
This unique journal reflects the new Europe. Founded and edited with the aid of scholars and church leaders from many European countries, it offers to ministers, students and theologians a new European focus for their theology. Publishing articles and reviews in German, English and French, the *Journal* seeks to reflect the diversity of European evangelical theology.

Edited by Justin Thacker
EVANGELICAL REVIEW OF THEOLOGY
96pp., 210x145mm (Quarterly),
ISSN 0144-8153
Published on behalf of the Theological Commission of the World Evangelical Fellowship. Some issues contain articles and reviews selected from publications worldwide for an international readership, interpreting the Christian faith for contemporary living, whilst others contain original material with a thematic focus.

All USA and Canada subscriptions to:
EBSCO Subscription Services, P.O. Box 1943, Birmingham, AL 35201-1943, USA

All UK and other international subscriptions to:
Paternoster Periodicals, c/o AlphaGraphics, 6 Angel Row, Nottingham NG1 6HL, UK
Tel UK: 0800 597 5980 • Fax 0115 852 3601
Tel: Overseas +44 (0)115 852 3614 • Fax: +44 (0)115 852 3601
email: periodicals@alphagraphics.co.uk

Subscriptions can be ordered online at:
www.paternosterperiodicals.co.uk (non USA and Canada subscriptions only)
All orders placed via our website will receive a 5% discount off the total price.
Rates displayed on the website will reflect this discount.

Paternoster Theological Monographs
(All titles uniform with this volume)
Dates in bold are of projected publication.
Condensed details are given for volumes published before 2004.

James N. Anderson
Paradox in Christian Theology
An Analysis of the Presence, Character, and Epistemic Status of Paradoxical Christian Doctrines

Dr Anderson develops and defends a model of understanding paradoxical Christian doctrines according to which the presence of such doctrines is unsurprising and adherence to paradoxical doctrines can be entirely reasonable. As such, the phenomenon of theological paradox cannot be considered as a serious intellectual obstacle to belief in Christianity. The case presented in this book has significant implications for the practice of systematic theology, biblical exegesis, and Christian apologetics.

James N. Anderson is a Research Fellow of the University of Edinburgh, Scotland, UK.

2007 / 978-1-84227-462-0 / xvi + 328pp

Emil Bartos
Deification in Eastern Orthodox Theology
An Evaluation and Critique of the Theology of Dumitru Staniloae

'This book deals with a major topic of importance—Staniloae is the greatest Romanian theologian of the twentieth century', Kallistos Ware.

1999 / 978-0-85364-956-4 / xii + 370pp

Paul H. Brazier
Barth and Dostoevsky
A Study of the Influence of Fyodor Dostoevsky on the Development of Karl Barth (1915–1922)

A work of historic and systematic theology *Barth and Dostoevsky* examines the influence of Dostoevksy on Barth. It demonstrates that the writings of Dostoevsky effected the development of Barth's theology. This influence was mediated by his friend and colleague Eduard Thurneysen and was in the form of a key element of Barth's thought: his understanding of sin and grace. This study, therefore, explicates: first, the reading of Dostoevsky by Barth 1915–16, and the influence on his understanding of sin and grace; second, a study of Thurneysen in so far as his life and work complements and influences Barth; third, Barth's illustrative use of Dostoevsky, around 1918–21, the period of the rewriting of his seminal commentary on Romans.

Paul H. Brazier originally trained in the fine arts. He holds degrees from King's College, London, where he completed his PhD on which this book is based.

2007 / 978-1-84227-563-4 / xxiv + 246pp

Graham Buxton
The Trinity, Creation and Pastoral Ministry
Imaging the Perichoretic God

In this book the author proposes a three-way conversation between theology, science and pastoral ministry. His approach draws on a Trinitarian understanding of God as a relational being of love, whose life 'spills over' into all created reality, human and non-human. By locating human meaning and purpose within God's 'creation-community' this book offers the possibility of a transforming engagement between those in pastoral ministry and the scientific community.

Graham Buxton is Director of Postgraduate Studies in Ministry and Theology, Tabor College, Adelaide, Australia.

2005 / 978-1-84227-369-2 / xviii + 310pp

Iain D. Campbell
Fixing the Indemnity
The Life and Work of George Adam Smith

When Old Testament scholar George Adam Smith (1856–1942) delivered the Lyman Beecher lectures at Yale University in 1899, he confidently declared that 'modern criticism has won its war against traditional theories. It only remains to fix the amount of the indemnity.' In this biography, Iain D. Campbell assesses Smith's critical approach to the Old Testament and evaluates its consequences, showing that Smith's life and work still raises questions about the relationship between biblical scholarship and evangelical faith.

Iain D. Campbell is Minister of Back Free Church of Scotland, Isle of Lewis, Scotland, UK.

2004 / 978-1-84227-228-2 / xx + 256pp

Daniel Castelo
The Apathetic God
Exploring the Contemporary Relevance of Divine Impassibility

This book attempts a view of God and suffering that takes the testimony of the early church seriously while also considering with equal vigour the contemporary climate. It emphasizes divine impassibility because a balance between impassibility and passibility requires establishing space within a contemporary climate that all too easily assumes passibility.

Daniel Castelo is Assistant Professor of Theology, School of Theology, Seattle Pacific University, Washington, USA.

2009 / 978-1-84227-536-8 / xvi + 152pp

Tim Chester
Mission and the Coming of God
Eschatology, the Trinity and Mission in the Theology of Jürgen Moltmann

This book explores the theology and missiology of the influential contemporary theologian, Jürgen Moltmann. It highlights the important contribution Moltmann has made while offering a critique of his thought from an evangelical perspective. In so doing, it touches on pertinent issues for evangelical missiology. The conclusion takes Calvin as a starting point, proposing 'an eschatology of the cross' which offers a critique of the over-realised eschatologies in liberation theology and certain forms of evangelicalism.

Tim Chester is part of a church planting initiative in Sheffield and was previously Research and Policy Director for Tearfund and visiting lecturer in Christian Community Development at Redcliffe College, Gloucester, UK.

2006 / 978-1-84227-320-3 / xviii + 264pp

Sylvia Wilkey Collinson
Making Disciples
The Significance of Jesus' Educational Strategy for Today's Church

This study examines the biblical practice of discipling, formulates a definition, and makes comparisons with modern models of education. A recommendation is made for greater attention to its practice today.

Sylvia Wilkey Collinson is a Visiting Lecturer, Morling College, Sydney, Australia.

2004 / 978-1-84227-116-2 / xiv + 278pp

Darrell Cosden
A Theology of Work
Work and the New Creation
Through dialogue with Moltmann, Pope John Paul II and others, this book develops a genitive 'theology of work', presenting a theological definition of work and a model for a theological ethics of work that shows work's nature, value and meaning now and eschatologically. Work is shown to be a transformative activity consisting of three dynamically inter-related dimensions: the instrumental, relational and ontological.
Darrell Cosden is Lecturer in Theology and Ethics at the International Christian College, Glasgow, Scotland, UK.
2005 / 978-1-84227-332-6 / xvi + 208pp

Oliver Crisp
An American Augustinian
Sin and Salvation in the Dogmatic Theology of William G.T. Shedd
Shedd's theology is arguably one of the richest resources in the American Reformed tradition yet it has not received the attention it deserves. Shedd was a theologian unafraid to think for himself, even if this meant he ended up with views that were not held by others with whom he had a natural affinity. His theology of sin and salvation illustrate well this creative innovation within a tradition. Crisp explores the relationship between sin and salvation in Shedd's theology, with an eye to both its philosophical and dogmatic significance for contemporary theology.
Oliver Crisp is Lecturer in Theology, University of Bristol, UK.
2007 / 978-1-84227-526-9 / xvi + 184pp

Garry J. Deverell
The Bonds of Freedom
Vows, Sacraments and the Formation of the Christian Self
This book proposes that Christian worship is a key source for any theology seeking to understand the covenant between God and human beings in the Christian tradition. Through a detailed examination of phenomenological, biblical and theological sources, the author seeks to write a theology in which the selfhood of God and human beings is seen as essentially 'vowed' or 'covenantal'. This claim is then explored through a detailed examination of eucharistic and baptismal practices within the worship life of the church. Eucharistic worship is understood as a 'non-identical performance' of the covenant established between God and human beings in baptism. Here, then, is a theology that understands Christian worship not simply as 'form' or 'event' but, more radically, as a mutual act of promising and commitment between God and human beings.
Garry J. Deverell is a minister of the Uniting Church in Australia and an Honorary Research Associate, Centre for Studies in Religion and Theology, Monash University, Victoria, Australia.
2008 / 978-1-84227-527-6 / xvi + 214pp

Paul G. Doerksen
Beyond Suspicion
Post-Christendom Protestant Political Theology in John Howard Yoder and Oliver O'Donovan
By pursuing a critical comparison of the political theologies of John Howard Yoder and Oliver O'Donovan, the present work shows how post-Christendom Protestant political theology has attempted to move beyond the suspicion that politicians corrupt morality, and that politics is corrupted by theology without putting forward some hidden attempt to reassert a contemporary version of Christendom.
Paul G. Doerksen teaches Christian Theology and Ethics in Winnipeg, Manitoba, Canada.
2009 / 978-1-84227-634-1 / approx. 300pp

Stephen M. Dunning
The Crisis and the Quest
A Kierkegaardian Reading of Charles Williams
'An invaluable contribution to our understanding of this extraordinary man', Glen Cavaliero.
2000 / 978-0-85364-985-4 / xxiv + 254pp

Keith Ferdinando
The Triumph of Christ in African Perspective
A Study of Demonology and Redemption in the African Context
'I am excited by this book', R.T. France.
1999 / 978-0-85364-830-7 / xviii + 450pp

Craig Gardiner
Melodies of Community
Christian Community through the Metaphor of Music, with Dietrich Bonhoeffer and the Iona Community
Gardiner adopts the musical metaphor of polyphony to articulate a new paradigm for exploring the nature of Christ and argues that the church can still affirm ecumenical unity while celebrating the diverse patterns of practice and belief. He weaves together Bonhoeffer, the Iona Community and a rich variety of further metaphors to suggest a 'Discipline of Counterpoint' with which the Christian community might perform divine melodies such as worship, healing, ecumenism, peace, justice and ecology.
Craig Gardiner is pastor of Calvary Baptist Church, Cardiff, a member of the Council of the Baptist Union of Great Britain and serves on its Faith and Unity Executive.
2010 / 978-1-84227-564-1 / approx. 300pp

Richard Gibb
Grace and Global Justice
The Socio-Political Mission of the Church in an Age of Globalization
What does it mean for the twenty-first-century church to conceive of itself as a community defined by the covenant of grace? *Grace and Global Justice* explores the ramifications of this central Christian doctrine for the holistic mission of the church in the context of a globalized world.
Richard Gibb is Assistant Minister of Charlotte Chapel, Edinburgh, UK.
2006 / 978-1-84227-459-0 / xviii + 248pp

Andrew Goddard
Living the Word, Resisting the World
The Life and Thought of Jacques Ellul
'The best introduction to Ellul's thought currently available', Alister E. McGrath.
2002 / 978-1-84227-053-0 / xxiv + 378pp

Andrew Hartropp
Economic Justice
Biblical and Secular Perspectives Contrasted
This book argues that a biblically-rooted account of justice in economic life has three great strengths as opposed to the confusing disarray of views evident in the secular world: it is harmonious; it is substantial; and it is contemporary. It indicates how a biblical understanding of production and exchange ('free trade' versus 'fair trade' and equality versus freedom) applies to contemporary topics such as the relationships between borrowers and lenders, and the use of monopoly power.
Andrew Hartropp has lectured in economics at Brunel University and is currently a Church of England Curate in Watford, Hertfordshire, UK.
2007 / 978-1-84227-434-7 / xvi + 222pp

Sharon E. Heaney
Contextual Theology for Latin America
Liberation Themes in Evangelical Perspective
In the context of Latin America, the theology of liberation is both dominant and world renowned. However, this context and the pursuit of theological relevance belong also to other voices. In this book, Sharon Heaney examines and systematises the thought of five evangelical theologians striving for liberation in Latin America.
Sharon E. Heaney teaches Religious Studies at Bloxham School, Oxfordshire, having completed her doctorate at Queens University, Belfast, Northern Ireland, UK.
2008 / 978-1-84227-515-3 / xx + 292pp

Timothy D. Herbert
Kenosis and Priesthood
Towards a Protestant Re-Evaluation of the Ordained Ministry
Herbert argues it is possible to re-imagine priesthood so that it becomes a useful way to understand the nature and importance of ordained ministry without undervaluing or negating the priesthood of all believers.
Timothy D. Herbert is Principal of the Carlisle and Blackburn Diocesan Training Institute, Carlisle, UK.
2008 / 978-1-84227-565-8 / xxii + 300pp

Roger Hitching
The Church and Deaf People
A Study of Identity, Communication and Relationships with Special Reference to the Ecclesiology of Jürgen Moltmann
'An excellent book', Jürgen Moltmann.
2003 / 978-1-84227-222-0 / xxii + 236pp

Mark F.W. Lovatt
Confronting the Will-to-Power
A Reconsideration of the Theology of Reinhold Niebuhr
'A constructive evaluation', Anthony C. Thiselton.
2001 / 978-1-84227-054-7 / xviii + 216pp

Neil B. MacDonald
Karl Barth and the Strange New World within the Bible
Barth, Wittgenstein, and the Metadilemmas of the Enlightenment (Revised Edition)
'Brilliant and nuanced', Christopher R. Seitz.
2001^2 / 978-0-85364-970-0 / xxvi + 404pp

Neil B. MacDonald and Carl R. Trueman (eds)
Barth, Calvin, and Reformed Theology
Barth and Calvin belong to the first rank of great theologians of the Church. Historically, Calvin's influence on Reformed doctrine has been much greater than that of Barth's. In contrast, Barth's Reformed credentials have been questioned—not least in his understanding of election and atonement. The question is: who should be of greater importance for the Reformed church in the twenty-first century in the light of recent academic research into the Bible? Who has the better arguments on the Bible? Barth or Calvin: who should carry the mantle of Reformed theology in the future? Doctrinal areas of focus are the nature of the atonement, scripture, and the sacraments.
Neil B. MacDonald is Senior Lecturer in Theology, University of Surrey Roehampton, London, UK.
Carl R. Trueman is Professor of Church History, Westminster Theological Seminary, Philadelphia, USA.
2008 / 978-1-84227-567-2 / xiv + 182pp

Keith A. Mascord
Alvin Plantinga and Christian Apologetics
This book draws together the contributions of the philosopher Alvin Plantinga to the major contemporary challenges to Christian belief, highlighting in particular his ground-breaking work in epistemology and the problem of evil. Plantinga's theory that both theistic and Christian belief is warrantedly basic is explored and critiqued, and an assessment offered as to the significance of his work for apologetic theory and practice.
Keith A. Mascord lectures in Philosophy at Moore Theological College, Sydney, Australia.
2006 / 978-1-84227-256-5 / xvi + 236pp

Gillian McCulloch
The Deconstruction of Dualism in Theology
With Reference to Ecofeminist Theology and New Age Spirituality
'McCulloch's informed and timely book fills an important gap', Christopher Partridge.
2002 / 978-1-84227-044-8 / xii + 282pp

Leslie McCurdy
Attributes and Atonement
The Holy Love of God in the Theology of P.T. Forsyth
'Skilful and nuanced', Trevor Hart.
1999 / 978-0-85364-833-8 / xiv + 328pp

David H. McIlroy
A Trinitarian Theology of Law
In Conversation with Jürgen Moltmann, Oliver O'Donovan and Thomas Aquinas
This book explores the neglected significance of the doctrine of the Trinity for the understanding of human law. Through interaction with the thought of Moltmann, O'Donovan and Aquinas, it argues that human law is called to play a positive but limited role in maintaining 'shallow justice' and relative peace. Human law is overshadowed by the work of the Son, included in the purposes of the Father, and used as an instrument by the Holy Spirit. However, the Spirit works in those who are in Christ to effect 'deep justice', a work of sanctification which culminates in glorification – the experience of perfect, free, willing obedience in heaven.
David H. McIlroy is a practising barrister and a theologian and an Associate Research Fellow of Spurgeon's College, London, UK.
2009 / 978-1-84227-627-3 / xxii + 262pp

John E. McKinley
Tempted for Us
Theological Models and the Practical Relevance of the Impeccability and Temptation of Christ
How could Christ be tempted to sin despite his divine impeccability? How could Christ experience temptation in a way that makes him truly empathetic for others who are not impeccable as he is? How could Christ resist temptation in a way that others can reasonably follow his human example? Historical theology yields several models for working out the apparent dilemmas that follow from the traditional affirmations about Jesus' temptation. In response, McKinley explores the biblical and theological evidence for Christ's impeccability and temptation with the goal of formulating a contemporary model. Doing this clarifies both the full humanity of Christ and the true relevance and implications of his earthly life for Christian sanctification in conformity to Christ.
John E. McKinley is Assistant Professor of Systematic Theology, Biola University, La Mirada, California, USA.
2009 / 978-1-84227-537-5 / xxii + 346pp

Nozomu Miyahira
Towards a Theology of the Concord of God
A Japanese Perspective on the Trinity
'A profound contribution to East–West dialogue', John Macquarrie.
2000 / 978-0-85364-863-5 / xiv + 256pp

Eddy José Muskus
The Origins and Early Development of Liberation Theology in Latin America
With Particular Reference to Gustavo Gutiérrez
'Fills a crucial gap', D. Eryl Davies.
2002 / 978-0-85364-974-8 / xiv + 296pp

Jim Purves
The Triune God and the Charismatic Movement
A Critical Appraisal from a Scottish Perspective
All emotion and no theology? Or a fundamental challenge to reappraise and realign our trinitarian theology in the light of Christian experience? This study of charismatic renewal as it found expression within Scotland at the end of the twentieth century evaluates the use of Patristic, Reformed and contemporary models of the Trinity in explaining the workings of the Holy Spirit.

Jim Purves is pastor of Bristo Baptist Church, Edinburgh, and serves on the Baptist Union of Scotland's national leadership team.
2004 / 978-1-84227-321-0 / xxiv + 246pp

Anna Robbins
Methods in the Madness
Diversity in Twentieth-Century Christian Social Ethics
The author compares the ethical methods of Walter Rauschenbusch, Reinhold Niebuhr and others. She argues that unless Christians are clear about the ways that theology and philosophy are expressed practically they may lose the ability to discuss social ethics across contexts, let alone reach effective agreements.

Anna Robbins is Lecturer in Theology and Contemporary Culture and Director of Training at the London School of Theology, UK.
2004 / 978-1-84227-211-4 / xx + 294pp

Ed Rybarczyk
Beyond Salvation
Eastern Orthodoxy and Classical Pentecostalism on Becoming Like Christ
At first glance eastern Orthodoxy and classical Pentecostalism seem quite distinct. This ground-breaking study shows they share much in common, especially as it concerns the experiential elements of following Christ. Both traditions assert that authentic Christianity transcends the wooden categories of modernism.

Ed Rybarczyk is Assistant Professor of Systematic Theology, Vanguard University, California, USA.
2004 / 978-1-84227-144-5 / xii + 356pp

Signe Sandsmark
Is World View Neutral Education Possible and Desirable?
A Christian Response to Liberal Arguments
(Published jointly with The Stapleford Centre)
'Bold, balanced and sensitive', Andrew Wright.
2000 / 978-0-85364-973-1 / xiv + 182pp

Alison Searle
'The Eyes of your Heart'
Literary and Theological Trajectories of Imagining Biblically

This book develops a theory of imagining biblically that explores the contributions scripture can make to new ways of thinking about creativity, reading, interpretation and criticism. The methodology employed in order to demonstrate this thesis consists of a theoretical exploration of current theological understandings of the 'imagination' and their implications within the field of literary studies. The biblical text locates the function generally defined as 'imagination' in the heart ('the eyes of the heart', Ephesians 1:18). This book assesses what the biblical text as a literary and religious document contributes to the concept of 'imagination'.

Alison Searle is a postdoctoral research associate on the James Shirley Project at Anglia Ruskin University, Cambridge, UK.

2008 / 978-1-84227-627-3 / xviii + 232pp

Andrew Sloane
On Being a Christian in the Academy
Nicholas Wolterstorff and the Practice of Christian Scholarship

'Accurate, meticulously researched, lucidly presented and critically sympathetic', Nicholas Wolterstorff.

2003 / 978-1-84227-058-5 / xvi + 274pp

Damon W.K. So
Jesus' Revelation of His Father
A Narrative-Conceptual Study of the Trinity with Special Reference to Karl Barth

This book explores the trinitarian dynamics in the context of Jesus' revelation of his Father in his earthly ministry with references to key passages in Matthew's Gospel. It develops from the exegeses of these passages a non-linear concept of revelation which links Jesus' communion with his Father to his revelatory words and actions through a nuanced understanding of the Holy Spirit, with references to K. Barth, G.W.H. Lampe, J.D.G. Dunn and E. Irving.

Damon W.K. So serves as an adviser of the Oxford Chinese Christian Church having studied at London Bible College and the University of Oxford, UK.

2006 / 978-1-84227-323-4 / xviii + 348pp

Daniel Strange
The Possibility of Salvation Among the Unevangelised
An Analysis of Inclusivism in Recent Evangelical Theology

'One of the best comprehensive surveys of this debate', Gavin D'Costa.

2002 / 978-1-84227-047-9 / xviii + 362pp

Scott Swain
God According to the Gospel
Biblical Narrative and the Identity of God in the Theology of Robert W. Jenson

Robert W. Jenson is one of the leading voices in contemporary Trinitarian theology. His boldest contribution in this area lies in his use of the Bible's narrative structure both to ground and explicate a panentheistic doctrine of the Trinity. *God According to the Gospel* critically examines Jenson's proposal and, through an engagement with canon and creed, outlines an alternative way of reading the biblical characterization of the Trinity.

Scott Swain teaches Theology and Biblical Interpretation at Southwestern Baptist Theological Seminary, Fort Worth, Texas, USA.

2010 / 978-1-84227-258-9 / approx. 300pp

Justyn Terry
The Justifying Judgement of God
A Reassessment of the Place of Judgement in the Saving Work of Christ
Terry's argument is that judgement, understood as the whole process of bringing justice, is the primary metaphor of atonement, with others – victory, redemption and sacrifice – subordinate to it. Judgement also provides the proper context for understanding penal substitution and the call to repentance, baptism, eucharist and holiness.
Justyn Terry teaches at the Trinity Episcopal School for Ministry, Ambridge, PA, USA.
2007 / 978-1-84227-370-8 / xvi + 228pp

Graham Tomlin
The Power of the Cross
Theology and the Death of Christ in Paul, Luther and Pascal
'Here is the groundwork of constructive theology at its best', Stephen Williams.
1999 / 978-0-85364-984-7 / xiv + 344pp

Steven Tsoukalas
Krsna and Christ
Body-Divine Relation in the Thought of Sankara, Ramanuja and Classical Christian Orthodoxy
This work compares the Krsnavatara (Krsna in his *avatara* state) doctrines of Sankara and Ramanuja and the incarnation of Christ as represented by classical Christian orthodoxy, and draws out comparative theological and soteriological implications. The result is a demonstration that many of the popularly held similarities between *avatara* and incarnation are superficial, and that therefore careful consideration of epistemologies and ontologies should be undertaken when comparing theologies and soteriologies pertinent to *avatara* and incarnation.
Steven Tsoukalas is Adjunct Professor of Comparative Religion and Theology, Wesley Biblical Seminary, Jackson, Mississippi, USA.
2006 / 978-1-84227-435-4 / xvi + 310pp

Adonis Vidu
Postliberal Theological Method
A Critical Study
The postliberal theology of Frei, Lindbeck, Thiemann, Milbank and others is one of the more influential contemporary options. Vidu focuses on several aspects pertaining to its theological method, specifically its understanding of background, hermeneutics, epistemic justification, ontology, the nature of doctrine and christological method.
Adonis Vidu is Associate Professor of Theology, Gordon-Conwell Theological Seminary, South Hamilton, Massachusetts, USA.
2005 / 978-1-84227-395-1 / xiv + 270pp

Adonis Vidu
Theology after Neo-Pragmatism
How are theological claims justified? What is the meaning of Christian talk about the non-empirical and the transcendent? Should Evangelical theology continue to hitch a ride with realism? These important contemporary issues are approached by way of a theological conversation with neo-pragmatic philosophers such as Davidson, Rorty, Putnam, McDowell, and others. This is an introduction to an influential philosophical trend and a critical and constructive theological proposal, at once scriptural and historicist, pragmatic and realist.
Adonis Vidu is Associate Professor of Theology, Gordon-Conwell Theological Seminary, South Hamilton, Massachusetts, USA.
2008 / 978-1-84227-460-6 / xx + 308pp

Graham J. Watts
Revelation and the Spirit
A Comparative Study of the Relationship between the Doctrine of Revelation and Pneumatology in the Theology of Eberhard Jüngel and of Wolfhart Pannenberg
The relationship between revelation and pneumatology is relatively unexplored. This approach offers a fresh angle on two important twentieth-century theologians and raises pneumatological questions which are theologically crucial and relevant to mission in a postmodern culture.

Graham J. Watts is Minister of Albany Road Baptist Church, Cardiff, Wales, UK.

2005 / 978-1-84227-104-9 / xx + 230pp

Nicholas J. Wood
Faiths and Faithfulness
Pluralism, Dialogue and Mission in the Work of Kenneth Cragg and Lesslie Newbigin
Wood offers a critical account of two key twentieth-century missionary-theologians who addressed the issue of pluralism within a confessional framework. He argues for a reconsideration of the biblical themes of fullness and fulfilment, which may offer a way of holding together the traditions of continuity, which Cragg shows can never be total, and of discontinuity, which Newbigin argues can never be absolute. He contributes to the development of an appropriate missiological approach to inter-faith issues which takes people of faith seriously while allowing faithfulness to the Christian gospel.

Nicholas J. Wood is Fellow in Religion and Culture, and Director of the Oxford Centre for Christianity and Culture at Regent's Park College, University of Oxford. He is a member of the Faculty of Faculty in the University of Oxford and a President of the National Christian Muslim Forum.

2009 / 978-1-84227-371-5 / xviii + 220pp

Nigel G. Wright
Disavowing Constantine
Mission, Church and the Social Order in the Theologies of John Howard Yoder and Jürgen Moltmann
'A strong-minded, original contribution', Alan Kreider.

2000 / 978-0-85364-978-6 / xvi + 252pp

Terry J. Wright
Providence Made Flesh
Divine Presence as a Framework for a Theology of Providence
Traditional discussions of the Christian doctrine of providence often centre on the relation between divine agency and human freedom, seeking to offer an account of the extent to which a person is free before God, the first cause of all things. Terry J. Wright argues that such riddles of causation cannot determine the content of providence, and suggests a unique and alternative framework that depicts God's providential activity in terms of divine faithfulness to that which God has made. Providence is not God as first cause acting through creaturely secondary causation, rather providence is God's sovereign mediation of the divine presence across the whole world, achieved through creaturely faithfulness made possible and guaranteed by his own faithful action in Jesus Christ.

Terry J. Wright is an Associate Research Fellow at Spurgeon's College, London, UK.

2009 / 978-1-84227-632-7 / approx. 300pp

Theodore Zachariades
The Omnipresence of Jesus Christ
A Neglected Aspect of Evangelical Christology

Omnipresence is the key to unlock the kenosis question. The popular view of the incarnation whereby Christ possesses but does not independently exercise divine relative attributes is shown to be problematic and cannot be maintained with Christ's omnipresence, which by definition demands possession and use. Drawing on historical studies from the early church and John Calvin's christological exposition utilizing such concepts as *communicatio idiomatum* and *extra calvinisticum*, this work argues for a robust Chalcedonian incarnational christology that avoids all forms of kenotic thought.

Theodore Zachariades is founding pastor of Sovereign Grace Baptist Fellowship, Tullahoma, Tennessee, and teaches for Luther Rice University's distance learning program, Lithonia, Georgia, USA.

2010–11 / 978-1-84227-531-3 / approx. 300pp

New and unscheduled titles:

Nicholas John Ansell
The Annihilation of Hell
Universal Salvation and the Redemption of Time in the Eschatology of Jürgen Moltmann
978-1-84227-525-2 / approx. 300pp

Laurence M. Blanchard
Will God Save Us All? [Provisional title]
An Assessment of the Historical Development and Contemporary Expression of Universalism in Western Theology
978-1-84227-638-7 / approx. 300pp

David Hilborn
The Words of our Lips
Language-Use in Free Church Worship

Studies of liturgical language have tended to focus on the written canons of Roman Catholic and Anglican communities. By contrast, David Hilborn analyses the more extemporary approach of English Nonconformity. Drawing on recent developments in linguistic pragmatics, he explores similarities and differences between 'fixed' and 'free' worship, and argues for the interdependence of each.

978-0-85364-977-9 / approx. 300pp

John G. Kelly
One God, One People
The Differentiated Unity of the People of God in the Theology of Jürgen Moltmann

The author expounds and critiques Moltmann's doctrine of God and highlights the systematic connections between it and Moltmann's influential discussion of Israel. He then proposes a fresh approach to Jewish–Christian relations building on Moltmann's work using insights from Habermas and Rawls.

978-0-85346-969-4 / approx. 300pp

Robert Knowles
Anthony C. Thiselton and the Grammar of Hermeneutics
The Search for a Unified Theory
978-1-84227-637-2 / approx. 300pp

Esther L. Meek
Contact with Reality
An Examination of Realism in the Thought of Michael Polanyi
978-1-84227-622-8 / approx. 300pp

Myron B. Penner
Subjectivity and Knowledge
Self and Being in Kierkegaard's Thought
978-1-84227-406-6 / approx. 300pp

Murray A. Rae (Ed.)
Critical Conversations
Michael Polanyi and Christian Theology
This volume offers a series of theological engagements with the work of Michael Polanyi. Polanyi's sustained explorations of the nature of human knowing opened a range of questions and themes of profound importance for theology. An epistemologist and philosopher of science willing to acknowledge the theological dimensions of his inquiry quickly caught the attention of theologians. His insistence on the need to recover the categories of faith and belief, emphasis on the importance of tradition and the necessity sometimes of conversion are themes explored along with Polanyi's social and political thought, anthropology, hermeneutics and conception of truth. Several of the essays set him alongside the work of other thinkers, particularly Barth, Newbigin, Gadamer and Girard. While all the essays are appreciative they do not shy away from critical analysis, and take further the critical appreciation of Polanyi's work.
978-1-84227-671-6 / approx. 200pp

Hazel Sherman
Reading Zechariah
The Allegorical Tradition of Biblical Interpretation through the Commentary of Didymus the Blind and Theodore of Mopsuestia
A close reading of the commentary on Zechariah by Didymus the Blind alongside that of Theodore of Mopsuestia suggests that popular categorising of Antiochene and Alexandrian biblical exegesis as 'historical' or 'allegorical' is inadequate and misleading.
978-1-84227-213-8 / approx. 300pp